IN PRAISE OF NEW TRAVELERS

Cultural Memory
in
the
Present

Mieke Bal and Hent de Vries, Editors

IN PRAISE OF NEW TRAVELERS

Reading Caribbean Migrant Women Writers

Isabel Hoving

STANFORD UNIVERSITY PRESS

STANFORD, CALIFORNIA

2001

Stanford University Press
Stanford, California

© 2001 by the Board of Trustees of the
Leland Stanford Junior University

Printed in the United States of America
on acid-free, archival-quality paper.

Library of Congress Cataloging-in-Publication Data

Hoving, Isabel.
    In praise of new travelers : reading Caribbean migrant
women writers / Isabel Hoving.
        p.   cm. — (Cultural memory in the present)
    ISBN 0-8047-2947-6 (alk. paper) — ISBN 0-8047-2948-4
(pbk. : alk. paper)
        1. Caribbean fiction (English)—Women authors—
History and criticism.   2. English fiction—20th century—
History and criticism.   3. Immigrants' writings, English—
History and criticism.   4. Women and literature—
Caribbean Area—History—20th century.   5. Caribbean
Area—In literature.   6. Women in literature.   7. Emigration
and immigration in literature.   I. Series.
PR9205.4 .H68   2001
813'.5099287'09729—dc21   00-045812

Original Printing 2001
Last figure below indicates year of this printing:
10   09   08   07   06   05   04   03   02   01

Typeset by James P. Brommer in 11/13.5 Garamond

Grace Nichols's work is reproduced with permission of Curtis Brown Ltd.,
London, on behalf of Grace Nichols. Copyright Grace Nichols 1989.

Thanks to Marlene Nourbese Philip and Ragweed Press for their kind
permission to quote the poem "Discourse on the Logic of Language" from
She Tries Her Tongue: Her Silence Softly Breaks by Marlene Nourbese Philip.

Acknowledgments

Twelve years ago, this study began as a project of eager reading and tentative writing—a project based on the urgent wish to obtain a transnational, intercultural understanding of women's insights and expressions. Looking back, I can see that the project has become more and more the background for talking and listening. Whereas I am much indebted to a wealth of authors, a wealth of texts, I begin to feel increasingly obliged to thank speakers, discussions, conversations. Indeed, I am the child of a poet and a musician/painter, and both endowed me with a fondness for aspects of orality. I thank my mother for giving me a wonderful language, lively speech, and with it the knowledge of the deep complexities of motherhood and daughterhood. I thank my father for acquainting me with those other languages of rhythm and color that I do not yet fully comprehend. I hope that I may continue to explore the field of orality in which these different inherited semiotics can be approached.

Twelve years is a long time, and very many people have guided and supported me on the way. I wish to thank Professor J. J. A. Mooij of the University of Groningen for his capable scholarly guidance, and Peter Zima, now a professor at Klagenfurt, long ago the inspired, erudite, and socially committed scholar who kindled the spark of my passion for literary theory. Rosi Braidotti's women's studies colloquium at the University of Utrecht served as a cordial, exhilaratingly intelligent temporary abode. I am grateful to the Onderzoekszwaartepunt Vrouwenstudies and its successor, the Belle van Zuylen Institute of the University of Amsterdam, which made possible the research project on which this book is based by accepting and funding it. I owe many thanks to Inge Boer of the Belle van Zuylen for guiding me with such passion into the field of postcolonial criticism and for reading different stages of this study and offering me many valuable comments. Selma

Leydesdorff, director of the Belle van Zuylen Institute, also offered her criticism of this work, and I thank her for it. The Department of Comparative and General Literary Studies of the University of Amsterdam offered me an academic home; I have greatly profited from my contacts with my open-minded colleagues. I would like to thank especially John Neubauer, Professor of Comparative Literature, and Helga Geyer-Ryan, Associate Professor of Literary Theory, for their welcome critical remarks on an earlier version of this work. For the same reason, I am grateful to Christel van Boheemen, Professor of English at the University of Amsterdam. The Institute for Development Research Amsterdam (InDRA), in which I participated as a teacher, proved to be a warm, hospitable, and inspiring place. I have learned much from the InDRA's exploration of South-North relations. In addition, I thank my students at the InDRA, the Vakgroep Algemene Literatuurwetenschap, and the Werkgroep Vrouwenstudies. Their often unexpected, original, and valuable comments and questions from a variety of perspectives did much to sharpen or change my own research questions and insights. I am glad to be a member of the excellent Amsterdam School for Cultural Analysis (ASCA), which offers me new opportunities for debates with colleagues in the field. Of my many friends at ASCA I mention especially Frans-Willem Korsten, Wilma Siccama, Patricia Spyer, and Markha Valenta for their supportive criticism and warm encouragements. I thank Mineke Schipper, Professor of Intercultural Literary Theory at the University of Leiden, for sharing with me her love for African and Caribbean (women's) writing, especially when I had the honor to be her colleague at Leiden. I also thank the University of Antwerp for granting me the much-desired space and time to finish this book. I am honored by, and grateful for, the attention great specialists in the field have given to an earlier version of this study. I thank Carole Boyce Davies, professor in the Departments of English, African, and African-American Studies and Comparative Literature at the State University of New York at Binghamton, and Gayatri Chakravorty Spivak, Professor of English and Comparative Literature at the Columbia University. I am privileged to have been able to benefit from their deep insights and probing questions; they have shown me how much I still have to learn.

My deepest and enduring gratitude is for Mieke Bal, first my supervisor, now a dear colleague and friend. She has shaped and hastened the process that changed me from an ambitious reader into a scholarly writer.

She made me lose my fear of "high" theory, supported my exploration of less prestigious theories and perspectives enthusiastically, stimulated me almost out of my wits, and is still fueling my ambitions.

It may not have been the academic institutions that were most important in forming this project. An intercultural reading group, organized and moderated by Roline Redmond in Groningen in 1988, gave me the first decisive feeling for cultural and ethnic differences in reading positions. Indeed, while working within the academy, my conversations with friends inside and outside the academy have helped me immensely in grasping the issue of intercultural exchange. Among many, I want to thank Marnel Breure, Kathleen Gyssels, Claire Moll, Thelma Ravell-Pinto, Garjan Sterk, and Gloria Wekker.

In an early stage of this study, Rosa Knorringa was willing to comment on the chapters on orality. Maaike Meijer and Laura Niesen-de Abruña helped me find my way into the community of Caribbean literary scholars. My discussions with my Caribbean colleagues and their intense evaluations of my work have been most valuable. I want to thank in particular Kathleen Balutansky. Of my nearest colleagues, I wish to express my fond thanks to Babs Boter, Maartje Geraedts, and Ineke Mok. I thank Jan Duinkerken for sending me all those incredible, outrageous calypsos. Louisa Trott, Mario Caro, and Maggie Bowers took meticulous care of my English, and improved it tirelessly. When this long project reached the stage in which it began to turn into a book, Helen Tartar of Stanford University Press was there, showing me the great, passionate importance of our kind of scholarly work. With great friendship, she helped me find my cross-cultural voice, a guidance and support for which I am deeply grateful. I would also like to thank Kate Warne and Mary Ray Worley at Stanford, who have shown great patience and precision in the last stages of the making of this book.

I thank my son, Jesse, for his patience with my absences, for messing up my studious life in the most miraculous and essential way, and for teaching me about the unexpected depths of love and motherhood. And, finally, my sweetest thanks are for her who doesn't want to be thanked, Annemarie Behrens, who does more than support me; she shares with me the three basic vital arts: gardening, reading, and mothering. All these arts we practice in lopsided ways, in unnatural ways, awkwardly, waywardly, and very happily.

Contents

IN PRAISE OF NEW TRAVELERS

1

Introduction: Place, Voice, and Silence

Entering the Scene of Caribbean Writing

A South-African voice:

Yet for me there is an uninhibited euphoric experience when I do write. It is as if I was deaf before and can now hear; I was mute, now I can speak. When people come up to me and say, "I enjoyed your book," "I read your article," "I thought your speech was good," "I heard you on the radio"—each time I am liberated, for someone is listening; someone has taken time to hear me. (Ngcobo 1988: 138)

And a North-African voice:

Writing is like killing, because it takes a lot of courage, the same courage as when you kill, because you are killing ideas, you are killing injustices, you are killing systems that oppress you. Sometimes it is better to kill the outside world and not kill yourself. (El Saadawi, quoted in Grewal et al. 1988: 4–5)

As the starting point of my long tale about reading on the East-West axis, I draw a South-North line, linking two very different statements on women's writing. Euphorically, South-African writer Lauretta Ngcobo sings of the empowering liberation induced by her successful effort to claim a voice through dialogue. From Egypt, Nawal El Saadawi speaks of liberation too —but her clipped, angry discourse is full of violence. Here are two views on the dialogue in which Black women's writing is engaged. One writer celebrates the invigorating dialogue with her readers. The other acknowledges the violent dialogue with muting and destructive dominant discourses.

In this twofold discourse about the dialogue two points become exquisitely clear: First, one cannot talk about Black women's speech and writing without talking about listening and reading too. Second, one cannot talk about women's voices without discussing liberation and imprisonment, violence and resistance. This goes for all those who read or listen, write and speak, but especially for those involved in the professional practices of intercultural interpretation in the academy. In the last two decades, postcolonial criticism and theory have taken up this challenge, too.[1]

The results of their readings are varied, frequently celebrated and school-forming but often highly contested too. Perhaps the most vehement critique of postcolonial theory as a frame for reading can be heard when Black women's writing is concerned. Read, for example, Caribbean scholar Carole Boyce Davies's passionate and rich study on Black women's writing in which she emphatically dismisses postcolonial theory as a possible approach and argues that Black women's texts cannot be adequately addressed by this often Eurocentric, universalizing theoretical practice (Davies 1994). In a recent book about Caribbean women writers by Haitian scholar Miriam Chancy the term *postcolonial* doesn't even appear in the index (Chancy 1997). These Caribbean scholars have a point: Caribbean women's writing is irreducibly *different*. One reason for this difference lies precisely in the fact that their writing takes shape by their engagement in complex, vehement dialogues with their many audiences, dialogues inevitably structured by power, violence, and resistance.

The complex nature of these dialogues can already be understood from a historical literary perspective. In the 1970s, when Caribbean women writers began to articulate their literary voices as a recognizable group, they did not enter a culturally and geographically closed male history; they entered a wide universe of several intertwined or completely unrelated literatures. As Selwyn Cudjoe remarked, "The rise of women's writings in the Caribbean cannot be viewed in isolation. It is a part of a much larger expression of women's realities that is taking place in the postcolonial world and post–civil rights era in the United States" (Cudjoe 1990a: 6). Caribbean women write within a radically transnational literary context. Caribbean literature in itself is already a diasporic, transatlantic, multilinguistic practice. Caribbean literature is the name given to a multitude of literatures that often hardly know each other, for Caribbean literature is written and spoken in Spanish, Papiamentu, Sranan, Dutch, Hindi, Portuguese, French, English, or others of the many languages of the Caribbean. Even within one language, Caribbean writers are positioned between many registers, cultures, and genres. But Caribbean literature is also plural because it addresses many other literatures: African-American, European, African, Asian. This transnational orientation is acutely visible in women's writing. Not only do the new women writers emphasize the hybrid and diasporic nature of Caribbean literature, but they also suggest that, as well as being linguistic, cultural, and ethnic, the diversity of Caribbean literature is gender-specific.

Though men were most visibly active in the field of Caribbean writing, women have always been a part of it. Davies and Fido suggest that, if Caribbean literary histories tend to focus on male writers, it is not that women were not writing, but rather it is an effect of a masculinist perspective (1990: 2). Many studies of the last decade prove that a differently inclined focus has no trouble perceiving a female literary tradition (Chancy 1997; Cudjoe 1990a; Davies and Fido 1990; Mordecai and Wilson 1990; Wilentz 1992; Nasta 1991). For women have been writing, just as they were —at least as much as the men—part of the degrading slave labor, the struggles against oppression, and the struggles for independence.[2]

Caribbean women were so from the very beginning. When in the nineteenth century Caribbean writing emerged in the form of slave accounts, women were among those who had their narratives published. Cudjoe mentions three slave narratives by women published between 1831 and 1857, one in Spanish, two in English. As the next female appearance on the scene, he points to the impressive number of poems by Cuban women published in the second half of the nineteenth century (more than one hundred). This accomplishment can be understood as a close effect of Cuban women's involvement in the Ten Years' War (1868–78) and the uprisings thereafter, which eventually led to Cuban independence in 1902. As before, literature and political and social activism are indissolubly connected. This writing is highly transnational, not unlike the first slave narratives: the Cuban women poets are influenced by the emancipatory movements in the United States (feminism and abolitionism) (Cudjoe 1990a: 15).[3] In the French Caribbean too, works by women of color were published already in the last decades of the nineteenth century (Wilson, quoted in Davies and Fido 1990: 2).

Twentieth-century Caribbean writing is often described as having a slow and sparse beginning until it finds a clear, exhilarating direction in the 1930s. Its new Afrocentric focus expresses itself, for example, in the transnational event of négritude, which springs from the meeting of French-speaking Caribbean and African intellectuals in Paris. As an antiassimilationist movement, driven by the desire to highlight and celebrate the specific essence and mission of the Africans in Africa and the diaspora, it had an important effect on Caribbean culture as a whole. Nevertheless, négritude's Afrocentric focus must be situated within a larger context of political movements that all share an interest in Africa: Haitian nationalism, the Jamaican Marcus Garvey's international "Universal Negro Improvement Association" (in the 1920s), Pan-Africanism (in the first half of the twentieth century). These political developments had their cultural counterparts. In the United States, the Harlem Renaissance of the 1920s had a lasting, transnational impact, though its influence on Francophone Caribbean writing diminished when négritude made itself felt. The early part of the twentieth century also saw the rise of European modernism, with its enthusiasm for African art and "primitive" art in general. The histories of Caribbean writing in this period are dominated by the names of male writers: Aimé Césaire; Léon Damas; Edouard Glissant, answering Césaire and Damas with an emphasis on hybridity, articulated in the notion of "antillanité"; and in the Anglophone areas at a later time writers as diverse as George Lamming, V. S. Naipaul, and Sam Selvon (Condé 1979; Ramchand 1983; Cudjoe 1990a).

But even during the first six decades of the twentieth century women writers have been active. In his account of early-twentieth-century writing, Cudjoe is able to summarize the works and lives of several active women writers. He speaks in more detail about Una Marson (also presented as a foremother in Cobham and Collins 1987) and Louise Bennett as pioneers of a woman-centered and Caribbean-centered literature. As a white Creole writer, Jean Rhys is given a comparable, though very different, prominent place. These women's importance for Caribbean women's writing is independent from their actual presence in the Caribbean: Rhys and Marson spent large parts of their lives in the United Kingdom. Louise Bennett kept writing and performing while two new generations of women writers entered the scene. But there is no slow waxing of women's presence here; the 1940s and 1950s were also an epoch of growing male dominance, expressing itself in the nationalist movement and resulting in an "increase of female oppression" (Cobham-Sanders, quoted in Cudjoe 1990a: 29).

Nevertheless, the 1950s and 1960s saw the shaping of a women's tradition in the Anglophone Caribbean: Phyllis Shand Allfrey published a novel, *The Orchid House*, which is now seen as a feminist classic; Clara Rosa de Lima wrote about sexuality, thematizing homosexuality too (*Tomorrow Will Always Come*); Sylvia Winter's famous *The Hills of Hebron* saw light; and in 1966 Rhys's *Wide Sargasso Sea* appeared together with Rosa Guy's *Bird at My Window*. These novels anticipate and parallel the rise of the African-American feminist/womanist novel in the United States. Moreover, many of the Caribbean writers in this and the following decades lived in the United States or the United Kingdom. If a masculinist nationalism informed cultural and political life in the 1940s and 1950s, the late 1960s and especially the 1970s opened up to Caribbean feminism (Cudjoe 1990a).

Cudjoe picks 1970 as the start of a new epoch in women's writing, as that was the year in which Merle Hodge's *Crick-Crack Monkey* appeared, a beautiful novel about a young girl's mangled departure from childhood in Trinidad, bringing together a strong critique of colonialism, an evocative intimacy in the depiction of family relationships and childhood experience, and language experiment. These aspects are echoed in many of the women's novels to come. In the Francophone Caribbean, the new era was prepared by writers like Michèle Lacrosil, who thematized the alienation of women in the early 1960s. Maryse Condé, Myriam Warner-Vieyra, and Simone Schwarz-Bart published their woman-centered novels in the 1970s and 1980s (see Shelton 1990 for a short overview, and Gyssels 1996). As Marie Cristina Rodriguez states, even in the last decades of the twentieth century, women in the Spanish-speaking areas tended to write and publish poetry rather than stories and novels. She nevertheless mentions, among others, the novelists and story-writers Aida Bahr, Rosario Ferre, and Mayra Montero (Rodriguez 1990; Davies 1998). In the Dutch-speaking area prolific writer, poet, and playwright Astrid Roemer demonstrates her passionate interest in women's experiences in a variety of texts and genres, all marked by an intense love of language experiment (Phaf 1990; Redmond 1993). Other women writers and poets from Surinam, the Dutch Antilles, and Aruba are carving their own trajectories, sometimes in the Netherlands.

The prominence of language experiment in the new women's writing is observed by many scholars of Caribbean women's writing (e.g., Davies and Fido 1990; Gikandi 1992). To a certain degree, language experiment has been a consistent characteristic of Caribbean men's writing, too. Simon Gikandi argues that "the linguistic crisis the Caribbean writer faces . . . is similar to that which confronted European high modernist poets at about the same time Laleau, Laforest, and Césaire began to write: how can literary language face the pressures of its objective conditions and yet liberate itself from them?" (19). One of these pressures for the Caribbean writer has been, indeed, the language of European high modernism. Aimé Césaire's famous poem *Cahier d'un retour à mon pays natal* (1939) is a case in point; Gikandi shows that Césaire used modernist forms to attack and explode the European French language from within (21–24). As I will show in the rest of this work, Caribbean women writers are engaged in a comparable project. But just as women's experience of life differs from men's, their struggle with language differs; their strategies of appropriation and abrogation of both national and colonial languages and discourses are always specific, and therefore we find a different perception of voice and silence in women's novels and poetry, different images of space and time, another relationship to oral genres (such as calypso), different images of the mother, of sexuality. This difference cannot be explained as a mere response to male predecessors. When Simon Gikandi states that the "new generation of Caribbean women writers is revising the project of their male precursors who had, in turn, revised and dispersed the colonial canon" (32), he pictures a particularly ill-fitting image of Caribbean women's "belatedness." Women did not enter a struggle initiated and already half accomplished by men. They have been part of the struggle all along. Moreover, the model of women addressing just this one masculinist tradition is obviously all too simple; women are addressing many other traditions, harking back to a long, multiple, diasporic, and transnational female tradition of Black writing. Therefore, the multiplicity and hybridity of their writing is unparalleled.

Reading Well: The Crisis in Postcolonial Theory
and Caribbean Migrant Women's Writing

The extraordinary position of Caribbean migrant women's writing asks for an extraordinary theoretical approach. And such a specified approach has asserted itself in the debates at the Caribbean women writers conferences (from 1988 on), in the many papers in journals and collections, in book-length studies and handbooks. This body of theory and criticism often identifies itself through a highly critical evaluation of postcolonial theory, even if postcolonial theory focuses on many of the same issues, such as hybridity. It is true, though, that postcolonial theory is in crisis, not only because of its universalism and Eurocentrism, but also, as Moore-Gilbert points out, for a host of other reasons that are related to the crisis in cultural criticism as a whole. There is an "increasing disenchantment with 'high' theory," and "a reaction against the new forms of political criticism which emerged in the late 1970s and early 1980s and, more particularly, a weariness with the issues of gender, class and race which these brought to the fore." In answer, one discerns new ways of establishing an interdisciplinary approach, or, in contrast, a return to the literary (Moore-Gilbert 1997: 186). The fact that postcolonial theory is criticized from so many perspectives that might also have been subsumed under the descriptor *postcolonial* is perhaps a sign of wear rather than a sign of its provocative vitality.

But postcolonial theory and criticism are too broad and even too successful to just be dismissed. Postcolonial thinkers from Fanon and Gandhi to Said, Bhabha, and Spivak have offered pathbreaking analyses of many crucial issues within colonialism and its subsequent phases, even if they sometimes framed their insights in dominant Western discourses. Some critics are inclined to embrace their favorite theorists as "not really postcolonial" and to dismiss others by labeling them postcolonial. But deciding whether theorists in this field can be defined as postcolonial or not is a tricky matter. Fanon appears in most handbooks on postcolonial theory, but Leela Gandhi is one of the few to discuss Mahatma Gandhi in this context. For most, Spivak's is one of the three big names in postcolonial theory, but Davies points out that her work also exceeds postcolonial theory—and her argument is an example of the slippery nature of the debate about the label (Davies 1994). Nigerian critic Chinweizu of course explicitly opposes all efforts of appropriation by Western academic discourses, but Caribbean writer and theorist E. K. Brathwaite—who is also searching for a specifically *regional* perspective—is mentioned in Ashcroft, Griffiths, and Tiffin's 1989 handbook as the advocate of a promising postcolonial perspective (146–48). Such a struggle about definitions depends of course on one's definition and evaluation of postcolonial theory and criticism. I would prefer not to define postcolonial theory too narrowly as a neocolonial master discourse, but rather as a broad field of varied approaches in which thorough, specific critique serves to stimulate a necessary self-reflection (and here I follow Moore-Gilbert's nuanced position).

Stuart Hall's fabulous 1996 reflection on the complex nature of the concept *postcolonial* allows us to answer the more substantial critiques, to wit, the critiques slating the poststructuralist tenets in postcolonial theory. Hall's elegant demonstration of the perfect relevance of poststructuralism in any anticolonial, anti-Enlightenment project is highly convincing. The most important point in his argument is an intelligent intervention in the recurring debates about the meaning of *post* in *postcolonial. Post* means *after*, the argument of antipostcolonialists goes, but colonialism has by no means disappeared; it has merely taken on a new shape (Davies 1994; Hutcheon 1995; McClintock 1992; Shohat 1992). But *post* does not just mean *after*. Hall quotes the ambivalence signaled by Peter Hulme and Ella Shohat, who see, respectively, a temporal as well as a critical dimension in the word, and a chronological as well as an epistemological aspect (1996: 253). Lyotard's discussion of the implications of the term *postmodern* is also very useful here in understanding the difference between these dimensions. First, Lyotard sees *post* "in the sense of a simple succession," that is, as *after*. He comments: "this 'breaking' is, rather, a manner of forgetting or repressing the past. That's to say of repeating it. Not overcoming it." (Lyotard 1993: 171) Next to this interpretation Lyotard sees the possibility to understand *post* as "a working through—what Freud called *Durcharbeitung*—operated by modernity on itself . . . the 'post-' of postmodernity does not mean a process of coming back or flashing back, feeding back, but of *ana*-lysing, *ana*-mnesing, or reflecting" (Lyotard 1993: 173). A combination of Hulme's observation of a critical dimension and Lyotard's and Shohat's differentiations leads to a threefold interpretation of *post*: (1) after; (2) anti; (3) *durch*, or *ana*, that is, a critical working through.[4] The three interpretations are indissolubly intertwined. Lyotard's comments emphasize that postmodernity should be understood as an ongoing process. This is precisely the point Hall makes when explaining that the shift to the epoch of postcoloniality does not mean a clean break. Following Derrida and Gramsci, Hall speaks of a "reconfiguration of a field, rather than . . . a movement of linear transcendence between two mutually exclusive states" (Hall 1996: 254). The postcolonial, then, should also be seen as a process, not as a finished, definitive state. This interpretation implies that postcolonial theory cannot but use concepts that have already been thoroughly criticized; but these concepts, when used self-reflexively and critically, can still be useful in an analysis. On the level of the sociopolitical, this triple understanding of the concepts implies that the colonial is now a contested but inevitable part of decolonizing states too, and that postcolonial nations or texts cannot but "mark their 'difference' in terms of . . . the over-determining effects of Eurocentric . . . systems of representation and power" (Hall 1996: 251). The colonial, then, is an integral part of the multiplicity of the postcolonial, which, as Hall adds, also orients its difference to other discourses.

I think Hall's arguments are very convincing. Poststructuralist insights will be of great help in theorizing the multiplicity of identity by forming a safeguard against easy reductionism. Poststructuralism can be especially productive in those moments when it offers the means for its own self-critique. For just like all other discourses criticized by poststructuralism, poststructuralist discourse constructs its own realities. Even the productive concept of multiple subjectivity can be seen to create, in practice, a certain debatable perception of Black women's writing. As Donna Haraway explains in a discussion of different readings of the Nigerian writer Buchi Emecheta, all positions in the debates about subjectivity are interest-bound (Haraway 1991)—and so is Haraway's own in the context of her argument (Moore-Gilbert 1997: 201). And indeed, one possible response of Western students to Black women's writing consists of the Procrustean effort to fit Black women's texts into a poststructuralist framework. While dismissing all clearly nonpoststructuralist aspects in their work, they insist on recognizing in Black women's writing implicitly poststructuralist deconstructions of unified subjectivity. Thus, Black women writers are appropriated to sustain a white Western critical self-reflection (see Haraway 1991; Homans 1994).[5]

Such appropriation is clearly the wrong answer to the question this study seeks to answer: how to read with respect, how to read in a manner that is truly dialogical? These questions have decided my topic. My focus on Caribbean *migrant* writers is motivated by my wish to discuss writing in the contact zones; it is there, I suspect, that the dialogue can be studied in its highest acuteness.[6] How is the unyielding "otherness" of Caribbean (migrant) women's writing read, and how can my own reading connect to these diverse manners of readings, from the contested postcolonial to the assertive Caribbean/Black feminist modes? The theoretical issue at stake here has a strong ethical and political dimension, as the following quote from Caribbean poet Aimé Césaire shows, warning against certain reading positions: "And I should say to myself: 'And most of all beware, even in thought, of assuming the sterile attitude of the spectator, for life is not a spectacle, a sea of griefs is not a proscenium, a man who wails is not a dancing bear'" (Césaire 1971: 60–62). As an exercise in reading, this study is written in answer to Césaire's challenge. I want to show that it is possible to be something other than a tourist, a spectator, or an eavesdropper eager for the stereotypically exotic. My inquiry into Caribbean women's multiple, hybrid identities tries to feel its way into the nuances in the literary exploration of these identities. It is often through close readings that these nuances can be found. Here, the potential for cultural analysis in the field of postcoloniality assesses itself; for in contrast to postcolonial theory, cultural analysis is based on the insight that it is only in direct dialogue with cultural products that the theoretical reflection on the present post- and anti-colonial, intercultural, transnational, and national cultures can develop. This is my tentative answer to the crisis in cultural criticism: let's turn back to the text, indeed—but let's read *certain* texts, texts that are marginalized, texts that may oppose certain Western aesthetic standards, texts that are self-reflective and that articulate their own theories of writing and reading. And let's listen to the ways in which these texts refuse the isolation and reification of the literary; let's hear the political and social dimensions in these texts too, if they ask us to. Such reading should imply what Spivak calls "doing one's homework": reading about the social, political, and economical context of the texts, and about the theorizing that has been done already, from within the same context especially. Reading self-reflectively, then, to avoid easy appropriation, and responsibly, by learning about the text's context; that is my answer to Césaire. But above all, reading closely and attentively and entering into a real dialogue with the text might be a way to revitalize the very necessary debate about the postcolonial condition, a debate that is nonetheless urgent even if the manner in which it has been conducted has wearied some of its participants.

Reading Well as a Critical Strategy Within Postcoloniality

Perhaps the vehemence of the critique against postcolonialism can be understood as an angry despair about the marginality of "other discourses" within the academy, that is, about the academic refusal or inability to listen and read well. The anger is justified—for that marginality could well be an inevitable effect of postcolonial criticism if, as Gayatri Spivak suggests, "[t]he general mode for the postcolonial is citation, reinscription, rerouting the historical" (1993b: 217). A focus on such a mode doesn't leave much space for unheard discourse—unheard, that is, by many in dominant positions within Western academe. And although these "other discourses" are part of the multiplicity and doubleness evoked by Hall, even he mentions them only in passing, without rendering them audible. If a poststructuralist postcolonialism is part of the analytical frame I am building here, the need to discern these other discourses and concepts about difference is certainly part of that frame too. Christopher L. Miller offers the sharpest articulation of this imperative that I've come across when he warns against a certain understanding of deconstructive theory, by which

> this negative model of interpretation takes on a life of its own, enjoining the Western reader to assess only that of which he/she can be sure—his/her own reading processes . . . the only positive object of knowledge left to be trusted is not an object at all but the solitary subject, paralyzed by its own power. When this point has been reached, a kind of blindness results. (Miller 1990: 8–9)

Yet, critics should strive to acknowledge the difference beyond the boundaries of their knowledge, outside the self. For if they do not, Miller wonders, "What becomes of difference in a methodology that trusts only self-reflexivity?" (1990: 10). This study responds to Miller's analysis by aiming at venturing a little beyond such self-reflexivity and freeing a space for the noncolonial and anticolonial, resisting discourses of which there are many.[7] Davies's valuable polemic work on Black women's writing asks for kindred spatial moves: the global space of postcoloniality should not always be centered around Europe, for Europe is not always the preferred addressee (Davies 1994: 86). With sensitivity and insight, Davies suggests that other discourses may have a definitely nonpostcolonial energy and vitality (108). They are often bent on organizing their reflection around race and gender, thus countering the postcolonial tendency to erase both. Despite these shared projects, Davies emphasizes that these discourses can not be brought under a common denominator (be it postcoloniality or another). Davies offers the concept "uprising textualities" as a tolerant signifier for this inappropriate plurality (107–12). I am answering Davies's challenge by highlighting the names and concepts offered by the texts themselves to describe their very specific hybridities.[8]

In the texts discussed in this study, there is always something that escapes the interpreting force of either postmodern, or feminist, or postcolonial discourses. Even Davies's concept of "uprising textualities" is not meant to provide a safe home to this evasive elsewhereness, this slipperiness. The readings in this work acknowledge the impossibility of a stable theoretical home for the miraculously multiple writing by Caribbean women. Instead of constructing a theoretical framework, the space for the analysis and interpretation created in this work is necessarily a plurality of intersections and borders rather than a field. The postcolonial does not have a territory of its own. The two following quotes capture this perhaps somewhat abstract insight beautifully. First, as Lata Mani and Ruth Frankenberg put it in a passage quoted by Hall, the postcolonial "'is in effect a construct internally differentiated by its intersections with other unfolding relations.'" (Mani and Frankenberg, quoted in Hall 1996: 245) This statement has direct consequences for a theory of writing within postcoloniality: it should be multiple, self-reflective, and tuned to both the theorized and untheorized aspects of this writing's hybridity. Therefore, I am continually crossing or confronting theoretical practices: Caribbean feminist literary theory and postcolonial theory, Caribbean nationalist approaches and orality studies, psychoanalysis and Black criticism, and all these with cultural analysis.[9] A second statement by Homi Bhabha depicts the object of study in a time of transnationality and postcoloniality:

Where, once, the transmission of national traditions was the major theme of a world literature, perhaps we can now suggest that transnational histories of migrants, the colonised, or political refugees—these border and frontier conditions—may be the terrains of world literature. The centre of such a study would neither be the "sovereignty" of national cultures, nor the universalism of human culture, but a focus on . . . "freak social and cultural displacements." (Bhabha 1994: 12)

Nevertheless, a focus on transnationality and border conditions might paradoxically demonstrate the need to acknowledge the indispensable local force of a form of nationalism (as in Merle Collins), or to acknowledge the radicality of the claim of universality (as in Wilson Harris). I will examine these possibilities no less than criticize certain liberal notions of pluralism and hybridity. Here, too, Bhabha can be quoted; he speaks of the need to understand "human action and the social world as a moment when *something is beyond control, but it is not beyond accommodation*" (Bhabha

1994: 12). This study does not look for control, but it wishes to offer an accommodation, a provisional space for confrontation and dialogue.

Three Issues

I have crossed an ocean
I have lost my tongue
from the root of the old
one
a new one has sprung
— Grace Nichols

This short text, the motto of this book, is constituted by three elements crucial to the creation of this unprecedented voice: "place," "voice," and "silence." These three issues name the three parts of my book.[10] I will present readings that attempt to explain the role played by "place," "voice," or "silence" in the novels, and how these texts rewrite or deconstruct these issues. By also examining the theoretical underpinnings of these readings, I wish to trace the complexities of the intercultural, interdisciplinary, and interdiscursive reading of Caribbean migrant women's writing.

"Place," "voice," and "silence" are not just "issues" or "themes." They are also important aspects of the different levels in the narrative structure of literary texts. Examining them brings one closer to the grain of the text itself, that is, to its narrative structure. Though I sometimes adopt the view that literary texts can be read as theory, it is equally important to read them in their specifically literary aspects. It is there that one finds the complex work done to help a postcolonial female voice come into being. Only by studying this complexity is one able to move beyond overly abstract, overly general statements. The emphasis on narrative aspects, structures of address, language, and even "plot" is indispensable for an insight into this complexity. Moreover, narratological elements and aspects like focalization, place, and space are at the heart of this study's concerns. An analysis of focalization, for example, clarifies the dominance of certain situated perspectives in a text and the relationships between them; thus, such an analysis helps elucidate the crucial issue of reading positions. In addition, the treatment of place and space in a novel is often connected to either imperial or anti-imperial figurations of global space. Even such apparently neutral elements are imbued with strong colonial or anticolonial connotations (Said 1994: 88–95). In this case, a narratological analysis is necessary to prepare an interpretation inspired by cultural analysis. Narratology, then, is the first methodology I call upon. Second, the perspective of interdiscursivity allows me to examine the crucial manipulations of different discourses. Third, and mainly in the last chapters of this study, I establish a relation to psycho-analysis, which appears less as a methodology than as a field of intense debates to which texts and readings may ambiguously relate. Finally, my deconstructive moves serve to explore the signification of the texts for other theoretical and philosophical reflections on "place," "voice," and "silence."

Place

"Place" (as an element of the textual level of the fabula, as "location") is not the same as "space" (as an aspect of the textual level of the story, and as lived, perceived, practiced place). What critical effects could be anticipated from a concentration on place and space by contrast to time?

In postcolonial writing, the issue of "place" is often thematized as displacement. Displacement is an ambivalent concept: it is a sign of loss, but also a potential for personal transformation, and thus an opportunity to choose new subject positions. This ambivalence is characteristic of postcolonial writing, especially in the Caribbean, where George Lamming spoke of the "pleasures of exile" in his collection of essays from the 1960s (Lamming 1992). As Sandra Pouchet Paquet states in her introduction to that work, "Exile is a site of both alienation and reconnection" (Lamming 1992: ix). In much Western thought about modernism, not only are the exiled and migrants characterized as displaced, but exile is often seen as the very condition of modern and postmodern subjectivity. Instead of fixed, full subjects one finds anxiously split and displaced subjects; talk about identity has developed into a spatial discourse of splits, gaps, and shifting subject positions. Even if ethnography and cultural studies are traditionally the very disciplines of identity, they also have recourse to the spatialization of subjectivity.[11]

French scholars Gilles Deleuze and Félix Guattari's theory of signification known as nomadology represents such a shifting, moving, displaced subjectivity. It understands exile as inevitable and ultimately invigorating. The critical comments by postcolonial scholars on this postmodern theory of mobility form an important point of reference in my discussion of place (Miller, Kaplan), as they open up a space for other, postcolonial discourses of mobility. The notion of homelessness figures not only as a postmodern but also as a crucial postcolonial condition (Bhabha 1994: 9). Giving up the desire to be accommodated altogether and learning to be a nomad, becoming a Hindu homeless sage or a lady tramp is a possible response. However, many postcolonial discourses of mobility can be criticized for their specifically masculinist and ethnocentric aspects.

There are women's discourses of travel, too. Scholars like Teresa de Lauretis and Luce Irigaray have argued that in Western thought femininity is often understood as passive space, whereas masculinity is associated with mobility.[12] Postcolonial and Black women writers and critics, also critical of this binary opposition, imagine feminine or feminist discourses of mobility, pairing these with a critique of the notion of "home" as women's place.[13] Acknowledging that the connection between "home" and "femininity" does not have to be discarded altogether, many critics search for other patterns according to which women relate to "homes," and to exile and movement in general. Sometimes women are definitely less enchanted by promises or experiences of travel.[14] They may even reappropriate the home to articulate new concepts of bound motion, or delegated motion. In this study I will discuss many examples of such anxious, ambivalent, often subverting homemaking.[15] These deconstructions of the notion of home do not only enable feminine discourses of mobility, but also allow us, first, to rethink the home and, second, to criticize those masculinist ideologies of free mobility that dismiss the home as a place for growth or contact.

If femininity is traditionally associated with place, masculinity is related to time, especially in Western discussions of time, history, origin, and genealogy. Postcolonial critics suggest that postcolonial place and space may function as a postcolonial disturbance of the Western privileging of genealogies and time.[16] This argument is appealing and often illuminating. However, a critical reading of several theories of space and time (among others the influential theories of M. M. Bakhtin and Yuri Lotman) taught me that space and time can never be separated. Therefore, it appears a more productive approach to study time as a factor of place and space, and space and place in their interrelation with time. Often it is imperative to go even further in situating and connecting concepts of time and space: within the Afro-Caribbean context these concepts cannot be disengaged from concepts of action, participation, and community.

Through such deconstructions a shift occurred: rather than a fixed entity, place is increasingly defined as a practice.[17] Thus, the processes by which these places came into being become the object of inquiry, just as the agency involved in their construction. This line of inquiry may lead to a critique of certain Western ethnographic practices of othering, which situate peoples as immobile natives in a fixed territory that is clearly and rigidly separated from other territories. In a comparable vein, "others" are situated in another time, either outside "history" altogether or in a remote historical period, like the Stone Age.[18] Such clear localizations and delineations are motivated constructions. As Christopher L. Miller advises, cultural studies (and studies of postcolonial writing such as these) should take it as their task to think through constructed borders and identities like these (Miller 1993: 21). And this critique of dominant discourses of space should be brought even further. For if borders can be examined with healthy suspicion, as they offer revealing insights into the power-infested processes of spatializing practices, they also represent an opportunity to imagine alternative concepts of mobility. Women writers are often engaged in such an imaginative project.

Chapter 2 traces alternative discourses of women's mobility, home, and collectivity. It does so through reading two pioneering collections of Black and migrant women's writing in Britain in the late 1980s,[19] and several novels published in roughly the same period (predominantly Johnson 1988 and Riley 1985). After an exploration of Western notions of the journey as a means of determining modernity, Chapter 2 proceeds with a rhetorical analysis of the tropes of space and mobility in Black women's writing in Britain. Black and migrant women's rhetorics of the journey are closely related to a politics of identity, just as Western postmodern poetics of travel are connected to the construction of the shifting, mobile identity of (post)-modernity. Chapter 2 shows how Black British women writers construct their concepts of identity by relating the trope of the struggle to the trope of the journey, or by introducing the trope of moisture. By evoking a feminine, sexual concept of bound motion, the trope of moisture helps in reconstructing the identity of individual Black women as fluid, transgressive, and yet centered. It may refer to alienation as well as belonging.

Chapter 3, turning to the ambivalently opposed theme of the home, concentrates on a detailed reading of one novel, Beryl Gilroy's *Frangipani House* (1986). Mama King, the novel's heroine, escapes from a confining and killing "home" for the old to share the harsh life of a group of beggars, finally turning to her family to find a relatively safe, but not fixed, position. Chapter 3 examines the implications of her adventures for a feminist/womanist theory of space and time. Not only does the novel bear upon imperialist strategies (including a specific white European feminist approach), but it also criticizes the Caribbean tradition of seeing the home island as a (repulsive) mother (Césaire), and the mother as immobile, receiving, passive. I will explain how the novel questions these approaches by a subtle manipulation of the narrative categories of time and space. The novel does not present places such as the house as a plot-space, but as a practice, or even as protagonist. This approach is already contained in the novel's use of Creole languages, which often imbue inanimate matter with a life of its own. The language strategy results in the impossibility of considering Mama King as "place." In a parallel manner, the novel displaces the destructive linear and cyclical times it also presents. By calling on anthropological insights into Afro-Caribbean concepts of time I propose an interpretation of the novel's efforts of installing a vigorous alternative concept of woman's time and history that is critically opposed to dominant destructive temporalities.

Voice

Voice and place are closely connected: voices either fit places, or they do not; places destroy voices, render them obsolete, or they offer a space for voices to come into being. How can this complex relationship be theorized? It is a general argument among postcolonial writers that colonial languages and literary conventions are just not capable of representing postcolonial places. Homi Bhabha, however, objects that this argument still departs from the assumption that unmediated realism is possible. But every "reality" is always necessarily a construction, and writing has its own material qualities, which interfere with any mimetic projects (1984b: 96–98). Following Foucault, one can say that the truth of any representation is decided by the discourse in which it is articulated. Thus, a text setting out to contest certain representations is often engaged in a deconstruction, destruction, or transformation of a discourse from *within* that very discourse. Chapters 4, 5, and 6 measure the dependency of Caribbean migrant women's writing on colonial discourses. I understand the different ways in which texts relate to colonial discourse as efforts to create a "voice":

by ventriloquism, by an ironic echoing, or, in contrast, by developing one's most intimate vernaculars.

Within postcolonial criticism, sometimes two positions on the issue of language are discerned. Those in the first position emphasize the inescapable dominance of colonial discourse, and the irreversible influence of colonial discourse on the languages and cultures it has dominated. They study postcolonial efforts to carve out their own speech positions by subverting colonial language from within. Their opponents hold that people from the former colonies can effectuate their decolonization by turning away from colonial language to their native languages (e.g., African languages, Creole languages).[20] They criticize the opposed position as negative, for it locks its adherents in the gaps and interstices of colonial discourse, leaving them with nothing but the strategy of irony and subversion.

However, such a binary opposition between the two strategies is a questionable construction. Chapters 4 and 5 discuss why: it is never possible to isolate positions as absolutely "positive" (authentically, purely "native") or "negative." For all languages are hybrid. There is no such thing as a pure, uncontaminated language. And all discourses are built from heterogeneous elements. This inescapable hybridity is one of the main tenets of postcolonial theory, but also—and in a more specific manner—of Caribbean theory. Creole languages, which in Caribbean writing are transformed into "nation languages" (Brathwaite), are highly hybrid. Caribbean poet and novelist Edouard Glissant even describes Creole as a "network of negativities." Nevertheless, this does not mean that Creole languages cannot function as highly anticolonial discourses. The use of Creole languages in women's writing may well be considered as a literary and feminist counterpart of nation building. Brathwaite's concept of nation language implies precisely this.

Exploring the specific otherness of Creole languages through their relation to oral practices can be rather problematic: on the one hand, orality is often appropriated by Western critiques of modernity and idealized and essentialized as the "warm," primitive counterpart of "cold," individualist Enlightenment and rationalism, which are associated with and rooted in literacy. On the other hand, Creole languages are more than merely the embodiment of orality. First, they have their very specific characteristics. Second, they function in a specific, important way in the realm of writing as well. For example, for over six decades at least, they have functioned as literary languages, and they are beginning to be used as the medium of criticism. Nevertheless, a comparison between Creole and oral practices helps uncover an aesthetics associated with both, privileging aspects of performance and dialogue and emphasizing structures of address. In addition, Creole languages, as strong communal languages, have a special capacity of binding its members to a shared but diverse tradition. Caribbean women writers are expanding the expressive range of Creole languages. Their creative experiments show how much women are involved in the development of these languages.

Chapter 6 is dedicated to a discussion of the different narrative and discursive strategies Caribbean women writers have chosen as the means to carve themselves a position as speaking subjects within colonial languages and discourses. The first point of reference of this discussion, then, is colonial discourse. Instead of concentrating on the project of defining this difficult concept—a project that would have resulted in quite a different study—I prefer to use the term in a broad and general sense, and to shift my attention to the postcolonial strategies that subvert colonial discourse. In the course of the argument that runs through the chapters, different elements of colonial discourse will be discussed in some detail.[21]

With Bhabha, I hold that the most important function of colonial discourse has been the creation of a "space for subject people" (Bhabha 1990: 75). Postcolonial and Black theorists have amply discussed a range of strategies used to subvert and split this dominant discourse with the aim of creating other spaces for those controlled and marginalized by it. Most of these theorists insist on the inescapable, powerfully domineering position of colonial discourse. When reflecting on the colonial condition, Caribbean critics often refer to the antagonistic pair Caliban and Prospero, two opposed characters in Shakespeare's play *The Tempest*. Caliban himself has this to say on the subject of his colonization, and the words are famous:

> You taught me language; and my profit on 't
> Is, I know how to curse. The red plague gird you,
> For learning me your language![22]

This quote testifies of the inescapable character of the English language; but it also testifies of the subversive use the colonized may make of it. Subversion, however, is too vague and poetic a term. Can this postcolonial subversion be analyzed in its diverse forms? Which concepts describe the specificity of different postcolonial strategies of splitting or exploding colonial discourse from within?

Three difficult concepts will give a sense of the precarious subtlety of these complex practices. Homi Bhabha offers the first concept, "colonial mimicry," to refer to the strategy of appropriating dominant discourse while adapting it simultaneously.

Bhabha, however, has described the phenomenon of mimicry not so much as a postcolonial strategy, but as a mode of colonial discourse.[23] I prefer to focus on the strategies of the colonized, who are appropriating or transforming the spaces offered by colonial discourse, instead of those of the colonizer.[24] The concept of *catachresis*, current in Spivak's work as it is in Bhabha's, highlights another aspect of the position of the formerly colonized. The concept refers to a word for which there is no adequate referent. Spivak, appropriating this Derridean concept to explain the condition of the postcolonial, reads the concept as a displaced postcolonial use of terms and concepts from colonial discourse in the different postcolonial context. An example is the concept of *democracy* when it is used in a postcolonial nation wrestling itself free from a colonial plantation economy, never having know any democracy in the European sense. Spivak explains the position of the postcolonial in this vein: "Claiming catachreses from a space that one cannot not want to inhabit and yet must criticize is, then, the deconstructive predicament of the postcolonial" (1993b: 64).

Here we find again the poststructuralist understanding of postcoloniality as a process in which colonialism is deconstructed, criticized, "worked through," and still very much present. The concepts of "mimicry" and "catachresis" both refer to the very close but curiously suspended relationship of the colonized to colonial discourse. They convey the notion of a split within postcolonial discourse that either can take the form of the ambivalence already present in colonial discourse itself (Bhabha), or can be understood as the loosened link between signifier and signified, as referred to in Spivak's account of catachresis. The critical potential inherent to this position can be used to create and maximize an anticolonial drive; the split can be energized into a subverting, splitting movement at the heart of colonial discourse. Such subverting practices can be captured under the common denominator of "irony." Linda Hutcheon explains: "the use of the trope of irony as a doubled or split discourse which has the potential to subvert from within . . . as a double-talking, forked-tongued mode of address, irony becomes a popular rhetorical strategy for working within existing discourses and contesting them at the same time" (Hutcheon 1991: 170–71). At first sight, irony seems an excellent concept to indicate the postcolonial balance between repeating colonial discourse and overcoming it. However, the concept is not very specific. Irony can be used as a postcolonial trope, but it is also the privileged mode of the postmodern, and even the mode of the colonialist, as Bhabha's work on the irony and mimicry in the discourse of the colonialist demonstrates. As Hutcheon underlines, in Bhabha's work, mimicry "is the strategy of 'colonial power and knowledge.' . . . Bhabha sees irony as appropriating the colonized Other, and implicitly therefore as part of the ambivalence and hybridity that characterize the colonial . . . in . . . its inescapable and complex mutual interrelations with the colonized" (Hutcheon 1991: 176–77). Irony, then, is a tricky instrument. It cannot be applauded as a subverting mode in itself. Postcolonial writers using irony to effectuate a liberating transformation of colonial discourse will therefore pair it with other literary devices.

It is tempting to look for that literary "otherness," for an invigorating total alterity. But no avid close reader will ever be able to surprise this alterity as a pure, undiluted difference within an otherwise hybrid text. Still, if it is useful to heed the ways in which the colonial is still resounding in every postcolonial text, it is as enlightening to study the inscription of the noncolonial discourses one has lived in. Eloquent terms such as *interstices* and the *in-between* do suggest that there are different discourses in postcoloniality, all demanding scholarly attention. Nondominant discourses and strategies can play the role of an ironic subversion of colonial discourse and thus cause a split within language.[25] And so I end with the argument with which I began my introduction to the issue of "voice": postcolonial writing is characterized by the intertwining of anticolonial strategies of deconstruction and nondominant languages and strategies. Any reading of postcolonial texts will take this twofold strategy into account. This means that readers unacquainted with nondominant discourses will have to do some additional study. The three chapters on "voice" reflect on the way in which this can be done.

Chapter 4 focuses on Merle Collins's *Angel* (1987), a novel about the lives of three generations of Grenadian women during a period of political turmoil. I approach the novel as a politically motivated project of creating a communal voice. This voice draws from the traditions of Creole and oral practices, but also from the potentials of both writing and the critical use of Standard English for the emancipation of the community. Reading this text within a larger discussion of postcolonial, Black, and/or feminist theories of orality and Creole, I discuss the language and subject theories in *Angel* through the themes of community, conflict, and violence. *Angel* presents the community's dialogism not as harmonious but as conflictual and often violent. Yet, Creole is endowed with a great flexibility, capable of regulating all communal conflicts and bearing on many aspects of life. The novel lays bare the class and gender differences by concentrating on the working-class women. Thus, it installs Creole as a language that predominantly expresses women's positions and experiences.

In Chapter 5, I demonstrate how the Guyanese novel *Whole of a Morning Sky* by Grace Nichols (1986) constructs its voice through an approach to orality and Creole that is different from Collins's text. My reading of the themes of conflict and community is now shifted to the theme of the outsider to the community. This theme is established through the thematizing of the act of looking. A narratological analysis shows how focalization is distributed among the protagonists, who, by virtue of their age, social status, or gender, are eager or reluctant observers on the fringe of the Creole community. The theme of looking is extended in a discourse about the emancipatory effects that the *reading* of both anticolonial and colonial discourses (as a specific manner of looking) can have on a young woman; reading can offer her the means to turn away from a passive, unaware colonial mimicry and gain a subject position as an independent adult woman. The practice of reading can be understood as the art of having oneself addressed—which is an ability rooted in the practice of oral performance. The novel can be read as an effort to reconstruct both Creole and Standard English as contexts for identification of which invigorating elements of orality are a part (like the openness to being addressed by others or the pleasure in certain forms of language play). It does not develop an oral aesthetics, but a specific aesthetics of sensuality, and consequently a sensual, playful, double voice.

Chapter 6 studies Jamaica Kincaid's essay *A Small Place*, to which Bhabha's concept of "colonial mimicry" is wonderfully relevant. The chapter opens with a discussion of the postmodern, postcolonial, and feminist labels often given to Kincaid's writing. I argue that a mere labeling does not yield insights into Kincaid's construction of a voice. Instead, I consider the complex process by which Kincaid works both with and against postmodern, postcolonial, and feminist aesthetics to create a voice. Sometimes, postcolonial texts are said to oppose the aestheticism of postmodern and modernist texts and to display a form of antiaestheticism. My reading of Kincaid's rhetorical strategies shows that it is quite possible to employ postmodern devices and even an unmistakably postmodern aestheticism to effectuate a postcolonial critique. The text does not employ any anticolonial counterdiscourse to articulate this critique. An interdiscursive analysis shows that Kincaid situates herself firmly within colonial discourse but criticizes it from within by confronting it ironically with a discourse that mimics a colonial, Christian discourse of decency. After considering the essay's structure of address, it becomes clear that the text links its irony to an unsettling and rigid identification of neocolonial victims and criminals.[26] Through confronting Kincaid's presentation of gender with Black and postcolonial theories of Black womanhood, I demonstrate that even Kincaid's apparently ungendered texts offer insights into the position of women in (neo-)colonial structures. Kincaid's voice, then, is less a voice than a highly idiosyncratic and elusive discursive strategy of appropriating and resisting elements from feminist, modernist, postmodern, colonial, and postcolonial discourses.

Silence

In much postcolonial writing, silence, not speech itself, plays the crucial role in the process of finding a voice. For many, especially women, silence is the condition of (obedient) muteness and self-effacement that has to be overcome, and thus it serves as a negative phase in a process. This silence appears as the inability to make an authoritative use of dominant or even nondominant discourses, or as an inarticulated blabbering and madness. Some postcolonial writers, though, celebrate this form of silence as an indispensable device to mute an alienating language, such as the Queen's English. By this distancing they create a space in which the meaningful rhythm of an (as yet unexisting) new, appropriate language becomes perceivable (Ashcroft, Griffiths, and Tiffin 1989: 141–43).

Silence can be seen as an obstacle to speech, but also as an instrument to find a new voice. Silence can also refer to a certain modesty in a writer's endeavor to represent otherness, and to an acknowledgment of the otherness of a (racially, ethnically, culturally) different person who cannot be captured in the writer's dominant discourse. In this vein Bhabha interprets Nadine Gordimer's representation of the Black wife and mother Aila in *My Son's Story* as a silent protagonist (Bhabha 1994: 13–15). However, Thelma Ravell-Pinto criticized the novel for repeating the racist stereotype of the silent Black woman who is placed beyond the realm of political discourse and beyond the realm of desire, and that of the Black male susceptibility to white women's sexual attractiveness (Ravell-Pinto 1993). Indeed, representing Black women as silent or stating their irrepresentability may be a very ambivalent solution, evoking stereotypes of a denigrating colonial discourse. Instead of insisting on the impossibility of representing the female, Black, or postcolonial otherness, Black women writers work hard to find a way to express this otherness—and in the process they, paradoxically, often take recourse to a form of (textual) silence. But this silence then takes on new meanings.

Nevertheless, a considerable amount of postcolonial writing departs from the premise that (female) postcolonial otherness cannot represent itself, nor can it be represented in any way other than through a subversion of colonial discourse, and through silence. Spivak's statement "the subaltern cannot speak" is one of the articulations of this position. The argument runs along the following lines: from the dominant perspective of colonial discourse, "the native" (as a fixed and unified identity) is a colonial construction, and therefore no unequivocal anticolonial position can be taken. He or she can be known only in the moments of escape from dominant languages and discourses: in the silences and gaps in this discourse. The opposite position holds that it is productive to assume that people in formerly colonized areas have unified identities that are not determined by colonial discourse. Thus, South African scholar Benita Parry draws on Fanon's theory of the politically unified self of the resistant native to sustain this view. The voice of politically unified collectives of the (formerly) colonized is represented in effective anticolonial discourses (Parry 1987).

The preceding account implies that a discussion of silence is closely linked to theories on the subject. Some postcolonial women writers may respond to colonial practices of unifying the subject by carefully expressing the multiplicities of their identities.[27] Even then, it may appear that this multiplicity cannot be expressed completely or simultaneously (for example, because it is the result of conflicting colonial and noncolonial dominant discourses). Then, the text will take its recourse to silence. At another point in the text, however, the narrator may suddenly, in an unequivocal voice, speak in unmistakable words about oppression. Indeed, nuanced analysis of multiplicity and hybridity and politically effective identifications of antagonisms do not exclude each other.

A comparison of Kincaid's rhetoric (in *A Small Place*) and that of Jamaican writer Michelle Cliff brings to light how the choice of stressing either multiplicities or antagonisms is related to the text's intended reader. Kincaid addresses the colonizer and his offspring, the tourist, and therefore chooses to emphasize antagonisms. Cliff, speaking to and of the Jamaicans and Black women, underlines multiplicity. But postcolonial writers will inevitably address a multiple audience, which hears the rhythms of the text in different ways, and will therefore repeat, disturb, or fail to respond to them accordingly. As Harry Belafonte says on observing the failure of parts of his audience to join in correctly: there is quite a *lag*.[28] In contrast to Belafonte, Kincaid and Cliff cannot just order their audience to give it another try. They have to keep addressing different groups of their audience simultaneously. Whereas some of their readers may find reminders of the binary structure of (neo-)colonialism and racism not only superfluous but even insulting, another part of the audience may find the emphasis on antagonisms an annoying theoretical complication; it disturbs poetically seductive narratives of multiplicity.

It may be useful to stress that an analysis of multiplicity must necessarily be paired with the identification of unequivocal antagonisms. The assumption that the theoretical understanding of language and identity as always hybrid and plural is incompatible with straightforward political agency seems to be a very persistent misunderstanding within postcolonial and/or feminist discussions. It is especially tenacious in the classroom. However, the acknowledgment that languages and identities are always plural should not lead to the conclusion that each and every statement one makes or position one takes has to be plural, fragmented, innerly contradictory, and endlessly nuanced too. As Spivak explains in a recent interview that touches on the issue of essentialism, there are mobilizing slogans such as "Third World" (in which the many differences within that large part of the world are erased) that come "in response to specific policies of exploitation"; using these slogans "is rather different from essentialism" (Spivak 1993b: 13). So, it is often important to differentiate between the practices of theorizing and those of political action, and to acknowledge the strategic force of clear, unambiguous, and even essentialist statements. Ultimately, it may even be more important still to recognize the theoretical work done in the different politically (or even therapeutically) motivated practices of defining the self, and to deconstruct the Eurocentric dichotomy of theory/political action altogether. Such a recognition may lead to a nuanced approach to the concept of (an embodied) self, in which the materiality of the self is neither diffused into discursive multiplicities, nor unambiguously essentialized.[29] Chapter 7 will explore this issue in the work of Michelle Cliff.

Basically, one can discern two approaches to the issue of the colonial relationship: one chooses a materialist position; the other situates the issue within a psychoanalytical context (Bhabha 1994: 229).[30] If the first position is inevitable in the context of Caribbean writing, where the issue of identity is intimately related to social and political developments, the latter seems as pertinent for a discussion of identity, subjectivity, and language. Yet, the use of psychoanalysis in a postcolonial context is contested. My discussion of silence and identity is therefore organized by the need to consider the relevance of psychoanalytical theories for the reading of postcolonial literature. If the need for such a reflection were not already self-evident, the work of Marlene Nourbese Philip, which is discussed in Chapter 8, would surely make the question unavoidable. By relating language to sexuality, by relating knowledge to castration and to the womb, Philip situates her narrative in the same area in which Western psychoanalytical theories operate.

In traditional psychoanalytical theory, (post-)colonial subjects—for example, Africans—have often been studied through the concept of narcissism. Therefore, one of the ways in which this study explores the opportunities and the limits of a psychoanalytical approach in a postcolonial context is by critically examining the use of the notion of narcissism for a reading of Philip's text. But feminist, Black, and/or postcolonial revisionings of psychoanalysis do not restrict themselves to the deconstructions of such Eurocentric or even blandly racist approaches. Caribbean women's writing has also created concepts that function as critical counterpoints to Western psychoanalytical notions. Thus, the Caribbean feminist concept of the *kumbla*[31] may be confronted with Kristeva's concept of the *chora*. Both concepts refer to the womb; both refer to a nondominant use of language. Both can be used in a reflection on silence. Although I do not present (Philip's implicit rewriting of) the kumbla as an (alternative) postcolonial psychoanalytical concept, I will discuss it as a trope that brings together psychoanalytical narratives of the construction of subjectivity through language and silence, with the issues of gender, "race," and colonialism.

In women's writing in the postcolonial, silence is often the privileged space through which the construction of subjectivity and the issue of representation is thought. But the concept of silence does not merely refer to the impossibility of (self-)representation. It is also used to open a space where the counterdiscursivity and the materiality of the female postcolonial embodied self can begin to be written.

Chapter 7 interprets the occurrence of silence in the work of Jamaican writer Michelle Cliff. I approach this silence in two ways: first as a condition that is to be represented, hence, as an object of representation; second, as a strategy of representation. The first approach connects Cliff's association of silence to the act of "passing" (that is, passing for white, and, in Cliff's work, for heterosexual too). Cliff's texts link silence to invisibility and to the secrecy of passing; the breaking of silence is linked to an anxious, reluctant looking into a closed interior. At the same time, the text analyzes the complex identity of the narrator as too innerly contradictory to be expressed. The ambivalent wish to retain both silence and the full complexity of one's identity appears as a rhetoric of indirectness. Finally I argue that the silences and gaps in her texts cannot merely be explained away by applying a critique of ideology. The silences do not testify of an unsuccessful attempt to cover up a suspect ideology. On the contrary, the silences are part of the plurality of identity. The complexity cannot be expressed without these silences.

In the playful texts by Marlene Nourbese Philip, which are central to Chapter 8, representation is an issue, too. First, I argue that these texts can be read as postcolonial, gendered theories of language and silence. Second, they explore the relationship between self-knowledge and knowledge of the other and are consequently about the representation of self and other too. Silence can be understood as an alternative, complementary language; both words and silence are needed to express postcolonial subjectivity. To examine these views on silence, I situate Philip's texts within the context of feminist and/or postcolonial debates about psychoanalysis. Philip's writings can be read as an ironic strategy of citing, exaggerating, and reversing Western psychoanalytical and other sexual discourses on Africa. Philip uses concepts common in psychoanalytical theory (such as "womb" and "castration"), but she situates these within a complex reflection on race, ethnicity, coloniality, gender, and sexuality. I demonstrate that this strategy results in a redefinition of both the feminist Caribbean notion of the kumbla and Kristeva's understanding of the chora. Finally, by shifting to a narratological and rhetorical approach, I argue that Philip employs two distinct narrative modes relating to the two crucial concepts of womb and castration. Within the context of this critical reflection on postcoloniality, sexuality, and psychoanalysis the postcolonial and feminist courage of Philip's revisionings becomes exquisitely clear.

2

Tropes of Women's Exile: Violent Journeys and the Body's Geography

> I have crossed an ocean
> I have lost my tongue
> from the root of the old
> one
> a new one has sprung
>
> —Grace Nichols

> I crawled to land like a creature from the ocean
> I breathed air—unconsciously changing
> I could not forget the waters
> So I am trapped—
> Two halves of two opposite worlds.
>
> —Prachi Momin

One's identification of oneself as a speaking subject is highly dependent on one's sense of place. For Caribbean women writers in Great Britain, the United States, or Canada, this sense of place often implies a sense of placelessness, displacement, continuous motion, or exile. To capture their revision of the issue of place and placelessness, the following pages will scrutinize different narratives and theories of travel and exile. I will show that cultural, racial, and gender identities are often constructed by means of the notion of the journey. One's definition of the notion of the journey, though, varies according to one's gender, and one's cultural and racial identification.

I will begin this discussion as one might begin a pleasure trip: by reading a narrative that already points seductively to the place one wishes to reach. Instead of opening in grand, historical style by first focusing on Columbus's enterprise and its detrimental aftermath, and instead of opening by referring to the gruesome Middle Passage, which is an equally important turning point in world history, I will turn to a journey of decidedly minor historical importance. Yet, in the light of my intended discussion of feminist postcolonial critiques of travel theories, the story about this feminine journey is highly significant. It has a bearing on some of the issues central to these theories and critiques: the ambivalence of exile, the relationship between identity and travel, and the role of gender.

In *Annie John*, a novel by Antiguan writer Jamaica Kincaid, a girl from the Caribbean sets sail for the United States.[1] She sets out on a journey of her own. In addition, however, she also offers a short but effective critique of the journey of Columbus, which played a decisive role in the generation of the modern age. If anyone can be said to have herself critically inscribed into Columbus's dominant narrative, it is this Annie John. As the location of her inscription, she picks a telling moment in Columbus's life narrative, a lesser-known moment of deep crisis: the episode when Columbus was put in chains. This happened in 1500, at the end of Columbus's third voyage to what he called the New World. A delegation from Spain came to look into the colonists' rebellion against Columbus and his brother on Española, and perhaps into Columbus's political loyalty, too. The brothers Columbus refused to acknowledge the authority of the delegation. They were arrested, put in chains, and brought back to Spain. There, Columbus was granted his liberty, but, as it had already become clear that he was a bad governor, he lost the title of viceroy. Under the picture of Columbus in chains in her schoolbook, Annie John writes: "The Great Man Can No Longer Just Get Up and Go" (Kincaid 1985: 78). Here, she repeats the words her mother used to mock her own father, who was slightly immobilized by an illness of his limbs.[2] Her act of mocking the immobility of the disliked patriarch is in line with other acts of defiance of authority, acts in which she and other schoolgirls explore the sensual, vital, and erotic aspects of life. Although this offensive behavior vexes her mother, Annie took the very words of her anticolonial blasphemy from her mother's mouth. Her mother is the main point of reference for her challenge of and escape from (colonial) authority. Her mother even plays a central role in Annie's dreams of escaping her mother, and her adolescent condition of tormented alienation from, first and foremost, her mother. The chapter following "Columbus in Chains" bears the title "Somewhere, Belgium." Reading about cruelly treated girls, she envies them their happy escape: "In the end, of course, everything was resolved happily for the girl, and she and a companion would sail off to Zanzibar or some other very distant place, where, since they could do as they pleased, they were forever happy" (86). Annie too longs for an escape to some "very distant place."

My most frequent daydream now involved scenes of me living alone in Belgium, a place I had picked when I read in one of my books that Charlotte Brontë, the author of my favorite novel, *Jane Eyre*, had spent a year or so there. I had also picked it because I imagined that it would be a place my mother would find difficult to travel to and so would have to write me letters addressed in this way:

> To: Miss Annie Victoria John
> Somewhere,
> Belgium
> (92)

Annie's dreams of exile are indeed self-willed dissociations from the dominant colonial, patriarchal, and matriarchal structures she does not want to be part of. But in her young woman's dreams, her escape is foremost an escape from her mother, whom she can no longer love without hating as well. Even so, she is caught within her desire for her mother, as becomes clear in the quotation. Annie leaves so that her mother may write to her. A very radical separation is the only way to remodel her relationship with her mother according to the discourse of literature, which she has found enabling, liberating, and offering a sense of direction. She is now the absent addressee, of whom no answer is required; she has won the freedom of the reader.

When Annie finally leaves home, she does not even do so as a future reader.

I had made up my mind that, come what may, the road for me now went only in one direction: away from my home, away from my mother, away from my father, away from the everlasting blue sky, away from the everlasting hot sun, away from people who said to me, "This happened during the time your mother was carrying you." If I had been asked to put into words why I felt this way, if I had been given years to reflect and come up with the words of why I felt this way, I would not have been able to come up with so much as the letter "A." I only knew that I felt the way I did, and that this feeling was the strongest thing in my life. (133–34)

She escapes from an oral history that will always place her in her mother's womb and thus will immobilize her within the history of someone else. She has no history of her own; there is no narrative to guide her into exile. The very basics of reading, the alphabet, are now lost to her, even if she tries to read and write the strongest, simplest elements of her own story.

From a blasphemous rewriting of Columbus's narrative, guided by her mother's parodic discourse, the novel leads to a concept of escape into a larger postcolonial world in which one can be a happy, unencumbered reader of even colonial tales (like *Jane Eyre*), which one may consume just for the pleasure of knowing to be a desired addressee; but it ends on the wordless awareness of exile as a necessary zero point, which leads away from stifling histories as well as from (known) language.

This short consideration of a girl's departure raises several questions about the relevance of the issue of the journey for the Caribbean women writers' enterprise of constructing their literary voices. First, one might object that Kincaid's story could very well be read as a story of a girl's coming-of-age. As Teresa de Lauretis reminds us, Sigmund Freud has offered a Western psychoanalytical model of a woman's journey, even as according to other Western fantasies she cannot be imagined as a traveler, but only as immovable place: "Freud's story of femininity . . . is the story of the journey of the female child across the dangerous terrain of the Oedipus complex" (Lauretis 1984: 132). Simply put, this journey consists of a gradual forsaking of the mother. The girl's destination would be passivity; her reward motherhood. It seems that it is quite common to conceive women as travelers, but only to reach the site of womanhood and motherhood. Once arrived, they are fixed in their identity as passive space. According to this interpretation, Kincaid's story does not really have a bearing on the issue of the journey for Caribbean women. It would be relevant to the adolescent girl's journey in general.

Nevertheless, I propose to complement the reading suggested above with another, postcolonial reading. Such a reading offers itself because of the unmistakably postcolonial elements in the story, like Annie's rewriting of Columbus, the interweaving of the notion of identity and that of the journey, and the evocation of a Caribbean discourse of the ambivalence of exile.

Kincaid's narrative sometimes reads as a provocative study of these issues. The story demonstrates that traveling and displacement can be understood as practices by which one deconstructs or creates an identity as a speaking subject. In addition, the novel presents the process of breaking with one's mother, which is generally seen as necessary for constructing an autonomous identity, as a painful, intense displacement, that is, as a journey. This kind of approach to identity through a discourse of spatiality and mobility is by no means unusual. It is apparent in Freud; and it is apparent in many other writings about modern Western identity.

For many historians, the modern Western age is triggered by one specific, paradigmatic journey: Columbus's journey to the Americas is described as the event that inaugurated modernity.[3] Columbus's misled expedition led to radical changes in European images of world geography and humanity. Many recent critical analyses of modernity abound in terms like "exile," "displacement," and "schizophrenia" as metaphors for the changed human condition in the modern age. In current postmodern, postcolonial, and poststructuralist critical practice, these metaphors of displacement even seem to proliferate.[4] Marxist interpretations situate this divided and displaced modern subjectivity within the context of the development of the capitalist world market, which brought about the "emancipation of the possibility and sensibility of the individual self" as well as the alienation and atomization of society, with the threat of the destruction of cultural and political values (Anderson 1988: 318). Marxist literary scholar Perry Anderson cites Marshall Berman's pictorial description of the context of this modernist disposition from Berman's book *All That Is Solid Melts into Air* (1983): "expansion of experimental possibilities and destruction of moral boundaries and personal bonds, self-enlargement and self-derangement, phantoms in the street and in the soul—is the atmosphere in which modern sensibility is born" (Berman, quoted in Anderson 1988: 319). This evocation makes it clearly felt that modern man is a haunted person, a view that fits well with depictions of modern Western ways of confronting the newly found other—confrontations structured by greed, repression, destruction, fear, and anxiety. The year 1492, when Columbus first landed on the coast of a Caribbean island, is designated as the moment in which the seed for this modern subjectivity was sown. Thus, the anxiously split identity of Western modernity is constructed by a journey, by violent cross-cultural contacts, and by radical displacements of the Western self within its sense of world geography.[5]

However, rather than tracing the modern back to the elusive historical reality of Columbus's ambiguous endeavors, I would prefer here to

question the construction of the modern by means of the trope of the journey itself. Australian scholar Simon During offers an illuminating argument for such a critique. He shows a deep mistrust toward all definitions of
the "modern," as they often come down to tautologies: "the West is modern, the modern is the West" (During 1991: 23). During argues that the distinction between the modern and the nonmodern is constructed *in* and *by*
journeys. It appears that the event of displacement itself offers the tempting opportunity to differentiate "there" from "here," "them" from "us."
Moreover, "the journey brings into view that crucial but extraordinarily
elusive difference between what I am calling, skeptically, the modern and
the nonmodern" (24). To illustrate his point During discusses the journey
of Dr. Johnson and James Boswell to the Hebrides in 1773. From their
comments on the Highlanders he infers the impossibility of fixing the constructed difference between modern and nonmodern in any cultural,
racial, biological, evolutionary, political, or economic theory about the
Highlanders' otherness. In the writings of the two travelers, During discovers a desire to construct hierarchies as such, partly motivated by their
desire to write interesting texts about their observations. The West, then, is
claimed as modern by the mere fact of its reflection upon, and representation of, the other. But it can be so only by virtue of displacement. The
journey itself is the marker of the boundary between the modern and the
nonmodern. It is virtually impossible to define the modern by means of
any unequivocal qualifications. So, for Europeans, the journey—any journey—is a means by which modern human subjectivity is constructed. This
approach to the journey is based on Columbus's paradigmatic displacement;
it assumes Western explorers and travelers as subjects of the journey.

The trope of the journey can also be studied in the context of the
other journey I mentioned: the Middle Passage. Instead of the trope of the
self-chosen journey of the explorer and tourist, then, the trope of the un-
willed displacement of exile becomes central to my discussion. Here I start
to comment on the last crucial point touched on by Kincaid's narrative,
that of the African-Caribbean discourse of exile. Before situating the notion of exile within the context of Caribbean modernity, I will explore the
signification of the Middle Passage for the understanding of Black identity.

Columbus's journey marks only one side of the triangular trade that
links the new and the old worlds together. The Middle Passage marks another side, without which the new world order cannot be apprehended. In

his study of African-American concepts of place, Houston Baker reflects upon the dialectics between the Western experience of the exploration and exploitation of Africa and the New World and the experience of Africans forced into this Western adventure. In a scrutiny of Richard Wright's *12 Million Black Voices: A Folk History of the Negro in the United States* (1941), which also describes the Middle Passage, Baker remarks that the position of the enslaved African within modernity was that of a terrible hole—the coffinlike confinement within the suffocating holds of the slave ships. "The hole, thus, stands as an ironic indictment of the commercial birth of modern man" (Baker 1991: 107). One of Wright's critics described this dialectic as the "determinative tension between 'blackness and the adventure of Western culture'" (107). So, the profitable journey of the European traveler is at the same time the killing Middle Passage for the African.

The choice for a double, not single, marker of the transition from one era to another leads to a different understanding of the way the modern age is understood. Others have done important work toward explaining how the modern age is rooted in the brutality of this colonial encounter, so that debasing perceptions of the racial and cultural other are already implied in Enlightenment thought. From their work, one comes to understand how European modern culture can be understood as cross-cultural in essence.[6] This cross-culturality is rendered explicit in Caribbean concepts of modernity. But European modernity and Caribbean modernity cannot be equated. Simon Gikandi, who has written a book-length study on the forms modernism takes in Caribbean writing, and whose argument I am following in this section, proposes to differentiate between European and Caribbean forms of modernization.[7] He situates Caribbean modernity in the creative schizophrenia embodied in creolization, which he defines as the modernization of African cultures in the Caribbean. Thus, he outlines a split, an inner dichotomy in Caribbean culture that is akin to the Western modernist experience but must be understood in quite different terms. The ubiquitous trope of "exile" in modernism, for example, receives a specific meaning in the Caribbean context, "because of its overdetermination by colonialism" (Gikandi 1992: 35). This specific exile of Caribbeans of African descent has its beginnings in the Middle Passage. Citing Edouard Glissant, a writer and scholar from Martinique, Gikandi points to the crucial awareness of Africa as the land from which those in the Caribbean are exiled. Next to the exile from Africa, Gikandi states, Caribbean people of African descent are also exiled from their own birthplace, because the colonial system does not offer them an opportunity to participate in the community. And last, if Caribbean people leave for the "mother country," that is, the site of colonial power, they will experience yet another state of exile as a second-class citizen in hostile surroundings.

Nevertheless, exile can also be seen in a more positive light. A self-chosen form of exile signifies a renouncing of the confinement in the "hole," the assigned birthplace of the modern Black man. Gikandi discusses statements by C. L. R. James and Guyanese writer Jan Carew that make clear that leaving one's birthplace also means a dissociation from a dominant, destructive culture, which threatens one's very subjectivity. Exile can also be interpreted as a self-willed entry into history, as Carew underlines (Gikandi 1992: 37 ff). This understanding lies at the base of Kincaid's story about Annie John: to enter history, Annie had to escape from the place that continually situated her in her mother's womb.

The Caribbean concept of modernity does not come into being by just one journey but by a complex exile from Africa and the Caribbean as well as Europe. Modern Caribbean identity, then, constructs itself through negotiating the often centrifugal forces of these different forms of displacement. Thus, one finds in Caribbean literature many rewritings of the displacements in the Triangle Trade that brought about this exile. Some, like Caryl Phillips, focus on the travel from the Caribbean to Europe, or they imagine the passage back home from Europe. Others aim at making the Middle Passage in reverse. Kincaid's narrative proves that these revisions may also bring with them a disruptive retelling of the narrative of the ill-fated seafarer from Genoa.

If women writers in the African diaspora offer such rewritings of the different concepts of the journey, these will often also explore the gender-specific aspects of traveling. I have argued above that Black male identity is already constructed as confinement, as immobility. But not only "race" immobilizes. Gender does too. Against all odds, then, these Black women writers aim at reappropriating the notion of travel as a Black women's experience. Like male Caribbean writers, they, too, redefine the journey not only as a sign of their loss, but also as a means to construct new identities and, therefore, as a trope for personal and social change. They are working toward a cultural critique based on a discourse in which tropes of (qualified) mobility are central, while these are nevertheless considered as feminist and Black. I will come back to the critiques and rewritings of Black women writers in Britain in a later part of this chapter. First I will consider some general, academic, feminist, Black, and postcolonial critiques of dominant discourses of travel, which explicate the ethnic and gendered nature of the dominant discourses now being challenged by women writers in the African diaspora.

Questioning Nomads and Tourists

In many narratives in the West the postmodern subject is recreated as a homeless traveler who no longer constructs meaning by relating to his or her origins. These influential and often appealing discourses of mobility have nevertheless been criticized for their ethnocentrism. These critiques are to be taken seriously, all the more because they lead to professional self-reflection. How should the identity of the Western literary scholar who wishes to situate herself or himself in the changing postcolonial, cross-cultural world be defined?

Probably the best known "poetics of travel" today is that developed by the French philosopher Gilles Deleuze and psychiatrist Félix Guattari. Key concepts of their writings are "nomadism" and "deterritorialization." The first concept, to which I will return, points to a philosophy of signification based on a poetic interpretation of the nomadic condition of violent mobility. The latter term is coined to refer to the postmodern movement of continuous displacement of significations, languages, discourses, and identities, a shift that implies constant deconstructions and reconstructions.[8] The term opposite *deterritorialization* is *reterritorialization*. This is the second movement in a dual movement, by which one positions oneself temporarily, to break away again afterward. It is a nomadic way of traveling or signifying, not the imperialistic one that would be aimed at settling and appropriating. By situating the alienation in language itself, Deleuze and Guattari use the notion of deterritorialization to indicate a general condition that affects "us all." They seem to formulate a discourse of displacement and travel of universal validity.

In an influential essay, Caren Kaplan has criticized Deleuze and Guattari's poetics of travel as a model for postmodern subjectivity for not recognizing the power relations causing differences in alienation (Kaplan 1987). She argues that they repudiate any notion of origin or point of departure:

Deleuze and Guattari are suggesting that we are all deterritorialized on some level in the process of language itself and that this is a point of contact between "us all." Yet we have different privileges and different compensations for our positions in the field of power relations. My caution is against a form of theoretical tourism on the part of the first world critic, where the margin becomes a linguistic or critical vacation, a new poetics of the exotic. . . . Theirs is a poetics of travel where there is no return ticket and we all meet, therefore, en train. (Kaplan 1987: 191)

Kaplan holds that not all those Deleuze and Guattari call alienated have the same access to power and privileges. She suggests that the inevitable moment of reterritorialization is just not possible without adopting a form of imperialism. Even the kind of free mobility advocated by Deleuze and Guattari cannot be realized outside the sphere of imperialist power relations. In short, Kaplan criticizes their negation of the fact that power is unequally divided.[9]

Kaplan is not the only one to oppose this implied opinion that the meaning of the condition of alienation would be the same for "all." If the French philosophers relate nomadism to a condition of freedom, Caribbean writer Edouard Glissant utters a bitter comment on this optimism: "L'inquiète tranquillité de nos existences, par tant d'obscurs relais nouées au tremblement du monde. Quand nous vaquons, quelque chose se détache quelque part, d'une souffrance, d'un cri, et se dépose en nous. Le sel de mort sur les troupeaux taris, au travers d'un désert nomade qui n'est certes pas liberté" (1981: 12). Later, in the same work, Glissant returns to the writings by Deleuze and Guattari in a short critical passage on the way Western thinkers theorize the relativity of "the Same" ("le Même," as opposed to "le Divers"). He says this about their work:

Malgré des comparaisons entre civilisations ou expressions (mais toujours généralisantes: l'Occident, l'Orient), cette rapide incursion des deux auteurs dans la Relation (le relais, le relatif, le relaté) ignore beaucoup *les situations autres.* Il y a là aussi un a-priori abstrayant dont nous nous méfions. Celui qui dit se nomme, il lui reste à nommer celui qui se tait, c'est-à-dire à concevoir son épaisse existence. Non pas à parler pour lui, mais à attendre sa parole. Toute autre attitude introduit à une vacation qui se prend facilement pour liberté. (Glissant 1981: 196–97)

Glissant criticizes Deleuze and Guattari's penchant for abstraction and accentuates the need for specificity and concreteness. Moreover, he offers his opinion that their rhetoric obliterates the discourses of the other cultures they evoke and appropriate. Such silencing would indeed jeopardize the legitimacy of the philosophers' references to freedom.

This same point has been taken up and developed by Christopher L. Miller (1993). Miller situates Deleuze and Guattari's work within the ethnographic discussion about the representation of the other. He seriously considers the French philosophers' claim of radical nonrepresentativeness, which would allow them to disengage notions from their cultural contexts and to use them to create a highly personal poetics. Miller, however, argues convincingly that their discourse of nomadism leans heavily on an implicit claim of ethnographic authority. Thus, in spite of their desire to steer free of ethnography, their manner of appropriating other discourses and strategies can be criticized as a questionable ethnographic practice of representation. In Glissant's words, they do not adequately "name" those they silence, and they refrain from creating a space for the discourse of others. Miller sides with Glissant when arguing that Deleuze and Guattari's practice of universalizing and abstracting collides with the postcolonial conviction that all notions, and so also the notion of free mobility, are situated. However, he does not condemn their antirepresentational attitude in itself. Instead, he criticizes the fact that their practice of representation is implicit. Therefore, they represent uncritically and without the required ethnographic integrity.

Postcolonial critic Yasmine Gooneratne gives an illuminating and concrete example of the situatedness of all notions, including that of placelessness. To sustain her point, she discusses the preference of critic Meenakshi Mukherjee for the author "who has . . . abjured 'place' and elected to wander" (Gooneratne 1986: 18). Gooneratne argues that one's judgment about such uprooted authorship depends on one's "sense of place." In this case, Mukherjee follows the norms of "the Hindu respect for the 'homeless ones,' the sages of India" (18). Deleuze and Guattari do not localize and relativize their equally situated predilection for the notion of nomadism; neither, as has been argued above, do they situate the forms of nomadism they refer to. In consequence, their poetics of nomadism and deterritorialization is criticized for what can ultimately be called its ethnocentric denial of the importance of "place."

In spite of these critiques, such discourses of light-footed, unhindered motion remain unabatedly seductive. Postcolonial scholars may be attracted too by their potential to describe their own theoretical practices.

If certain forms of signifying can be understood as if they are forms of mobility, then the process of *theorizing* the shifting, multiple identities of postcoloniality through deconstructions and rewritings is certainly a form of *moving* through often unfamiliar, inappropriated areas, too. But the concept of nomadism does not do justice to the specific situatedness of this group of Western intellectuals. Could there be a more suitable term to catch these institutionalized Western scholarly practices? Or should scholars renounce the quest for a postmodern position of free mobility altogether? For the sake of argument, let me begin by considering the possibility of finding an adequate term for such a position. What about *tourism*? Indeed, the term fits the way in which the Western middle-class intellectuals are situated surprisingly well. As Jonathan Culler states, speaking about the tourist's view of traveling, "for most of us, the world is more imperiously an array of places one might visit than it is a configuration of political or economic forces" (1988: 153). Culler suggests both the attraction of this discourse (for how much more attractive it is to visit places than to ponder economical or political structures) and its drawbacks. If this "us"[10] were to refer to the community of literary critics, they would be endowed with a scholarly habit of casually shopping around for (once-situated) concepts. But the political and economic forces referred to in the quote cannot be willed away by merely inscribing oneself in a discourse that negates them. On the one hand, then, scholars may not want to play the tourist for long—apart from the fact that tourists are not exactly held in high repute. On the other hand, Culler has pointed out that the very desire not to be a tourist is also part of the discourse of tourism: the dichotomy tourist/traveler serves to address the tourist's desire of, and their willingness to pay for, authenticity. For white Europeans in general it is not easy to escape the position of the tourist. Even for Caribbean creative writers in Europe it is sometimes impossible to be anything else. Therefore, one need not be surprised that, while Jamaica Kincaid in Chapter 6 uncompromisingly lashes out at the tourist, Amryl Johnson often almost identifies with tourists, though often shunning them too, when she tries to reconnect to the islands of her birth (see below).[11] Western scholars of cross-culturality, who are necessarily constantly engaged in acknowledging and, to a certain extent, appropriating concepts and theories from other cultural contexts, are in a comparable situation. If they emphasize their intellectual freedom to appropriate, they are close to the position of tourists—rather than nomads.

This position has one unexpected advantage. Paradoxically, if they (or we) prefer to be blind to the discourse of tourism in which they are thus inevitably implicated, they miss the opportunity to become aware of the very political and economic structures Culler refers to above, if only because of the tourist's bad reputation. This awareness will often result in a scholarly concentration on the global processes by which margins and centers are endowed with special signification, and by which borders are created, and on his or her involvement in these.[12] As soon as such scholars stop their preliminary exploration of their cross-cultural position and settle down to engage in extended, serious studies, they stop being tourists. But in that moment they are already less interested in free mobility than in critical (self-)reflection. It seems to me, then, that discourses of free mobility will be effective only if they do not merely open up to other discourses but also are balanced by self-reflection.

When Western scholars begin to study the varied international processes that regulate the distribution of global power, they are coming close to the many Black and feminist postcolonial scholars whose work explores the processes involved in the construction of borders. These borders may be, for example, the confining walls of their exclusion, or the painful split within the identity of bilingual women. The varied borders they are confronted with are, most certainly, also related to their gender. Often, these very borders are also the sites of their creativity. After this short consideration of the ethnocentrism implied in a Western theory of travel, the next section will discuss the feminist critiques that draw attention to the aspect of gender implied in the spatial discourses that center around borders and mobility.

Female Space, Sitting Ducks, and Mothers in Motion

Black women writers can relate to dominant travel discourses only by contesting and rewriting them. This is not only because these travel discourses are ethnocentric, but also because they bear upon gender. Often, men are cast in the role of travelers; women are deemed to be passive residents by nature. Indeed, several feminist scholars have pointed to the masculinist character of the motive of travel and mobility in much Western discourse. In a 1984 essay, Teresa de Lauretis scrutinizes the opposition between (female) space and the (male) traveling hero in structuralist narratology, and she shows how spaces and movements in narrative texts have been gendered. She mentions Yuri Lotman's contribution to the rigid gendering of these categories. Lotman argues that every story consists in its most abstracted form of a chain of two functions: entering a closed space and emergence from it. This closed space can be a house, or a tomb, or a womb, or a woman; in any case, it has to be understood as female. The hero entering and leaving this space is by definition male (Lauretis 1984; Lotman 1990).

In Western philosophy at large one finds a tendency to associate femininity to inactive, immobile space. Luce Irigaray states in her *Ethique de la différence sexuelle* (1984) that sexual difference is based on the interaction of time and space. God, being time itself, created space as something outside him, to embody himself within it afterward. Therefore, time is inherent to the subject, and space is outside it. As space is the site of creation, it is characterized as feminine and maternal. Recently, Mary Gordon has taken up a similar argument in an essay on American fiction. Janet Wolff cites her in her own essay on the masculinist character of the vocabulary of travel in cultural criticism: Gordon "notes the centrality of the image of motion connected with the American hero. . . . At work here is 'a habit of association that connects females with stasis and death; males with movement and life'" (Gordon, quoted in Wolff 1993: 231). Gordon makes an even stronger point: "men's journeys should be construed as a flight *from* women" (Wolff 1993: 230–31). Wolff acknowledges that Gordon is not the only one to point at the gender-specific character of travel metaphors; she mentions, for example, James Clifford and Meaghan Morris.

This tendency of associating men with motion and women with homely stability has a serious impact on the construction of literary history. As an example, consider a study by a scholar who has worked on the relation between exile and literature. Simon Gikandi states that the first great works in Caribbean literature were written in exile. For him, the early literature of exile is the zero point of Caribbean writing (Gikandi 1992: 33). However, when he proceeds to discuss the texts written in exile, which he considers as the masterpieces of Caribbean literature, it becomes clear that this great literature of exile is produced by male writers and males alone.[13] After reading Jamaica Kincaid's work, also written in exile and very much about *woman's* exile, it seems urgent to consider the ways in which women are implicated in this larger discourse of journey and exile. For they *are* implicated: Columbus's ships bore Spanish women's names[14]; and during the

Middle Passage, contrary to the men, African women were obliged to stay on the quarterdecks so as to be accessible for rape (Baker 1991: 124–25). They were assigned specific places in these journeys. So, how are women included in the cruel double beginnings of "our" modern age?

Kincaid subordinates Columbus's narrative to a girl's story of escape from her mother, which is also an escape from a doubly colonizing discourse. For her, as much as for her male colleagues, exile means an enabling escape from immobilizing dominance. However, her journey is in part a flight from her mother, which, as I will argue below, is in itself a traditional masculinist configuration of the journey. Kincaid uses this trope while transforming it, for instance by her insertion of the mother's discourse as the source of her own revolt, and of exile as a site oriented toward her mother's discourse.

In addition to Kincaid's story, there are many other narratives of journeys and exiles in which women—and even mothers—are involved as travelers. To appreciate these, it is important to differentiate between these feminist and womanist narratives and the masculinist stories from a Eurocentric modernist or postmodernist perspective, also used by women writers. For the widely used (post)modernist discourse of travel, displacement, and deterritorialization is also very attractive to European feminist critics working within the context of postmodernism.[15] Yet, uncritical adoption of certain tropes of mobility may bind critics to a limited, masculinist, and ethnocentric discourse. Let us rather inquire into the possibilities of a feminist or womanist discourse of travel.

For women do travel, as Janet Wolff rightly notes, and they do construct their identities around notions of travel and motion. When they do, they apparently put their very gender identities at stake. In the case of the Victorian lady travelers, "their activities positioned them in important ways as at least problematic with regard to gender identification" (Wolff 1993: 233). Traveling women of different classes, sexualities, "races," and ethnicities are negotiating their identities in their own ways.

This statement can be illuminated by the specific narrative of Black women's mobility formulated by one of the best-known women writers in the African diaspora, Alice Walker. In this narrative, Walker links the ability to travel to "race," gender, and a certain form of motherhood. She even articulates the necessity of women's mobility as a part of her definition of Black womanhood. In the late 1960s, Walker coined the word *womanist* as a Black counterpart to *feminist*, and the last lines of the second entry of her definition of the concept are as follows: "*Womanist*. . . . Traditionally capable, as in: 'Mama, I'm walking to Canada and I'm taking you and a bunch of other slaves with me.' Reply: 'It wouldn't be the first time'" (1984: xi).

Being a responsible, committed Black woman means, among other things, that one is capable of moving oneself and others away from oppression; it means that one is willing to go and to lead into (another) exile. For Walker, this aspect of femininity is quintessential, so much so that her very name testifies to its centrality: "My great-great-great-grandmother walked as a slave from Virginia to Eatonton, Georgia—which passes for the Walker ancestral home—with two babies on her hips. . . . (It is in memory of this walk that I choose to keep and to embrace my 'maiden' name, Walker.)" (1984: 142). From this fragment, we learn that Walker is Alice's "maiden" name, that is, her father's name. Even if her ancestor was a mother-in-motion, I detect the suggestion here that women should partly keep their "maiden," maybe androgynous qualities of unburdened freedom of motion to claim the fullness of Black womanhood. Literal, biological motherhood threatens Walker's concept of the mobile female. Nevertheless, women, whether they are artists or not, should have children; but Walker pleads for having *one* child, and one child only, in a famous essay dedicated to the topic. "'Why only one?' . . . 'Because with one you can move,' I said. 'With more than one you're a sitting duck'" (1984: 363). Mothers bear the curse of being known as the most sedentary variety of women imaginable, and therefore, Walker implies, also the most vulnerable. But this goes only for mothers of more than one. By concentrating on a "light" variety of mothering, that is, the mothering of one child, Walker creates her image of mobile motherhood. In this way, Walker creates a concept of female migratory identity around the notion of a purposeful mobility.

Reading Walker's argument about the necessity of only *one* child, one encounters other reasons for not having more than one, relating to the pain of giving birth and the concentration needed for work. At the same time, the essay is an eloquent defense of the importance of having this one child. Walker affirms motherhood as an active, politically empowering position. She does so by making a *mother* the main protagonist in a narrative about encounters with racism from white feminists, and about the Black radical responses to those and other instances of racism and sexism: "our young mother," who is Alice Walker herself, gains from the birth of her daughter a deeper understanding of the world than she had before. Walker offers an important contribution toward a theory of Black female mobility. She leans upon the assumption that free, unencumbered mobility is most desirable, and that this mobility is not easily reconcilable to those aspects of femaleness she values otherwise, that is, motherhood. But she is also prepared to discuss this ambivalence. First, she informs her readers that the ancestor from whom she took her name carried *two* children on her hips while performing her striking journey, not one. Second, she openly ponders the implications of Buchi Emecheta's identity as a writing mother of *five* children for her own theory of *"one* child" (Walker 1984: 66–70). Thus, she opens the possibility of other theories about femininity, motherhood, and mobility.

It occurs, of course, that women from Black or migrant communities dismiss discourses of travel, unconcerned with the fact that they might thus ally themselves with dominant definitions of women as space. Within all ethnic or cultural communities, discourses about traveling may appeal differently to men and women, and their strategies of adopting or resisting them will therefore differ. In her essay about the construction of migrant identities, Keya Ganguly makes the point saliently (1992). She reports a conversation with two Indian men living in the United States, on the subject of travel: "For ordinary middle-class people like themselves, travel 'back home' consisted of a long series of queues, bribes, third-class compartments, and dirty accommodation. In contrast, they said, here they could 'drive up to a ticketing window, charge the ticket to their American Express cards, and go wherever they wanted to, *in style*" (Ganguly 1992: 33). Upon which Ganguly asks them critically: "what about the fact that as Indians, we have to go to extraordinary lengths to prove our visa or citizenship status, proof of residence, reasons for travelling, and so on, every time we crossed a border?" (33) And she comments: "The metaphoric references to travel, railway stations, and tea-drinking—in the context of thinking about identity—seem to me to be tied up with sublimated odyssean fantasies of masculinity and self-authorization" (34). For these men, "[e]migration as a search for mastery is another trope in the text of the recovery of selfhood" (37). The first quote shows how Western travel discourse appeals to the men, who apparently enthusiastically embrace the image of the mobile American hero as analyzed by Mary Gordon. Nevertheless, for the Indian women whom Ganguly listened to, the case was different. In their stories, the past before the migration was glorified; traveling had cut them off from supporting family structures in which their status was secured. In this case, the discourse of travel has no appeal for them. Their rejection of travel discourse implies a critique of such a discourse, rather than a "natural" inclination to the home.

In the work of women writers, the notion of womanhood as naturally related to homeliness is sometimes taken up and appropriated to submit it to a radical deconstruction. Jamaica Kincaid is a case in point. She describes the importance of domestic activity for her writing. Then she says about her motherhood: "But I have these two children and yet I wrote one book in a year and three months. . . . you see, being so interested in domestic activity, having children can only add to my feeling of domestic life. I am beginning to see their life as going out into the world, whatever it is. But I can only see that from the kitchen table" (Perry 1990: 504–5). Here we find a sitting Black woman who is nevertheless creative. I must add that Kincaid has a way of translating history into domestic activity, as she tells in the same interview (504). This means that she does not exclude herself from the outside world, but that she refigures the outside according to her own need of the domestic and personal scale.

Both Walker and Kincaid contest travel discourses that define (Black) women, and especially mothers, as nontravelers and passive space. Walker draws on the history of Black resistance to offer her alternative narrative of Black motherhood as a condition of mobility. Nevertheless, she underwrites the discourse privileging free mobility. Kincaid dismisses this discourse altogether. Instead of contesting the notion of motherhood as passive space, she rewrites it as the condition of sedentary creativity. By deconstructing the opposition between inside and outside, she also changes the nature of the border deciding her condition as kitchen dweller. Both writers take up aspects of gender, generation, and/or "race."

Kincaid is at least ambivalent about the advantages of traveling. To a certain extent, this ambivalence is shared by Janet Wolff, the author of the exploratory essay already referred to above. Wolff argues that feminist critics should keep their distance from the gendered vocabulary of travel when looking for an adequate discourse for their own work in cultural criticism. Even in an adapted version, she warns, most travel discourses will still be rooted in a resistance against fixed subjects, and consequently still lean toward the mistaken and impossible ideal of free mobility. Feminists should always be conscious of the situatedness of critiques and theoretical enterprises; thus, they should acknowledge that the dominant center should be the main object of critique, and the margins should be seen as the place where this criticism is articulated (Wolff 1993: 235).

Nevertheless, Wolff praises certain alternative metaphors of space and motion.[16] She offers an appropriate characteristic of the different tradition in Black women's writing about mobility by referring to the recurring notion of bound motion. A Black feminist travel discourse, she argues, often centers around the notion of "dislocation from a given, and excluding, place" (Wolff 1993: 235). This notion echoes Davies's definition of Black women's mobility, to which I am turning now. Wolff's essay, however, testifies to one of the problems common in cultural critique: by focusing on a critique of dominant travel discourses, the vigorous spatial tropes and discourses used by postcolonial and/or Black feminist or womanist writers are relegated to the margins. Unfortunately, Wolff's text too refers to these discourses only as an afterthought, anonymously, and thus reinforces their marginal status.[17]

In contrast, Carole Boyce Davies offers an account of the relation between gender identity and motion that is rooted in an abundance of Black and migrant women's texts. In her rich, very informative study *Black Women, Writing, and Identity*, Davies introduces the concept of "migratory subjectivity" to describe Black women's identity. She explains: "Black female subjectivity then can be conceived not primarily in terms of domination, subordination or 'subalternization,' but in terms of slipperiness, elsewhereness" (Davies 1994: 36). This concept insists on the *difference* of Black female subjectivity. It should be differentiated from the "nomadic subjectivity" articulated by Deleuze and Guattari: "It is not so much formulated as a 'nomadic subject,' although it shares an affinity, but as a migratory subject moving to specific places and for definite reasons" (Davies 1994: 36–37). In this way, the concept admirably brings together the mobility of Black women's identity and its specificity. In addition, Davies's definition (and especially her emphasis on the "elsewhereness" of Black women) offers a remarkable guideline for those who wish to listen to and address Black women scholars, which I will discuss in some detail. After leafing through many volumes of postcolonial theory, one might exclaim, with Davies (80, 88): where are "the women . . . in the discourses of post-coloniality?" Whereby he or she will refer especially to Black and migrant women. Davies's terse answer is that "they are somewhere else, doing something else" (88).

It is tempting to accentuate the outsiderness of Black and migrant women's reflections on the self. Indeed, it is quite common to show how Black women writers always evade discourses and definitions meant to situate and confine them. This approach, however, doesn't do justice to the complex quality of Black women's writing. It implies that Black women's writing can be studied only as a critique that inhabits dominant texts in an elusive way.[18] But the force of these texts lies as much in their articulation of culturally and gender-specific notions and discourses. They are not merely critiques. It seems wise, therefore, to refuse to understand all literary expression from, say, Africa or its diaspora as reactions to dominant Western discourses. If one does, the following suggestion by Christopher L. Miller will be of use: he urges scholars of, say, a specific African literature to learn about the relevant African literary traditions, African epistemologies, and theories in which the object of their study is embedded. This, he states, is the only way one may encounter the difference of other discourses.[19] In the same vein, Black women's discourses of spatiality are not just "outside" and "elsewhere." They often refer to or create some specific *inside* space as well.

In art as well as in theory, then, there are Black women's discourses of travel in which the concepts of femininity, motherhood, traveling, and home itself are redefined. Acknowledging these discourses will lead to a better understanding of Black migrant women's writing, as this writing is often shaped according to nondominant notions of the relations among gender, "race," exile, and writing. Such considerations may eventually result in different literary histories of the writings of the African diaspora. Let us therefore continue where Davies leads us, and begin to outline some of the complex Black and feminist metaphors and discourses of space and motion.

Journey as Struggle

Writing is like killing

—Nawal El Saadawi

In the late 1980s, several collections of Black British women's creative writing appeared. In these publications, a conscious effort is made to evaluate the shaping of a specific aesthetics that is directly linked to the experiences and visions of Black British women. Containing literary criticism (by the editors) as well as creative writing, these publications teach a lot about the crucial debates within the field of Black British women's literature. Many of these debates focus on the relations among gender, "race," and mobility discussed in this chapter. It can even be argued that in their poetry, prose, and essays Black women in Britain reappropriate the notion of travel as a Black woman's experience. They try to represent their efforts of forging new (collective) identities and literary voices through the trope of the journey. These women's journeys are explicitly situated within global power relations.

The first subject of my inquiry is the collection *Charting the Journey: Writings by Black and Third World Women,* which appeared in London in 1988. This collection is especially noteworthy as it constructs the (literary) voices of Black British women by means of a specific use of the trope of journey. Thus, an aesthetics is developed in which the journey, writing, and struggling are closely interrelated. Two types of imagery surface in the short introduction: one is connected to the notion of "journey," the other to that of "struggle." Both, however, refer to the larger context of the construction of identity. Here and in the shorter introductions to the book's separate sections, the editors engage in many elaborate deconstructions of the (often spatial) notions used to describe the situation of migrant women, by others or by themselves: journey, home, time, borders, frontiers, food, diversity, and wholeness. Most of these are apparently linked to a discourse of travel; others are connected to the body and a sense of identity. More often than not, the editors of *Charting* discuss these notions within the context of political struggle. This association is made from the very first page of the introduction. There, the editors set out to define "the idea of Blackness in contemporary Britain" as an idea and a process that is rooted "in the arrival, and creation of a life in this country, of three to four million people . . . from the former British colonies" (Grewal et al. 1988: 1): "And since the 'new life' was one of opposition, of struggle, it was inevitable that the old, taken-for-granted notions of 'black' and of 'woman' would be questioned and subject to change" (2). The imagery of struggle is taken up and maintained. Thus, the postcolonial displacement lands migrants in a discourse of struggle. This struggle is in its turn imagined as a journey. The two discourses are apparently entangled. Through their interrelation, they serve to articulate a postcolonial account of strategies of identification and signification.

Because they are placed within the context of Black women's political struggles, these efforts to find new images of Black womanhood are described as weapons in a struggle in their own right. Nawal El Saadawi's radical statement, which I used as an epigraph to this section and which I have taken from the introduction to *Charting*, stresses the violent context within which Black women's creativity has to operate. Saadawi compares writing to killing. To her, the situation in which the writer finds herself is violent anyway; it is not she who initiated the violence. She has to defend herself to survive. To some, this may not seem a female position. However, in a piece in the collection, based on workshop discussions around 1986, Kum-Kum Bhavnani challenges this assumption already in the title of her piece: "Is Violence Masculine?" Her answer is no. She prefers to define violence in relation to the state rather than in relation to gender. As many Black women are daily confronted with the brutal violence of racism, they just cannot afford to exclude violent struggle against it as a viable strategy. Even the discussion about political strategy itself may be aggressive and violent. "If white women claim they are non-violent and assert the need to only develop non-violent resistances, they are then denying themselves the right to express any solidarity with our struggles" (Grewal et al. 1988: 265). This close relationship between signification and struggle points to a semiotic perspective in which power relations are deemed paramount in the construction of meaning. This view refers to Foucault's opinion of discourse, but it is articulated in a highly radical way. However, if these strategies of identification are part of a struggle, they are also described as a journey.

Ours then is a journey. . . . It is a migrants' journey not simply in the commonly accepted sense, but also in the sense of migrations from past to future lives. It includes that other form of migration—movement across the frontiers of life into new, uncharted territories of the self.

Like all momentous journeys it is full of fits and starts, gains and losses. Yet to grasp the substance of this journey is the political challenge. (Grewal et al. 1988: 2)

The initial, alienating experience of migration is appropriated and reforged into a discourse of ongoing, willed transformation. In this way, the two metaphors from the collection's title ("Charting" and "the Journey"), the issue of traveling itself and the issue of representation are both brought under the heading of the political struggle.

The interweaving of the journey and the struggle should not come as a surprise. Indeed, the association of these concepts is an illuminating deconstruction of implicit assumptions in common Western definitions of the journey. From a Western perspective, the Western traveler leaves the civilized center of the world for unknown, uncivilized areas that have not yet been charted. This unknown territory is then charted according to Western norms, or submitted to Western imperialist norms. In this imperialist concept violence is inextricably bound up with traveling: the inhabitants of the unknown regions will be confronted according to the traveler's project, and more often than not he will see them as a threat to his schemes, and force them to submit or annihilate them. In a similar way, unknown landscapes are often seen as territory to master: rapids must be mastered, mountains will be conquered. By taking for granted that violence, force, and travel are always necessarily blended, the editors of *Charting* offer an implicit critique of both the travel discourses of the naive tourist and the concept of nomadism.

The last point needs some elaboration. Deleuze and Guattari's nomadology speaks extensively about the nomad war machine. They do, therefore, relate mobility to violence. But, as Miller argues, the authors do not discuss it within a representational context (1993: 26–30). Therefore, they are able to associate war with "multiplicity, smooth space, becoming-animal" (29). It will be apparent that this is not the way in which most Black women writers understand violence. Black women writers who are searching for strategies of representation will often inhabit a representational level, and seek to confront their individual and collective experience of different forms of violence.

The struggle for identification, then, is imagined as a violent journey. But the trope of the journey is in its turn complemented and sometimes overlaid by the notions of transformation and growth. In their introduction, the editors motivate the need for such a journey by analyzing the actual difficult position to which the Black women's movement in Great Britain has come after a period of successful self-organization and political action. "We failed to grow" is the editors' (self-)criticism (Grewal et al. 1988: 3). And this sentence contains their program: change, growth, and transformation are now the tasks set for politically motivated Black women in Britain. As the failure to negotiate the diversity within the Black women's community is seen as the cause of the crisis, the object of change is the redefinition of Black womanhood as a diverse, multiple identity. The editors want to strive toward "our own, ever-changing image" (5); Black women's identity should be seen as variable, and impossible to freeze.

This imagery of a mobile identity is nevertheless well rooted in a specific social context. In fact, it seems as if the editors try to wed a discourse of mobility to a Marxist discourse. Much in line with Janet Wolff's observations, the editors shun an indefinite spatial imagery and use situated tropes instead, even if they have to take these tropes from discourses they criticize. Two of the recurring images in their discourse are the "border" and the "frontier." The editors are well aware of the imperialist discourse from which they stem, but they allow for quite different connotations.

What does the word border make you think of? A hem at the bottom of a skirt, the divide between Scotland and England, the thick line between rich and poor, living on the border line, the tenuous line between young and old.

And frontier—apart from *Star Trek* connotations? (Grewal et al. 1988: 117)

The existence of imposed frontiers, defined here as man-made constructions in the realm of the social and political (instead of the geographical), makes efforts and struggles necessary for those who want to travel and cross them. The acknowledgment of the plural and contradictory character of identity leads not to just any free mobility but to the struggle to cross imposed boundaries.

The imagery of necessary, permanent transformation comes back in many comparable deconstructions, such as that of "home": "Home is where you're safe. / Home is where you're scared to be. / Home is a place of mind./ Home is a foreign land. Home is homelands" (Grewal et al. 1988: 9); and "time": "Time is a kind of space. We move with it and through it, for it and against it. . . . It is a measure of frontiers traversed, jobs fulfilled, changes endured. . . . 'Time is money.' . . . Time is frozen in the migrant's memories" (Grewal et al. 1988: 55–56). These deconstructions are brought about in poetry and prose as well as in more analytical and journalistic writing. The collection aims at offering sociological rather than literary insights. So, even if the struggle for identification is seen as a semiotic enterprise, *Charting* does not try to find a specific *literary* aesthetics. It is dedicated to the socially and politically motivated semiotic work by Black women in Great Britain, as "a contribution to the documentation of Black womanhood at a specific moment in this place called Britain" (Grewal et al. 1988: 4). As the journey to be represented is an individual as well as a diversely collective journey of a political nature, the writing expressing it cannot be restricted to either literary or nonliterary genres only. The editors include poetry (47 of the 75 texts), essays (20), and prose (5), as well as interviews (3). Thus, they acknowledge that poetry may be an excellent medium to express diversity, ambivalence, and multiplicity, while on the other hand they insist on the unambiguous nonliterary statement of political and social wrongs.[20] The literary sections of the collection mirror this contradiction. For example, the poem "Social Change" by Eveline Marius castigates those who do not directly engage in social struggle:

> Everyone wants social change,
> but you won't get it
> blaming everything and anyone except yourself
> taking up photography
> arts and crafts
> painting
> video making.
>
> —Eveline Marius (Grewal et al. 1988: 260)

Contrary to the editors' text, which places writing and other signifying practices alongside struggling, this poem seems to suggest that producing art does not lead to the desired social changes. I discern a certain paradox in the choice of poetry as the medium to condemn creative acts (such as writing poetry, one wonders uneasily?) by comparing them to "taking drugs / hanging around in coffee bars / making excuses / moaning / moping" (Grewal et al. 1988: 260).

An opposite stance is taken in another poem, two pages further. In the wonderful poem "Among Tigers" by Suniti Namjoshi, a distance from struggles and causes is expressed:

> You see, I have survived so long,
> my habit of observation grown so strong
> that sometimes I think I almost belong.
> I know exactly how a tiger drinks,
> how a tiger walks, smiles and thinks,
> but find somehow that I cannot ape
> that unthinking pride or its manifest shape.
> I fully understand the Tigrish Cause
> and keep my distance from those massive jaws.
>
> —Suniti Namjoshi (Grewal et al. 1988: 262)

Here we find an exquisite expression of the position of the marginalized—be she a migrant, a woman (of color) among men (of color), a lesbian—which at the same time questions the usefulness of the muscular semiotics of struggle and Cause of this (relatively) dominant group for her own experience. It is one of the few moments in the collection when some distance from a "Cause" is expressed, without in turn referring to some other, worthy political cause of one's own.

This poem seems to imply that dominant, Marxist, or other revolutionary discourses may fall short of representing the experience of migrant women. In this, it is connected to statements such as the one by Audre Lorde, quoted in the introduction to the section "Frontiers": "What you chart is already where you've been, where we are going, there is no chart yet" (Grewal et al. 1988: 117). Migrant women who try to escape traditional definitions move outside the realm of known representation. Nevertheless, representation is possible; the possibility of representation is the whole point of this collection; the editors would never agree with those who would place (Black) femininity by definition outside representation. Like Fredric Jameson, who sees a certain kind of (cognitive) mapping as a means of coming to grips with modern society (Jameson 1988), the editors believe in the possibility of "charting" their journey. They do not claim to chart the totality of the world as they see it. They mean to chart the *journey*, a project that amounts not to the fixation of a space, but rather to the plural and flexible notation of an ongoing motion.

In *Charting*, then, the construction of a new identity is described as a violent journey. The editors of *Charting* rewrite the trope of the journey in such a way that it may express their strategies of identification: thus, one finds in their editorial comments a politically motivated celebration not of the journey itself, but of the continuous transformation and the diversity of Black migrant women's identity. However, the wish to see this ever-changing diversity expressed in complex poetry is at odds with the editors' conviction of the necessity of the political clarity in Black women's writing. This tension becomes visible in the paradoxes in some of the poems, and it is partly resolved in the editors' emphasis on the sociological value of the collected texts. Others, however, have opted for different ways to bring to light both the political and poetical aspects of the Black British women's journey to a new identity and a new voice. An interesting case in point is Cobham and Collins's *Watchers and Seekers*.

Journey, Space, and Sexuality

My black triangle
is black light
sitting on the threshold
of the world
  —Grace Nichols (Cobham and Collins 1987: 29)

At the risk of staging an unintentional and undesirable dichotomy between politics and sexuality, I will now consider Rhonda Cobham and Merle Collins's anthology of Black women's texts *Watchers and Seekers* (1987) under the heading of the interrelation between the journey and women's sexuality.

Watchers presents itself as a literary anthology. The introduction by Rhonda Cobham uses the context of worldwide migration and exile to picture a network of related women who link through time and space to form a literary tradition. To establish these links between present-day Black women writers in Britain and earlier experiences of migration and oppression, the introduction makes use of the image of the (fore)mother. Mothers are travelers as well as anchoring points; they connect the writers of today to the history of women living in earlier episodes in the African diaspora or other worldwide migratory movements; mothers connect today's writers to "the strong traditions of independence and creativity that have characterized Black female culture for hundreds of years" and to "a cultural tradition of survival" (Cobham and Collins 1987: 9–10). In contrast to *Charting*, the introduction places the collection unambiguously within the cultural and literary tradition of the "Black women in Britain" and their migrating foremothers, who moved between (for example) Caribbean and British culture. One of those is Jamaican poet Una Marson, whose work and person are presented in the introduction: "she was a Black woman, determined to fashion her own definitions of both these concepts—Blackness and womanhood—through her art" (4). Cobham does not speak about the way in which the two aspects of this identity might relate. She reports that Marson found "a new awareness of herself as a Black woman" (4) when she was confronted by British racism, and also by her racial and cultural solidarity with other Caribbean and African people in England. She then started to write poems to celebrate the international women's movement, alongside other poems about the destiny of African people within the political events around the 1940s.

Cobham uses negative terms to describe the way Marson must have experienced her Black *femininity*: she did not find a satisfying relationship, she did not have children, and she is presumed to have "missed out on some of the most important emotional experiences available between women" (6). The suggestion is that Marson's experience of sexuality, which is constitutive of her gender identity, must have been bitter and frustrating. Indeed, many of the poems in this collection testify to problematic experiences of sexuality. Sexual harassment, rape, abortions, and teenage pregnancy are topics alongside the intricacies of (heterosexual) love, childbirth, family life, mother-daughter relations, and also racist violence, imperialism, history, and political struggle.

The mother figure looms large in this collection. Sometimes she manifests herself in an angry outburst against those who want to collapse all aspects of womanhood into the comfortable notion of "mother":

Don't call me Mama
Don't call me Mother
See me for what I am
A Woman.

—Carole Stewart (Cobham and Collins 1987: 34)

In this poem, "mother" is analyzed as a reductive stereotype used, for example, in nationalist rhetoric. The text warns against the exaltation of the mother, which amounts to a denigrating reification and a denial of women's complex and plural subjectivity. However, I fear that the notion of Woman (with capital W) may prove equally problematic.

More often, though, the mother is present in a more positive way: in a Praisesong (Nichols, 101), or in a homage to a mother's wisdom (Griffiths, 95–96), or in an intimate address to one's mother, in a realization of sameness (Anyiam St.John, 83–84; Hawkins, 85–86). The different experiences of racial and sexual oppression lead to a sense of solidarity with mothers, who are a main inspiration to these women writers who are, as Meiling Jin words it, "Strangers in a Hostile Landscape" (123–26): "mother figures, whose strength and frailty assume new significance for daughters now faced with the challenge of raising children and/or achieving artistic recognition in an environment hostile to the idea of female self-fulfillment. . . . Such mothers, too, are our literary precursors" (6). Cobham places herself within Black feminist and womanist traditions when she thus relates creativity to motherhood, calling up Alice Walker's eulogy of her mother's art in *In Search of Our Mothers' Gardens* (1984) as well as Nigerian writer Buchi Emecheta's praise song of her mothers, who taught her the art of telling stories (Emecheta 1986).

However, as the diverse poems in this collection make clear, childbirth may not be the only central experience that makes women into women. There are many other aspects to Black female sexuality. To explore these, I now want to discuss one particular poem by Grace Nichols, which connects sexuality, gender identity, racial identity, and a critique of space and history.

MY BLACK TRIANGLE

My black triangle
sandwiched between the geography of my thighs

is a bermuda
of tiny atoms
forever seizing
and releasing
the world

My black triangle
is so rich
that it flows over
on to the dry crotch
of the world

My black triangle
is black light
sitting on the threshold
of the world

overlooking my deep-pink
probabilities

and though
it spares a thought
for history
my black triangle
has spread beyond his story
beyond the dry fears of parch-ri-archy

spreading and growing
trusting and flowing
my black triangle

carries the seal of approval
of my deepest self

—Grace Nichols (Cobham and Collins 1987: 29)

Read within the context of the tropes of exile used by Black women writers
in Britain, this is a remarkable and courageous text. Instead of lamenting
her displacement, the poem's "I" concentrates on the sign of her Black femininity as the nodal point of the world. Her "black triangle" becomes the
point of focalization (overlook) as well as the point that acts on the world
(seize, release). Like the mysterious Bermuda Triangle, it seizes and engulfs,
not unlike that other greedy Black hole, feared by men, the mythical *vagina
dentata*; but it chooses to release also. It wets the world; it spreads, grows,
and flows. Contrary to the dry and stable geography of the patriarchal
world, it is wet, fluid, and flowing. Its active nature is yet accentuated by its
definition as a whole of "tiny atoms."

The poet takes up the old imagery of woman as place by qualifying
her body as "geography," but represents the place as multiple. The place
consists, first, of the "geographic" body, which not only is space but also
holds "probabilities," that is, a future. The spatialized body is itself placed
within time and is subject to change. Second, the Black triangle marks the
body's threshold. As such, it is part of the body only to a certain extent; as
a go-between between world and body/"I," it does not completely belong
to either. The Black triangle is a commuter. Seizing, releasing, and flowing,
it communicates with its outside. This nodal element of body space, then,
is active, mobile, and oriented toward the exterior. It breaks down the image of the body as a unity of spatial passivity. There is yet another spatial
reference in the poem: there is a "deepest self," which, as the ultimate spatial point, counts as an anchoring point. The Black triangle can be understood as the active counterpart of this stable center.[21]

The central image of this spatial figuration, then, is the threshold,
the frontier. In this aspect, the poem is related to the important trope of
the frontier in *Charting*. The threshold functions even more strongly as a
woman's image, as it separates and links an inside—a home of sorts, traditionally a woman's domain—and an outside. Like Black women sitting on
their porch or veranda, the Black triangle is "sitting on the threshold." But
from that threshold, while never really leaving it, it undertakes its very specific journey, and it negotiates the world by spreading, growing, and flowing. Janet Wolff might recognize here another form of "dislocation from a

given place." The Black triangle reconstructs the site that it commands as a "contact zone."[22] The poem plays with the eroticism with which this zone of contact between, say, Europeans and Africans has been invested since the end of the eighteenth century, and which Pratt has described as the "eroticization of the contact zone" (Pratt 1992: 87, 90). This self-conscious Black, female journey does not lead to alienation, as it is always connected to a sense of self. Instead of the nostalgia that binds the Indian women in Ganguly's research to their former home and their sense of self, Nichols envisions a sense of self rooted in the body, which does not lead to an immobilization in nostalgia but makes possible an optimistic outward motion. This image of the presence of Black women in Britain naturally takes their presence as a given instead of describing it as displacement or alienation. The image rather traces the critical, disturbing effects of its dissenting presence and the displacement it effects itself. Thus, the poem reverses the postcolonial geography (which still organizes a shifting, eccentric empire around a stable cultural center).

According to Nichols's poem, the liquid nature of the Black, feminine self allows it to travel. This moisture is a sign of the richness of Black femininity. So, Black femininity is no obstacle to this restricted kind of journey. The moisture is presented as an active counterdiscourse, opposed to dry patriarchal discourses of history. It refers to a semiotics of sensuality, governed by the logic of personal desire. Instead of equating female subjectivity to fluidity, passivity, and lack of stability, Nichols sketches an active yet plural Black female identity, which defines itself by means of the fluid strategy of a self-conscious sexual desire. The trope of moisture has openly female, sexual connotations. But it also harks back to that other trope of liquidity cited in the two poems in the epigraph to this chapter. One, also by Grace Nichols, points to the ocean as the intermediary area between lost past, lost tongue, and alienated presence, wherein a new tongue is growing. The ocean, the domain of the Middle Passage of the slave trade, functions here as the prototypical passage causing a deterritorialization of language and identity. The other poem presents the ocean as the trope for alterity (instead of displacement). Rather than a fluid, plural identity, Prachi Momin describes the dual subjectivity of the migrant. Like Nichols in "The Black Triangle," she uses the oppositional pair dry/moist to designate dominant discourse and counterdiscourse. "The Black Triangle" recalls this latter connotation of water as the sign for alterity. Moreover, it retains the implicit references to femininity and sexuality. Thus, in this poem, the trope of moisture is brilliantly used to designate racial and cultural as well as gender difference.

Nichols's poem plays with a traditional notion of woman as place by blending it with a sensual discourse of the body. Thus, Black women's specific situatedness is elaborated as a geographical figuration in which Black femininity is seen as neither displaced nor immobile. The poem understands Black female identity foremost in its sexuality, which is centered and transgressively active at once. This is a beautiful instance of a Black woman's "migratory subjectivity." Its mobility is not nomadic, not free-floating; it is bound, and controlled. Is it elusive or slippery? Perhaps, but only if one thinks that elusive women take up space, claim the right to speak, claim the independence of their own minds, and refuse to follow dominant norms. I prefer to read Nichols's poem as a wonderful discourse of female identity that stands in its own right and that can be understood on its own terms, without situating it between the lines of other discourses.

Thematically, *Watchers* seems to stand in sharp contrast to *Charting*, but on second thought the collections appear to relate in a much more complex manner. I have read *Charting* as a politically motivated collection of texts that seek to express a Black female identity. *Watchers*, even if it is presented primarily as a literary anthology, does not lack this political dimension. But it is not preeminent. Cobham judges, for example, that "[s]ome of the collection's most memorable lines were penned in response to specific social injustices" (Cobham and Collins 1987: 10). In this formulation, politics is seen as one of the "texts" in a large intertextual field, to which one can respond in literary writing. It is the writing, finally, that is considered here. The shared experience of exile is connected with a certain tradition of literary expression, rather than with the problems of self-definition, as in *Charting*. Cobham explores "a cultural tradition of survival," which "is probably best seen in the poems on political themes and in the capacity for joyousness" (10). Hence, political engagement and joyousness both stem from the will to survive. The juxtaposition of the two is characteristic of the collection's approach.

As the literary is put at the center, the quality of the treatment of language is considered in the first place, and it is often characterized in terms of sensual enjoyment. Cobham's detailed attention to the use of diverse rhythmic patterns is a sign for this, but the predilection for a discourse of sensuality can also be observed in the terms used when describing styles of writing such as "fervour and poignancy" (10) and the "ebullient" character of someone's authorship (8). This preference is also clear in the following:

One of my favourite poems in this collection is a short one by Carole Stewart that contains the impossible lines, "But I love you and I loved Curly Wurlys/Mars bars and Fry's Turkish Delight. Now my sweet tooth is dead." . . . Add to that the intoxicating sensual power of Grace Nichols' poem "My Black Triangle" and the sheer delight in sound of Fyna Dowe's "De bubble still a bubble now de bubble burs." (10–11)

The pleasure in the sensuality of this literature is most clearly felt when Cobham finally uses the metaphor of the "home" to describe the collection:

each time I read through the collection, I have the illusion of being "back home" for that family reunion of sisters and cousins we've been promising ourselves for years; where we'll cook home food, laugh raucously at the most inane jokes, share political obsessions and spiritual insights, rap about relationships and generally heal each other of all the scars of all those years of achieving and surviving like the strong Black women we cannot always be. (11)

If this literature can be seen as a journey, then it is a journey home, even if it is a home that has yet to be created. Characteristically, this is a home of varied sensual pleasure, ranging from cooking and eating to intense female bonding. At first sight, this homey image seems to oppose the discourse of mobility in the other collection, *Charting*. The home in *Watchers* seems to be a place of healing, mirroring traditional definitions of the home as a secure interiority, almost a womb. But a closer look reveals that *Watchers'* definition of the home is much more energetic, and not far removed from the tropes of mobility in *Charting*. *Charting* chastises the Black women's movement for not being able to negotiate their differences, which keeps it from appropriating, transforming, and continuing the once-alienating journey into a process of growth and transformation. *Charting* wishes to offer an accommodation to the many different perspectives within the community. Thus, a shared but variable, "ever-changing" identity is created. This is exactly what the trope of the home in *Watchers* also purports to do: to indicate the space where a multiple, shared identity is recreated and where growth and transformation become possible.

The two groups of editors of the two collections employ different tropes and discourses to outline their vision of Black British women's identity and creativity. *Charting* considers the journey in its aspects of violence and alienation, and it envisages a homecoming of sorts by an entry into an ongoing process of identification. *Watchers* understands the journey as a shared experience that links generations, continents, and ethnicities. The editors use the trope of the journey to describe Black British women's identity, but in contrast to *Charting*, they link it to sexuality and sensuality. For them, the journey is always a bound motion; it is linked to a sense of self that is rooted in the body. The trope of the journey is therefore well reconcilable to that of the home.

Homecomings

In my examination of the rewritings of that specific journey that leads into exile, it has become clear that the journey *back* may be of equal importance to reconstructing one's identity. Narratives of homecoming abound in Caribbean women's writing. Indeed, the journey "home" may be as complex and painful as the journey "out." Many African and Caribbean writers in exile have written about the effects of the arrival and stay in unforbidding mother countries (to mention a few in the Anglophone tradition: Ama Ata Aidoo, Erna Brodber, Buchi Emecheta, C. L. R. James, George Lamming, V. S. Naipaul, Caryl Phillips, Joan Riley, Samuel Selvon). But there is also a strong tradition of writing about the journey "back." For the Caribbean, Aimé Césaire's *Cahier d'un retour au pays natal* (1939) has been most influential. It was translated into English in 1947, and recent fictional texts in English may echo his vision of the native island as the repulsive maternal body—"a fallen world, a defiled body" (Dash 1989: 22), with which the returning migrant can reconcile himself only after overcoming his disgust. Such is the case in the first novel by Britain-based Jamaican writer Joan Riley, *The Unbelonging* (1985). However, there is a price a writer must pay to imagine the migrant as a prodigal daughter returning to her defiled mother. Then, both female protagonists may be trapped in decay, immobility, and horror.

Femininity as Death, by Water or by Fire

The Unbelonging is about young Hyacinth, a Jamaican girl who is sent to England to live with her father. Having been quite happy with her protected life with her Aunt Joyce in Jamaica, she loathes her stay in England, where she is threatened with (sexual) abuse by her father. To escape her dreadful reality, Hyacinth starts to fantasize about Jamaica. She loses her grip on her real past, and her desire to return to her idealized home becomes an obsession. In a dramatic final scene, the story results in the return of the unhappy protagonist to Jamaica. Her homecoming turns out to be a nightmare.

"Lord be praised," the thin voice creaked out. "Is Hyacinth come back fram England! Hyacinth noh faget me. Come chile, come mek me look pan yu."

Hyacinth stared at her in horror. . . . The bony body shifted uncertainly on the bed, feet moving with painful deliberation. . . . Then it was standing, swaying uncertainly, movement unsure as it started towards her. The mouth opened in a grimace of a smile, showing gaps in the discoloured teeth, gold glinting just where her aunt's gold tooth had been. . . . This is not reality, her mind rejected. The reality is not here, this is the nightmare. (139)

In Jamaica, Hyacinth is suddenly exposed to a host of repressed memories of her own past, with all the poverty and cruelty she had wanted to forget. They now come back to her in the shape of the horrifying, soiled maternal body. Contrary to Césaire, the novel does not suggest how the protagonist can come to a possible acceptance or reconsideration, other than a desperate retreat into fantasy.

The novel is based on several related dichotomies, which bear upon some of the themes I have discussed above: mobility and fluidity, motion and struggle, sexuality. Another aspect is that of reality and knowledge as opposed to fantasy, repression, and blindness. I will discuss these aspects separately and show how they are related. The novel's remarkable representation of these aspects gives it a special place within a tradition of writing about women and mobility.

As the quotation above suggests, the horrifying maternal body plays a central role in the outcome of the novel. But this mother's body is part of a larger complex, as Riley thematizes not only the imperialism and its effects on the (ex-)colonized motherland but also the violence and oppression within the family and in the gender relations within this imperialist context. To develop this theme, the text uses the ambivalent image of wetness. The novel is structured around a very strong contrast between a reality of threatening wetness and atrocious parental bodies, and a futile, immaterial world of blessed fantasy. The first and most visible threat, portrayed under the trope of wetness, comes from the father's body. Hyacinth's sad life, led in terror of her father, is punctured by the appearance of the fluid that heralds bodily punishment: she wets her bed, and is beaten for it by her father. Hyacinth's constant fear of wetting her bed produces other fluids: it makes the bile rise in her throat; sweat breaks out; tears burn. Her father, excited by the punishments, manipulates Hyacinth into another vulnerable wetness: he has her bathe and wash herself in his presence to add to his arousal. Finally, after a long period of sexual threat, he rapes his daughter. The daughter's fluidity, then, points forward to the unspeakably horrifying, destructive father's sperm. Quite in contrast to Nichols, moisture refers to the reduction of the Black female body to a passive prey for a destructive male sexuality. The moisture betrays the girl into a panicking, utter passivity. In Riley's text, there is no way to imagine the fluid woman's body as the site of an active, sensual mobility.[23] All forms of fluidity are entrapping or threatening: the rain is threatening, and so is the sea, a crucial element in Caribbean narratives; it is "savage, a wild and angry grey," formed of "foaming and boiling" waves "groping their way towards the cluster of wooden houses," while Hyacinth watches "in alarm," "desperately," her "heart fluttering" (107).

This aggressive sexual wetness is not the only threat to Hyacinth, though. She is trapped between her fear of wetness and a terror of heat and fire. When she escapes from male threats into a fond fantasy of her life in Jamaica, she always hits upon a horrifying memory, which she hastily represses. Slowly, the novel uncovers that it concerns a tragic incident in which her childhood friend Cynthia died in a fire (66, 67, 86, 99, 122, 123, 138, 140, 142). Cynthia was sadly beaten and oppressed by a "big and aggressive" father (86), a "man going mad" (142), who is never mentioned but always "lurked in the shadows" (86). Hyacinth is guilty of "ignoring the pleading in Cynthia's brown eyes" (86), of leaving her burning (99). She suppresses her guilt of abandoning her friend to this killing complex of male aggression and devouring fire and backs away from her awareness of her complicity in Cynthia's death.

But the memory is tenacious in reemerging. The event is very significant to Hyacinth's narrative, as she and Cynthia can be not only juxtaposed but also identified with each other. Cynthia can be seen as Hyacinth's alter ego. They bear the same name, even if the letters are scrambled. The cry uttered by the girl caught in the fire is uttered by both: "the hard-faced man, the little girl's scream of terror, the way it choked, gurgled off. Had it been her, she wondered?" (123) Was it *her*, Hyacinth herself? Indeed, both girls are the victim of male oppression, be it associated with fire or with moisture. Hyacinth is Cynthia, reclaimed from the fire, displaced to England to undergo a repetition of her doom, but this time by water, not by fire.

The contrast between fire and water is reminiscent of the dichotomy of water and fire in Baldwin's text *The Fire Next Time*, where fire is understood as a trope for the violent Black revolution to be expected if no halt is called to racist oppression. This fire stands for a second annihilation of mankind, next to the biblical deluge. But if in *The Unbelonging* the fire (connoting active revolt) is the first destruction and water the second, Hyacinth's second distress can be understood as a regression. Hyacinth's narrative does not develop the state of the passive victim into that of a Black rebel. To the contrary: Hyacinth's role is always passive. She does not resist the fire any more than the moisture engulfing her. The opportunity for revolt went up in the fire with her other self. And Blackness, to Hyacinth, signifies only male aggression, squalor, and primitivity (89, 112). Fire and water refer not to racial aggression (as in Baldwin) but to sexual aggression within a racist context. Thus, *The Unbelonging* speaks not only of the repulsive mother's body, as evoked by Césaire, but also of the girl's body as defiled passivity, corrupted by Black male aggression.

Hyacinth's repression of the memory of Cynthia's death is needed to reconstruct her desperately desired ideal, motherly, Jamaican home, as a soothing contrast to the cold, destructive, male world of England. Apart from the memories of poverty and tension she negates, Hyacinth has hardly any material with which to build this Utopia. She has the memory of the "reassuring bulk" of her aunt (9, 32, compare 107). But she remembers her largeness, her bulk, and not her *body*; she remembers a sense of safety, but not the person her aunt was. Neither did she take from her aunt a strong enough women's language to guide her. No female counterdiscourse is offered as an alternative to the dominant, restricting, bullying word of the father.[24] The impotent discourse of home developed by Hyacinth is nothing but a blind reaction to the horror of her life in England, which is dominated by her father, who teaches her to hide and to lie. If met with racist remarks about her provenance from jungle or slum, she invents a more prestigious former accommodation to evade racist disdain. This becomes her standard tactic, so much so that the fantasy blocks her memory of her real past (19, 68, 71, 98, 110, 121).

Hyacinth's fantasy bears predominantly on *place*. All places in the novel have explicit and clear connotations. Not only is the defiled mother pictured as a "place" to return to, but the bleak, cold, bare rooms where Hyacinth lives stand for the desperate entrapment in her father's brutality. Thus, the squalor of her former living space (in Jamaica, but also in London) refers directly to the shameful secret of her rape, which she wants to hide at all costs. This connection between place and the secret of incest is articulated in a recurring phrase: "Incest flourished where the roads were bad" (49, 62, 91, 131, 137). If she were to tell people about her "place," this revelation would amount to disclosing her terrible secret, which would surrender her to the hatred and disdain of white and Black people alike. Secrecy and fantasizing become Hyacinth's inadequate tactics for dealing with reality; they have suffocating spatial effects. The secrecy forces her into isolation; the fantasy entraps her and blinds her. Hyacinth's silence not only leads to her own predicament but also affects her aunt, who feels neglected and deserted and consequently is driven to despair, drink, and self-neglect. The terrible body of this motherly aunt in her soiled hut on the "bad road," then, is ultimately defiled not only by colonialism (as Césaire suggests) but also by the sexual aggression that victimized, trapped, and muted Hyacinth.

Hyacinth's blinding and entrapping discourse of home is an obstacle to all knowledge of Jamaica. The question of knowledge of "home" is amply discussed in the last paragraphs, where Hyacinth's fictional discourse of home is contrasted to her fellow Jamaican students' political discourse about Jamaica. However, the text does not allow Hyacinth to learn from their narratives. No counterdiscourse has any signification. Curiously enough, not even intellectually is the studious Hyacinth allowed to be moved an inch outside the father's discourse. She has to return herself to the maternal sphere to acknowledge the extent of her repression, and the full horror of both (surrogate) mother- and fatherland.

In England, Hyacinth backs away from insight. In other words, she is absolutely unable to move, bodily or intellectually. Blindness and immobility are equated, just as knowledge and motion are related. But Hyacinth does not see, she does not speak, and she does not write—she does not send word to her aunt, for which she is reproved bitterly in the end. But how could she write? How could she step outside her own torture? Because, from the beginning of the novel onward, Hyacinth was already dead and turned to ashes. Her body was already lost in the fire that devoured Cynthia's body, locked in by the inescapable, omnipresent father. If the novel pictures the killed girl as the very image of cowardice, this means, above all, that she is reluctant to move. This characterizing robs her of her body as well as of her mobility. By killing her thus before the start of the story, the novel does not leave Hyacinth any possibility to escape, to move through real space. As an eternal victim, she is trapped in a doomed circularity, which comes down to immobility or futile motion.[25] She is incapable of moving through space as well as through time and memories. She reimagines her past by freezing it into an unchanging, eternal image of warmth, light, and protection. The only other option of mobility necessitates a radical breach with the matter in which her dead body is still caught, and to enter this make-believe world. Hyacinth often dreams of the liberating movement through an immaterial space: envying birds, she aims at a bodiless soaring to a level where all sensual experiences are blotted out (38, 40, 92). Only by freezing her past is she able to create an immaterial world in which "soaring" is possible.

The Unbelonging pictures women as location, and questions their mobility. Aunt Joyce could not survive her desertion by her niece; she was abandoned and she degenerated in the trap of poverty. Cynthia/Hyacinth are trapped by mad male sexual aggression and its effects on their racial and sexual identification, and they perish, entrapped, by fire and water. In the last instance, the novel identifies not only the two killed girls as exchangeable, but also the third childhood friend, Florence, who stayed in Jamaica. After the juxtaposition of Cynthia and Hyacinth in this fragment: "Florence, so unchanging and unconcerned, not like her and poor Cynthia. . . . Florence was better off than both of them, for she never had to worry about anything" (92), one finds another positioning on the final pages: "She shuddered at the thought that she might have been that woman. . . . Cynthia always better off than the two of them" (142–43). Florence decayed as well, abandoning her body to the toil of childbearing, aging before her time by suffering. It does not seem to matter whether women travel: they will always be trapped and victimized. The example of politically aware Perlene, Hyacinth's Jamaican student friend, does not balance this overall picture. A politically inspired courage to know and to move must necessarily disappear when confronted with the immobilizing terror of sexual aggression.

If Riley can be seen as rewriting Césaire by concentrating on the aspects of gender and sexuality, then she can also be read as an argument within another literary debate. Her texts are a reaction to tendencies to romanticize the migrant's experience.[26] Riley's novels[27] form an exertion to acknowledge the reality of the horror of this life in exile. If condensed into one sentence, the novels would come down to a: "Look! It is much worse than you dare to acknowledge!" But these statements do not go unanswered.

A direct reaction is to be found in Vernella Fuller's debut, *Going Back Home* (1992). Fuller explores the journey back by juxtaposing two sisters, who both give an opposite meaning to the notion of "home" and "the journey back." Fuller elaborates the different views on the "journey" in strings of dialogues. In her acknowledgment, she declares that she was supported and stimulated by Joan Riley. However, while she writes about similar themes, she does not follow Riley's pessimistic realism. Contrary to her predecessor, she enlarges upon the sensual delights of the homecoming in Jamaica; and she prefers to give free vent to very different perspectives of the qualities of the native island as a home. Her approach makes one reconsider the nature of Riley's realism, which I would rather classify as a Caribbean gothic, in which the body plays the role of a horrifying thing. This does not mean that her gothic approach would not be truthful: this horror is also displayed in other Caribbean novels that are otherwise quite realistic. Such is the case in Beryl Gilroy's *Frangipani House*, a text to which the next chapter is dedicated.

Home: Rhythm, Vibrations, Circular Motions

Another novel that can be understood as a reaction to Riley's perspective is a 1988 text by Amryl Johnson from Trinidad, who has lived and worked in England since her arrival at the age of eleven. Neither "a travelogue nor . . . a guide for those who wish to visit" (2), *Sequins for a Ragged Hem* concentrates on the writer's own experiences during her second visit to the islands of the region of her birth. In the introduction she tells about the first, difficult journey back to Trinidad, in 1982: "During those four weeks, I felt very much an outsider, almost 'foreign' to my own culture" (1). She made the decision to return, "and this time I would be better prepared" (2). Johnson implies that a homecoming has to be constructed, has to be won. The text itself is the outcome of her effort to win a conclusion from her ambivalent but urgent experiences, which force her to reflect upon her identity. Johnson's text negotiates the dialectics of being an outsider as well as a prodigal daughter.

In *Sequins* some of the themes of *The Unbelonging* return: *Sequins* is also about a difficult homecoming, about water, the sea, the intricacies of memory, sensuality if not sexuality, and the connection between "knowledge" and "belonging." Like *The Unbelonging*, this text is structured around the triangle of sensuality/mobility/knowledge.

The first sustaining element of the text that springs into sight is "rhythm." I am not referring to the narratological term used by Bal and others (which is about the level of the narrative), but to an aspect of the narrator's text itself. The text is riddled with a sense of urgent necessity, overwhelming the heroine, but staying largely unexplained to the reader. The author sheds some light on this condition when speaking about her receptiveness to "spiritual influences or . . . vibrations" (1), leading to a feeling of being urged by an ancestral figure. This sometimes cryptic intensity, displayed in short, feverish passages, often makes the narrative hard to follow. This narrative strategy is already present in the text's very first sentences:

> "Girl, when you get off the plane, run!"
> I stepped off the plane into Carnival fever. Even before my feet had touched the ground, I could feel the hot, pulsating beat of calypso music shoot like a bolt up the well which enthusiasm had pierced in my right leg. I was standing on the tarmac almost dancing on one foot. . . .
> "Girl, when you get off the plane, run!" . . . While I was doing my dance on the tarmac, the other passengers swept past. (3–4)

For the heroine, traveling is clearly not the detached dream of male autonomy discussed above. A direct (though mysterious) experience of the rhythm of Caribbean life forms an obstacle to a smooth and clever tactics of travel, which implies swiftness, clever maneuvering, and jumping queues.

For Johnson's "I," her first experience of being "home" is "rhythm." This intense experience is often narrated in a sequence of short phrases, in which the key emotive utterance is repeated (twice or more). In the quotation above it is the phrase "Girl, when you get off the plane . . . "; elsewhere, it may be a recurrent "Go on!" (57), "Look!" (106), "No!" (124), "Stop!" (256), or "Stab!" (272). The technique of repetition may be associated with the repetition of phrases in the calypsos (quoted in the Trinidad chapter, 14, 27, 28, 33, 34, 43, 51, 52) that herald the famous, impressive Trinidad Carnival taking place shortly after the heroine's arrival. The carnival, with its compelling rhythms and its character of sweeping collectivity, functions as the narrative's framing device. The final passage returns to the first sensations felt during the carnival and thus endows the narrative with a circular structure. But long before that ending, the narrative has already deepened the significance of this rhythm by associating it with the experience of almost mystically significant "vibrations," that is, other sensual or even supernatural experiences.

The sense of emotional directness produced by the repetition of exclamations and the like also comes from the directly reported snippets of conversation, not introduced or mediated by the narrator. This narrative technique places the narrator amid a multitude of exciting statements, remarks, and questions, which she often takes as addressing her, directly or indirectly. In addition to these human utterances, the narrator will be confronted with other sensual stimuli, which she gladly regards as signs. "No matter how deep my preoccupation, the raw smell of fruit, vegetables, herbs and the babel of voices could not be straight-jacketed into any borders of alignment. Freedom" (254). Smells and sounds signify freedom, as she experiences in this marketplace in a too-orderly built town. Ultimately, this sensitivity to the temptation of music, food, and celebration signifies the heroine's Caribbean-ness. This becomes clear in responses like this one:

"Now, you sure you not too tired."

"Boy, behave yourself! I a born Trinidadian. How I go be too tired for Buccoo tonight?" (140)

A real Trinidadian simply cannot be too tired for such festivals, which to her are irresistibly invigorating.

In the end, the narrator hopes, these sensual signs, taken together, will amount to an insight into her position within this multiple culture. And they do. At the end of the book, an unseen presence urges her to reanimate her memories, to "[b]ring the colour back" (273), and not to leave the islands. She should not stop being "[h]ungry for the wealth of experience" (272).

Go on! Go on!

Bring the colour back. Give it life. Give it energy. Let it sparkle against any glimmer of light. Gold in the daytime. Silver by night.

Don't go!

Stab.

Stay!

Stab.

(273)

She responds by sewing the piece of cloth she picked up as a souvenir of the carnival, from which the patches of color have disappeared. Sewing it, she works to retrieve the colors. The story ends with her feeling of being in very close, lasting contact with a female ghost, who stands for all women on the islands.

In this last passage, the narrative technique of rhythmic repetition is linked to a powerful, vibrant, significant sensual experience. It links the narrative back to the initiating experience of the carnival, which only now receives its full signification. The trope of sewing also refers to the writing process, which enables the narrator to grasp the full sensual experience of her homeland, and thus, in a way, to "stay." When she leaves now, her writing will enable her to keep relating to her homeland, and to keep giving life to her memories. Her writing will keep her home.

Sequins links sensuality to knowledge in a way that stands in stark contrast to the relationship between sexuality and knowledge in *The Unbelonging*, where threatening sexuality forms an obstacle to knowledge of oneself and the island of one's birth. Johnson's text acknowledges that it is impossible to really come home. The text demonstrates clearly that, for a migrant, the elusive quality of "belonging" can never be more than gradual, partial, temporal. However, one can win a homecoming by gaining knowledge. Johnson accentuates this insight by contrasting her experiences on the islands outside Trinidad. There she is seen as a Trinidadian, so as someone who does not belong, but also as not-quite-Trinidadian, which saves her from being met with the same prejudice as "real" Trinidadians, and which therefore makes her a suitable person in whom to confide (146–47). Being an outsider, she is allowed to know inside things about people's lives. Moreover, she learns that whatever her exact identity may be, she will always somehow be an outsider to some aspects of Caribbean life.

Thus, *Sequins* disregards a quest for pure belonging in favor of a more detached project to learn about the area of her birth. The text regards "belonging" as inextricably bound up with knowledge of an area; when a Tobagan tells her about his island, she reflects upon his "ease in the place of his birth" (142): "It was his and he knew it. During those six months, I didn't meet anyone who didn't know their own island. They knew the soil and the plants and the fish and that little beach tucked away from prying eyes where you could go for a swim in the nude. . . . Firm as rock, man, woman and child, they had stood in their own grounding" (142). However, the protag-

onist's quest for knowledge is far from direct and purposeful. The text refrains from presenting events and sensations as metaphors. Traveling awkwardly, on a low budget, submitted to bureaucracy and mismanagement,
like other Caribbean people and sometimes like other tourists, Johnson's
protagonist travels and moves in with people for reasons of convenience or
for the pleasure of their company, but never because being with them would
mean a passage into a more authentic, more Caribbean way of life. Instead
of searching purposefully for the metaphorical nature of the details of Caribbean life, she enjoys this life as it happens to her. Significance comes to
her suddenly and uninvited. Even so, the account does not cultivate hap-
hazardness, anecdote, or idiosyncrasy as the funny narratives of more detached "innocent anthropologists" would do.[28] In contrast, the heroine is really keen to acknowledge sudden signs, sensations, and vibrations that will
finally offer her a strategy to reconnect her to her birthplace.

The traveler tries to gain the knowledge necessary for a relative homecoming by exploring all aspects of life. She experiences nature and food as
intensely as debates, company, other people's plights, politics, and poverty.[29]
The knowledge she desires is to a certain extent transcendental: presuming
a truth underlying the surface of daily life, she tries to comprehend it by her
receptiveness to its "vibrations." The text's intensity in dealing with the surface of life, nevertheless, to some degree, deconstructs the hierarchical or-
dering of knowledge into a superior "deeper" truth and an inferior "surface."
The traveler reads the surface of life eagerly, surrendering herself to what
Donaldson sees as a feminist postcolonial "hoodoo" reading attitude (Donaldson 1992: 18–20). Such a reading refrains from looking for metaphors,
but rather chooses to read metonymically. *Sequins* can be read in this manner, too. Instead of stating an unambiguous metaphorical relation between
appearances and deeper truth, then, the final note of the narrative offers a
metonymic relation: the piece of cloth she has picked up refers metonymically to the significant carnival where she found it; the act of sewing is in itself metonymic, as it links colors, sequins, and glitters to each other. These
colors do not signify a hidden truth. An ancestral figure coming close, not
replacing the heroine but complementing her, encourages her to endow the
revived colors with new life and energy. Thus, the colors themselves become
the bearer of force, energy, and signification. They do not point at any hidden meaning; they embody it.

Sequins's understanding of knowledge points away from the notion that "home" can ever be a full, secure identity, always present in one's deepest sense of self. Instead, one comes home by creating a relationship to a political, economical, social, sensual place, through continuous personal efforts. Sewing and writing are ways of establishing this relationship. The text thus represents one's relationship to one's home as relative and shifting. But it also represents the Caribbean itself as a state of continuous mobility.[30] After having traveled with a group of market women who continuously move from one island to another to sell their merchandise, the narrator muses that Caribbean people have always migrated between the islands; she calls them a "people on the waves, of waves" (212). The Caribbean, "home," is a location for constant, awkward crossings to and fro. The protagonist can testify to its awkward nature: she experiences the discomfort and dangers of boat crossings, and often her plane bookings go hopelessly wrong. Even for those born and bred in the Caribbean, "home" can be a large, shifting, uncertain notion.

The protagonist receives her insight into the nature of the Caribbean home through her close contact with commuting market women. Their gender matters to her; as they are women too, the narrator is able to relate to their experiences. As a heterosexual woman she also bonds easily with men, even if her friendships with them are not as extensively narrated as her contacts with women. The narrative function of gender and sexuality in *Sequins* differs greatly from that in *The Unbelonging*. Despite their differences, both novels relate sexuality to fluidity. In *Sequins*, sensuality is part of the quest for identity, and it is explored through the recurring, structuring trope of fluidity. *Sequins*'s central trope of fluidity is the sea. The sea does not represent an aggressive male or active female sexuality. It is both frightening and sensually delightful; it is a place for quiet meditation, but it is also a place that literally robs the heroine of her sense of self. At a certain point in the story, the protagonist lingers in the sea some distance from her company, standing upright with only her head surfacing. Then, she looks down and finds that, probably through the effect of reflections on the water, her body has vanished. She feels decapitated and is overwhelmed by a sudden loss of identity (83). The image occurs once again, when, upon attempting to board a plane, she discovers she has been omitted from the passengers list (268). Again, she feels erased. This image of being erased by the sea invokes the hierarchically ordered image of surface life and underlying, deeper truth referred to above. The protagonist cannot reach that part of her identity that is rooted in a collective, unconscious, ancestral past. However, the incident with the passengers list demonstrates that she also feels swallowed up by anonymous bureaucracy, thus disturbing the solemnity of the first interpretation. The textual interest in sociological and political dimensions, and in the anecdotal, consistently hinders a reading that concentrates exclusively on vertical structures and sacred hierarchies of truth.

Finally, the text restores to the protagonist that submerged part of her self she had lost in the sea. The return becomes possible when the protagonist has established an intense, personal relationship with the people on the islands, gained knowledge about the conditions of people's lives and the violent colonial history. In a dense, significant sentence all the aspects of these relationships and connections are articulated: "See. The sea. The sea—of faces. Ghosts" (272). The sea, which has robbed her of her identity, is now transformed into the people she has met and the history that claims her. The multiplicity of her (real and only sensed) encounters is reduced to the final identification with the female ancestor through whom she connects with the totality of Caribbean present and past. But, as I have argued above, this identification has to be won through the continuous work of sewing, writing, and seeing. Her eager acts of seeing things and people lead her to a complex understanding of her home place, and thus all parts of her identity are reconnected.

In this way, *Sequins* links the crucial aspects of female Caribbean homecomings summarized above: the narrative represents gender, sensuality, and sexuality as the means of bonding necessary to obtaining the knowledge that creates a sense of belonging. Here, *Sequins* stands in contrast to *The Unbelonging*, where sexuality takes the form of male sexual aggression, and thus has the function of immobilizing women. The sense of belonging gained in *Sequins*, however, is shown to be a gradual, uncertain state, as the Caribbean itself is a shifting, mobile area, to which one belongs often by virtue of a laborious moving through it. Johnson's literary voice responds to the difficulty of the intended homecoming by speaking in a highly intense, dense, emotional voice, which summons up an underlying reality through which a relative, dialogical discourse of home can be created. Her predominant interest in the anecdotal, however, disturbs the verticality and seems to argue that there is no homecoming other than a constant intimate engagement with the people of the Caribbean.

Conclusion

African-American, Asian, and Caribbean women writers in exile create new discourses of travel and homecoming, through which they articulate their search for a new identity. None of the writers discussed surrenders with eagerness to a discourse of free mobility. But they do find ways to express invigorating forms of bound motion. Rhonda Cobham and Merle Collins (the editors of *Watchers*), Grace Nichols, and Amryl Johnson all consider feminine sexuality and sensuality as the forces that enable women to travel, to explore the world, or to create a sense of belonging. In women's sexuality, in the female body, and in the experience of motherhood, these writers find a new, nonalienating point of departure for women's (bound) mobility. In contrast, however, Joan Riley studies how sexual violence restricts feminine sexuality and prevents women's mobility.

In addition to this emphasis on the crucial role of sexuality in Caribbean women's discourses of travel, and in addition to Riley's discussion of male violence, writers may examine the function of violence as a women's strategy to escape the constraints of either forced movement or forced immobility. This is one of the aspects of the discourse of travel in the collection *Charting*. Here, the concept of the journey is related not only to women's strategies of identification but also to women's political struggles. A violent struggle is necessary to create the space for new (collective) identities or, in other words, to engage in self-chosen patterns of movement. Caribbean women in Britain inevitably move in relation to opposing forces, constraints, and boundaries. Their journey toward new, mobile identities itself is already a struggle. In their narratives, the notion of free mobility does not fulfill the function of an inspiring ideal, as in some Western discourses of travel. The acknowledgment and exploration of the restricting boundaries are much more urgent, as is the struggle to overcome them. What these authors offer, then, is a discourse of specific, bound motion.

These discourses of travel, in which sexuality and violence play crucial roles, are essentially different from the discourses of mobility through which certain Western European scholars understand signification and identification. Caribbean migrant women's discussions of the issue of mobility imply a severe critique of the racism and sexism responsible for their anxious, undesired immobility. In consequence, Caribbean women writers refrain from adopting Western literary forms of (presumed) free mobility, like certain postmodern practices. If they do relate to postmodernism, they will also qualify and criticize it.

Sometimes, Caribbean migrant women writers create very effective narratives of travel by appropriating existing discourses of travel. Kincaid's narrative about Annie John's departure is a good example, as it connects to existing narratives about the girl's journey into adulthood. I discussed the story at the beginning of this chapter as it offers an excellent image of the relationship between exile and writing. But it is also a narrative about a girl who has not yet gained full womanhood. The next chapter is dedicated to a novel in which the travels of an old woman are narrated.

Homemaking, Woman-Talk, Time-Waste:
Beryl Gilroy's *Frangipani House*

Anyone who came upon the house sitting sleek and comfortable on the town's edge, stopped . . . as if under a spell. It was that kind of house—eloquent, compelling and smug. . . . it was the ring of frangipani trees . . . which named the house and caused folk to whisper darkly 'Over yonder—Frangipani House! People dies-out dere! They pays plenty to die-out inside dere! Death comes to lodgers in Frangipani House!' . . . Those who still felt the pulse of life, however weakly, found soon enough that not only did the walls of the house recede to leave them exposed and vulnerable, but suddenly it compressed them enough to cause consternation before they adjusted to their new surroundings. The hopes and emotions the women shared grew hazy with the passing of time. Finally they disintegrated leaving only faint smudges when they were finally blown away. (Gilroy 1986: 1–2)

Whatever sweet connotations the notions of *home* and *house* may have for some, here we are far removed from the house that harbors and protects in a warm embrace of intimacy. What kind of house is this that strangles and eradicates with brutal finality? Frangipani House, a haunted and haunting house, treacherous and deadly, is a cynical comment on what a house might mean as a home, a sign for one's own identity. This chapter will unravel the terrible secrets of this killing home for the old, set in the Caribbean, and founded upon the crimes of people torn apart by changing global structures.

    To pursue the discussion about the home that I began in the preceding chapter, I will now focus on the notion of home from the perspective of the mother, she who did not leave. This chapter is organized around Beryl Gilroy's novel *Frangipani House* (1986)[1], from which the above quote is taken, as it can be read as a very perceptive Caribbean feminist rewriting of restricted but dominant narrative concepts of time and space. Let me then begin with a reflection on homes and houses. There are surprisingly many different discourses built around this notion. Within Caribbean criticism, the house has been studied as a culturally specific topic.[2] The theme of the house occurs throughout Caribbean literature, which is not surprising considering the prevalent problematization of notions of identity, belonging, homelessness, and "home" in this writing.[3] Homi Bhabha reads in Naipaul's *A House for Mr. Biswas*, a novel that in many respects is paradigmatic for its treatment of the theme of the house, "the desperate wish to be *accommodated*, to defy a primal lack, but the object of desire is always deferred" (Bhabha 1984b: 95–96, my emphasis). Bhabha explains this frustrated desire as a reaction to the alienating discourses and institutions of English literature. Here, then, the house stands for (cultural) identity.

In the work of other Caribbean writers, however, this rather general understanding of the trope gets a more gender-specific signification. There is, prominently, the vision of Caribbean poet Aimé Césaire, who captures the meaning of "home" within the context of Caribbean exile in the compelling but restricted image of the defiled mother's body as the home into which the exiled should painfully reintegrate. Césaire is not the only one to associate mothers with a place to which others return. Houston Baker repeats this image in a critical review of (among others) Richard Wright, in whose work "mother does seem a black-determined *place*," associated with domesticity, albeit no "reliable place of refuge" (Baker 1991: 118–19, my emphasis). Wright and Césaire, as poets of spatiality, show the relevance of Beatriz Colomina's statement that "[t]he politics of space are always sexual, even if space is central to the mechanisms of the erasure of sexuality" (1992). Both Césaire and Wright choose to sexualize and gender "place" and to spatialize a specific gender and sexuality, motherhood.

Next to these masculinist figurations, influential female and feminist perspectives on the relation between gender and space stand out. Sandra Gilbert and Susan Gubar's seminal study on white British women's writing examines white female narratives about being locked up in stuffy rooms, thus metaphorizing white women's restricted identities through their existence in, rather than as, confining space. Looking back through the well-

known essay by Spivak (1986) about the novel central to their argument—
Jane Eyre (1847), by Charlotte Brontë—it becomes clear that the choice of
this pivotal text has important implications. For it is not just a text by and
about "a woman," but a crucial English protofeminist text in which English
femininity emancipates itself at the expense of a woman from the periphery. (Neo)colonialism and feminism intertwine in this image of place. In
order to free themselves from their confinement, English white women
confined within small places have, in their turn, locked up a Caribbean
woman to have her burn the house and jump to her death. If this is acknowledged, then the house can no longer be studied as the place where
only white men have imprisoned only white women. It is also the place
where white women installed their Caribbean sister as a threatening other
and made her annihilate herself. Between European and Caribbean women,
then, the house is a place of violence.[4]

In recent gender-oriented studies of Caribbean and British-Caribbean
women writers, however, the theme is used ambivalently. On the one hand,
the creation of a literature of one's own is described as the building or making accessible of a familiar house ("Come then into our house for a reflection of yourself," as the invitation in *Charting the Journey* goes [Grewal et
al. 1988]). On the other hand, a house can embody confinement. This is
one of the statements of Elisabeth Wilson, who studies the trope of closed
spaces in Francophone Caribbean women's writing (Wilson 1990). She
finds that closed spaces in these texts function as "a trap which forces a
confrontation with self, a confrontation often too painful to endure" (49).
Wilson also highlights the more positive aspects: the closed space may offer a temporary protection, too. In the end, however, the enclosure keeps
its occupant from full participation in life and community.

A certain ambivalence is endemic to the trope of the house, which, for
women, isolates from the community in destructive ways, as well as contains and identifies the community, such as in the quotation from *Charting*.
This precarious relationship to both the community and to dominant colonial structures is often imagined through the presentation of Black dwellings in Black women's writing, where one often finds houses as dilapidated
huts on the plantations, in the yards, in poor villages, and in slums, and as
depressing, dark, damp city rooms and apartments.[5] Two lines of action are
taken to cope with these living conditions: a refusal to live in them, and the
acceptance and reappropriation of these spaces as potential homes.

Through his exploration of the work of Nobel Prize winner Toni Morrison, Houston Baker has offered an illuminating perspective on the tactics of reappropriation. In his discussion of "place" in Black male and female writing, Houston Baker differentiates a female vision of "place" from the male approach he criticizes. In his reading of Morrison's writing (especially *Sula*) he discerns a female, domestic writing of place, which strives for an intimacy in which contact can be established with "ancestral energies of survival and a poetic consciousness" (Baker 1991). However, to appropriate this interiority it must be "cleaned"—and Baker explains this act of cleaning as a refusal of the dominance of white male masters/rapists over Black dwellings. In Morrison's writing I find reference to a strategy as well as a counterstrategy, that is, a tactics[6] of "placing" people (especially mothers) and "spatializing" gender and race. First, there is the oppressive spatializing of slavery and colonialism that put African women on the mid-deck of the slave ship, then in crumbling sheds and cabins on the plantations, and thus, always, in a partial confinement that is left open to allow rape.[7] Second, I find a female counterstrategy that reappropriates this closed space, which closes it to oppressors from outside, and which at the same time roots it in a communal past. Closing it leads to openness to another time-space.

I understand this closing and opening as a discursive strategy, too. To explain this, I will repeat Morrison's words on the subject, as quoted in Baker:

I felt a very strong sense of place . . . in terms of the details, the feeling, the mood of the community. . . . I think some of it is just a woman's strong sense of being in a room, a place, or in a house. . . . I do very intimate things 'in place' . . . writing about being in a room looking out . . . is probably very common among most women anyway. (Morrison, quoted in Baker 1991: 133)

Morrison seems to take up the discourse of "woman as place," but only to change it carefully in a discourse of "woman *in* place," suggesting a potential as a female counterdiscourse. Here she implicitly relates to Gilroy's (and others') strategy of refusing the equation of women and passive space. However, the understanding of women as being *in* place is not necessarily a critical and politically enabling notion in itself, as the critique of Gilbert and Gubar's work reveals. Morrison, therefore, carefully situates and qualifies her discourse of woman-in-place. She speaks about the African-American community and implies that the understanding of Black culture as *housed* (in Bhabha's words, accommodated) in domestic spaces is a gendered counterstrategy. One of its aims could be to allow women to gather the community within the sphere of female domesticity, so that they might partake of it through the mediation of their own domestic discourse.[8]

This perspective on "space" defines houses not as isolation but as sites of intensified contacts with a spatial and temporal whole. Nevertheless, this strategy can never be wholly successful. Defining women as being "in place" differentiates them from, say, men "at large": thus, women are excluded from those communal events that take place "outside." Sometimes they must restrict themselves to a mere "looking out." Morrison accepts the drawback of such spatializing, as she emphasizes the larger advantage of the house as a site for a sense of the community's mood, and thus as a starting point for a woman's discourse on Black identity. Women's position, then, is irresolvably ambivalent.

Houston Baker articulates this ambivalence within the context of institutionalized racist sexual aggression. Speaking about the oppressive spatializing of Black women, he concludes: "Interiority and the frontier of violation coalesce in the accessible body of the African woman" (1991: 133). In his view, Black women are placed in a half-opened interior, which gives access to the oppressor but offers the enclosed women no escape. The way in which the Black female body is conceived would be a result of this spatializing. Baker stresses the enforced "accessibility" of the enclosed woman.[9]

In his analysis of female rewritings of women's place, Baker turns to Lacanian psychoanalysis. He centers his readings around the way the literary texts present the female position toward the phallus, thus associating the interior with the womb. However, this means that escape from this confinement entails a negotiation of the phallus. Baker implies that women must escape *through* (a rewriting of) heterosexuality. This interpretation defines interiority always in relation to the phallus, as if interiors always refer to wombs.

They might, indeed.[10] But there are also strategies of enclosing that are not immediately dictated by the phallic desire for accessible female bodies. *Frangipani House* is dedicated to the discussion of a more complicated kind of enclosing, in which no entry for rape is left. It is a desexualizing spatializing, used for old age. The enclosed bodies are closed off from sexuality, which is one of the reasons for their fast annihilation. In contrast to the strategies of space described by Baker, in *Frangipani House* bodies are desexualized by their confinement. Therefore, I would also consider the destructive total confinement as a violent act against those inside, especially against older people.

My discussion of *Frangipani House* will take sexuality into account, but I will not make it the central theme. Nor will I consider houses and homes necessarily as wombs. In my argument, I will concentrate on the complexities of the ambivalent African-American women's perspective on the house, as a willed interiority, closed against the exterior to find revitalizing connections to a community on the one hand, as well as a destructive confinement on the other. The house is the result of spatializing strategies of imperialism, in which sexism, racism, and ageism work together to deny the subjectivity of its victims. But it is also the site of identity and transformation. It can be a dominant, destructive discourse, but as a woman's place, it can also serve as a counterdiscourse.

Through a detailed reading of the novel, this chapter will develop the argument begun above, and work toward an understanding of spaces as identifying practices. I will argue that the notions of time and space developed in the novel imply a view of signification and textuality. Thus, a feminist postcolonial concept of the text is outlined. This approach makes it possible to understand the entangled relation between space and speech. It leads to the recognition of a vigorous narrative energy in Gilroy's novel, which culminates in the radical refusal of the concept of space as suffocating immobility, and in opening the possibility of escape from spatial, temporal, and discursive confinement.

Localization

There is nothing innocent, then, about the representation of homes and houses. Writing about houses appears to be an act of assigning people to places and of seeing them *as* places. Wright, Césaire, Gilbert and Gubar, the editors of *Charting*, Wilson, Morrison, and Baker all engage in a (repressive or liberating) form of localizing. A critique of dominant strategies of "localization," the "placing" of people in space and time to allay and secure their otherness, need not be expressed in scholarly discourses; it can be articulated as literature, too. *Frangipani House* is a case in point. *Frangi-*

pani House can well be considered a warning against enclosure, against *houses*. It is, among other things, the story of an escape.

Here is the story: Mabel King, Mama King to most of her close friends and family, is sixty-nine when her dutiful but absent offspring place her in an expensive home for the old, after a lifetime of toil for her children and grandchildren. In this home, Frangipani House, where the harsh director called Matron rules, Mama King threatens to lose her sanity. She escapes and joins a group of beggars until she is beaten up by some young men in the marketplace. She recovers and is then taken in by the family-to-be of one of her granddaughters, with whom she will emigrate to America. In addition to this story line, the novel offers many glimpses into other old and young women's lives, especially that of Matron. Here and there, Matron's story even threatens to take over the story of Mama King.

This text can be read as a narrative about the escape from localization into a migratory subjectivity, which is very much a Black and Caribbean feminist concept, as we have seen, and has little to do with nomadism. The first step in my reading of this text consists of analyzing the kind of confinement presented in the novel and its relation to oppressive spatializing strategies. To grasp the full signification of Mama King's confinement, it is helpful to consider the critique of "localization" that is now being articulated in ethnography and cultural studies. One instance of this problematic practice of linking people and cultures to places is criticized by Akhil Gupta and James Ferguson.[11] They criticize the anthropological habit of collapsing space, place, and culture: groups that form a cultural unit are associated with "their" territories:

thus, "the Nuer" live in "Nuerland" and so forth. The clearest illustration of this kind of thinking are the classic "ethnographic maps" that purported to display the spatial distribution of peoples, tribes, and cultures. But in all these cases, space itself becomes a kind of neutral grid on which cultural difference, historical memory, and societal organization are inscribed. It is in this way that space functions as a central organizing principle in the social sciences at the same time that it disappears from analytical purview. (Gupta and Ferguson 1992: 7)

Gupta and Ferguson unveil an uncautioned use of a concept of "space" that considers space a neutral, given category.

James Clifford signals the same strategy of cultural localization, the making of "natives," when criticizing the "excessive localism of particularist cultural relativism," which entertains "the notion that certain classes of people are cosmopolitan (travelers) while the rest are local (natives)" (Clifford 1992: 108).[12] Clifford shows that these Western views often link "race" or ethnicity in a restricting way to the concept of immobility. This holds for gender too, as I have shown. *Frangipani House* offers some insight into the way in which "localization" relates to age as well as to ethnicity and gender. It does so not only by its thematization of the confining, destructive house but also by its other figurations of space as well as of time. The infamous Frangipani House after which the novel is named works as a medium for localization by brushing aside references to a space outside the home. Listen to Matron, the home's voice, when she answers Mama King:

> "Where my dress? You thief my dress. My dress is American dress. I will know it. I will drag it off youback."
> "Sit down Marma King," said Matron is [*sic*] a softer tone than usual. . . . "I'll ask about you Merican Dress. Is dat what you call the material?" (8)

America, the place where Mama King's children emigrated to, is one of Mama King's points of orientation, the place from where she expects letters (in vain), and some sign from her family. At the same time, it is a place of high standing. When Mama King refers to the American origin of her dress, she implies that she used to associate with high quality before entering the home. Thus, she reconfirms her independent, superior identity. In her answer, Matron rejects both meanings. America doesn't exist, either as a place of hope, from where Mama King's happiness should come, or as the place of origin of the quality of her past life.

Matron, the personification of Frangipani House, denies the existence of the outside space. But the lodgers are granted another space in which to seek refuge: they can turn themselves in upon themselves and escape "inside." *Frangipani House* uses spatial metaphors to depict this inner world, this self that has turned in upon itself. Inside Mama King there is a graveyard (18). She fears bursting open "like a ripe calabash" (19). Mama King experiences pain "all over"—"Inside and out" (39), and this expression shows how distinct boundaries (even between self and outside world) melt away and spatial order breaks down. Sometimes Mama King wanders in this unmeasurable interior self, where she can move without any effort in a limitless space. It is not a smooth, flat surface: within her there are "cracks of heart" (24) and other crevices and fissures where memories lie.

Above all, there is inside the older people "a dark space . . . in that space all the feelings of old age had solidified into a ball of disappointment" (34, see also 8).

This dark space brings the "black hole" to mind, the cosmic phenomenon where time and space are compressed, ultimately to disappear. In this inner space there is no differentiated place to support and direct a narrative. There is no way out for the inhabitants; the escape inside and into the past leads to death. In Frangipani House one is stuck in a claustrophobic present that is inescapable. This total confinement opens not to a fertile communal past but to a Black hole of disillusion and death. It is a "hole" like the one in the slave ship, in which, according to Hortense Spillers (1987), who differs from Baker in this respect, men and women were enclosed together, regardless of their gender. Thus, their gender is erased: both subjects are taken into account as *quantities* (Spillers 1987: 72). Spillers differentiates "flesh" from the "body," and she sees "that distinction as the central one between captive and liberated subject-positions. In that sense, before the 'body' there is the 'flesh,' that zero degree of social conceptualization that does not escape concealment under the brush of discourse, or the reflexes of iconography" (Spillers 1987: 67). Within the context of the Middle Passage, the gendered bodies of women become "'ungendered'" flesh (68).

Thus, this particular localization of elderly people (not irrelevantly, women, as I will show later) makes them into "flesh"—into already dehumanized bodies. This strategy of localization is similar to the strategies criticized by Gupta, Ferguson, and Clifford. "Old people" live in "a home for the old"; and thus, in a process similar to the "making of 'natives'," they are made into zombies, dead souls, nonsubjects. However, this localization is a spatiotemporal strategy, not merely a spatial one. An important aspect of this double strategy is related to time and could be described as "temporalization." I will explain how it works.

Anthropologist Johannes Fabian has talked about the act of localizing (without using the term) to include similar and simultaneous strategies of placing people in *time*.[13] He argues that "others" are often situated in a remote place, which is also set in a primitive past (Fabian 1983, 1991: 32 ff). And indeed, if Frangipani House functions as an oppressive institute, it is mainly because of its treatment of time. Within the confinement of Frangipani House time is suspended. No change ever takes place—and, because in a certain view[14] change can be seen as an essential characteristic of time,

time does not exist anymore. It is impossible to find traces of past times (2, 5, 44). Mama King complains about the time in Frangipani House: "You don't see it going. But you wake up one morning and it all gone. Wha kinda place dis is!" (5). Another inmate says, "I hate this place. It makes me forget" (36). But that, exactly, is the very thing at which the treatment in the home aims. Matron exclaims in another passage: "Memories! She mustn't have memories. She can't cope with them. I wish I could get them out of her but I can *not*" (34). It is only on visiting days, when visitors come from outside, that time is reinstalled.

Mama King identified Sunday as the day when her hair was combed, her false teeth soaked in cleansing solution, and when Nurse Douglas paid more than scant attention to her personal hygiene.

At precisely three o'clock, a quiet dignity descended like a dust-cloud, and enveloped the place. (20)

But even so, time functions only as the signal for the temporary installation of a mere pretense of a normal time, in step with the real life outside. This alignment of time is the precondition of a fleeting contact between two mutually exclusive worlds: the residents and the outside.

This temporal aspect of the localization in *Frangipani House* deserves special attention: it plays an important role in the novel's critique of spatiotemporal localizations and of the concepts of time and space that make these possible. Because of its emphasis on time, the novel closely relates to the "homemaking" tactics as deployed in Morrison, in which the home forms a means to touch a deeper, communal past. In Morrison, enclosure is transformed into a means of establishing a fruitful manipulation of time. Morrison presents this temporal tactics as a countermove, working against the destructive temporalizing that cuts people off from other times and histories. One of the key phrases in *Frangipani House* suggests that the novel's countertactics lies in its specific interweaving of time and place. In the last but one chapter I find: "The women from the lane often stopped for 'woman-talk and time-waste'" (105). A fleeting, everyday trope like "time-waste" would of course not be explained in the text. Even so, it is tempting to give it a special, postcolonial and feminist significance: I read the trope as if "time" refers to the linear notion of time that places Western Europe and the United States in the present while confining all other continents to a primitive, timeless past. This linear time is the condition of the

Western masculine subject, as I have suggested in the preceding chapter; it is a patriarchal time, conceived of as generational chains of fathers and sons. It is a time one measures mathematically, in years, so that one can calculate at what age one is put outside time, outside history, outside the space of humanity. This is the time, I argue, *Frangipani House* wants to be finished with.

The strategy Mama King uses to counter her confinement is simple and effective: she escapes the home and enters the life of the homeless poor. However, this simple move can be studied on different levels of the text. It can be brought to relate to different notions of place and time. I will consider several well-known approaches to study literary place and time to show that the choice for one of these approaches rather than another makes it possible to read Mama King's escape as a useful intervention in the postcolonial debate on these issues.

Plot-Space, Chronotope, Spatial Practice

Time, place, and space function on different levels of the literary text: the level of the text, the story, and the fabula. Thus, on the level of the fabula the element of "place" or "location" will be studied, while an analysis of the level of the story will concern the aspect of "space."[15] In structuralist terms, *Frangipani House*'s fabula can be described as a series of boundary crossings between the different areas of the fabula: the home itself, the latrines, Mama King's own house, the outside world of roads, fields, and sheds to sleep in, the market. However, if I were to concentrate on the level of the fabula and restrict my argument to the text's treatment of *place*, I would miss the point. The critique of time and space in *Frangipani House* cannot be read on all levels. I will explain why this is so by confronting two possible approaches to space and time.

Within literary theory, these approaches appear as two different influential currents of thought. The first one is rooted in the work of Yuri M. Lotman and other members of the Tartu school. Lotman's influential semiotic theories were developed from an understanding of culture as a spatial metalanguage. When Lotman studies culture as a spatial structure, he does not deny the importance of temporality, but he understands "time" as evolution and development, as the succession of different states, which can and should be analyzed synchronically. Before studying the dynamics of a system, his approach implies, one should articulate its basic laws and grammar; only then will it be possible to study the processes of change.

For my discussion, Lotman's spatial approach is at first sight eminently relevant, as he studies the occurrence of spatial concepts, such as "house" and "home," on the smaller scale of the literary genre and individual texts. He understands these concepts as members of a dichotomy: the opposition between "home" and "wood" is allegedly a universal folkloric theme (Lotman 1990: 105). There are also other possible dichotomies. Thus, "home" is sometimes opposed to "journey"; Lotman also discusses the dichotomies "home"/"antihome" in Gogol (as in home/brothel), and Gogol's contrasting of "home" as a place of egocentric introversion with a more positively valued "homelessness."

Lotman's presentation of the dichotomies based on the notion of "home" is open to critique. A first (still harmless) observation is that even the most apparent dichotomies through which the concept of home is understood have no fixed relevance. Lotman himself acknowledges this fact. For example, in a Caribbean context, the dichotomy home/journey is problematic. Two Caribbean critics of women's writing, Pamela Mordecai and Betty Wilson (1990), argue that the journey is a part of Caribbean identity; hence, Caribbeanness is rooted not in a particular place but in a specific set of experiences, to which the experience of "home" and "journey" both belong. From this point of view, "home" and "journey" are not opposed. Within the Caribbean they are entangled.

With this insight, however, Lotman begins to deconstruct the notion of home. For this observation implies a critique of his own method of understanding the home through a dichotomy of fixed spaces, separated by boundaries. Instead, he suggests that "home" is always a relative construction, dependent on its counterpart. Nevertheless, Lotman doesn't question explicitly his strict understanding of the trope as a spatial one, that is, as a frame for events, a plot-space.

Lotman's approach does not catch the specific function of the home in *Frangipani House*. Here, the home functions not just as a spatial setting but as a spatiotemporal *practice*. A Lotmanian reader may object that the home can be understood by opposing it to the life-giving "outside." But "home" and "outside" are not simply two opposite places: the "outside" is primarily defined by its specific time. Moreover, the home can best be understood in its activity of localizing and temporalizing. Understanding it as a mere place does not do justice to its active role in the story. To see the home in its role as a haunting, killing house, you'll have to renounce the level of the fabula as the relevant object of inquiry in favor of that of the story. The home, then, cannot be seen as just a place in which things happen. On the level of the story, I see the house as a devilish construct, a creation, a growth; and part of the novel's enterprise is to slowly uncover the mechanisms by which it has come to life.

Clearly, a concept of space and place different from Lotman's is called for. I can obtain it only by means of some interdisciplinary shopping: at de Certeau's (philosophy and cultural studies), at Mieke Bal's (narratology), at Gupta and Ferguson's (anthropology), and at Bakhtin's (philosophy of language and literature). The concept of "practice" helps to understand the space in *Frangipani House*. I have taken the concept of "practice" in this context from the philosopher Michel de Certeau. In his study *The Practice of Everyday Life* (1984) he examines the everyday practices used by consumers to manipulate imposed social and cultural patterns. He also refers to the manipulation of space; when giving some examples of such practices, he mentions among others reading, speaking, cooking, *living in a house*, and *walking*. The last two examples concern me here. They are especially illuminating because of their relation to reading and speaking; and the close connection between dwelling/walking and speaking/reading is central to any understanding of *Frangipani House*. The crucial connection between space and speech springs forth from de Certeau's definition of space as distinguished from place:

A place (*lieu*) is the order (of whatever kind) in accord with which elements are distributed in relationships of coexistence. It thus excludes the possibility of two things being in the same location (*place*). . . . A place is thus an instantaneous configuration of positions. . . . A *space* exists when one takes into consideration vectors of direction, velocities, and time variables. . . . Space occurs as the effect produced by the operations that orient it, situate it, temporalize it, and make it function in a polyvalent unity of conflictual programs or contractual proximities. On this view, in relation to place, space is like the word when it is spoken. . . . In short, *space is a practiced place.* (de Certeau 1984: 117)

Michel de Certeau articulates the relationship between place and space as analogous to that between Saussurean *langue* and *parole*.[16] His perspective has other potentials for a reading of *Frangipani House*, but I will leave them for the moment to focus on the narratological interpretation he offers.[17] Mieke Bal's definition of space runs as follows: "The story is determined by the way in which the fabula is presented. During this process, places are linked to certain points of perception. These places *seen in relation to their perception* are called space" (Bal 1985: 93). This definition is remarkably close to de Certeau's; space is situated place, *observed* place.

In *Frangipani House*, places tend to lose their autonomy. Their importance as autonomous cultural spheres, accessible and influential, is underplayed. Instead of presenting places as real towns, countries, or landscapes, the novel offers perceptions and discourses of place: words behind which the materiality of places disappears. "America" is less a geographical place than a space that holds a possible future for Mama King and Nurse Carey (7 and 90); it is also the promised land for those who wish to escape from Guyana's poverty. "Aruba" is the mythical space where Mama King's late husband would have gone, a place that is as little demonstrable on a map as is "Cove and John" in the Calypso (11). "Africa" is for some a way of life in which communality is central, and which could offer an alternative to a miserable present, that is, a future (95, 99–100). For others, in contrast, Africa is the sign for inferiority that has to be shunned. In this space, places are evoked from other places; "Africa" is a possible lifestyle for the Caribbean, "America" is a quality to be found in a dress and a mailbox, and "Aruba" is virtually a name for nowhere, for "gone, never to come back again." Geographical distances and proportions are not very relevant in this perspective, where Guyana seems to lie closer to Africa than to the never-never land of Aruba.

The destructive home works as a narratological suicide machine: it works on the deep level of the text by destroying *place* as a meaningful setting for dramatic events, that is, as the place where the events of the old people's histories are set. At the same time, however, the novel reinstalls this place as (acting) *space* on the level of the story and the text. In this respect, the textual space resembles the alternative concept of space proposed by anthropologists Gupta and Ferguson. They argue for a notion of space as always intrinsically connected:

The presumption that spaces are autonomous has enabled the power of topography to conceal successfully the topography of power. . . . if one begins with the premise that spaces have *always* been hierarchically interconnected, instead of naturally disconnected, then cultural and social change becomes not a matter of cultural contact and articulation but one of rethinking difference *through* connection. (Gupta and Ferguson 1992: 8)

This notion stands in contrast to the traditional view of space as a field of autonomous places, defined and delineated by their association to one particular culture. The notion helps to bring into focus the peculiarity of the space in Gilroy's novel, which is neither traditional nor quite what Gupta and Ferguson describe. The space in *Frangipani House* differs from the interconnected spaces as proposed by Gupta and Ferguson in the way it is conceived as a series of incommensurable time-spaces. In the novel, all different spaces have their particular times, which do not correspond. Moreover, they are all situated in the same geographical sphere. They cannot be differentiated by staking them unambiguously off against each other. Their difference lies in their construction as a spatiotemporal whole. With Mieke Bal, you could say that they represent different points of focalization of space and time.[18] So, spaces are no mere geographical points, but rather cultural and historical spheres that represent cultural, ethnic, racial, and class identifications. Within literary texts, such spaces function to organize fabulas into stories with their specific experienced and perceived time and place. The home, then, must be seen as a (discursive) practice rather than as a place. For an understanding of this concept of literary space I will turn to the work of Mikhail Bakhtin.

Bakhtin can be seen as the exponent of a second theoretical tradition of thought about space (as opposed to Lotman's), which prefers to consider space and time as essentially intricate. In a long essay written in the late thirties, Bakhtin introduces the concept of the "chronotope," which he borrows from Einstein's theory of relativity. Literarily, it should be translated as "time-space." Bakhtin uses the term for "the intrinsic connectedness of temporal and spatial relationships that are artistically expressed in literature" (1988b: 84). Following this definition, he writes a paragraph that clearly shows his difference from Lotman, who would publish his views some decades later:

What counts for us is the fact that it expresses the inseparability of space and time (time as the fourth dimension of space). . . . In the literary artistic chronotope, spatial and temporal indicators are fused into one carefully thought-out, concrete whole. Time, as it were, thickens, takes on flesh, becomes artistically visible; likewise, space becomes charged and responsive to the movements of time, plot and history. (Bakhtin 1988b: 84)

For Bakhtin, then, quite in contrast to Lotman, space and time cannot be separated. For him, time must indeed be seen as the fourth dimension of space, a view Lotman explicitly rejects. Following the statement quoted above, Bakhtin discusses in detail several chronotopes from classical times to his own present; for example, he describes the chronotope of the meeting; the chronotope of the journey, which, according to Bakhtin, is so widespread that it might be traced in any novel; the folkloric chronotope; and the idyllic chronotope. He then shows how these chronotopes work to organize the different literary texts and genres. He also examines the particular views of time that are common to the period and the location where these texts were written, so as to situate the texts within a specific cultural thought. In this way, the essay slowly unravels a history of chronotopes and conceptions of time and space in literature.

For examining postcolonial texts, Bakhtin's perspective of time and space in literature as blended together into the spatiotemporal device of the chronotope that organizes the narrative structure of the text holds great value.[19] The house as it appears in the novel can be understood as a chronotope, that is, a spatiotemporal device that organizes the text. Bearing in mind that a chronotope is related to a larger cultural context, I will situate the device of the destructive home/house in *Frangipani House* within the context of Caribbean women's literature. Here, we find many instances of the metaphor of the *kumbla*, a term taken from the novels by Erna Brodber. The kumbla (literally, calabash) connotes a small enclosure, offering protection and safety like a womb or a cocoon, and possibly a preparation for growth and transformation. But it can therefore also be a site of suffocating distress and an obstacle to entering the outside world.[20] The chronotope of the kumbla occurs in several Caribbean writings by women (see, e.g., its occurrence in the title of a collection of essays on Caribbean women's literature, *Out of the Kumbla*). Here, the chronotope is often used to refer to the necessity of breaking out of a confinement that was brought about by sexism and racism. In the case of *Frangipani House*, the chronotope of the kumbla certainly operates. However, the confining house is a very complicated device that operates in complex ways that need to be carefully considered. It cannot just be equated to a kumbla.

Bakhtin's concept of the chronotope makes it possible to relate a certain literary time-space to the concepts of time and space that are current in the historical and geographical context of that specific literary work.

Within the Caribbean context, then, concepts of time and space are closely linked to action, participation, and community. The direct implication of this suggestion is that the chronotope of the house in *Frangipani House* must be understood as an active principle, almost a protagonist; and in its turn, the house must be seen as the effect of the activities of others. So, even while the concept of the chronotope is helpful in our understanding of Frangipani House as a kumbla, I need de Certeau's emphasis on practice, in particular, speech, to illuminate the critical charge of spatial concepts such as the home in *Frangipani House*. The next section starts from his assumption about the relationship between space and speech.

Space and Speech

Frangipani House's representation of space steers away from concepts of space and time used in strategies of localization of women, (de)colonized people, and aging people. This critique of oppressive concepts of space comes about by the novel's refusal to define place as "plot-space." Instead, the novel organizes itself around the chronotope of the confining, killing house, which is seen as a localizing device that has to be escaped. But there is yet another way the novel counters restricting representations of space, and that is by adopting a certain perspective on space as a semiotic practice. This makes an unexpected development of the story possible. I have suggested above that space, in *Frangipani House*, is largely discursive. But this does not mean that space is merely "textual." On the contrary, in the novel, a "text" is significant only insofar as it is more than a visual representation. Texts are like spaces in that they, too, must be *practiced* to have meaning. My analysis of this approach to the notions of text and fiction leads me to argue that the novel can be read as a critical comment on postmodern discourses of textuality, which is based on a gendered African-Caribbean understanding of space and time. One trope stands out as a particularly significant metafictional image: the window that creates fiction. It will be the focal point of the next argument.

Many Black women writers employ spatial discourses that center around notions like border, frontier, and boundary. One of them is Grace Nichols. In her poem *The Black Triangle* the poet posits herself on the threshold and confronts dominant discourses from there, never abandoning her own sense of a rooted self. The threshold is a site of negotiation, and as such it can be a specific place for a woman as well, like the porch of some of the homes in the South. It offers the possibility of bound motion. Mama King, too, is seated on a threshold: a window. It is a site of contact, but it is also a boundary; and this makes it different from Nichols's woman's place. If one sets Gilroy's threshold against Nichols's sexual, fluid threshold of fertile femininity, one can argue that the window is the place for *old* women.[21] "Since her entry into the home, she had begun to see the world through the glass window of her room as was the destiny of many old people. Mr Carey the druggist told her once, 'Too often old people get to see the world through window. To make it interesting—they must pretend it's magic'" (5). Here, the dichotomy between isolated interior and forbidden exterior is installed. In addition, this division is linked to a problematics of observation and fictionalizing. The narrator's text, as well as the character Carey's text, points ahead at the particular kind of observation through the window, which will be elaborated later in the novel. In the words of the druggist, this forced circumstance of observation receives unexpected significance: old people who have no choice left but to look through the window to make an effort to render the world interesting by pretending it is magical.

Magic is a very complicated concept, and when I relate it to "fiction" I take into account only some of its aspects, not necessarily the most important ones. In this context, I choose to understand magic as the miraculous, more or less frightening effects of the hidden manipulations of the (super)natural by others. Magic differs from religion in that the magician seeks to master and manipulate the spiritual forces, whereas the priest submits to them (Alleyne 1989: 15). The exact proceedings of the magician are hidden from the public. The person who acts is invisible behind the effect. Here one finds a similarity to escapist fiction, also producing an entertaining illusion; (lighter forms of) magic, as well as fiction, may be enjoyed as entertainment and distraction, for which the conditions of its production must be hidden to keep the illusion intact. The reader does not understand how the effect is created and adopts the comfortable position of the consumer. In the case of the old people Mr. Carey refers to, it is the old people themselves who create the situation in which they play the part of the audience that has to be entertained. Their role is not merely passive. They posit themselves not as stage directors, authors, actors, or fictional characters but as "readers."

One can make a comparison between the position of the elderly who observe the world through the window and a definition of fictionality as the process in which an extratextual reality is transformed into a textual one (Gorp 1980: 63). The window can be seen as the screen onto which the world is projected, or as the surface on which the world becomes readable. By the mediation of the window, the chaotic, inaccessible reality is transposed into a semiotic structure. However, this move simultaneously renders this reality inaccessible. It can no longer be experienced directly. It can now be read as a possibly interesting, but for one's own life always rather irrelevant, picture, which, like magic, is also more or less threatening. The novel represents this situation as one of hampered observation. The window is often misted over, and often it is too dark to look outside.

By the motif of the window, the "reading" of the reality is represented as an alienating deed, which nevertheless does lead to some deeper insight into the self, even if only into one's fading away. But that, of course, is not really surprising: obtaining identity always occurs through a series of alienating identifications. Here, identity is constructed within a dominating discourse—and this discourse does not identify old age in a very promising way. The fragment about the picture card is an instance of this interpretation of the self.

Mama King looks outside through the window, where a torrential rain is coming down. The motif of rain often expresses desolation.

Only a picture card at the mercy of the rushing water held her gaze. "That card like me. Going wherever rough water push it." Now picture side up, the card had no control over its route or its fate. It came to rest behind a stone but the respite was brief. There it was again—water-logged and disintegrating, raindrops falling upon it like stones and seeking truly to destroy it.

Mama King cupped her head in both hands and closed her eyes. When she opened them again, the window was clear. Everything had vanished. (31)

The card has two sides, of which here only one is visible. The side on which text is written (or maybe not) cannot be seen. The water will certainly efface the text before it effaces the picture on the other side. The symbolism is not hard to point out. In addition to the similarity in the ways both the card and Mama King are helplessly left to the vagaries of destiny, another comparison is obvious: Mama King, too, has sides hidden from view: one can no longer read her "text," that is, her orderly narrated life history, and with that her capacity to communicate. All those are erased. This interpretation is reinforced by those passages in which Mama King writes (rather peculiar) letters that are never posted by those she trusts to do so. One can argue that the aged self may be represented in the outside world, on the other side of the window, but only as a memory, an empty sign of the past without relevance to the present.

The following quote will enable me to make a comparison between the observation through the window and the observation of another time through a comparable but different transparent surface. It will bring me onto the theme of the landscape.

She chuckled softly, and in her imagination walked until she reached the pond. The water hardly stirred but some dragonflies hunted close to the surface. From the depths of the pond she could hear voices of women long dead and gone—the washerwomen she used to know, singing as they beat the dirt from the clothes with their faithful wooden beaters. They had left the echoes of their songs to tell how life had robbed them of their youth, of their spirit and then of their lives. (53)

In many Caribbean and African narratives the pond is represented as a magical place, associated with women, spiritual forces, and death.[22] The window and the surface of the pond resemble each other because they are both flat, even, transparent, because insects circle over both surfaces (6, 24), and because they both separate two worlds of different time-orders. If the druggist is right in speaking about the connection old people make between observation through such a surface and magic, then his statement holds even more true for the pond. In it, Mama King imagines hearing the voices of women long gone. She hears the echoes of their voices, not the text of the songs they sang. These echoes in themselves tell the story of frustrated and destroyed women's lives—not by what they say, but by their mere presence. The surface of the pond lets through only those traces that refer more to the loss than to the past itself. The pond is related to the many significant tropes of wetness in *Frangipani House*, which all refer to destruction, erasure, and death: rain is coupled with sadness, and it erases traces; the sea is an amorphous space without origin, time, or shelter, and as such is a sign of death (28).

Combining the trope of the pond with that of the window, one could argue that this is the way Mama King imagines herself: sunk behind her window in a space outside life, where there are no living sounds but only traces and shreds of memory, pointing at an absence. And indeed, Mama King identifies with the women in the pond: vividly, she suddenly reexperiences the sensations of soap, starch, and cotton she had herself when doing the family laundry in the past.

Thus, as a kumbla, the home for the old is also a pond, in the magical African sense of the word. Mama King emerges as someone who is gifted with the special power to "see" into another reality, a past reality that is now more real to her than the present. This "seeing" is hearing and feeling rather than literally seeing, and as a complex form of sensory perception it is superior to mere visual observation. One aspect of Mama King's predicament in *Frangipani House* is that she can only (and often only imperfectly) *look* at the outside world, instead of feeling, smelling, or hearing it. This restriction of the senses turns the outside world into mere words, mere fiction. But this bare, empty kind of fiction does not hold any promise for "localized" subjects.

Confinement separates from and thereby fictionally *shows* the outside world. However, confinement is double-edged: as it creates an outside *and* an inside, it creates an inside space in which a specific discourse might take shape. Is there such a discourse in the novel? This question is all the more urgent because I read Mama King's destructive confinement as an effect of neocolonialism (I will have more to say on that later). Ultimately, then, my question is whether some kind of postcolonial speech can exist within this restricted, "post-"colonial space. Maybe there is some counterdiscourse possible, an invigorating fiction, and thus a position as a speaking subject. Can the "localized" speak?

If the answer to this question were the same as that to Spivak's famous query (1988), the next part of this section would have to be on a pessimistic note; and it is. Perhaps this inquiry into the speaking conditions within the confined space of *Frangipani House* might even enhance one's sensibility to the delicate question of whether a postcolonial counterdiscourse is possible at all. Speech as such is not impossible, at least: the elderly in Frangipani House utter several kinds of speech. I differentiate three forms. But none of them is liberating or critical. To decide their nature and force, I will take the theories by the characters themselves as guidelines.

When Mama King is talking and calling out to herself in her room, Matron wishes to interfere. Nurse Carey then pleads with her not to:

"She's only talking. All old people talk like that. She's saying the things she never said. That is old age!"

"I wonder if reading a romance to her would help," chirruped Miss Mason. "That's what happens when women can't have something they once had. That's my imagination at work again." (10)

"She's only talking"; there is, then, a first way of speaking that is without consequence, that is *only* talking, without danger, principally insignificant and monological—because it is meant as such, but also because the addressee just walks out of earshot (4). This speech is wasted, just as the old women's time now is. This kind of talking may be an incoherent or aggressive monologue ("Mama King . . . menacingly continued her soliloquy," 11), which in its ultimate form is screaming:

Just then Miss Tilley started screaming and as if to ease their own anguish several other old women joined in—their voices blending the guilt, remorse and resentment of old age.

There was nowhere to hide from the screams, they formed an invisible barrier around her. (5)

The voice of this old age is characterized by remorse and bitterness. It encloses the women destructively, just like the home itself.

"She's saying the things she never said," is the second aspect of this speech named by Nurse Carey. Indeed, the older people often surrender to boundless talk, which is no longer restrained by any taboo. Miss Mason, for example, speaks as freely about sex as demonstrating uninhibited sexual behavior (13). This talk brings unsaid, hidden truths to the surface. As such, it is a mad, testifying speech—"like a drunken preacher" (10)— which is reminiscent of the speaking in tongues analyzed by Mae Henderson.[23] For the character, this raving heralds destruction. "She's saying the things she never said" means that the old woman is no longer who she was. It is the sign of the destruction of her former identity, which she had constructed by suppressing certain realities in her life.

Even so, for the reader the raving is most significant. It is so, of course, by its mere contents: one learns something about the old person's past. But in addition, one learns something else. The voice of this enclosure, like the echoes in the pond, tells a lot about the *nature* of and *reasons* for the confinement. If Frangipani House is an eminent example of "an artificial, constrained practice of fixation," as Clifford articulates it, then someone must have brought it about; and it may not be just "old age" that explains the need for destructive incarceration. Just like gender, ethnicity, and "race," "old age" is a complex construction that cuts through other categorical identifications. The anger and frustration heard throughout the narrative, presented as if quite obvious and natural, point to the reasons for that rage, which I will address shortly.

"I wonder if reading a romance to her would help," proposes Miss Mason. I interpret "reading a romance" as a form to be subsumed within the third category of speech (the first being futile, incoherent speech; the second the unrestrained uncovering of hidden truths). This is a form of active reading and consequently a form of writing and rewriting. It is a certain process of fictionalizing, actively engaged in by the residents. It can be understood as the creation of illusions, and it takes different forms.

Mama King recreates her past in a form that is considerably nicer than the testimony of others suggests. This is especially the case for the role she assigns to Danny, her lost husband, as a devoted lover who brought her happiness. Mama King's best friend, Ginchi, and a less dear acquaintance by the name of Ben Le Cage offer a comment that shows there is something wrong in Mama King's story. According to the far-from-perfect Ben Le Cage, Danny was "the cruellest, most ignorant man in God's world" (33), who "bumped, bruised and boxed you face and kick you about worse than a football" (33). Miss Ginchi's depiction of Danny is part of a secret she confesses to Mama King shortly before her own death: she confesses to have had a hand in Danny's death. These are the last words she says to her friend before dying: "He was a brute. All he ever do is to break women will, break women back, and drink rum" (76).

All this throws doubt on the sustainability of Mama King's version. But if Ben Le Cage calls her merely "a crazy old woman dreaming of an imaginary man" (34), he does her an injustice. Mama King recreated a desirable past, by which she makes an important statement about her life. It is the same statement we find in the fantasies of another inmate, Miss Mason, who has never had a love affair.

Nobody was good enough for me. "No," said my mother, "men are evil. Men are bad. Men are the devil." I never married.

I was never in love except in my imagination. I could build a man like you build a house and then fall in love. (9)

Now she amuses herself by avidly reading "romances" about love: "'I want another romance,' she said. 'A true romance then tonight I can dream of things you people indulge in. If I were young again I would love every man who was willing until he screamed for mercy'" (10). Thus, she creates a number of fictional levels, which she clearly differentiates from her real life in past and present. She knows perfectly well that her former "men-building" was only a surrogate for the love and sex she could have had. The way she speaks about her reading, and her dreaming of love then and now, shows that her life was a delusion. In her case it was her mother who stood between her and her fulfillment. It will become clear that her case was far from isolated.

For Mama King, her husband Danny's desertion of her seems more important. In her story, his desertion consists only in his sudden departure. The advantage of her narrative is that (with the help of the reverse movement of her logic) it enables Mama King to conclude from his absence that she misses him, and, in consequence, that he must be a beloved absentee. It makes him, in retrospect, the fulfillment of her desire for a true, loving husband. This fiction shows that Mama King desired love, and the context shows that this love was absent. This is the important signification of her narrative, which is kindred to the echoes of the washerwomen in the pond, the romances of Miss Mason, and also the bitter, remorseful ravings of the old. They are all significant not by what they say but by their indication of an absence, and of an unfulfilled desire.

These voices and narratives are comments on closed, painful histories, which are not easily remembered. These narratives do not articulate a critique, but they are merely desperate, destructive, mad illusions, which lead away from the cruel stories and histories, and away from historical time. When time stops, it is impossible to develop a story. This, then, is the voice of those who are "localized" by old age in the periphery. Its impotence is the result of the way the novel relates speaking subjectivity to space and time. It does so by letting the fact of fixation in a secluded spot and in a frozen present render speech and the narration of stories and histories impossible. Thus, the text presents fiction within fixation as a destructive illusion. Within confinement and isolation, a counterdiscourse cannot be found. But there are ways out of this predicament. Such an escape is at the same time a reconceptualization of space as a text. As it turns out, "landscape" is the ideal textualization of space.

Escape into Landscape

The narratives told by the screams and ravings of the residents in Frangipani House are inconclusive. They only help do what the home hoped to accomplish: secluding the elderly to their deaths, moving them outside time and history. Words do not help to reintegrate these people into history. In the novel, there is only one way to reinscribe oneself into history, and that is by engaging directly and unmediatedly in the events that form the history of a community. This move becomes possible if one connects to the specific time-space in which the collective history is laid down. Perhaps unexpectedly, in *Frangipani House* this time-space takes the form of the *landscape*. The function of the landscape will be understood best through the novel's perception of time and history.

The novel's presentation of time and history as practices to engage in evokes certain African or African-Caribbean concepts of time. In *Roots of Jamaican Culture* (1989), Mervyn Alleyne discusses a concept of time that, according to him, is as much West African as Jamaican, and by extension, may also be Afro-Caribbean. He bases his argument on several African scholars (Mbiti and Nhiwatiwa) when he writes: "[I]n the African world view, the time concept is based on natural events. Time is defined in terms of the events that are taking place or have taken place. Time is not an imposed mathematical formula; it is a phenomenal event" (Alleyne 1989: 155). Quoting Nhiwatiwa, he repeats: "Time is the event that has taken place or is taking place. It does not matter how long it takes the event to finish or start. The most important thing is the individual participation in the event taking place" (156). He then clarifies in his own words: "It is not important how long you spend at (say) the barber shop: what matters is the quality of social interaction there" (156). Thus, one is situated within time when participating in a certain event. This event should not merely take place; one should engage in it actively.

According to this opinion, time is strictly related to the experience of events and is not to be measured as an abstract category. Even while a strong critique of the generalizing and essentializing tendencies in Alleyne's explanation would be justified, his intervention is useful as a critique of Western abstract notions of time.[24] Instead of using Alleyne to baptize *Frangipani House*'s treatment of time as somehow "African," I refer to Alleyne to suggest that the abstract, Western time concept the novel criticizes is culturally and ethnically specific. I will refrain from outlining an "African" or "Afro-Caribbean" time except by trying to capture the specific notion that is visible in this Caribbean text. Here, then, time is always narrative; that is, it is experienced on the (narratological) level of the *story* and not on that of the fabula, where time exists only as the principle that arranges events in a certain order. When Mama King finally escapes, under the wing of a group of beggars, she escapes from Matron's evil narrating voice, which articulates the temporal context of her story in a destructive way ("'June 28 in the year of our Lord, far into time,' said Matron with a chuckle," 40). Moreover, she escapes from the inner voice that tries to narrate her own past again and again. At the moment of Mama King's escape, one sees Frangipani House as it is: a story undoing itself by shedding its narrative aspects (time and space). Fleeing the house, Mama King escapes a discourse that separates space from time.

Mama King then lands in the semiotically rich space of the outside world, where the narratively promising "road" and "market" are situated.[25] It is the "wide world," a spatial arrangement of a series of semiotically rich places. It is also defined by its different time order. The past, paramount in the home, recedes and fades away (62). In the beggars' life, shared by Mama King, time is not cumulative and linear but cyclic. So, the absence of time within the home's confinement is opposed not to the dominant linear time of historiography but to the cyclic time of a very vitalizing present. "When I run away I was happy," Mama King says later. "I go forward. I never look back. Life was risky. It like going to catch fish at high tide on rough water" (96). This time order is not idealized. It is not the folkloric or idyllic chronotope described by Bakhtin.[26] The cyclic time cannot be understood as the novel's Utopian moment. Concepts of circular time can be very traditional in a literary text,[27] as in the case of the two chronotopes I mentioned. Whether an alternative concept of time functions as a critique against dominant time concepts, in whatever way, is highly dependent on genre, and historical, cultural, social, and literary context.

This other time order is a semiotic order that is also "readable," but only in a very specific sense: that is, if the concept of "reading" is interpreted as connoting "understanding" and "awareness" so that the concept is in fact independent of written or printed symbols.[28] To the deadly ways of reading in Frangipani House, then, the novel does not oppose a supposed impossibility to read and speak about real life. The novel rejects the easy dichotomy of reading/living. There is a way this outside reality can be read, but it is completely different from the way the world was read through the window in Frangipani House. This text is read by experiencing it with all senses, not merely through the eyes. Thus, Mama King decides she no longer needs her glasses (61). The space becomes a readable world she can relate to: a landscape.[29]

The novel offers two ways in which this landscape is read: *working* and *walking*. In the passage about the pond, I have already referred to the function of working. The kind of reading that is done in the act of working does not lead to new, bubbling flashes of insight. It entails a kind of interaction with the materiality of life that is opposed to the empty, meaningless observation of life from outside. As such, work is defined as a relationship with life, that is, an understanding of it in the sense of an insight into "how it works."[30] But work can also numb (80). So, "working" is not romanticized, even when it is presented as an essential feature of Mama King's identity, which is taken from her only at the cost of her disintegration and alienation from life.

"Walking" is more explicitly presented as the second kind of reading; de Certeau has proposed a similar equation. At the start of the narrative, Mama King walks over the terrain of the home while reading the many prohibitions and laughing about them. These written texts, such as "Keep off the grass," restrict her freedom of movement, while she recalls the feeling of grass under her bare feet, and the time she lay in the grass with her husband, talking. The literal act of reading prevents her from reading the world, that is, getting in touch with it. According to Alleyne's definition of time as the concrete experience of, and participation in, events, a direct experience of the meaningful landscape is the first step toward reentering time.

I compare this semiotic, sensory experience to "reading" because I want to argue that here a critical, counterdefinition of the *text* is being prepared. This different conception may be related to a different (possibly characteristically postcolonial) understanding of literature. The postcolonial counterdefinition of the text I discern links to the novel's representation of the landscape as a text: alternately, texts may be defined as landscapes. Texts are considered as specific textures, shaped by specific histories, and rooted in, and opening out to, a specific past. The crucial link between landscape and text, between walking and reading, is that both serve as (the domain of) *practices* to relate to a vivid temporality: a present made significant by the past, a significant past, connected to the present. The specific materiality of these domains (words, space, earth) is less important than the *effect* they are pursuing (i.e., the effect of reestablishing a link with significant time). Both landscape and text can be seen as performance: the landscape, too, sensually addresses its audience of walkers. I consider the emphasis on aspects of performance and effect as proper to a postcolonial perspective. Because texts are seen as reaching outward to the world, they do not lose their material relation to their places and times of origin, even if these may be many.[31] In contrast to certain postmodern theories of signifying (notably Deleuze and Guattari's nomadology, discussed in the preceding chapter), this approach insists on the importance of the *situatedness* of texts in space and in time.

Reentering time by experiencing the sensual aspects of landscape is not only a very effective action performed by characters. It appears to be a basic condition for the production of meaning: writers, too, use the close association between landscape, time, and memory to create their own narratives of past and present. Toni Morrison is, again, an eloquent example of the relation between memory, writing, and the sensual experience of landscape:

> You know, they straightened out the Mississippi River in places, to make room for houses and livable acreage. Occasionally the river floods these places. "Floods" is the word they use, but in fact it is not flooding; it is remembering. Remembering where it used to be. All water has a perfect memory and is forever trying to get back to where it was. Writers are like that: remembering where we were, what valley we ran through, what the banks were like, the light that was there and the route back to our original place. It is emotional memory—what the nerves and the skin remember as well as how it appeared. (Quoted in Zinsser 1987: 119)

The past is not lost to us, then. But not because it has been written down. It is still there because it is inscribed in the body, because it is inscribed in landscape. Landscape is saturated with (often repressed) collective memories. Because of its sensual materiality, it can be touched and experienced. Thus, the past is evoked, brought into the present, and revitalized. This reviving of the past has the effect of revitalizing the present, too. The experience of the present is dependent on one's experience of the past; as long as the past is frozen, the present cannot but be dead too. Whoever brings the past back to life, reinstalls the movement and sensuality of time itself.

The problem is, of course, that it is so very hard to *touch* that lost past. Usually, texts, movies, and other narrative and visual practices perform the task of bringing a meaningful past back into the present. But the African diaspora has not been documented in such a way. In discussing the slave narrative of Fredrick Douglass, Henry Louis Gates Jr. states that African slaves in the United States did not have the means to know anything about their own history: "The knowledge the slave has of his circumstances he must deduce from the earth" (1987a: 90). Deprived of time and history, then, slaves have to rely on meaningful space for their identification. Not surprisingly, this need for landscape and space as an alternative site of memory is felt in Caribbean literature too, where the absence of a meaningful history is felt most acutely.

Some even wish to see the privileging of "place" as a general characteristic of postcolonial writing. In a modest but influential essay in 1965, D. E. S. Maxwell already analyzes the function of landscape depictions in texts by Achebe and Stow, and he argues that landscape in (what he terms) Commonwealth literature "comes to signify the qualities of the society that inhabits it, and prompts the imagination to see in it the imprint of the past which the present must try to understand" (Maxwell 1965: 89). Maxwell relates landscape to the past, that is, to history, a history urgently needed in postcolonial writing, as dominant Western historiographies leave the peoples of these landscapes hardly any possibility but to relate their identities to the history of the Western centers of the world. Landscape is the space in which the past has inscribed itself.[32] Ashcroft, Griffiths, and Tiffin, authors of a pioneering survey of postcolonial theory and practice, go even further: they suggest a dichotomy between time, privileged in European texts, and space, privileged in postcolonial texts. With grand gesture they state: "In post-colonial thought, however, as the Australian poet Les Murray has said, 'time broadens into space'" (Ashcroft, Griffiths, and Tiffin 1989: 34). Following this poetic but rather inexact formulation, they mention the strategies several authors use to mobilize "space" against "time": some novels "run European history aground in a new and overwhelming space which annihilates time and imperial purpose" (34), whereas, in another essay, an author "makes a plea for an escape from a prison of perpetual recriminations into the possibilities of a 'historyless' world" (34). Yet another holds that "hybridity in the present is constantly struggling to free itself from a past with stressed ancestry. . . . It replaces a temporal lineality with a spatial plurality" (35–36). Thus, Ashcroft, Griffiths, and Tiffin bring together very differently situated authors from Australia, the Caribbean, and Canada in one postcolonial enterprise to structure texts around the concept of space instead of time.[33]

Morrison's and Gilroy's texts show that instead of merely turning the hierarchy of time-space upside down by privileging space instead of time, a more ambitious deconstruction is called for: by shattering the dichotomy altogether, by insisting on the inescapable interweaving of space and time, and by understanding space and time as lived signifying practices. Thus, the specific "sense of place" of postcolonial authors (as analyzed in Peggy Nightingale's *A Sense of Place in the New Literatures in English*, 1986) can be understood as the authors' deep feelings of belonging to their (post)colonial cultural environment, that is, to a (multiple) community and a (broken, but significant) past. If their "sense of place" motivates some authors to make the landscape their explicit theme, they use the theme as a means to imagine their elusive, broken past as rooted, material, sensual, significant. We're talking not about the relation between abstract time and abstract place but about the role of spatiotemporal strategies in the construction of (cultural, national, communal) identity. Together with Caribbean time, space is a necessary site of identification, as important as language in much related Western scholarship. In this light, the seemingly obvious remark by Nigerian author Chinua Achebe's takes on new significance. When Achebe speaks of the crucial importance of knowledge of the geographic and cultural "place" to an understanding of a literary work, and insists on the "writer's oneness with his or her place of origin,"[34] he is not pleading for a sociological or biographical approach to literature. In essence, he connects to what Adrienne Rich dubbed "a politics of location" (Rich 1984). By insisting on the spatial nature of literature and identity, Achebe opposes a form of universalism that seemingly approaches literature as a transcendental phenomenon but keeps submitting it to Western norms and values (Achebe 1975). Again, a Bakhtinian understanding of literature as heteroglot, and therefore always still testifying of the manifold contexts from which it has sprung, helps to understand the weight of Achebe's plea. An emphasis on "place" in itself is not the differential sign of postcolonial literature. But the insistence on space as "inhabited, always already meaningfully constructed place," and, moreover, as materialized history, is a sign for the ineffaceable difference of the postcolonial subject.[35]

Here lies the significance of the landscape in *Frangipani House*. It is the specific time-space in which history is laid down and through which one can reenter history, that is, the events of the community. The landscape, then, is a space testifying of its history. We find the landscape in the novel represented as the cultural text in which local history is preserved and made accessible. When Mama King touches grass, her own past in which she walked on grass or laid in it is recalled. Her memories spring to life by this sensual contact. Sometimes she remembers the events linked to a certain place, such as the pond; the mere memory of a certain landscape is sufficient to recall the past linked to it.

This understanding of landscape as a spatiotemporal text may sound nostalgic, but it is not. Even if the memories of this situated past are fond, the history thus "read" is hardly rosy. The illusions about Mama King's Danny are replaced by a repressed narrative of a past of drudgery and toil for her children and grandchildren. The landscape itself is not merciful, certainly not for old women who need a definite protection. As a text, it is hardly more beneficial than the mediated fictional text produced by the window. Mama King realizes this very well, even at the very moment she is confronted with the destruction of her identity, symbolized by the empty picture card. When, in the passage about the picture card, the window suddenly opens to a void, Mama King shiveringly prays for help: "'The sun so bad, it killin' and shrivellin'. The rain so bad it floodin' and drowndin'. Lord help me'" (31). This significant utterance contrasts strangely to the recurring metaphor of the vitalizing, phallic light celebrated elsewhere in the text.[36] The statement about the destructive forces of sun and rain is reinforced by other crucial associations, like the one about the sea and the cold trade wind:

> Mama King seemed to have frozen in time and was now by the sea. The wind blew across her face. It was January.
> "*The wind so cold, Dan,*" she said. "*It trade wind, blowing from different place. Some place goes cold with snow and ice. Winter I believe they calls it.*"
> "*I love sea water. You can't see where it come from and where it go. It like life and death. It keep going on.*" (28)

Danny praises the beauty of a sea without origin or aim, without beginning or end, like life and death. As a dead man, he would; Mama King imagines him to collapse life and death into this infinity. Mama King complains about the cold, and it is quite befitting for a living mortal to shiver

at the confrontation with infinity. Even so, this infinity is spatially defined
in that it contains "places." Mama King refers in her evocation of those
places to the North, where the centers of colonial power are located, which
make their destructive influence felt at the Caribbean seacoasts. Mama
King's sea is the sea of the African diaspora and the sign of female desert-
edness, not the infinite placelessness of Danny, the dead and deadly, placeless, shifty male.[37]

The sea is not the only element of "landscape" that testifies to a past
(and present) of imperial interference. The novel shows gradually that the
vitalizing text of the landscape is also the site of a homelessness old women
cannot occupy without danger. It is a space of violence and poverty, and
even if Mama King welcomes the marginality of life in the open as an invigorating condition, this life doesn't offer the marginalized any protection.
But the insight into the rawness of this condition does not mean the sad
end of Mama King's desire for life, as I will show. This insight is represented as a necessary step toward an alternative, female manipulation of
speech, space, and time.

Haunting Houses

In the end, the landscape is forbidding. Yet it seems the only place
where a counterdiscourse can be forged. However, the discursive force strong
enough to counter the destructive localizations exposed in the novel comes
from elsewhere, as I will show. But before this force can come into its own,
a daring, doomed intermediary voice must be created as if in a necessary rite
of passage. Only after nearly having succumbed to this preposterous voice,
and only after having forsaken it, can the protagonist find her place in a sustaining narrative.

As if in opposition to the futile voices of enclosure I have discussed
above, the novel presents a different kind of voice that makes itself momentarily heard within the new condition of dislocation and homelessness.
At one point in the story, Mama King leaves the bothy where she usually
stays to accompany one of the beggar women, Sumintra, to the fish market. The market is an intensified semiotic landscape, overwhelming to the
senses. In literary theory, the cultural significance of the concept of the
market is evaluated differently. Bakhtin approaches the market as the space
of heteroglossia central to his concept of language. Czech literary scholar

Peter V. Zima, who departs from Bakhtin's exploration of the market, argues instead that the market is the location of the mechanism that emphasizes exchange value over use value, which leads to the ambivalence of meanings and values and, ultimately, to indifference (Zima 1981). In current literary discussion, much use is made of Bakhtin's inspiring insights. However, in Caribbean literary debates, Bakhtin's perspective is sometimes criticized because it does not pay enough attention to the power structure of the network of different, competing, dominant, and marginalized voices.[38] Zima, who uses Marxist insights, does precisely that. Mama King lands in Zima's market rather than in Bakhtin's. Her story shows how language loses its meaning in the market, which may be a danger to the continued existence of identity. The market in *Frangipani House* is a landscape of danger, a "choke-and-rob place" (65), especially so for marginalized women, like Sumintra and Mama King. Even if in West Africa the market may be the site of the powerful class of market women, the market is here the young men's territory, the space of "their wild manifestation of youthful strength" (66).

And yet, this is the location where Mama King, for a short while, finds a new voice. Mama King suddenly reveals herself as a fortune-teller. She reads a woman's hand in exchange for some money. "The first time I tell fortune. God forgive me for tellin' lie" (65–66). In the light of Gates's optimistic theories about the speech strategies of signifying associated to the trickster figure, this voice appears to have special potencies. But Mama King's exhilarating, creative, and profitable speech is not represented in the text, and before it is developed it is brutally punished.

This is what happens: lured by a swinging praise song about the caring grandmother to which a group of young men dance, she moves one step too close to the deceitful, empty discourse of the market. Two of these young men beat her up, attracted by the sight of her fortune-telling money. Mama King, unconscious, lands in the hospital. Apparently, Mama King breaks a taboo when she thinks she is able to live within a language that has lost its meaning. She did not yet fully realize that the language of the market exists only as entertainment and a means of exchange, or, maybe, as a discourse of male violence and rhythm unreadable to her. She almost had to pay for her trespassing with her life.

This episode can be understood within the context of the rites of passages in folk narratives. Mama King's passage is another articulation of the widespread theme of the temporal death as a passage from one state to a higher one (Lotman 1990: 160).[39] With reference to Propp, Lotman mentions the initiation rituals of the shaman, which include a form of dying associated with being ripped apart or cut to pieces; to create this effect, parts of the body are perforated, or a snake is brought into the body. After having passed through this rite, the shaman receives the gift of prophecy (160). Mama King assumes the art of fortune-telling without having been initiated in such a manner, and she pays a proper price: by dying *after* (instead of before) prophesying. Her (temporary) death does not bring her the gift of prophecy or the authority of the shaman, but it does work as a passage for her. It gives her the position of the more or less detached grandmother. Detached from a killing confinement and thrown out of the beggar's located homelessness, she is now prepared to position herself within different times and spaces. But she will never again totally abandon herself to any absolute confinement, localization, or position.

Mama King's short stay in the marginal time-space of the beggars, and her unconsciousness after the attack, can be compared to other intermediate stages in African and Afro-Caribbean women's narratives of escape. For example, in Nigerian writer Buchi Emecheta's well-known *Second-Class Citizen*, heroine Adah's stay in the maternity ward in the hospital is also such an intermediate stage, a passage, in which she learns to lie and delude with language (and other means of make-believe) in a comparable way. It is as if women in migrant women's writing need to go through an episode of raving and screaming before they find themselves in a new discursive position. This new position is characterized by the insight into the ambivalence of language, which can now be manipulated to obtain desired positions. These passages through the breakdown of discourse and identity lead not to a homecoming but to the ability to situate oneself temporarily and to name oneself accordingly. Therefore, these narratives are less geographies of women's confinement and escape than stories about the practice of manipulating space and time, and speech. This point must be made in order to understand the novel's account of an alternative, counterdiscursive voice.

Above, I have set Mama King's passage tentatively within the context of folk narratives. But far from being a mere rewriting of a folktale, the novel appropriates traditional structures, as many other recent narratives told by women do, in order to shape women's own strategies to find new positions in society, and to negotiate the mechanisms that pin women down in certain confining conditions. Thus, I consider their narratives as practices, not as structures. As de Certeau puts it, after the study of linguistic systems the study of signifying practices became possible; the study of the codes and taxonomies of spatial order enables us to pass on to the study of spatializing practices (1984: 116). This chapter is a study of practices, then, and not one of systems. It doesn't have the choice: the novel radically refuses to consider *anything* as object, structure, passive space. Instead, it sees agency and effects all around.

One of the ways in which *Frangipani House* practices place is to refrain from installing the outside world as "plot-space," but instead it presents an animated *landscape*. The landscape becomes a protagonist in its own right. It is not the only nonhuman entity in the story with the privilege of being considered able to act. The narrative style of the novel often presents matter as acting subject. There are many examples, in the narrator's text as much as in the characters'. They include hardly conspicuous fixed expressions such as "her secret died" (8), as well as elaborated personifications of "work" as in "but since when work turn its back on poor, old people? *'If work come now and stan' up before me, I give her a big-big cuffing'"* (19) and "'Work has scrawled its name all over her. It owns her'" (94). This style of endowing inanimate matter, occupations, and characteristics with the privilege of the acting subjectivity of the protagonist seems to be common in Caribbean Creole speech. Again, Bakhtin's work helps to understand the radical difference of the novel's strategy of narrating. In his article on the chronotope, Bakhtin has studied the folkloric time of the agrarian collective: "This time attracts everything into its orbit; it will not permit any unmoving or static setting. . . . All objects are thus attracted into life's orbit; they become living participants in the events of life" (1988b: 209). The objects here are natural phenomena, like sun, stars, and sea. They are present not as the object of "poetic perception" but "as part of the collective process of labor and the battle against nature." Thus, Bakhtin contrasts this vision with an aesthetic approach. Later literary developments restrict the power of time and, in consequence, of "narratability."

Bakhtin's remarks enlighten Gilroy's literary choices to a certain degree. Gilroy knows how to make effective use of this unbridled narratibility; and, steering free from all traces of nostalgia to an earlier organization of life, she rejects the aestheticism that privileges distance and visuality.

The fact that a large part of the novel is written in Creole demonstrates already that Gilroy situates her narrative strategies in another history of chronotopes and narratives than that described by Bakhtin. Gilroy exploits the "narratable" potentials of Creole admirably.[40]

An important, perhaps unexpected aspect of Gilroy's technique is the downplaying of human agency. The novel's human characters have relatively little influence over their circumstances. They are determined by that which surrounds them, and they are the products of their past; more often than not, this makes them feel driven into a corner. They are often worried about the way others will see them (especially Matron and Mama King's daughters, Cyclette and Token). In fact, only nonhuman entities seem to act in carefree and purposeful ways. By this narrative strategy, people may associate on equal terms with matter and abstractions. Memories can be greeted, work and toil can be seen as (maybe troublesome) friends, work can put its seal on someone's appearance, and trees may name a house.

Gilroy sketches an aesthetics in which it will be more difficult to treat women like objects and places, thus opposing the narratological definitions of the patriarchal story, where woman appears as space and thus is excluded from subjectivity.[41] The novel enables all narrative categories and all attributes to step forward as protagonist. Within the novel, it is impossible to speak about woman as passive place, because on the one hand place is never passive, and, on the other, all human beings, in their turn, are also defined as space. Thus, the text opposes the patriarchal plot recognized by Irigaray. In fact, the text acts in a way that stands as the symmetrical opposite against the home it depicts: it endows the inanimate with life. And, conversely, it does not take life from animated characters but places them into surroundings where they can enter into relationships with everybody and everything.

This brings me back to the chronotope of the house. Above, I recalled the recurrent literary definition of "house" as a trope of identity. *Frangipani House* makes specific use of the trope. Here, houses are not locations to harbor identities, but they have their own identities, their own life. The house is always an "other"—it is animated by the repressed aspects of the history of its inhabitants or owners, just as Frangipani House is the creature of the past with which Matron has not come to terms. But if houses are "other," they are not radically so. The story of Mama King's own house shows how the representation of the house wavers between identity and otherness.

When Mama King left her house when she stopped taking care of others, her identity as caretaker collapsed and her house turned "other." This "otherness," however, is also her lost identity, based on the painfully missed family life ("I want go home," 17). If she feels whole, the home is just an empty shell unrelated to her, and then she tends to give it away (81). The birth of her great-grandchildren in her own house renames it. This makes a new relationship to the house possible and thus enables her to move back into the house again.

In this narrative, Mama King's house does not function as a protagonist, like the destructive Frangipani House. But every house is presented as a kind of identifying narrative to which one can relate, and which shows a certain tendency to encase and to appropriate. The house is not the sign of an inalienable identity but the mark of another identity, albeit a former self; as such, it is something to live in temporarily and then to leave, maybe to return sometime. The novel uncovers houses as localizations that may suffocatingly encase and fix fatally. Mama King, for one, kept herself at a safe distance from the house she shared with her husband, to sit instead on the clean sand and watch and listen to the river and the trees (14).[42] *Frangipani House* is not only the story of an escape. It is also a warning against houses, against the institutions that hamper observation, and the institutions of imperialism and patriarchy, which are ultimately responsible for the repressed fears that come to haunt Caribbean houses. The novel is a plea for a continuous escape.

Paradoxically, escaping appears to be the only way to participate in a community, either that of the beggars or that of a new part of the family that orients to new values. The only way to exist within history lies in one's active engagement in the community's events. The next section studies the specific history and time that are at work in *Frangipani House* and that make this manipulation possible.

The Genealogy of Women's Betrayal

Frangipani House has a happy ending, even as it is not Utopian or definitive: Mama King, after her recovery, is adopted by her heavily pregnant granddaughter and husband. She is reinstalled as a grandmother. The text of the song in the fish market comes true; language becomes significant again.

In (grand)motherhood lies the key to the counterdiscourse on time, space, speech, and gender presented in *Frangipani House*. In the enclosure of Frangipani House one cannot be a mother. The name of the mother is erased. On the one hand there is Matron's stubborn garbling of Mama King's name to "Marma King" ("'Why you callin' me Marma King? I am Mama King. Mama mean mother. Don't call me dat stupid name! Marma King! I ask you! What kinda name dat is?'," 4) On the other hand there is the harsh title of Matron. Between those two names the unuttered name of the mother is lost.

Rather than lost, however, the mother's story is repressed, only to surface in the incoherent, spiteful screams of the old women in Frangipani House. There is no lost, happy, fulfilled story of the voice-endowed mother to which life in Frangipani House would stand in shrill contrast. For one, Mama King is complimented with her past quietness and altruism, which implies that as a wife and mother she was not encouraged to speak her mind as she wished. Next, her motherhood did not amount to much: "Regret for the cursory care she had given her children made her restless. Work had been the culprit that wrecked her life, robbed her of her perspicacity and deprived her children of her love" (80). Only as a grandmother was she able to speak warmly to her eager grandchildren: she told them stories.

For Mama King, the time outside Frangipani House does not exist as an evolution from a disastrous past to a more and more sunny present, nor as the opposite, though both are evoked by the text. The novel shows that in past, present, and future there are only related stories about the relations between the generations. In these stories mothers are abandoned by their children, especially by their daughters, and betrayed or kept hostage and starved (72); mothers neglect and sell their daughters; the grandmothers take care of the grandchildren. Sons, who may have been abandoned by their mothers too, do not blame their mothers for it with the same bitterness, which enables them to escape the cycle of reproach and revenge (94).

Instead of a chronological, linear time order, we find a bitter genealogy of the continuing reciprocal betrayal between mothers and daughters. Daughters and mothers find their ill-fated relationships repeated and mirrored in the lives of others; and long after their mother's death they still call her up in those they meet in their old age. Even then, they still identify with her. In *Frangipani House* there is a clustering of stories that evoke and echo each other.

This is the reason Matron's story threatens to overshadow Mama

King's, as I stated in the second section. Frangipani House appears to be the product of Matron's deep feelings of spite and revenge for her mother. After reminiscing about the way her mother bargained her away coldly and her own deep hatred of her mother, Matron says, "'I look after these old people to find peace from what I feel in my heart. But they ungrateful too. . . . All my life I have to say I love her to please this place—to please this world'" (72). Matron established the house in order to make amends for her hatred, but in fact, unconsciously, to be able to give it free rein. But what is repressed may return in intensified form. For this reason, Frangipani House turns into a gruesome place of decadence and revenge: "Matron . . . went from bed to bed, her eyes moving over the captured women like a torch. She saw not only them—single and isolated—but all their physical progenitors that the beds had served. Their distorted faces, their decrepitude, their dependency, their illness, their senescence, their odours; all leered at her from the eyes of those who now lay there" (43). It is the mother, multiplied in time and space, who represents the horror experienced in Frangipani House. Indeed, this is the fallen, defiled, repulsive body of the mother, who in this case is still half alive and threatening and who is abandoned by her children. They do not dare come back to her, just as Mama King's children are appalled by what they find on returning to their mother. But it is also the cold and cruel mother with whom Matron identifies to harden herself against these fears. "What would she [Matron's mother, IH] have done?" (88). She defends herself in the same way as her mother against her fear of old age, which is also the fear of becoming like her mother and being treated like her and other old women: "her harshness with them [the older women] was an attempt to build fortifications against the relentlessly encroaching tide of her own old age" (88). The story of Matron's hate for her mother and the power of the unscrupulous mother over her daughter lies at the base of the narrative of the haunted house that is Frangipani House.

Spatiality is the key to this horror story about the mother. According to Laura Mulvey, "Enigmas and secrets generate the image of closed hidden spaces which generate in turn the divided topography of inside and outside" (1992: 58). The same process operates in *Frangipani House*. The time-space in Gilroy's novel is built around the theme of a series of secrets that have to do with the (grand)mother. Always indirectly, but sometimes directly, here they concern Danny's true nature, his murdering, the various cruel acts mothers and daughters commit against each other. This theme is close to the issues that move Toni Morrison to her writing: the necessity of looking into the eye of the unspoken horrors of the past of African-American women and to speak of them. With a variation on Mulvey's argument, I would say that the textual space is constructed not according to an "aesthetics of curiosity" (Mulvey 1992: 65) but rather according to an aesthetics of repression, of returning to and allaying the past. Even so, this aesthetics also produces closed spaces, kumblas—the rooms in the home, the dark holes in the old people's inner world, they all harbor the terrible secrets of the mother.

The mother is a particularly central figure in Caribbean feminist and womanist studies, as well as all the concepts derived from this notion, such as "motherlands."[43] The Afro-Caribbean concept of the mother differs in important ways from European concepts, as it has taken its form through the catastrophic experiences of the African diaspora, slavery, and (neo)colonialism. It is a very complex concept, and Caribbean women have to negotiate the many colonial, racist, sexist, ageist definitions and stereotypes, as well as empty exaltations, to find a way to talk about Caribbean mothers, their history, and the relation between these mothers and grandmothers and daughters. As many women are well aware of the pains and hardships of (often single) motherhood, these discussions do not eagerly give way to shared, harsh criticisms of motherhood and the mother (such as has been the case in parts of the Dutch women's movement in the 1970s and 1980s). And if much of Caribbean women's literature is written from the daughter's perspective,[44] Jamaica Kincaid's ruthless grievance against the atrocious mother, seen through the eyes of a passionately loving and hating daughter who had to rip away from her, is certainly no standard of the way the mother is represented in Caribbean women's writing.

In Gilroy's novel at any rate, there is no such explicit critique. Nevertheless, in some passages the memory of the mother is depicted as a terror, in others, reference is made to fears and intense anger, whereas fragments of the terrible stories of mothers and children are dispersed throughout the text. By this narrative strategy, the image of a problematic, terrible motherhood is evoked without sullying the figure of the mother itself. This image is represented as a series of secrets located in places. From there, the text is divided into closed spaces from which it is hard to escape to an outside world.

Even Mama King does not stand for the blameless mother, who, as the opposite of Matron, innocently enters the hell of the mother-daughter revenge. She, too, had to neglect her children. Her daughters, maybe in response, abandoned her in turn, leaving their children with her (95). Her daughters, Token and Cyclette, are absent mothers in their turn. Their names and personalities bear the stamp of absence, plurality, elusiveness: Token is appearance; she is an empty strife for status, and is without "familiar mark by which to identify her" (86). In contrast, Cyclette is overwhelming, plural, a fierce energy without a fixed center: "her limbs appeared ready to break away from her body and take on lives of their own" (86). Neither of them is stable enough to take on the care of others, least of all the care of their mother, whose lack of care they reproach. Their caring for their own families is restricted to their catering to material needs.

All these mother-daughter stories are characterized by the desertion of either one of the two. The time of this story of repulsion is not the patriarchal, Oedipal time, which is the time of succession of the father by the son (or by the son-in-law, or even of the mother by son or daughter) and the transfer of the home. This time is supported not by a series of appropriations but by a series of escapes, emigrations, and desertions.[45] However, contrary to other interpretations of the birthplace as the repulsive body of the abandoned mother, in this novel the mother is not reified. She is alive, she can speak, she can be spoken to, she has a will of her own; she can even get up from the bed and escape, not as a zombie nor as a haunting spirit but as a living human being to whom her lost children can speak. In Gilroy's text, the traumatizing return is an event in which, on both sides, subjects are involved. Here, Riley's horrendously thinglike aunt is blessed with subjectivity and a strong name of her own: Mama King. Space becomes person. And if time becomes the collective site of desertion, it is consequently also that of a possible return.

In *Frangipani House* we find time, then, as a bitter genealogy of daughters following/leaving mothers, a chain of generations that in the final analysis is corrupted by the colonization and neocolonization compelling people to emigrate, and which is the cause of the breaking up of families. But there is also the suggestion of the possibility of halting this destructive cycle and opening up space for other stories of time. To do so, the relationship with the terrible mother has to be restored.

This is no easy task. For the relationship between mother and children is very much a degenerated one. Fortunately, in the face of the degradation of the mother and the daughter, there is one position that stays un-affected: that of the grandmother. As a grandmother Mama King plays a healing and binding role. After her spectacular escape from Frangipani House and her intermediate stay with the beggars, she finds some rest with the family of her granddaughter Cindy. This rest is only relative; she will have to move with them to America, a movement announced but not rep-resented in the text. If, on her reentering the history of her community, Mama King finds that this community is moving—combining the jour-ney and home in its migratory identity—she has no choice but to move with them. Amryl Johnson's account of the market women who continu-ally travel between Guadeloupe and Dominica (Johnson 1988: 230) teaches that this movement is not homelessness but a migration according to a fa-miliar pattern: it is part of Caribbean identity. The (grand)mother now shares this aspect of mobility, even if the novel refrains from depicting this new condition. So, she does not find a home in a new *place*; rather, her new dwelling is situated in time, in the chain of generations.

Her new position as "old woman at peace at last" (104) is definitely no safe homecoming. "'But,' she added fiercely, 'my heart brittle—like eggshell. It easy to break'" (109). The statement of her vulnerability shows that her escape and metamorphosis did not teach her the masquerades of the clever, elusive trickster evoked by Gates. Even if she has stayed on the boundary between two worlds (inside and outside, present and past, life and death, Caribbean/America), she has not acquired any full mastery to move in these dangerous borderlands. She is no magician, and neither is she a shaman. But she may well be close kin to Maroon Nanny, the leg-endary figure in Caribbean history also known as Granny Nanny.

Mama King shows her grandchildren what it means to be supported by the community (105–6), and by that she actualizes the communal val-ues the American husband of her granddaughter suspects to be African: in this way, she links a remote past (Africa) with the past and the future (America). She also links a remote generation to the youngest: Mama King's own mother was a twin, and Mama King's granddaughter gives birth, with her aid, to the twins Mama King predicted: "Twin skip gener-ation" (105). They are born in her own house, the house she kept on after moving to Frangipani House. In a sense, she helps to bring into the world (and into her house) again the generation of her mother, but this time redoubled, in the vital form of male twins. As men, they may have more chance to escape the cycle of betrayal and birth than girls would have had.[46] The new father of the twins shows that he has understood the lesson: he names one of his baby sons after Mama King's deceased brother, Abel, a man who chose to care for his family.

Calling back former generations is no alien thing to grandmothers. In Frangipani House, some old women slide back to their youth, thus disturbing a linear chronology and calling into life again their own mother as a young woman. Mama King also brings back a past into the present, but she does not let them coincide: the new generation that brings back her mother's generation is male. Moreover, she does not dissolve herself in her act of calling up the past, because she does not turn into a child herself but proudly assumes the precarious role of the ([great]-grand)mother. This makes the difference between dementia and a vital, regenerating manipulation of the past.

In addition to its refutation of the notion of woman-as-place, Gilroy's novel explores the ambivalences of woman's state of being in-space, a state evoked by Morrison. The novel examines the conditions that allow women to create a beneficial home. Mama King has "cleaned" her own house by assisting at the birth of her great-grandchildren there and thus situates her house in the specific temporality of the cycle of returning generations. Thus, she has reappropriated her home by defining it as a specific temporality. This strategy is quite close to the strategy of linking to the past by means of the home discussed by Morrison. But as a Caribbean tale, Gilroy's novel does not accentuate the necessity of one specific place as the site of contact with the communal past. In the Caribbean, homes will often be shifting, traveling, hardly permanent.

In the same way that Mama King helped to ensure the survival of the family, and thus the continuation of the generational time, by escaping Frangipani House she also prevented time from becoming rigid and deadly. Thus, she could evade the evil side effects of a time (neo)colonization had unsettled. The spectacular escape of Mama King rewrites many former escapes in the Caribbean, from colonization, from murder, from slavery, from zombification—she also rewrites the escape of Maroon Nanny, the grandmother of all those who strive to escape and fight imperialism.

Conclusion

I have been indicating some of the ways that *Frangipani House* redefines notions of space and time. I have outlined the great significance of
these rewritings by placing them within the larger context of literary approaches of phenomena as space, place, and time in relation to gender,
race, and age. However, I have read them tentatively as indications of the
possibilities of new definitions, not as the definitions themselves. My style
of reading is inspired by the little sentence at the end of the novel, where
women stop for "woman-talk and time-waste." "Time-waste" is a kind and
modest indication of an alternative time that exists already in women's
lives. She who wastes time, only wastes the patriarchal, measurable, Western notion of time. For according to certain African/Caribbean interpretations of time, time cannot be wasted at all, as it exists in action and interaction alone. Saying that you are coming over for a nice bit of "woman-talk
and time-waste" means that you define the time you spend in this delicious
and indispensable act of talking and bonding as outside dominant, imperial time—that is, you define it as a counterdiscourse. To the dominant notion of time these women around Mama King oppose their own modest
time-waste, knowing well that they are responsible for the continuing re-
generation of the human race—I would not know of a more fundamental
base for a concept of time. The women, though, do not explicitly stage it as
a defense against the exigencies of the dominant definitions of time. That
story remains to be told.

She who talks about "time-waste" also acknowledges the oppressive division of labor, which describes women's proper way to pass time as cleaning, cooking, housekeeping, giving birth, nursing, caring, and also growing
food, trading, and even road building, depending on one's race, class, and
ethnicity. Work—this is the other important connotation in the concept of
"time-waste." In *Frangipani House*, work has a negative as well as a positive
meaning. It is the only fixed center for a stable identity, but it also tears families apart and turns people into senseless drudges. However, it is also a
means by which one can relate to the world in meaningful, fruitful ways. It
is here that I would place the aesthetics the novel (not unambiguously)
seems to aspire to. It would be based on a semiotics that understands significance as interaction; semiosis would result from situated action, that is, action situated within the practice of making spaces for oneself and one's com-

munity, a practice that at the same time temporalizes, as it causes the events on which time (in the Afro-Caribbean sense) is based. For this text, saying things is not so much doing things,[47] but doing things is kindred to speaking in that they are both practices, spatializing and temporalizing practices.

However, the radical project of the novel is most visible in its choice of heroine, the stubborn grandmother. Mama King "wastes," that is, disturbs and destroys a certain time: she foils the dominant notion of a neat chronology of generations by short-circuiting past and present. In this way, and in refusing to be a repulsive place, she saves herself, revitalizes time, and saves the story of the generations. The story of her escape shows that it is possible to displace place and time, however tentatively. Hence she shows it is possible to continue telling stories. And the telling, the eager manipulation of the level of the narrative that transforms space into practice and places into persons, inspired by a vigorous, enabling narrativity, is what makes the refiguration of womanhood in the African diaspora possible.

Writing for Listeners: Merle Collins's *Angel*

> We don't always have to write for readers,
> we can write for *listeners*.
>
> —Ama Ata Aidoo

"book, not stupidness"

Angel was in Standard III. The youngest in her class. She didn't like it at first. The children kept shouting "country-bookie" and telling her to speak properly. . . . Angel told one of her young tormentors that she came from Aruba.

"Liar!"

"Is true! Is why ah caan speak so proper."

"Say something in Aruban."

"Pappia doto."

"What is dat?"

"It means, 'Ah have to go.'"

Maria was impressed. "Say something again."

"Mammie say I mus talk English all the time now so as I could learn quick," said Angel, trying hard to keep in her mind what she had said, so that she could say the same thing again if asked to say "I have to go" in Aruban.

"I feel if was me I woulda talk a lotta Aruban."

"Ah don know. Ah tink . . . "

"We always tellin you not to say 'Ah don know.' It soun real country. Why you caan say, 'Me en know'?"

Angel asked Doodsie to teach her Aruban. Doodsie brushed her aside, impatiently.

"In Aruba we used to talk English same as here and a little bit o Pappiamentu."

"Ah don even know Patwa. Allyou does only talk Patwa for us not to understand."

"What you have to study is you book, not stupidness. Go and do you homework!" (Merle Collins 1987: 90–91)

The seven-year-old girl Angel is surrounded by many languages in Grenada: her own despised "country" english,[1] Maria's superior english, the Standard English used by the primary narrator, Angel's mother Doodsie's english ("English" in the text), Papiamentu, her parents' patois, the English in which she has to do her homework, and the nonexistent Aruban of her own invention, the weapon with which she tries to protect her sense of self. The quoted passage shows that all of these languages are linked to social positions—they are either "real country" or a parental privilege. However, instead of offering a contrast between a superior, colonial Standard English and a Creole expressing a postcolonial nationalist consciousness, the text presents a continuum of voices. There are different Creoles that are opposed to each other rather than to a Standard English. Nevertheless, Doodsie makes a contrast that will be central to the argument in this chapter: not only does she point at the hierarchy between the different voices, but she makes the more important contrast between "book" and "stupidness." "Book" refers to schooling, literacy, English, social success. "Stupidness" refers to the sphere of vernaculars, english, Creoles, a low social standard. Doodsie's view, echoing colonial norms, conceives of literacy as the key to a better life.

Doodsie's statement about the importance of literacy over orality occurs in a novel in which the spoken Creole is unmistakably all-encompassing. The narrative unfolds in the characters' reported speech, which is always a form of Creole. The novel, then, seems to choose Creole—that "stupidness"—as its medium. Could it be the case that Doodsie as a character disagrees with the novel as a whole about the value of Creole and orality? Would she have preferred to play her part in a novel in Standard English? But that would have been foolishness. She would have been silenced. Yet, Doodsie is not just the odd alienated colonized character that is kindly begged to leave the premises of serious postcolonial theoretical debate. For even the best-known advocate of the use of Creole (i.e., as nation language[2]) in Caribbean writing, Edward Kamau Brathwaite, admits the need for English literary devices to create worthy West-Indian literature. Indeed,

Doodsie's words point at the vital, productive unresolved tension in Caribbean writing between Creole and orality on the one hand and Standard English and literacy on the other. This tension is the subject of this chapter, which is the first of three discussing the issue of "voice" in Caribbean migrant women's writing.

If Doodsie proposes a dichotomy through which to understand orality and literacy, she echoes both a traditional figure in an influential body of European reflection about the nature of orality and the binary model sometimes evoked by Black and postcolonial critics. This model is evoked when, for example, references to oral practices in a written text are evaluated as "positive" elements, as opposed to the negativity of those critical discursive practices that consist of an ironic, deconstructive adoption of colonial discourse. Moreover, orality demands a phonocentric approach, and as such it opposes the scriptocentrism of much of today's postcolonial theorizing. In a way, then, orality exceeds postcolonial theory; it can be mobilized to act as a vital, free space that has not been appropriated by a Eurocentric, scriptocentric, invading postcolonialism. By virtue of its strong polemic force, this opposition of oral positivity versus scriptocentric negativity is appealing, and I will keep referring to it.

On the other hand, the fruitfulness of the binary model is questioned widely, by Western scholars of orality as well as by Black and postcolonial critics.[3] In the context of the Caribbean, the dichotomy orality/literacy (translated as Creole versus Standard English) is overlaid with the theory of the Creole continuum as a more accepted (though not unproblematized) context for any consideration of the Caribbean language situation.[4] And yet, the tensions between dominant colonial languages and the languages of the periphery will always be relevant. There is no smooth escape from that field into either a happy multiplicity or a politically inspired choice for one of the poles of the dichotomy. As I have stated above, even the most fervent nationalist pleas for the use of Creole testify of the need for colonial notions of language and culture; moreover, an emphasis on orality as the expression of nationhood (which will often be defined in gender-, class-, and ethnically specific ways) can also suppress the plurality of the Caribbean community itself (see Edmondson 1994). For orality and Creole are also associated with a sometimes very conservative macho working-class perspective, as Carolyn Cooper shows in her rich study of Jamaican popular culture (Cooper 1993).

This, then, is the paradoxical situation Caribbean women writers enter into. They have to come to terms with the inevitability of Standard English as both a "lingua franca" and liberation, and as an alienation and negation of Caribbeanness. They also have to envisage the potentials and restrictions of Creole. They have to negotiate the significations of orality and writing, all the while being aware that these language practices are defined in gender-specific ways.[5] Somehow, they have to work through the pull and push of the cruel opposites book/stupidness, modernity/backwardness, culture/slackness (Cooper 1993), alienation/authenticity.

Two interesting novels, written in the 1980s by two Caribbean women writers in London, offer rich opportunities to explore the connections between orality and writing. The argument in the following two chapters is constructed around a reading of *Angel* (1987), a novel about three generations of women in Grenada by the Grenadian writer and performance poet Merle Collins,[6] and *Whole of a Morning Sky* (1986) by Guyanese poet and novelist Grace Nichols. This chapter discusses several forms in which the dichotomy between orality and literacy is deconstructed; after revisiting traditional Western approaches to orality as the opposite pole of literacy, I'll consider the deconstruction offered by *Angel.* The third section of this chapter is about *Angel*'s use of Creole to picture the Creole community as an inwardly conflicting but unbreakably cohesive complexity. I relate this view to another Afrocentric perception of the oral community as a multivoiced structure, bound together through dialogism. Through that comparison, some of the differences between "orality" and "Creole" come to light. The fourth and last section takes a critical look at some opinions about a specific aesthetics connected to the oral community (which is also a working-class community). Orality and Creole are often connected to the body and sexuality. Even if these associations can be celebrated as the liberating return to unencumbered authenticity (e.g., by male Caribbean singers), they are often expressed in a conservative, masculinist view of sex and gender. I will discuss different efforts to experiment with the languages of oral and, especially, Creole communities to show that there exists an ongoing experiment to broaden the scope of Creole, not in the least to have it embody a nonmasculinist experience of sensuality. This experiment helps to dismiss the definition of the vernacular as essentially marginal, lower-class, macho, concrete, and confining. In addition, it offers a critique of the scriptocentrism inherent in much postcolonial theorizing.

Praise Song for the Creole Community

Doodsie may have her thoughts about the stupidity of the vernacular, but the novel she is a part of is itself a very vernacular, very "oral" text. It continues a Caribbean literary tradition of representing collective talk that has been initiated by novels such as *Minty Alley* (1936) by Trinidad writer C. L. R James, a novel placed in a "yard" and representing the Creole of ordinary people, as observed by a middle-class character (Ramchand 1983: 69 ff). Among the many other novels in this tradition is Roger Mais's early novel *Brother Man* (1954), in which a "chorus of the people in the lane" offers its anonymous comments on everyday events. In *Angel,* however, the "chorus" has lost its anonymity and its marginality and has become the main protagonist. It is no longer observed and characterized by an external narrator using Standard English: it narrates its own story, characterizing and observing itself.

Angel is the daring enterprise of narrating three decades of political turmoil in Grenada from the point of view of the Grenadian working class. It covers the period during which Eric Gairy ("Leader," in the novel) began his activities as the founder of the Grenadian Mental and Manual Workers Union in 1950 and his subsequent rise to power. It reports the undemocratic developments during Gairy's government, the establishment of the New Jewel Movement (NJM), and the "Revo" brought about by the NJM and the revolutionary government headed by Maurice Bishop ("Chief") (1979–83). Finally, it treats the tragic and confusing events of the party's internal conflicts, the murder of Bishop, and the American invasion that ends the revolutionary endeavors.[7]

In popular Western publications about the area during this period, like tourist guides, one usually finds positive or neutral evaluations of the American invasion that is said to have been approved by the large majority of the Grenadians, who are reported to refer to it as "rescue." *Angel* takes an alternative stance, offering a rather different picture. It tells about the effect of the events on the ordinary people, their role in the developments, the conflicts and confusions, and the bitter disappointment in the failure of the revolution and the U.S. military intervention. This anticolonial, politically committed position translates into a specific language politics. Most important, it results in a choice for a highly "oral" text.

Angel is primarily a book in which one finds endless streams of talk.

It brims over with directly reported talk, always in a Caribbean vernacular. Standard English is present, but in a modest way: it most often serves as a vehicle to sustain the narrative, and it does not interfere with the vivid confrontations of the Creole languages that form the narrative.[8] There is so much directly reported speech in the book that the reticent primary narrating voice hardly keeps any authority among the many varieties of the regional vernacular, often referred to as Creole. The primary narrating voice restricts itself mainly to describing the immediate actions that accompany the talking. Reflections immediately shift to the Creole of the free reported speech. All relevant information is given in Creole, in the endless, sometimes anonymous conversations that comment on the events. The events are hardly described in any other way. The comments seem much more important than what actually happens.[9] As the bare facts of its history are general knowledge, Collins's novel is particularly significant in its narrative choices: the decision to place the focalization with the ordinary people, and the related decision to choose Creole as the novel's main language and a special kind of "orality" as its mode. This is an orality with a difference. By comparing it to other reflections about orality, I'll show that it situates itself outside the dominant space of scriptocentric postcolonial theory.

First, this orality is not opposed to writing, and therefore it cannot be understood in terms of writing (i.e., as its antipole). Even if *Angel* is a highly oral text, instead of merely dismissing writing altogether, it offers a natural, everyday, but very effective deconstruction of the dichotomy orality/writing. The novel often refers to the act of writing and to written texts. Fourteen letters appear in the novel, most of them are quoted literally in parts and thus occupy several pages each. Yet, they are made part of an oral exchange: all letters are either written or read, often in the company of others, with interruptions for meditations or closer comment, or for loud laughter or curses:

She looked at her sister, intent upon the letter. "Where de part? Read it, lemme remember."

They lay off Leader. And he just finish have a elaborate wedding wid that airess from the big family home that he engage an bring up here to married . . .

"E eyes big. E aimin high!"

That man is the limit. He so like a show that he had the most biggest wedding possible. They say it had enough shampain to bathe in . . .

"Dat sweeten me. Girl dat really sweeten me. Me an Cousin Maymay say 'Wee-ee-ee! Imagine all dis people an dem bathin in champagne!' Well dat was fete yes!"

"Girl, was real pappyshow weddin. Dey say there never was a weddin like it an never will there be again!"

. . . And you know who his best man was? Guess nuh. His boss . . .

"Uh huh! Papa Boast!" (16–17)

Doodsie's children advise her not to write so stiffly when writing a letter to her best friend, but rather to *talk*:

Dear Ezra,

How are you? I hope fine . . .

Doodsie paused, looking at what she had written. She thought of what the children always said to her when they saw her begin a letter. All of them, even Carl now, laughed and said, 'Mammie, dat look like school book ting. Write as if you know er, non!'. . . She turned the page. Started again.

Dear Ezra,

How's tings, girl? Over here is as if they gettin worse. (206)

The new generation teaches Doodsie that the talkative effect needed to express the intimacy she feels can be conveyed only by a greater mastery of the art of writing. The shift to the familiarity of speech goes together with a shift to a more Creole register. The oral is not the quality of an older generation, as Western studies of orality suggest, but it has to be gained through the very act of writing. "Write as if you know er": this advice could be read as the novel's main writer's statement. So, the novel thematizes writing not by opposing it to speaking but by considering the ways it is appropriated by a vernacular community that has become literate.

To understand *Angel*'s important innovation, let's turn to two somewhat removed theories of orality, one a famous African-American theory, the other a constellation of traditional European views. Henry Louis Gates Jr. offers a term to describe Doodsie's writing strategy. In his words, one can say that Doodsie strives for a "speakerly" effect. By a "speakerly" text, Gates explains, "I mean a text whose rhetorical strategy is designed to represent an oral literary tradition, designed 'to emulate the phonetic, grammatical, and lexical patterns of actual speech and produce the illusion of oral narration'" (1988: 181). The concept seems to suit the novel remarkably well. However, Gates's definition of the speakerly text harbors two kindred but differing definitions, one of which especially suits *Angel*. On the one hand, Gates uses the term to designate a text that masks itself as an oral narrative, a part of an oral tradition. In such a text one might find formulas and other specific stylistic characteristics, such as repetitions, or the presence of songs. On the other hand, the speakerly text is defined with the help of the Russian concept of *skaz* (derived from *skazat*, to narrate), which refers to a "[l]iterary procedure by which a story is put into the mouth of a narrator who suggests, in a vivid oral narrative style, the atmosphere of a certain milieu" (Gorp 1980: 156, my translation). Following this description, one expects a text in which the day-to-day speech of ordinary (or less ordinary) people plays a central role. Of course, this everyday speech can be artistically elaborated and can respond to specific aesthetic norms. Edwards and Sienkewicz even argue that it is only from a Eurocentric perspective that one would oppose a "performance," in the strict sense, to ordinary conversation (Edwards and Sienkewicz 1990: 15). Nevertheless, I make the distinction to be able to differentiate between this Eurocentric approach and Gates's much more critical approach, which takes into account the power-infested field in which orality and literacy interrelate. For the first description fits texts that are traditionally the object of orality studies. This orality is then studied as an alterity, as a crucial difference to Western means and modes of expression and even to Western consciousness. It has traditionally been understood not on its own terms but as the opposite of literacy. As the well-known scholar of orality Ruth Finnegan remarks, even as the more traditional forms of this kind of scholarship have made way for less Eurocentric approaches, they are still influencing Western concepts of orality and writing (Finnegan 1988: x). These views inevitably play a role in Western readings of texts such as *Angel*. Therefore, I will present a short discussion of the main tenets so that I may give a more acute picture of the specific alternative perception of orality offered by *Angel*.

In Europe, orality has long been studied as a characteristic of texts that are removed in time and space. This kind of scholarship, often bearing on the oral production of communities that do not have access to writing, or in which a recognizable oral tradition can be discerned, seeks to understand the nature of orality by situating it as a distinct cultural sphere (Ong 1987; Goody 1977; Lord 1960). The concept of orality is often appropriated to function as antipole in the opposition spoken/written, which is central to Western thought. Jacques Derrida shows how this oppositional pair can

be traced back to Plato's *Phaedrus*, which narrates the invention of writing
—the first of three landmarks that mark the history of logocentrism (Derrida 1976: 97). In this text, script is characterized as a rather ambivalent invention. Thus, skepticism is articulated at the very moment its origins are narrated. Whoever controls the script possesses only a pretense of knowledge, not true wisdom. For one possesses wisdom only if one has actually digested it and made it a part of one's person; true wisdom is ranged with the body, orality, and speech. The notion of speech as more authentic, as if standing in a more direct relationship to reality than writing, has become the implicit or explicit assumption of many subsequent treatises about language and language use. The best-known scholar in the tradition of logocentrism may be linguist Ferdinand de Saussure. Derrida argues that de Saussure's approach made the spoken word appear unproblematic and thus undebatable: the relation between spoken word and experience, and meaning, is considered transparent to the degree that the word fades under the overwhelming presence of the reality it has evoked.

According to this perspective, references to an oral tradition can be understood as signs of authenticity. Indeed, Western orality studies have suffered from a desire for authenticity: they have been hunting for more original versions of certain narratives, for stable mother plots, or for the tales of a yet more "primitive," more "untouched" people. But this hierarchization of orality as authenticity over writing has lately been the object of severe criticism. Derrida's influential critique of logocentrism shows the questionability of the assumptions on which the dichotomy between transparent spoken word and derived written sign is based. But there are also scholars of orality in a stricter sense of the term who undertake an emancipation of orality from its enforced definition as the antipole of literacy. Birgit Scharlau and Mark Münzel, for example, authors of a study of Latin-American Indian oral traditions (1986), argue that the dichotomy oral culture/literate culture merely rests on the European preoccupation with writing, which after 1950 became a central criterion of civilization in the West. Absence of the script then became the primary characteristic of the "alien" cultures under anthropological scrutiny. The opposition oral/written was and still is connected to that between primitive/civilized, authentic/alienated, and warm, personal/cold, anonymous. The point is that orality is thus disengaged from the society in question, of which the culture remains undiscussed, and annexed to an internal European critique of civilization. In fact, Scharlau and Münzel state with some venom that Europeans are quite incapable of understanding how a people without script think. If Europeans assume that logical, abstract thought becomes possible only with the introduction of writing (Goody 1977; Ong 1982), if they assume that thought in oral cultures is necessarily simple and concrete, then these opinions might be explained by the fact that they are merely capable of grasping the simpler aspects of the utterances of an oral society and that the more abstract and complex concepts elude them.[10] These and similar critiques result in the acknowledgment that the oral can no longer be defined as the antipole of the written. Now, emphasis shifts to those approaches that seek to describe certain styles of verbal artistry in their specific local and historical forms. These verbal arts are situated in their social and cultural contexts, of which the absence or presence of writing is merely one aspect among many, not the crucial factor of difference (Finnegan 1988: 55–58).

Angel offers its own comment on the dichotomy between orality and literacy, not only by showing that it is untenable but also by criticizing the related assumption that orality is connected to vernaculars and literacy to the colonial language. Doodsie's struggle to appropriate writing for her vernacular uses shows that speaking and writing cannot be opposed as a parallel scheme to Creole and Standard English. In the novel, it is not only Standard English that is written—on the contrary, all letters are in a form of Creole. The act of writing in itself is not endowed with any innate authoritative or alienating quality. Doodsie's writing does not fix Creole in an authoritarian Standard. There are as many ways of writing Creole as of speaking it. Moreover, the written Creole does not produce the same kind of distance and absence as the poststructuralist concept of "writing" suggests. Written and spoken texts are listened to in the same way. That is, listeners talk back to both; writing does not fix speaker and listener in a position of sustained activity or passivity any more than speaking does. In both modes of communication the word occurs as a moment in an exchange, as address, and as an invitation to react. This seems to me the central characteristic of the use of orality in *Angel*: it is a multiple dialogue, an ongoing interaction.

In the incident of corrected letter writing, Doodsie seems to depart from her own assumption about the hierarchical opposition between "book"/writing and "stupidness"/speaking. In the context of the keeping up of the Creole community—and that is what her letter writing is about, the maintenance of cherished family ties and friendships against the odds of invading international politics—writing and speech take on meanings different from those in the context of schooling, to which the quote that opened this section testifies. Writing and "book" are no longer connected to social climbing and the plot to leave the community, but rather they are associated with the construction of the Creole community. In this way, Doodsie appropriates writing as a postcolonial instrument for nation building.

This appropriation of writing for the expression of a Black identity seems to be comparable to the appropriation of writing in the African-American tradition from the early slave narratives onward, as analyzed by Henry Louis Gates Jr. I will follow his argument in detail to point out the difference with Collins's project. Gates considers many texts in the African-American literary tradition as implicit critical comments on the hierarchy between speech and writing that is central to the dominant Western reflection. The opposition between writing and nonwriting, between those who master the script and those who do not and, in consequence, those who master the dominant language and those who do not was of great relevance to the ideological defense of slavery. Gates explains how during the Enlightenment a systematic argument was construed to prove that writing is the eminent sign of civilized humanity: those who could not write were not considered human and did need not be treated as such. To counter this allegation, Black people have been writing from the times of slavery onward. By the very act of writing, they proved themselves to be civilized human beings. Gates recapitulates: "Black people could become speaking subjects only by inscribing their voices in the written word" (1988: 129).

The crucial point lies in this "voices": for not only did the early African-American writers adopt the dominant language for their writing, they also exerted themselves to inscribe the Black vernacular in their texts. Gates discusses the nature of the tension that is always present between the oral inscribed in the text and the writing itself, between the Black vernacular and white literary discourse. In the African-American tradition, he states, Black vernacular is "the black person's ultimate sign of difference." In this context, two different but complementary literary strategies may be discerned. On the one hand, African-American texts try to endow the Black speaking voice with a scriptorial form. On the other hand, they also seek to escape their written nature: the text wishes to be an oral tale, testifying of what Gates calls "the black quest to make the text speak" (1988:

240). Thus, if African-American writers use vernacular or other references to orality in their texts, this style of writing cannot be merely understood as an endeavor to bring an element of authenticity into their texts, or even as an unambiguous sign for an African-American racial specificity. The scriptoral character of the text is in itself already a challenge to the denial of African-American humanity, as much as it also denies the opinion that the African-American is only and specifically oral. Written orality, then, is the site of paradoxes bearing upon the African-Americans' very existence as human subjects.

Gates analyzes the textual strategies Zora Neal Hurston and Alice Walker adopted to establish the vernacular as a literary medium in its own right. In her famous groundbreaking work *Their Eyes Were Watching God* (1937), Hurston has her characters *speak* instead of write their way into full speaking subjectivity. Gates approaches Walker's *The Color Purple* (1982) as a radical revision of Hurston's work. He highlights the ingenuity of the intervention to write a whole novel in Black English, a strategy that undeniably installs the vernacular as an autonomous literary language. The main protagonist of Walker's well-known novel, Miss Celie, attains her position as a capable speaking and acting subject by writing her own vernacular, just like Doodsie. This means that the dominant literary tradition no longer forms the necessary context of the formation of subjectivity. In this way, Walker gave an important different direction to Hurston's project of revaluing the oral tradition. If Hurston's writing imitates speaking voices, Walker urges spoken pieces to join into a written text. As such, they obtain the prestige that until then only texts written in Standard English could claim.

For Gates, the addressee of Walker's text is the written (colonial) tradition, the "book" celebrated by Doodsie, and the flow of Gates's argument toward this last point is a sign of its (well-motivated) scriptocentrism. In the same vein, *Angel* can be read as a successful example of those Caribbean texts that establish the vernacular as an appropriate, complete vehicle for the literary expression of crucial events in the community's history. But it is more than that, as Gates's analysis enables us to see: it not merely inscribes the vernacular and the community to whom it belongs in dominant literary history but also forms a strong, radical contribution to an alternative postcolonial literary tradition in which the vernacular is valued over the dominant colonial languages of schooling. The interesting point about

Angel is that it is not primarily critically oriented toward the dominant literary discourse. It asks for a much more phonocentric, Creole style of listening. In this novel, the vernacular is not primarily the "ultimate sign of difference," as Gates has it. It stands instead for the community, for "us," or, to use more literary-political terms, for nation building. Rather than a critique of scriptocentrism, it is a praise song for the Creole community. *Angel*'s difference lies exactly in its endeavor to be more than just difference—which would always secure it in a dominant Western intellectual discourse. In the next sections, then, I will explore the hybrid and plural Caribbean context that necessitates a more specific Caribbean understanding of the relations between oral and written practices. Here, tensions need not always spring forth from binary oppositions, nor is orality inevitably addressing the grand universe of "book."

The Voices of a Community in Conflict

Difference is a crucial concept in *Angel*. It is not the difference between the Grenadian community and the colonial powers, though, that demands the most attention: instead, the many differences within the community are carefully weighed. The speaking community in which the narrative is situated hardly consists of an undifferentiated mass: conflicts between generations, political and religious views, women and men are fought out in intense and sometimes violent dialogues. In the same way, differences between social status and class (often related to differences in education) are negotiated.[11] These conflicts and differences do not break the community down. Discord is the norm. We do not even find a tragic rupture between alienated Westernized youngsters, say, and the authentic but powerless Afro-Caribbean illiterate elders. Angel, the representative of the youngest generation in the three-generation novel, an academically educated daughter, does not break with the collectivity. She keeps talking, venting her irritation, challenging, ostensibly running away and coming back again; she keeps inviting address and she keeps responding. When the language-loving daughter goes through her education, she begins to master Standard English, and she begins to teach and write her letters in that language. Nevertheless, she does not move away from the community. In contrast, her path through the educational system leads her right into the heart of the community's struggle. She manages to use her education as a revolutionary instrument, negotiating the alienation it implies.

Angel appropriates Standard English as an instrument for intellectual, revolutionary education. However, the novel clearly chooses Creole as its main language. This choice is inextricably linked to the choice of the community of ordinary people as the main protagonist in the novel. As Caribbean linguist Morgan Dalphinis says, "The Creoles have traditionally been the means of providing a platform for the discussion of local events" (Dalphinis 1985: 10). A Caribbean speakerly text that makes prolific use of Creole is often also a text about the social and political history of the working classes. These create a textual context that did not exist before; they establish an as yet unwritten everyday space as the site where politics is rooted. The ongoing popular political debate is shown to be an organic part of the divided, dialogic Grenadian community.[12] All protagonists seem to share the novel's standpoint on the unity of their views, even if they insist on highlighting the differences. It is often the working class and the older generation that have the more acute understanding of the people's unity-in-diversity, and they will convey this opinion to the younger people, sometimes by stressing the differences the young do not wish to acknowledge. For example, as a student, Angel makes a visit, together with her politically active friends, to the families at the low end of the Jamaican social ladder to "make the links that we must make and know exactly what we're fighting for" (160). However, these Jamaicans show her the difference between them: "'An we know dat oono a come, nyam up de ital,[13] reason wid we good good an den move back up a palace fe continue de nice life! Is like ting different for oonoo, see?'" (160). Not only does the statement show that it is not easy to make the connections necessary for the struggle—Angel is conscious of that already—but it also shows that the students may be a burden to those they want to support, if only by eating their hard-won or hard-grown food. The students insist on their kinship, while the Jamaican people question it:

> "Nyam the ital, young bway! Is how you a push de yellow yam roun you plate like you fraid for touch it?"
>
> "Non, man! I accustom eatin yam!"
>
> "Eh heh? An is how it look to me like it strange to you?" (160)

Food is culture, in a very direct, physical way; it stands for the shared Caribbean reality the Jamaicans know about and the students are (now, or as yet) uneasy with. Indeed, food is a shared language the students have to re-discover. It is as ordinary and plain and as material as Creole talk.

Angel also offers other semiotic systems besides language and food to express the general statement that the Creole semiotic systems are strong enough to embrace all kinds of social conflicts. The Creole community is pictured as an elastic semiotic system, in which food, as well as words and images, may serve as means of communication. It is at one point in the story effectively imaged in the battle of the portraits Angel wages with her father (188–93, 199–203, 208). Angel removes the portrait of the politician Leader her father values so much from the living room. Her father hangs it back up, after which Angel refuses to enter the parental house, in protest against his political judgments. In contrast, her father criticizes her wall dec-oration: for example, the portrait of a rasta boy. The conflict ends when the father gives in and removes the portrait. The crucial point is that all stand-points translate into the choice of wall decoration. Walls, or even houses, are not questioned as necessary commodities, as they are in *Frangipani House* (Chapter 3). Houses are characterized not by their function as enclosure but by their function as sign bearer, or semiotic system: they are defined by what hangs on their walls. In the houses of others, pictures of the Good Shep-herd, the Holy Heart, and the like are indexes for the milieu Angel herself comes from, for her "home" (161). These religious images, signs of what she, at a certain point, considers an obsolete view of life, will begin to refer to something else she keeps her faith in: the Caribbean community. Thus, there is never the need to break with the sign system itself. New political views, in the form of posters, take possession of the rooms of her friends, then of her own room, which originally had "bare white walls" (131). Rooms (sites of the community's identity) are often associated with the women's world, but not always—Angel's father's political views are voiced by the por-trait he hangs in what he apparently considers his living space. More often, however, the posters hang in the girls' rooms (see, e.g., 137, 160, 163). The lack of posters in the room of a young man is emphatically worded: "Three years and not one poster?" (141)

This is the form of consensus in the oral community in *Angel*: the in-terpretant (in a Peircean sense) changes but is linked to the same sign bearer. If a reference is no longer effective, as in the case of the Christian pictures that do not appeal to Angel anymore, then the interpretant changes (to "home") to keep the sign bearer intact. If an individual sign is no longer valued, such as Leader's portrait, then the *kind* of signs can be maintained, and another one of the kind can be used: another portrait, in this example. Thus, the vernacular in *Angel* has a kindred flexibility to represent varied views, and to be the means of expressing political as well as religious, domestic as well as relational and literary opinions. Creole stands metonymically for the whole of the people's (Creole) culture. Orality, then, cannot be understood as an absence (of writing, of modernity) or as one of the poles in a dichotomy; neither is it the decisive characteristic of Caribbean popular culture. It can be studied only as the specific language philosophy rhetorics of the Creole culture of the community.

Cynthia Ward offers a highly polemic Afrocentric attempt to make a comparable point for the West African context. She clearly addresses Western orality scholars, but she makes some valuable points for my discussion of Caribbean vernaculars. I will therefore discuss her contribution at some length. Ward places the concept of orality back into the context from which Western scholarship has disengaged it, namely the (in Ward's texts, West African) oral community. This community is first characterized by its multilinguality and not by the absence of writing. The script may fulfill some function in the community: many West African peoples have long possessed a form of writing, even if it was sometimes used for ritual uses rather than for common, popular use. Recently, another form of literacy entered the oral community in the wake of a European colonial language. A socially significant dichotomy was the result. In West Africa, people often speak several regional African languages, whereas they write in the European language, being fully aware of the deep social, cultural, and political differences between both types of language use. The members of the community consequently hold nuanced, subtle views on their linguistic and semiotic situation (see also Finnegan 1988: 56). If Ward articulates these views, they evoke structuralist and poststructuralist insights—but they derive from quite a different semiotic context. Ward states in a direct polemic with a poststructuralist standpoint that in the multilingual oral context the sign is considered as obviously arbitrary and ambivalent. Language is seen as subject to change; the borders between speech communities as questionable, variable, ambiguous. The oral community holds an antiessentialist notion of subjectivity and meaning as plural constructions. "In a part of the world where widespread multilingualism is the norm, the arbitrariness of the sign is no great revelation" is Ward's dry comment (1990: 88). Ironically, she claims that the member of the oral community has a knowledge of language practices that is superior to that of the citizen of the literate center: "we can also use their language and the kind of thinking that goes along with it. There is this difference: we have the choice and we know it. To hear their structuralists and poststructuralists speak (excuse me, write), they don't have the choice" (Ward 1989: 133). This last statement is, among others, directed at Walter Ong. It contains two points of critique: the first is her directly opposed opinion about the group that knows more about language and consciousness; the second is her strategy of reversing his use of "we" and "they." Both points come clearly to light if one compares Ward's statement with the following fragment from one of Ong's essays, a text Ward does not mention explicitly:

Knowing the effect of writing on ourselves, knowing how much of what we consider simply human is due to the appropriation of writing, we can enter into the state of consciousness of oral peoples—never directly, but reflectively. And reflective entry has some advantages over direct entry, for primary oral cultures can hardly reflect on orality as such by contrast with the literacy they do not know. (Ong 1987: 375)

In both quotes *we* are in the know, whereas *they* are not. But Ward's *we* is not Ong's *we*. Their crucial disagreement concerns the relevance given to the notion of purity and intactness. Ong recognizes "primary orality" only in the form of the untainted oral culture, where writing does not yet exist, and he applies the concept of "secondary orality" only in the context of Western literate cultures, where audiovisual technologies bring the spoken word back into prominence. Ward, in contrast, shows that there are other forms of orality that are rooted in the everyday life of all societies. Therefore, she thinks Ong's general view of orality defendable only if it concerns the everyday verbal interaction of everybody, in oral or in scriptoral societies. Clearly, this is not what Ong intends to say. Ward's intervention reintegrates Gates's artificial differentiation of two kinds of orality (as described in the second section). From a non-Eurocentric perspective, the two are one, as Ward underlines.

Ward's use of the word *we* can be understood in a new, inclusive sense, as she argues that her interpretation of orality approaches it as a phenomenon belonging to "us": a very common language practice, shared by everybody and open to everybody, eminently unauthoritarian: "This orality is the history of, presence of, and possibility of multiple, often contradictory stories, fictions, realities, meanings—none being allowed to have precedence over the others without being marked as overtly coercive" (Ward 1990: 87). This description serves as the starting point of her sketch of the West African oral community and the oral antiaesthetics of some West African texts and other texts in the African diaspora.[14] She characterizes the oral community as a democratic network of equivalent voices. Ward describes the oral community in political as well as semiotical terms. She considers it as a principally antiauthoritarian community: words and texts receive their meaning in the open discussion conducted by the collective. "The oral is rather the 'always already' possibility of being responded to by Clara's tale, Sam's tale, or a baby's fart, or a discussion, with no one person's 'reading' being allowed to have precedence, or authority, or the power of legitimization, over another's reading. The oral narrative is not privileged over other oral discourses" (Ward 1989: 134). The oral nature of texts lies in their accessibility to the reactions of their listeners, in their capacity for inviting comments. The community, not the text, decides the orality of the text. So, the apparent dichotomy between the spoken word and the written letters in *Angel* to which I referred above is misleading: when the letters are read within the oral community, they are responded to with the same directness as spoken words would be. They are made part of the verbal exchange, and the mere fact of their being written instead of spoken does not change the fact that they are now part of an oral communication. If one studies "orality," then, one has to shift attention from the text to the context of the exchange. In the oral community language can never be disengaged from its speakers and listeners. This argument leads to an insight that has been advanced recurrently in the preceding chapters; it has a bearing on the importance of the acknowledgment of the situatedness of texts and language practices.

The value of Ward's intervention lies in her radical approach to orality, which she defines as a complex of interactional practices. However, her qualification of this practice is questionable. She projects upon the interaction within the oral community democracy, collectivity, openness, fluidity, and other positive qualifications. It is tempting to read her description of the oral community as a Utopian proposal for a non-Eurocentric, non-scriptocentric literary polysystem in which the multiplicity of cultural utterances is preserved and valued.

It is much harder to accept her description of existing oral communities as valid. In every oral community uneven power relations designate who has the right to speak. African women writers have been clear enough in pointing out the obstacles women have to fight before gaining the right to speak their mind, even if these writers may also praise the inspiration they find in their oral communities (James 1990). Dialogism may be more relevant to the understanding of oral practices than the technology of expression, but it would be preposterous to define this dialogism in a Bakhtinian way. In Africa or the Caribbean, it is hard to find arguments to support the notion of a harmonious equivalent dialogism within the vernacular community. One should rather understand Caribbean dialogism as a dynamic, divided, contesting plurality. Conflict and violence are important factors in this dynamic.

In *Angel,* even in its most intimate moments, "confusion" (which here equals quarreling) is the norm: "'Well everyting in place,' pronounced Jessie. 'Once you hear confusion start, everyting awright again'" (286). Ward presents "orality" yet again as fullness and positivity. Her starting point is the unwarranted assumption that authority and power are absent from the oral exchange. Even if she uses the potent concepts of interaction and practice, she reduces them by erasing their implication in the construction of power relations. Instead of defining "orality" as the deducted antipole of alienated Western literacy, she bases a dichotomy on the opposition (very much contested)[15] between public and private, adding the semantic markers [+ power]/[− power]. She deduces the nature of orality by placing it in opposition to the public sphere of Western society, which is structured by power relations. Ward seems to be motivated by the desire to depict the West African orality as radically different from a prestigious postmodernism that looks down on it, to the degree that she defines West African orality as the real thing, from which postmodernism is only a weak derivation. Ward's utopian approach places orality again beyond scrutiny and interpretation. It is a severe obstacle to an analysis of the differences within the community.

Angel takes a less utopian stance. It treats difference, conflicts, and violence as often painful but real elements of the community's heteroglossia, as I have shown above. But it also depicts the tendency of the collective to maintain its cohesiveness. One of its binding forces is the bonding between members of a family, above all between mother and daughter.

For the gap between students ("high-up people") and poor families ("who low down," 160) is deeper than that between the educated and the uneducated members of one family. Between them, there will always be a common denominator. This holds true especially for Angel and her mother, Doodsie. For Angel is capable of negotiating the alienation caused by her education only by integrating her mother's views of life into the dominant and critical perspectives she is studying. Not her father's. For even if Angel is a self-willed child who looks very much like her father, it is her mother who encourages her to learn (99 ff). And Angel acknowledges the crucial part her mother plays in her intellectual and political development, even if she sometimes vehemently denounces Doodsie's choices in life (172–76, 188–90). Despite their apparent differences, Angel is able to use her mother's discourse very well to enter the communal political debates as a speaking subject. She is initiated as an adult politically conscious speaker by quoting her mother during a political discussion with her fellow students.

"But here in the Caribbean we have Black Power."

"But it not doin us no damn good," said Angel suddenly. "Look at Leader!"

"Exactly!" Kai went on talking, but Angel didn't hear what he said. I actually said that! she marvelled. It was a line borrowed straight from Doodsie in answer to arguments about Leader's control of the country. Jesus, thought Angel! I said that! (157)

Angel borrows her mother's statement, including the characteristic curse. It does not make her an adequate partner in the dialogue yet: she cannot listen to the responses, as she is too involved in the sudden consciousness of her own newly found position of speech, which, to her surprise, is connected with her mother. The relation to her mother is crucial to Angel's growing capacity to handle differences, as the following quote shows:

"Lord, Mammie, some of those teachers so damn backward is a shame. . . . All de same old stupid ideas. No new thoughts of changing curriculum and having new approach to language an . . . well you know what ah mean! I did jus feel like heavin dem out de window!"

"So what dat would o do? Change dey ideas or mash up dey head? Look, somebody move dis cat outa me foot before ah throw it to kingdom come, eh!. . . Move, cat! If you come back here, you dead."

"Leave de cat alone, non!"

"But I serious, you know, Angel. How allyou expect everybody to agree wid everyting one time? Me, I more revolutionary dan allyou." The crochet needles clacked. "Dammit! Look you make me drop a stitch!" (241–42)

Mother Doodsie and daughter Angel share kindred revolutionary and violent impulses, as the quotation shows. They correct each other's inclination for too rigorous solutions, whether they concern blockheaded colleagues or cats. The use of violence is not restricted to certain groups; in general, it does not mark the end of negotiation, nor the boundaries of the community.[16] It is cruelly present at the heart of communal life, at the heart of child-rearing (e.g., 111, 122), at the heart of marriage (e.g., 69, 89–90). But it is mitigated by the presence of others, especially if the marital violence appears to frighten the children who witness it (90). This violence highlights the conflictual nature of the differences by which the community is structured. In *Angel*, these conflicts are accepted as inevitable, even if their violence is mourned and abhorred. In her treatment of the vernacular community, Collins relates to the Caribbean notion of the tempestuous multiplicity of the Caribbean, in stark contrast to scholars like Cynthia Ward, who offer a more harmonious sketch of an African oral community. Collins's text pictures the bonding while refusing to erase difference, or to deny the violence in Caribbean lives.

Angel presents violence as the decisive moment in the difficult relation between "theory" and "action," the two fields that Angel moves between and that form the scene of her coming of age. To reconcile these two fields, she has to come to terms with the issue of violence. Doodsie tells her daughter that violence is not the answer to settling conflicts of a theoretical or ideological nature. But mere theorizing does not offer any solution either. Up to a certain point, Angel can integrate her theoretical position with an activist stance through her active involvement in the revolutionary movement. At the end of the novel, she hesitates to take sides when a civil war looms. Like many other Grenadians at the time, the destructive developments within the revolutionary government confuse her. She cannot stand for either one of the parties, cannot act on her conviction. It's not that she cannot argue quite well; she has grown into a capable speaking subject, but she doesn't stand up to act. Her younger brother, Rupert, blames her for hiding opportunistically in an ivory tower, abandoning the people she claims to be fighting for:

"Look, Rupert, the issues are clear . . . "

"Don give me no lecture. They clear to me, too. But you siddown dey wid you clarity. If you clear an everybody else unclear, what you go do? Go an siddown in the museum?" (270)

The American invasion of Grenada, which follows soon after the discussions above, forces Angel into resistance, even while disagreeing with her fellows in the struggle. Angel realizes first that the time for mere talk is over and that action is needed. This time, she doesn't take her cue from her mother (or father): her parents are not as averse to the invasion as she is. Her insight into the need for action comes from her grandmother, whom she suddenly remembers ("walking with determination towards the radio, a glass of water in her hand. De man inside dey only talkin, talkin . . . !" 275). She also realizes she is scared, and she says so. Her brother Rupert praises her for that. Now she shows that she accepts the inevitability of engaging violence at the same time as undergoing its full threatening force. She understands that recoiling from violence makes it impossible to act, just as the pursuit of theoretical/political clarity can be an obstacle to action. Her resistance to imperial violence is in fact a claim to the nation's right to its own national conflicts, confusions, and violence. An acceptance of the inevitability of violence together with an acceptance of the limited relevance of theoretical discourse is the necessary condition to grow into a full speaking, feeling, and acting subject. Of course, this is a theory too; it insists on the restrictions of (monological) speech. In this, *Angel* links to the semiotics presented in Beryl Gilroy's *Frangipani House*.

Thus, Angel's relationship to the different generations of her family structures her development as a full (though often dissenting) member of a community in conflict. Her growth becomes possible by her struggle to make the right choices. Just like the girl, the novel itself can be said to have made some remarkable decisions, which led to its particular position within Caribbean writing. To evaluate these decisions, I will now shift my attention to the level of the text in its literary context.

If seen as part of the larger project of Caribbean writing, *Angel* makes some significant choices. Those that first catch the eye concern the focus by which it presents Caribbean society. It makes the class and gender differences of the speaking community very visible by concentrating on the working class, and then especially (though not exclusively) on the women. Focalization lies continually with the knitting, cooking, cleaning, crop growing, and harvesting women, especially those of Doodsie's generation.

But as naturally as they involve themselves in household tasks, some of them join demonstrations to walk, dance, and shout, or recite revolutionary poetry during political meetings, and even take up arms. Their position is strengthened by the more than ninety Creole proverbs that are scattered through the text and that articulate their perspective. These proverbs function as subtitles for sections of the twelve larger chapters. They summarize the section, but they also put other points of view into perspective, or they offer a touchstone for the notions of the younger generation. Even if the older generation is inclined to accept the American invasion, the new generation is led by the sayings of its parents and grandparents to take up arms against the invaders. The older women's speech forms the Creole space in which an educated daughter can grow into a female speaking subject.

Women writers and critics often choose an approach that takes gender and class differences as its main preoccupation. By their choice to highlight, for example, gender, this community will then be presented as a (painfully) differentiated complex. Often, they will also relate their work to a vernacular community and its modes of expression. That does not mean that the "voice" these writers create is necessarily didactic, realist, or direct. On the contrary, they value language play and experimenting, without which the creation of an effective voice would not be possible, especially if the multiplicity of that communal voice is acknowledged.

Above, in my reading of *Angel*, I have explored the multiplicity of the Caribbean vernacular community, which is presented metonymically by the different registers and forms of Creoles and colonial languages. The novel refers to the oppositions between some of these languages, without establishing them as antipoles (e.g., between "Ah don know" and "Me en know" in the quotation on the first page of this chapter and between Standard English and Creole). The dichotomy between Creole and Standard English and that between speech and writing is undone by the text, especially by its postcolonial appropriation of writing, which is integrated in the specific semiotics of a Creole community that is working toward its nationhood. In this way, the art of "writing 'speakerly'" receives a positive value, in Kubayanda's words. This positivity is situated in the novel's radical decision to dedicate its appropriation of writing to the Grenadan community instead of addressing a larger transnational intellectual community of readers. *Angel* works toward that sort of Caribbean positivity, which is connected to the art of nation building within literature.

Orality, Creole, and the Languages of Criticism and Creativity

Angel points at a semiotics in which language has to be paired with (collective) action to be meaningful. This semiotical position is intertwined with the novel's effort to integrate personal and political aspects of women's lives. What else can we say about the novel's oral, Creole semiotics? Is it connected to a knowledge system of its own? Does it imply notions of language and identity that are radically different from mainstream postcolonial views? And is it possible to contextualize this semiotics as gender-specific, working-class, Black? Jamaican scholar Carolyn Cooper, one of today's most provocative specialists in the field of orality, offers a well-informed reflection on the situatedness of Creole and popular culture (Cooper 1993). Cooper's study, which offers a close reading of different forms of Jamaican orature (Louise Bennett's poems, Jean Binta Breeze's performance poetry, the explicit songs by Jamaican DJs in the dance hall) describes "the liberating path of Jamaican popular culture," which reestablishes a contact with its lost African homelands. This evocation of the African aspects of Jamaican identity is part of a larger creolization process in which a hybrid Jamaican cultural identity is shaped (Cooper 1993: 34). Cooper shows how Black working-class culture can be integrated with this identity while transforming it. Her study helps to understand *Angel*'s oral semiotics as specifically Black and working class. Both Collins and Cooper elaborate women's part in this culture. Cooper's study offers a relevant analysis of the collection of life narratives *Lionheart Gal* of the Jamaican Theatre Collective Sistren, a "process of communal disclosure" in which a development from personal to political understanding of the collective's lives takes place (Cooper 1989: 49). It is important that Cooper situates these life stories within the context of women's narrative modes: "the preferred narrative mode of many feminist writers is the guise of intimate, understated domestic writing by women: letters, diaries or what Sistren, in an oral/Creole context, simply calls testimony" (49). Cooper points out in the work of Sistren what we also find in *Angel*: the principal *ordinariness* of the exchange, the centrality of the collectivity, and the link between the personal and the political. In Sistren's text *Lionheart Gal* the Creole text serves to illuminate the gender differences within the community, and these shared narratives lead to a political understanding of personal lives.

Sistren's text is about and from a painfully divided Creole community, a dividedness brought to the fore by the choice to have women speak, just as in *Angel*.

Cooper's argument and the writings of Sistren and Collins all refer to an issue that has been addressing writers throughout the decades: what discourses and languages are suitable to express the experiences of women and members of the working class? *Angel* chooses an oral mode in which Creole plays an important role. Sistren chooses Creole and a written version of an oral performance, testimony. By situating their texts in a highly political context, they both implicitly repudiate an aesthetics that privileges language and the literary as such. Both celebrate oral, Creole culture as a Black working-class *women's* culture, too. The appropriation of this sometimes very conservative and macho popular culture as a women's space too is far from obvious. Yet, this emancipatory move is also part of other feminist projects. By discussing one telling debate in the United States I can highlight the specific aim and problematics of Collins's and Cooper's Caribbean project. I'm referring to a notorious exchange between Henry Louis Gates Jr., Houston A. Baker Jr., and feminist literary critic Joyce A. Joyce in 1987. Joyce's tentative (and sometimes, admittedly, naive) critique of some of the tenets of poststructuralism in an African-American context was vehemently dismissed by her opponents (Joyce 1987a, 1987b). Gates himself sympathizes much more with the radically opposed standpoint of one of his key texts, *Mumbo Jumbo*, by Ishmael Reed. Gates reads in this text "an argument against the privileging in black discourse of what Reed elsewhere terms 'the so-called oral tradition' in favor of the primacy and priority of the written text. It is a brief for the permanence of the written text, for the need of criticism" (1983: 705). For Reed, orality signifies rigidity and stifling conventions. He associates himself with those postmodern and deconstructive trends that, in the wake of Derrida, value the vigorous abundance of writing. From his standpoint, the concept of the authenticity and transparency of the spoken word is misleading. In the context of the African-American culturally and politically motivated interest in orality, Reed's stand is indeed quite spectacular and daring, as Gates does not hesitate to point out. But it leaves a lot of space for other possible views on the value of orality and writing, especially when these take gender and class into account, or wish to acknowledge the regional specificity of different vernaculars. This is a difference Gates passes over in silence.

Joyce, quite in contrast to Gates, refers to a Black aesthetics that would be outside the sphere of the poststructuralist revaluation of writing. She, like Grandma Ettie and Angel in Collins's novel, insists on the limitations of too exclusive a concentration on (written) language. In an attempt to suggest the context of an alternative Black aesthetics, she points to two illiterate characters in two novels by African-American women writers who are acutely aware of the wrongs committed against them. She comments: "Shared experiences like these can bond a people together in ways that far exceed language" (Joyce 1987a: 341). To make her point she creates an *oral* universe as the site of essential (nonverbal) Black experience. Hers is an effort to outline a nonelitist approach to Black literature. Gates's and Baker's reactions to these and many other points seem to me to be something of an overkill. Their elaborate arguments about the incorrectness of Joyce's views of poststructuralism, about the political merits of serious analysis of texts, the falseness of the dichotomies between theory and humanism, theory and "black men" (*sic*) are quite apparent, when reread after the considerable lapse of twelve years and more (Gates 1987b). But even if Joyce's argument can be criticized, it makes the very acceptable point of the specific view of language and the relation between writer/performer and audience that is implicit in the writing practice of writers who work from within and for a working-class community. Such a view will result in a specific aesthetical form.

Yet, this does not mean that this form is necessarily also simple, direct, or didactic. In this aspect Joyce's promotion of a Black tradition of intelligibility, of a direct and mutual relationship to the audience from whose midst one speaks, is a reduction of orality. For one, the assumption that a writer always addresses one clearly delineated community, his or her own, is questionable. Apart from the fact that "the writer's audience is always a fiction," as Ong has argued, communities are also always multiple, divided; and a writer will often address several "communities" simultaneously. Moreover, this perception of the relation between writer and audience is closely linked to an understanding of the writer as a teacher, and his or her work as didactic.[17] As Gates has shown, however, the pioneering African-American anthropologist and writer Zora Neale Hurston, who has done much to develop the voice of the Black Southern community by experimenting with it, was hardly interested in the didactic function of language. Her literary discourse is organized around metaphors, ambiguities, and the multiplicity of subjectivity. Hurston even experiments with language without an authoritative narrator: she uses free indirect speech as "a mood come alive," "words walking without masters." Yet, her pleasure in language play cannot be understood as a rejection of social commitment: her writing is far from irresponsible and negative. Hurston is driven by the need and desire to speak, and one of her sources of inspiration is the oral tradition of the Black community of her youth; in speaking, she calls this popular culture to life again. For her, the oral community and its oral traditions are not at all at odds with the multiplicity of the subject or the playful complexities of language. Her views are corroborated by other postcolonial critics, for example, Craig Tapping: "So-called primitive cultures . . . value what is told, not for its content but rather for its form. . . . A performative aesthetic operates: just as it does when we read the most up-to-date postmodern document or text. What we value is not what we're told, but the play through which the artist-creator reveals what we're told" (1989: 19). One does not need any so-called primitive cultures as a context to agree. Following Tapping, it seems to me that most oral performances, in all societies, are characterized by a seductive form. This seductiveness is logically connected to the element of address and openness to the audience in many oral practices I have discussed above—the performative aesthetic, as Tapping aptly puts it. Just as Ward does, Tapping insists on the complexities of oral exchange. And just as Joyce does, he insists on the *difference* of the cultural practice of a nondominant community.

The specific, performative aesthetic of the Caribbean oral, working-class community is thoroughly analyzed in a range of studies on Creole. Ashcroft, Griffiths, and Tiffin even consider Creole (if studied from a certain angle) as eminently suitable for gaining insight into postcolonial language use. They state, "The theory of the Creole continuum is an outstanding example of a post-colonial approach to linguistics because it reaffirms the notion of language as a practice. . . . The Creole continuum reminds us that a language is a human behaviour and consists in what people *do* rather than in theoretical models" (Ashcroft, Griffiths, and Tiffin 1989: 45–46, my emphasis). Thus, the theory of the Creole continuum offers a promising model for an approach that studies orality as an actual language practice instead of as an ideological referent for anticolonial resistance or as a sign of warm, maybe primitive authenticity.[18] A first advantage of such an approach is that it deconstructs the dichotomy between "speaking" and "doing" at work in some of the texts discussed above. As such, it offers a context to those who stress that signifying practices other than speaking are also important for community building, such as Ma Ettie, Angel, and Joyce. Here, the text testifies of the postcolonial insight into language as not only a practice but also as one of a complex of intertwined semiotic practices, which was discussed in the preceding chapter.[19]

Second, as this approach focuses on the variability of actual language use, in the flexible context of different registers and forms of Creole, it opens the possibility of acknowledging conflicts within the collectivity. Caribbean Creoles have been studied as speeches resonating with conflict. According to linguist Morgan Dalphinis, Creole is in itself "at least partly, a symbol of the historical conflict evident within Creole languages," and he explains, "the conflict between the European enslaver and the African enslaved" (Dalphinis 1985: 1). Edouard Glissant is even more vehement in his pained evocation of the conflict embodied in Creole, as becomes apparent in a quotation from his texts in an essay by Michele Praeger:

> The masters thought Creole a composite language, an oral language of resigned slaves but, in reality, says Glissant, it is the result of a "network of negativities recognized as such": "You want to reduce me to stammering, I will systematize this stammering, says the slave to the master, lets see if you can understand." . . . According to Glissant, unlike other languages, the function is not to communicate, to be useful, but to deconstruct, to subvert. (Praeger 1992: 42–43)

If one follows Praeger's interpretation of Glissant, it becomes quite impossible to consider Creole merely as the positive, unambiguous representation of national consciousness. Glissant approaches it almost as pure negativity, namely as a speech that is deconstruction and accusation in one. As such, it is the linguistic counterpart of those postcolonial literary strategies that aim at the deconstruction of Eurocentric, colonial myths and discourses from within.

Creole can also be studied not in its origins but in its actual function in present-day Caribbean literature. Then one finds that different forms of Creole are set against each other, each conveying, for example, a certain social or cultural class, or a specific social attitude. As Ashcroft, Griffiths, and Tiffin point out, Creole indicates "a communication between classes" (1989: 76), whereby the notion of class must be understood with its racial and cultural connotations. Many writers offer a flexible use of a range of Creole dialects, by which they picture a complex image of the manifold social relations within Caribbean society (for several examples, see Ramchand 1983: 96–114). Thus, Creole is used to convey differences, boundaries, and conflicts, but it also embodies the communication that negotiates these differences. *Angel* offers a good example of this dual function.

Creole, then, is the site of conflict. It is also the site of the pleasure of (even bickering) togetherness. It can be even more. Writers who have been experimenting with expanding the scopes of Creole languages want them to function as languages of consciousness, as high-standard literary languages and as languages for scholarly reflection. In fact, they address the question Gates asked in his reaction to Joyce: what language do Black writers use?

Cooper's answer to this question illuminates a feminist, Caribbean difference with the practices favored by Gates. Gates is as interested as she is in using a Black vernacular as the medium for criticism, but he chooses specific aspects that he then integrates into poststructuralist academic discourse. Cooper instead aims at broadening the range of Creole itself until it functions as an effective critical discourse. She carries Sistren's project of presenting women's life narratives in Creole a step further by boldly arguing that these texts can be theorized in Creole too—and she continues her essay in Creole. In this way, she intervenes in a more general discussion about the range of Creole, answering a question from an unpublished paper by Victor Chang, who wonders why Creole is "not used for internal musing and reflection." Chang provokingly states that "[p]erhaps it could be argued that the very spoken nature of the Creole, its very physicality, militates against its use for inner reflection and introspection" (Cooper 1993 52).

Cooper takes up this challenge. By convincingly continuing her analysis of Sistren's play in Creole, she also answers Gates and Reed, showing that criticism and orality are not mutually exclusive. But the nature of her oral/Creole criticism is definitely very different from Reed's postmodern discourse. Cooper enters into a direct dialogue with the texts she analyzes, in line with the dialogic demands of the oral situation, as Ward explains. Her criticism is much more dialogic, more personal, and more political than the kind advocated by Reed. Cooper's criticism takes on something of the ordinariness (the everyday, material) and political nature of Creole, and of much of the women's writing she referred to above.[20]

Creole appears to be an effective language of criticism, which is then transformed in a more material, everyday practice. The capacity of Creole to convey a sense of directness, intimacy, and—sometimes—sensuality is both an opportunity for women's writing and an obstacle; for this sensuality has been appropriated by a raucous machismo. In her 1993 study, Cooper develops this point admirably. She shows how the association between Creole and sexuality goes back to colonial times: by considering Jamaican the debased offspring of Standard English, European colonial discourse has endowed Jamaican language with the negative attributes of bastardy and corruption (40). This definition is extended to the notion of "talk" (versus book): "oral discourse leaves the tongue open to slackness; writing trims the tongue, curtailing linguistic looseness" (40). What interests me here is the almost overly explicit presence of sexuality at the heart of the notion of creoleness and syncretism. This presence is even more visible in the omnipresent postcolonial concept of hybridity, theorized by Homi Bhabha and evaluated by many others. Hybridity is a curious concept. As others have remarked, it has a history in biology, referring to notions of crossbreeding; as Robert Young has said, studies of racial hybridity are really about interracial sex (1990). The reference to heterosexuality in the concept of hybridity suggests that hybridity weds two opposites to create a synthesis. Hybridity seems to be dependent on the existence of two antipoles: male/female, Black/white, African/European, oral/written. But the concept itself is often used in an argument that is meant to break with binary thought. This in itself might be a good reason to dismiss the concept of hybridity altogether in favor of the notion of syncretism (Becquer and Gatti 1991), or the more precise notion of creolization. However, the ubiquity of sexuality and the body in the work of many Caribbean women critics and writers makes me appreciate the sexual connotations in the concept of hybridity. In my eyes it is precisely here that the problem of the full expression of Caribbean multiple identity lies.

Sexuality is one of the main themes in Black male orature in the Caribbean (such as the well-known Trinidad calypso, and the Jamaican DJs' lyrics examined in Cooper 1993). These loud, indecent songs testify of the need to claim an identity and save it from the threatening dominance of cultural and economical neocolonialism; the songs claim a Black macho identity by insisting on surprising Black male sexual prowess. As Cooper suggests, sexuality is the battlefield on which masculine identity is claimed, because in all other domains Black lower-class masculinity has been devalued (167). But sexuality is not just an aspect of individual experience; it is often closely connected to both group identity and cultural or national identity. Heterosexuality reveals itself as an important aspect of national identity, if one acknowledges that homosexuality, decadence, and femininity are often deemed (U.S.) imports (151). Thus, a cultural model of Caribbean identity makes itself known. Where the "créolistes" celebrate the manipulating talents of the cunning, masquerading masculine narrator, who is the Caribbean champion of indirectness (Arnold 1994), the Black working-class singers loudly identify with the explicit sexuality of the Black macho ramgoat. Cooper defends the subversive nature of this focus on sexuality: "Whatever belongs to the sphere of sensuousness . . . has the connotation of being antagonistic to Reason" (147). However, it may be that this eager talk of sexuality helps to construct a collective identity, but it is also a precarious way of doing so. The celebration of aggressive macho sexuality is often predicated on the devaluation or victimization of women and homosexuals, it is often sexist and conservative, and in addition, it is at odds with the emancipatory demand for respect. There is a tension here, nicely expressing itself in the notion of respectability (Cooper 1993: 167): white middle-class culture demands respectability before giving respect, but respectability implies the shedding of life's essential, much-valued sensuality, vitality, subversion, and rebelliousness. The emphasis on sexuality is at odds with the middle-class ideology that is often the dominant force in the difficult shaping of a Caribbean national identity. Sexuality is the hidden cause of hybridity, but it is also a threat to the articulation of a smooth, decent, coherent national identity (which has not yet been fully formed). This is the crucial, potentially most productive point in Cooper's argument. The tension between the celebration of sexuality and the construction of collective identity is also apparent in the difficult theorizing of hybridity and sexuality, for it seems to me that Western postmodern scholars may write with gusto and pleasure about the multiple, indecent, loud, hybrid body, whereas Caribbean scholars and writers have the more difficult job of negotiating the strategies of appropriating and subverting colonial myths of Calibans and presumed loose matriarchs, and the strategies of constructing more respectable and subtle cultural identities. How does one write about full, embodied Caribbean identity when talk of sexuality lands you in colonial, racist, and sexist stereotype, and silence about sexuality makes you complicit with the colonial middle-class desire to erase Black working-class views of life?

Angel situates itself within this debate. It solves the problem by in-

cessantly concentrating on the working-class community itself, and especially on the women, never exceeding the boundaries of their shared, public talk. The novel works hard at conveying a sense of communal closeness
and intimacy. The oral quality of the many loosely structured conversations in *Angel* has the effect of creating the sensual atmosphere of an infor-
mal exchange between people who are very close to each other. The novel
also takes pains to endow solitary musings with a certain intimate physical
quality. It does so by inserting many very effective short descriptions of the
physical context of the speakers and of the emotions that are the effect of
these surroundings.

In these short passages the thoughts and feelings of the characters are
presented in free indirect speech in Standard English or West Indian Standard, which then often shifts to Creole (see, e.g., pp. 30, 54, 86, 153). In
these moments, Creole becomes for an instant the language of consciousness, which, according to Ramchand, is still scarce in Caribbean writing
(Ramchand 1983: 105). But almost everywhere, Creole is reserved for directly reported speech. The result is that very intimate matters are never
conveyed directly, neither in Creole nor in Standard English. There are no
direct reports of sexual encounters, for example. Only in hindsight the
reader learns about the presence of sexuality. In a letter to a friend, Angel
writes: "But Janice! If at the tender age of twenty-one I've just *begun* to
grow up, then Jesus! I'll be forty before I'm of age. Of age to do what, she
asks? No, that's done, but I don't feel any different" (166). It is remarkable
that even this explicit admission of the event occurs in (reported, so distanced) Standard English, not in Creole. Creole seems to be the medium
for personal, intimate communications, but it is so only up to a certain
point. The reader has heard about unwelcome sexual advances and about
Angel's infatuations, even about friends staying for the night (160), but even
then the narrative declines to invite one into sharing the sensual details of
an erotic encounter. It is as if Creole is strictly respecting the boundaries of
communal exchange. The most private, intimate details of one's life are not
for open discussion, and the modest narrator, too, refrains from telling what
the characters do not convey. In *Angel*, this is where the private quality of
Creole speech ends. Here, Creole is community talk, not bed talk.[21]

Angel's careful linking of Creole to the open domain of shared communal life results in a text that is clearly speaking to and for both working-
class women and their upwardly mobile daughters, and that modestly ad-

dresses issues of intimacy, sensuality, and sexuality without succumbing to a masculinist eroticism. To keep this balance, the text has to renounce the possibilities of both open provocation of bourgeois norms, as well as the intimacy of introspection. This does not mean that Creole is by definition incompatible with the pleasures of the body. Far from it. Many novels show Creole's eminent suitability for evoking the sensuality of, say, growing up in the Caribbean landscape. But it is not self-evident. Authors have to work hard to find a voice to express the more delicate aspects of intimacy and sensuality. Grace Nichols's novel *Whole of a Morning Sky* shows that the tension between Standard English and Creole can be applied to create a sensual voice that also extends to the erotic.

Conclusion

Against the background of the above discussion, the value of *Angel's* specific voice can be assessed. *Angel* creates a language in which women (and men) can express a variety of positions, both progressive political and traditionally religious, both interior musings and terse sayings. This Creole, then, does not merely reflect the views of the working classes, the yard people. Above, I suggest that *Angel*, in a way, continues the tradition of the yard novel. Now it has become clear that the yard (as the location peopled with the objectified naive and the less educated) has been developed into the social community as a whole, a collectivity embracing both (gendered) laborers and intellectuals who speak for themselves—even if the justification of someone's claim to speak *for* or speak *as* other members of the community is often the subject of negotiation.

The focus on the dialogism of the community is part of the novel's aesthetics as a "speakerly" text. In other aspects, too, it testifies of its involvement in orality, for example, in its tendency to focus on comments rather than on descriptions. My interpretation has shown that this aesthetics necessitates a situated (perhaps) postcolonial approach, that is, Creole studies. A more general postcolonial approach falls short of analyzing the exact effects and nuances of the novel's multiple voice. Yet, even a speakerly text like *Angel* testifies of the twofold strategy by which postcolonial texts are structured: for even if the novel draws heavily on oral practices, it also engages in a deconstruction of colonial discourse. The latter strategy is visible in the novel's easy appropriation of writing and even Standard English as instruments for reinforcing the Grenadian community. Through this appropriation, the contrast between nondominant and dominant semiotic practices is neutralized. The effect is that the dominant perspectives are denied their obvious influence on the nondominant and that the vision of the latter is endowed with a self-evident central role.

Angel puts the postcolonial nation and its voice in the center. This move implies an important comment on those forms of general comparative postcolonial criticism that are geared against the privileging of the center and surrenders to the fascination of the margins. My discussion of *Angel* has shown that the margins' appropriation of the notion of a center, if only implicitly in the novel's thematization of the community as a centripetal force, can be as radical. It helps to deconstruct the (post)colonial model of center and periphery in a multicentered model (cultural aspects) while also insisting on the difference in power of different centers (geopolitical aspects). Indeed, I would even hold that an excessive critical interest in marginality might lead to an undervaluing of the historical *difference* of postcolonial nations, which can not always be explained from the site of their contact with the colonial powers.

In the last section of the next chapter, I will return to the novel's specific aesthetics as a speakerly text. Thus, a second conclusion is offered to this first chapter on "voice."

5

The Pleasures of Address: Grace Nichols's
Whole of a Morning Sky

Will Creole necessarily be at the heart of Caribbean writing? Let us not make the mistake of assuming that all Caribbean writing, or Caribbean migrant writing, is characterized by a Creole or an oral aesthetics. Nevertheless, all Caribbean women writers can be seen to relate to the gendered and ethnic tensions between the more Standard English and the more Creole registers in the Creole continuum, even if their works do not engage as explicitly and radically with the issues of orality and Creole as Merle Collins's *Angel* does. To show that aspects of more readerly Caribbean novels exceed a scriptocentric reading, this chapter offers a close reading of *Whole of a Morning Sky* (1986), a poetic novel by Guyanese writer Grace Nichols, who, like Merle Collins, resides in London. Taking up the challenge made in the preceding chapter, this chapter explores the ways *Morning Sky* makes the most of the tensions between Standard English and Creole to deepen the expressive range of both languages. A crucial aspect of this narrative project is the focus on contrasts and conflicts. *Morning Sky* treats conflict in an essentially different way than *Angel* does; it chooses to concentrate not on the centripetal but on the centrifugal forces in the community. Therefore, it is set on the borders of that community. Like Nichols's poem "My Black Triangle," discussed in Chapter 2, her novel studies the opportunities and the anguish of border conditions. This choice is related to a different aesthetics, which leans more on writerly devices than *Angel* does. For the sake of my argument, I will regularly take recourse to a comparison between the two novels. To wind up the argument built in these two chapters, the last section looks into the possibility of articulating an answer to the question of how we might understand orality in Caribbean writing. As such, it offers a comparative evaluation of *Morning Sky* and *Angel*.

An Appetite for Contrast

A striking difference between *Angel* and *Morning Sky* is that the Grenadian novel *Angel* grants Creole a much more important space than *Morning Sky* does. This language strategy, as we saw, is linked to the central position of the community in the narrative. If *Angel* chooses to situate the narrative right at the heart of the community, Nichols's novel places its focalizing characters at the borders of the community, thematizing the position of relative outsiders, and with it the centrifugal forces of the community. If the tensions and conflicts are treated quite differently in *Morning Sky* than in *Angel*, they are presented as of a comparable kind. Nichols's novel is also situated in a period of political turmoil, this time in Guyana. It follows the experiences of the Walcott family and focuses on the period between 1960 and 1964. In Guyana, this period starts with the preparations for the elections (1961), which are won by Cheddi Jagan ("Mohabir" in the novel), the candidate of the People's Progressive Party ("National Labour Party"), who has been premier since 1953. His most important rival is Forbes Burnham ("Atwell"). The British (who were still in control of Guyana) and the United States feared that Jagan's reelection would result in a Marxist government, so they initiated a period of political destabilization. Trade unions were infiltrated, and strikes against the government were financed with U.S. funds. Racial tensions were fanned. Conflicts took on a violent character, and they culminated in a very bloody period in the spring of 1964. The novel ends in the period following these troubles, when the British took over more and more of the government's power. There was no military intervention, as in Grenada; such an intervention (though in a less violent form) had already taken place in 1953. Independence was obtained in 1966, two years after the narrative's ending.

Whereas the Grenadian novel speaks about conflict and also about united resistance, *Morning Sky* concentrates on the conflicts themselves. This focus on conflict has a special effect. One might even feel that the novel emphasizes contrasts for aesthetic and rhetorical purposes—to be able to make clear and sensual characterizations. This narrative mode of emphasizing and creating contrast is crucial to the rest of my argument, as it allows me to relate the issue of conflict to our discussion of Creole's potential to express intimacy and sensuality. I will take some space to elaborate on it.

The model of contrast structures the narrative as a whole: the two main protagonists, Archie and Clara, patriarch and archfather and young, light-spirited, clear-eyed mother; lack versus fulfillment; cold discipline versus warm playfulness and sensuality; and Standard English versus Creole are sketched almost as two stereotypical antipoles. However, the oppositions are always fluid, temporal, and slightly paradoxical. Archie, who is a head teacher and a speaker of a nearly Standard English, for example, is really from a very poor family, whereas Clara, who is fond of the Creole community, spent her youth in a well-off, warm, middle-class family.

The principle of contrast can be observed in minute detail, too. For example, when Clara breaks with a friend because this friend is said to work evil against her, she feels guilty. "And Clara consoled herself on one of her mother's sayings—'there is more mystery between heaven and hell,' or something like that" (27). Clara or her mother do not accurately recall Hamlet's famous statement to Horatio: Shakespeare's protagonist speaks of "more things in heaven and earth." Clara is not the only one to change the more neutral "in" to "between," but it is less common to bring in hell. By structuring the statement around the oppositional pair of heaven and hell (in keeping with the novel's preference for contrast), and by adding the explicit "mystery," the statement is given a more outspokenly contrasting structure. It has also become more material: between heaven and hell one finds the earth, and it is there where the mystery lies, according to Clara's reading (or her mother's). Shakespeare acknowledges heaven too, but in *Morning Sky* the physical earth is the source of all pleasure and pain. This second dimension of the quote is linked to another aspect of the novel's appetite for contrast. For the contrast makes the statement more salient, more easily pleasing; and this joy in language use is crucial to the text. The novel uses contrast as a rhetorical device to make descriptions more explicit, and more appealing. Contrasting, as an effective aesthetical play, is similar to Clara's playful impulse to disguise herself hideously now and then to give her children an enjoyable fright; she obtains the desired impact by contrasting her familiar sweetness to frightening horror (24). It is this sensation the text is after, and it finds it in a close observation of actual language use. I would argue that the novel presents orality and Creole not as distinct linguistic and cultural spheres but rather as highly sensual practices, firmly embedded in ordinary life. This, too, is apparent from the short quote above. Clara does not appear to be overly interested in the accuracy of her quote, attributing it to her mother with a refreshing lack of respect for English literary history. One could relate her indifference to the novel's approach to orality.

In many oral traditions, the authenticity or originality of narratives may be irrelevant.[1] Texts are important in the context in which they are spoken, and it is rather pointless to search for a first, definitive version. Finnegan speaks in another context of an oral culture's little "respect for 'the word' that seems more typical in fact of cultures dominated by written forms" (Finnegan 1988: 57). All texts, regardless of their provenance, can be used to give meaning to the events of life. If *Angel* articulated the mother's perspective by inserting the many Creole sayings as subtitles, *Morning Sky* stages a quote from the preeminent canonical English text to give vent to the (grand)mother's view.[2] English literature is thus appropriated as a Caribbean text, quite suitable for use in the Caribbean vernacular community, even in relation to things as Caribbean as obeah. Nobel Prize winner Derek Walcott and visionary Guyanese writer and thinker Wilson Harris would agree; they, too, consider Caribbean and other postcolonial people the rightful heirs to classical and European literature. In Nichols's novel, orality lies not in language or text itself but in its use only.

And this actual use is always seductive, for speech is a material, sensual practice that is seeking to please (or to challenge, to enrage, but anyway to *move*). The central device of contrasting is one of the means by which Nichols strengthens the attraction of speech—any speech. Indeed, the novel insists on the sensual quality of speech, and if it does not convey this opinion implicitly through its rhetorical devices, it does so explicitly, as in the following quotation. Here, the text argues that even the Queen's English can be considered a vernacular, with all the sensuality of intonation and rhythm of Creole, differing only in its connotations: "Hartley had lived in England for a while and unfortunately for him his voice was more English than Guianese, full of subtle sarcasm and innuendoes which everyone saw as an air of superiority" (60). This does not mean that this English is recognized as a part of the Creole community. Nichols seems less interested in bringing the elements of the community together: she pictures the differences. But the text's approach to orality states clearly that Standard English cannot be opposed as a "high" written language to the "low" shared orality of the people. It functions as a socially significant speech among others. And its social function is never fixed. For Hartley, speaking Standard English is not linked to a strategy to side with neocolonial powers and to rise in the hierarchy. On the contrary, he speaks it to create some space between his colleagues and himself and to articulate his critique of persisting colonial structures. A different use of Standard English is made by a senior staff member at the Ministry of Culture. This man, who feels trapped between his affinity with the English and his imposed loyalty to the government (which is much too communist for his taste), speaks a Standard English to his subordinates. But when he enters into dialogue with a colleague on his own level, he smoothly switches to a familiar Creole, which now functions as the vehicle of middle-class male bonding. Thus, Standard English is used to emphasize hierarchical difference. It is not in itself a marker of social superiority; it is dropped in favor of the Creole that expresses direct bonding, direct intimacy with people he considers his equals. Then Creole becomes the sign for social superiority, as it testifies to his familiarity with high-class people. Indeed, as Jean d'Costa stated in a different argument, those who think that "[t]he continuum would possess a magical one-to-one correspondence with the whole range of life, generating without doubt or conflict all of the registers relating to 'any given social context'" (255) miss the subtlety and the paradox in the actual use of Standard English and the different Creoles as markers of shifting differences. So, *Morning Sky* forsakes the certainty of always matching one register or language to one sort of character. Instead, it concentrates on the subtleties of actual speech. The selection of and the switching between these forms of language use take on meaning within specific exchanges, within specific contexts. I'll elaborate some of the implications of this understanding of language as an always situated, relative practice below. What can be underlined already is that this notion of language as speech and address necessarily refers to the seductive aspects of language, too.

The novel revels in the pleasure that speaking, and listening to, all kinds of languages generates. Creole can function as the speech of closeness, certainly, but the novel endows all registers and languages with a rich, sensual quality. However, it leans not only upon the speakerly qualities of Creole or other forms of speech to attain a certain sensuality in its language use. It also brings into play other literary means to create this effect. Emphasizing and creating contrasts is one I have already discussed. Another device is the thematizing of focalization and the visual. This second device does not merely serve aesthetical ends, though. In fact, it forms a crucial knot in the novel's thematics of orality, visuality, isolation and belonging. The next section will develop this argument.

On the Borders of the Creole Community: Archie

Morning Sky situates the main point of focalization on the very border of the lower-class Creole community. The following fragment illustrates the situation:

Archie seized the opportunity to interrupt. "That woman has no regard for Sunday," he said, referring to Ivy Payne who has just put on her dukebox, playing Sparrow's "May-May—making love one day with a girl they calling May-May. Making love one day with a girl they calling May-May. I pick up May-May by the railway. . . . "

"This is the sort of thing I have to put up with every day," he added as the calypso got louder, "and the thing is she chooses all the vulgar tunes, none of the nice pieces."

"I know, old boy. They're from a different class," said Conrad soothingly. (134)

The bawdy song, in Creole, by one of Trinidad's most famous calypsonians serves here to represent working-class culture. In the eyes of the story's father, Archie, it is an unsuitable noise that does not respect the sanctity of Sunday; it shamelessly opposes loudness and vulgar sexuality to the required silence and spirituality of the Lord's day. Archie articulates his distance from this milieu. He is even opposed to it.

In this and many other parts of the novel, focalization lies with Archie, the father of the main protagonist, Gem. Until his retirement and move to Georgetown, with which the novel opens, Archie was a head teacher. At first sight he represents the language of authority. His narrative and that of his few friends (like Conrad) is most often rendered in a Creole that is very close to Standard English or West Indian Standard. Nevertheless, his authority is never stable. In the fragment above, for example, the offensive calypso is quoted in fuller length than strictly necessary, and, even if Archie is granted the means to utter his complaints in directly reported speech, the narrator makes it clear that his words are all but drowned by the roar of the juicy song. Here, as elsewhere in the novel, Archie is placed as a lonely and vulnerable figure against the turbulent and irresistibly obtrusive sphere of Creole. It is the sphere of a varied, multiple oral community, which the novel likes to present in colorful, tasty fragments. In this novel, all communality is connected to the ordinary people, those who live in the yards, and to the Creole they use. Those who do not belong to the yards are represented as individuals who stand in a distant relation to the Creole community, never as members of some other collectivity. In this regard, Archie differs from Allan, Angel's father, who is always part of the community (if only by virtue of his womanizing), even if his children sometimes think his political opinions obsolete or opportunist (200, 233, 283, but see 244 too). But Allan's daughter Angel is his very image, and she is as hot-tempered as he is. They root each other in the multiple collectivity.

Archie, then, is a loner. But he comes from poor stock himself: his parents were poor, he was an only child, and his mother died when he was still young; he has always needed to work hard, and he has always felt lonesome and isolated. If he feels closed off from the community, it is not because he is middle-class by birth. Archie's position is one of lack. His highly ambivalent attitude toward "his people" is expressed in his position as a headmaster, or the "Teach," as he is affectionately called. After his move to Georgetown, this kind epithet makes him feel nostalgic and mild (107, 154). But the name holds distance as well as intimacy, as it refers to schooling (the process that potentially alienates from the oral community), and thus to literacy, as well as to the familiarity that is characteristic of the Creole community of "his people." Archie is condemned to this ambivalence. He is excluded from an intimate, physical relationship on the basis of equality, such as Clara has with the people around her. Read from a psychoanalytical perspective, his is almost a classical situation; he, the male, is incited by the threat of his lack to identify with the phallic image of Power, that is, Standard English and aspects of the colonial power. Archie has learned to speak with authority and to climb up to the position of a head teacher. But he is never free of the anxiety caused by his initial lack. Therefore, he has become the anxious, often frustrated spectator of the sphere that, in his eyes, always refers to his lack. For the Creole community of which he is the observer stands for the poverty from which he has escaped. However, it is also the closeness and communality for which he has longed and that he had to miss in his own lonely youth. Archie adored his mother, who died when he was twelve, and he respected her so much that he sacrificed conformity to his classmates for her. Her death must have meant the ultimate condemnation to loneliness, even if her spirit still dwells with him. Therefore, I assume that his lack, partly projected in his isolation from the community, will always also refer to his missing her, too.

Archie sometimes peevishly dubs the Creole community a woman's world—"all this womanness" (10). In this way, it is connected not only to his mother but also to his wife, Clara, Gem's mother. Clara identifies much more with this oral community: "Clara herself wasn't averse to all the calypsoes and could be heard humming *Bury Me Under the Tray of Dalphoori* or *Love in the Cemetery*" (120). Her closeness to the people of the yards, who live with calypso, is not to Archie's liking: "When she came back into the bedroom Archie said 'Aieee' in a suffering kind of way. 'I suppose you know what you're doing. This is their way of trying to get close'" (46). In *Morning Sky*, Clara is the image of fullness and sensuality. Archie sees her as such, but he also fears that she will be contaminated by the abhorred poorer community, that "they" will come too close and get under her skin. And indeed, they come very close to that skin. The comment on "all this womanness" above is made on the occasion of Clara's belly being anointed by a woman from the village they left for the town. Clara surrenders easily to this sphere of sensuality. For Archie, who has worked hard to enter the sphere of order and authority, this women's world might pose the threat of the chaotic, presymbolic sphere of the womb—degraded by poverty. Indeed, adopting Archie's fearful yet eager perspective, the novel makes an effort to picture the community of the village and the yard as a physical, sensual, uninhibited, and irrational sphere. The intensity of this description makes it understandable why the poor, lower-class disorder causes Archie so much anxiety, while its feminine fullness also forces him to be an ambivalently longing observer of its unruly existence. The community that is also associated with the feminine is the ambiguous site of what he fears and what he misses.

If one understands this ambivalent situation, it becomes clear why focalization plays such an important role in the novel's presentation of Archie, especially if its role is compared to that in *Angel*. There, the focalization al-

ways lies within the community, even if the protagonist with whom the focalization lies tries to break away from the community. In Nichols's novel
the vernacular community is the object of the painful focalization of protagonists (Archie, but also Gem) who hover on its borders. The result is
that focalization in the novel becomes a difficult, anxiety-raising process. In
these moments, the novel closely follows Archie's focalizing. He is surrounded by disquieting sights and sounds he'd rather not remark upon; if
he sees or hears, then he also reflects on the distance he wishes to keep.
"Sometimes from the side of his platform window Archie could catch a
glimpse of a dress tail disappearing up his backsteps. And when the wind
blew he got a whiff of the provoking gales of kitchen laughter" (24). It is
not Clara's togetherness with the women of the community that is represented in this fragment but Archie's distanced, awkward observation of the
event. To elaborate the point, it is Archie's male gaze that genders the Creole community as female. By following his anguished gaze, the novel discloses this categorization as the effect of a partial, gendered perspective.

However, if in this novel the Creole community functions as a feminine sphere, it does not do so exclusively. *Morning Sky* does not lean too
heavily upon psychoanalytical schemes, even if it likes to play with some
of the contrasts offered by the Freudian tales. The community that plays
such an important role in Archie's life and in the novel is first and foremost
determined by class, ethnic, and racial differences. If it were the female
sphere only, then Archie would have been a much more tortured voyeur.
As it is, he himself often admits to being part of the unruly masses, as his
repeating complaint about "my people" indicates:

He was to make that comment, "My people, like they're cursed, man," throughout
the years in his Princess Street home.

He made it when the little shirt-tail boys tried to walk over the narrow
drinking-water pipe that ran alongside his bridge. He made it once when someone picked his pocket. And he made it at weekends when Ivy Payne held her
weekly Saturday night dances and Sunday picnics. (120)

Archie is part of the community not only by an act of his own will, but
above all because the Creole community does what all oral communities
do—address him. Archie is addressed as "Teach," and he is seduced by it
to acknowledge the people as his own.[3] Of course, this is not enough to
erase his (male, middle-class) lack. The importance of his role as outside

focalizer is not undone by it. Before going deeper into the role of focalization and the gaze in the novel, I will discuss the forceful sensuality of the practice of address.

The Sensuality of Being Addressed: Dinah

Archie is one half of the contrasting pair formed by husband and wife, but in fact the novel is structured around four different poles. In addition to the adult male and female, both occupying different spheres in the adult cultural order, there are the older daughter, Dinah, who is in the midst of her battle with the adult laws, and the younger daughter, Gem, who has not yet entered this adult world. There is also a little brother, but he never becomes a narrative agent. Instead of the son, the usual hero of so many coming-of-age stories, *Morning Sky* stages two daughters. With the help of different registers of Creole and an expressive Standard English, the novel depicts the space in which they will form their social and speaking subjectivity. Archie's distant attitude marks one degree of involvement with the oral community. Clara's intimate involvement with the women's collectivity establishes another point of reference. The shopkeepers, the children from the neighborhood, the colleagues, and the neighbors who form the context of their daily life offer other positions to identify with or to address. Gem's older sister, Dinah, is the one who actually engages in the process of identification and differentiation elicited by this social and discursive space. She is of the age to inscribe herself into the cultural space. She finds that her education and family background place her somewhere between the "low" world of the yard and the Creole to which her mother does not really belong but that she certainly refers to, and her father's "high" sphere (Christian 1990).

At first, Dinah is a schoolteacher, just like her father. Then she decides, against her father's wishes, to accept a position with the Ministry of Culture. Her work consists partly of proofreading texts that will be published. From a teacher/lecturer/speaker, she turns into a professional reader.[4] Yet this change offers her greater freedom; she no longer copies her father and does not strive for the rigid order of education and Standard English (9) anymore, but she finds a position as a reader of and a listener to other discourses with other kinds of authority. She enjoys having herself addressed by others and by other ideas, especially if they are subversive. Dinah may be compared to the protagonist of *Angel*. Dinah and Angel are both engaged in an often politically articulated battle with their fathers (Nichols 1986: 127; Collins 1987: 199 ff; see above). Gem, the secretive onlooker and eavesdropper, is still under the lee of the battles the older daughters are waging.

Dinah's position is revealing when compared to that of Angel. Angel turns out to be a teacher of English who enters into political discussions with her students. She allows them to talk "bad," commenting that their own vernacular is not "bad" but "a different language"—English "isn't better than our own language" (236). Angel's choice to leave the university and to enter professional life is a conscious political choice to be able to connect to social life (166). Dinah, however, started to teach when she was only fourteen (23). Her speaking in the classroom must have been a mere "citing" of a dominant discourse (Tiffin 1993). It is not an instance of a successful oral position, as Angel's revolutionary teachership certainly is. If Dinah chooses to become a reader, she becomes a reader of the anticolonial. It does not turn her into a member of the oral community, nor into a speaker of nation language. International Marxism (instead of the unsuccessful pretended socialism of the local government) is the medium by which she articulates her anticolonial critique, and it is not a Marxism rooted in a community of which she feels a part. It is clearly an imported notion, brought to her by the individualist and slightly condescending Hartley, who is also a speaker of a British Standard English. So, Dinah's turn away from colonial mimicry does not lead her into nationalism and "orality," as a more schematic postcolonial path would. Standard English becomes the medium by which she can take the distance she needs to grow.[5]

There is one important sense in which Dinah can be seen as approaching the oral community, and that is in her desire to be addressed. Following Ward's observation on orality, being open to address is an "oral" quality. But Dinah's desire is not vernacular. It is certainly sensual, though, as she likes the sinewy young man Hartley who guides her readings very much. And it inaugurates her as a speaking subject, as a subject of desire, and as a moving subject: she moves away from the universe of her parents, from colonial discourse, and from nationalist discourse, and, skipping work and obligatory organized protest marches, she prepares for the definitive move away from home. She may yet return, like Angel, and try to get in touch again with the community; but that move lies beyond the scope of the book. Dinah's desire to be addressed by anticolonial critical theories is a necessary phase for someone developing into a speaker in her own right, whether she is in a strange place (migrants in Europe or the United States) or whether she is in a place she does not belong to yet (Dinah).

This episode of opening oneself to address can have its sensual aspects, as Dinah's story shows. The story lingers on this episode, suggesting Dinah's involvement in her new openness in very subtle ways. This openness is pictured as the capacity not only to listen (and, already, speak) but also to *look* further than before. Consequently, even in times of threat and disaster she has an eye for details outside the sphere of violence, and the tenderness to share her observation with others. Thus, after a night of collective vigil against arson attacks: "But it was not until dawn that people ventured back to their beds. Gem sneaked into Dinah's bed and was surprised when Dinah placed an arm around her and said, 'Look,' pointing through the open window to a reddish-looking star in the early morning sky" (141). It is one of the very few instances in which the sisters share an intimate moment. They share a moment of vision. Their shared gaze is very unlike the tortured gaze of Archie. It is not restrained or difficult; they look through an open window, not a closed one. It has no voyeuristic nature but moves away from the restricted, narrow sites of the forced acts of voyeuristic looking to find the largeness of space, and with it the desire to move away from the confinements of one's own background. This escape, which in Dinah's case is also an association with other discourses, takes place through the opportunity to be addressed. Dinah has already become skilled in this oral art. She knows how to have herself addressed, even by a red star.[6]

Her little sister is the champion of another narrative skill ambiguously linked to the oral practice. In the next section I will elaborate on this skill and develop the link between the thematizing of focalization and the gaze, (Archie's) lack, sensuality, and orality.

Focalization and the Visual: Gem

In twenty very intimate fragments scattered among the chapters of the story, the girl Gem is made into a focalizer. In these fragments, the narrator addresses Gem with "you," and in a quiet, intense tone Gem's observations are told to her, as if the narrator is retelling her the events of her day when seated next to her bed, at bedtime. The voice is in a very slight Creole; sometimes only the -s of the third person singular is dropped ("Your mother tell you . . . to be careful," 39), or the auxiliary "to be" ("And your twelfth birthday coming up," 155). Gem hardly ever speaks. The narrator speaks to her and for her, telling her her own history. Sometimes the narrator's voice is indistinguishable from Gem's own words. In this closed address lies an invitation to adopt an identity as a speaker. Spoken subject (Silverman 1984: 47–50, 198 ff) is invited to become speaking subject. But she can become so only by learning to look for herself.

Just like Archie, Gem hovers on the borders of the community. In fact, they are both relative outsiders who focus on the community from a certain distance. But Gem is a child and has not yet had the chance to enter it. In contrast, Archie has left it (ambiguously) behind. Gem's focalizing is not structured by lack. Far from it. For children, the secret look (which is reminiscent of the voyeuristic look but does not yet obey the logic of voyeurism) is often determined by their desire to know and thus is related to their gradual entry into the adult order. The interludes that feature Gem show that she is an intelligent person who is eager to learn. The narrator reports how she digests all kinds of information, from jumbie tales to the exciting things to see in Georgetown. There is not the pained urgency of the anxious male in her gaze. Even if she is an outsider to the adult community just as her father is, she is secure in her position as a child. In contrast to her father, she belongs. In the fragments devoted to her vision, she is spoken to in her own words, and her vision is acknowledged as valuable in its own right. Gem lacks the male lack.

Nor does she suffer the failing, partial gaze ascribed to women in classical psychoanalytical thought (Silverman 1988: 31). Her child's gaze is merely one way of observing, and it cannot be isolated from a complex of different faculties of observation, like smelling, hearing, touching. There is no question of a privileged position of the gaze, as is the case with Archie. Gem's ways of observing are relatively autonomous, as they do not follow any adult patterns of desire and lack. But they are not innocent or without passion. The interludes testify of the lusts that go with Gem's observation. At first these are connected to the pleasures of motion and rhythm (1–2, 65), food (29, 75, 136), conjuring rituals (12), jokes and performances (49, 65, 75), smell (76), touch (21, 75, 90–91), until slowly the pleasure of looking establishes itself (38, 48) and takes on erotic overtones. When her gaze gains in intensity she becomes curious about what female bodies look like and spies upon the beautiful woman next door when she is half naked (101). Approaching womanhood, she then starts to look at herself, slowly assuming the position of the one who is looked at (101, 155).

Gem's capacities of observation are only relatively autonomous, for they are clearly infantile, and she will have to outgrow them. Therefore, she already follows adult examples of observation. It is especially her gaze (rather than her smell, etc.) that is directed by others. For example, she follows her mother's gaze.

Shortly after their move to Georgetown, Gem explores the beach while thinking of the stories about her mother's youth, one of these featuring the "four-eye fish." The short fragment ends with the following sentences: "You walk past the Round House with the militia band playing and you could see the lighthouse, a tall tall red-and-white striped building. You find a few dead four-eye fish washed up on the shore" (39). Gem's history is shaped against her mother's history. She finds the fish of her mother's story dead. First, her finding shows her mother's story to be true and palpable. Second, it also shows her mother's story to be history, past tense. The fish are dead. Her mother's gaze is no longer relevant. It is Gem's gaze now that counts, and it embraces her mother's past youth history as well as the buildings and creatures of her own life. Still, the fish she finds have four eyes: on these, Gem's eyes and her mother's eyes cross and meet; the fish links and preserves their gazes, bearing testimony to their close bond as observing girls in the same surroundings, which are dominated by aggressive male symbols.

There is another character who might have been an excellent guide for Gem's gaze. It is a character virtually embodying the notion of focalization. This is Archie's friend Conrad, formerly a photographer for the Criminal Investigation Department. "There is nobody else like him," Gem judges (75). Conrad is a focalizer by virtue of his occupation as a photographer and his monocle, but also because his house is full of radios and electric wires connecting him to the outside world (69). He loves to listen to speakers at political meetings. He does not speak about his own preferences, sexual or political. Rather, he makes a spectacle of himself and has others look at him and speak about him. He dresses outrageously. He keeps white mice as pets, and when he carries them with him, they unexpectedly shoot out of a sleeve; he could be a spy, or a private eye, taking on disguises and disguising his gaze. Gem is absolutely taken in by his person. Yet, she does not follow his gaze in the same way as she follows her mother's. To the contrary, her gaze is hindered by his adult gaze. But this experience holds a lesson. When she enters the darkroom in his studio she is taken into a total blindness, "alone in time and darkness with Conrad" (82). This does not intimidate her any more than his modest caresses at other times. But "Sometimes you're glad when he opens the door again though" (82). In fact, Conrad teaches her about the necessity of (temporary) blindness for an indirect, more lasting focalization: the darkroom is needed to develop his pictures, which represent and stabilize a process of looking. But Gem, who is not yet preoccupied with looking and representation, does not understand this lesson as one she could benefit from herself. She does not yet need to manipulate her own gaze or that of others. As far as she is concerned, the dark is Conrad's device for constructing his very personal representations that do not concern her. He takes her picture before she can fix her "mouth in a proper smile" (82), and he silently follows his own devices during the process of creation, leaving her free.

Gem, in return, makes Conrad the object of her own focalization, which is still very idiosyncratic and linked to her contained children's world on the edge of the community. She takes her own sensual pleasure from him; she sits on his lap, on his shoulders, eats the candy he makes for her, sniffs his smells. At a certain point she feels too big to loll on Conrad's knee anymore. Then her children's perspective is breaking open, and the dominance of adult discourses and adult desires begins to be felt. Gem needs sensualities other than candy and the caresses of a middle-aged unmarried man to engage herself in the erotics of address. Yet, it was Conrad who first addressed her and named her in terms of the adult world, by telling her "you were a clever child. You were going to be somebody great when you grew up. You're wiser than your ten years" (75). He is the first one who refers to an adult order in which she might find a relevant position. But he is no guide, no intermediary between worlds to her, no trickster figure. He has no real access to Gem's world. Moreover, Gem does not really see separate worlds. She is fully part of her children's world, just as the fragments in which she is addressed testify of her own story, running parallel to but not yet overlapping the adult narrative.

If Conrad is not suitable as a guide it is not because he occupies her father's position. His attitude of focalizing is very different from Archie's. It misses his reluctance and probable anxiety. Conrad is able to look at the most gruesome images because he can keep his distance by photographing them (he took "grisly murder photographs with meticulous care," 69). It seems that Conrad knows how to play with the gaze. He gives many examples of the playful manipulation of his own look and that of others. He does not feel excluded and isolated. If he is a loner, this may be by free choice. He lives outside the realm of heterosexuality. He never marries and lives in a close and devoted relationship with his elderly mother until she dies. Whereas Archie's lack originates in his devotion to and missing of his own mother (15–16), Conrad never leaves his mother. His insensibility to heterosexual laws of identification and separation makes him also unsuitable for the associated anxieties and urgencies of the look. He looks, exposes himself in deceitful, playful ways, and he speaks, listens, and is silent according to his own secret needs. Thus, he is an excellent partner for the childishly perverse Gem, who also revels in this kind of play. It is true that Conrad's erotics extend to Gem, but this does not separate them yet. He expresses it in such a way that it is very close to Gem's own way of satisfying her need for the pleasure of touch, taste, smell, sound, and sight.

The focalizer *par excellence* is a man: Conrad, the father's companion. One could place another character opposite him as a female counterpart: Rose, Clara's cherished bosom friend. In theory, she could also be an excellent guide for Gem. But she is not. Rose "sees" things, but in quite a different way from Conrad, who has largely invested in a technology of observation (his radio, his photography) and was paid for turning his observations into documents for the benefit of the government. Rose has visions and dreams. There is no need for her to spy or to use technology to gain knowledge about the goings-on around her, as she is considered part of the Creole community, which is the site of her interest. However, Rose's presence is not as central to the story as Conrad's. She takes the stage in the very first and the very last part of the story, in both cases especially to warn Clara of unseen dangers and to offer her a remedy. Conrad enters the story well before the second half, and stays in it until the last pages.

Both Conrad and Rose are protectors. Both dare to look very deeply, even into the face of death. Conrad learned to cope with human bodily violence in two different ways: by keeping his distance and by using violence—he hits well, and he carries a gun. Rose recognizes supernatural evil and as yet indiscernible diseases, and she uses herbs and probably obeah too to counter them. Thus, Rose's remedies are in line with the novel's presentation of observation as a practice that is basically sensual. It is rooted in the body; it aims for utmost intimacy and even identity (85). Rose and Clara occupy the female site of orality, with a specific female notion of focalization in which looking, touching, and smelling are closely linked.

The sensual approach to observation as a pleasurable, binding practice can be understood as a gender-specific view, and it echoes, for example, Kristeva's notion of the semiotic. The daughters who are coming of age are intrigued much less by this bodily focalization than by its male counterpart, but their interest is sensual too—it is awakened by the apparently greater detachment it offers from the daily life they are growing away from. The novel places the two different modes of observation next to each other as a man's way and a woman's way. It associates a relatively Standard English to the distanced mode of looking, whereas the close, sensual woman's way is related to the easiness and communality of a deeper Creole.

However, this woman's way is also structured by certain forms of lack and painful difference. For if there is bonding, there are also those whom one bonds against. Clara's relationship with Rose is deepened by their suspicion and rejection of another friend, who may be using obeah. And Clara's recognition of her closeness with Rose is told retrospectively, when their daily intimacy is already a thing of the past. So every girl has to enter an adult semiotic system that is structured by lack, be it the Creole community or the middle-class world of distance and Standard English. In this way, *Morning Sky* undoes the romantic notion of Creole as fullness, casting it as firmly established in the symbolic. The lack gradually installs itself in the life of Gem, too. This happens through the intervention of colonial politics and its associated violence. Gem's development illustrates the crucial impact of the gaze in one's growth into a full speaking subject—which, in *Morning Sky*, is a subject commanding Creole as well as Standard English. We have seen how the political and the personal are brought together by a flexible use of Creole in Collins's epic novel *Angel*. *Morning Sky* summons both (a slight) Creole and Standard English to take up the challenge of relating these very different aspects of life. However, it is important that it relies on the help of a subtle manipulation of childish gaze and adult gaze to offer a different but very effective solution to the problem of representing the political as an aspect of personal life. I will explain this narrative strategy by concentrating on the many interludes in which Gem's story is told.

Gem's narrative consists of a series of intimate sensual experiences, stories, and anecdotes about the people around her. Gradually, the political events start to have their effects on Gem's story in the interludes, too. The main narrative concerns the tensions around the general strike, the mass demonstrations and the pickets, and the police attacks on the people. The city bursts into violence, lootings, and fires.[7] The Walcotts decide to send their children to safety. Gem's perspective is caught in the following fragment: "As you walk you keep looking back at the skies too, counting all the orange blazes like billowing bottle lamps in the sky. You feel like a girl in one of those schoolgirl comics. A heroine looking back at her city in ruins" (108). Gem dwells on the colors produced by the destruction. She seems to weigh up the experience of taking flight and finds a suitable narrative form for it. Instead of panic, she feels "calm. Full of a calm, frightened excitement" (108). She savors the moments.

The next fragment is about the pleasures of kite flying, with only a minor reference to the fires and the troops that were sent in to control the situation. In the following fragments, there is much about food, and some hopeful children's considerations like these: "Every afternoon you listen for the voice of the Trade Union president on the radio. You're anxious to hear his last words after the singing of solidarity forever. It's always the same; 'The strike continues.' You want the strike to continue. Your heart lift at the words. No school" (131). The strike means hardship, lack of the necessary supplies, political tensions and violence; but none of this matters to Gem, who has her own priorities. Yet, a few pages later, Gem is trapped in a mass of people when a bomb explodes; the next moment, she is all but choked by tear gas. She is affected by the severe wounding of people she knows. Finally, she is shocked by the death in the fire of one of her playmates. When she first sees the house on fire, "you feel as if your heart is going to burst. Nothing can stop it from bursting now" (148). She witnesses the plight of people in the fire, "And you can't remember much else after that. At times when something too terrible is happening, your mind or your heart don't want to believe it and so you let everything become hazy and not real. Teddy and all his seven brothers and sisters burning to death and his mother and father. Only the one sister who jumped, escaping" (149). Witnessing this unspeakable event marks the end of Gem's youth. Death and violence have come right into her child's world, and they end feeling, and the capacity for sensual experience. At this moment focalization, the act of looking, unmasks itself as a potentially horrifying, unbearably gruesome act. Looking is no longer a sensual pleasure. It brings her face to face with death, which is clearly the site of the boundary of her own capacity to observe: she retreats from the act of looking and from reality altogether. Having stumbled upon a deadly barrier, her gaze will, from now on, change its direction. Only now can Gem learn Conrad's lesson of the need to manipulate one's gaze. With it, she starts to discover the benefit of distance, which is, among other things, implied in the use of Standard English.[8]

After the fragment about the fire, there is only one more fragment in which Gem's position as a focalizer is celebrated. It is also the end of the novel. This short text suggests the developments I indicated above. It begins with a short look at the burned space where Teddy's house had been. Gem in fact tries to "see" in the way Rose sees: she tries to sense her friend's spirit. Then, in several definitive moves, the fragment announces Gem's twelfth birthday, narrating her experience of growing breasts, her diminishing feelings for candy and for Conrad, and the approaching of the exams for entering secondary school. Her focalizing is averted from the boundary installed by death toward, first, sexuality, and, second, the more dominant forms of knowledge that are taught at school. It becomes a "Standard Focalization," as it no longer belongs to a complex of faculties of observation. Her taste changes, she doesn't crave candy anymore, and thus this faculty vanishes from a complex of childishly, perversely pleasant sensations. Gem moves toward a more sophisticated art of reading. It will bring her the capacity to manipulate her gaze and summon a distance that will guard her against physical confrontations with sights too horrible to behold. Distance is installed: the source of freedom and alienation.

The fragment ends on a characteristic view of the garden full of plants, fruits, and vegetables, which echoes the description of the lands around the house in the village the Walcotts left at the beginning of the story. However, this time Gem's view is doubled with her father's:

And your house is up for sale. Quite a few people come to look at it. Your father look at it too, walking round it, looking at it from the back garden where everything is blooming. The gooseberry tree laden with fat gooseberries, the pumpkins swelling big and heavy on the ground, the tomatoes ripe and plenty, and the bora climbing fresh and green as if it didn't care that the person who had planted it would be leaving. (156)

The person who had planted it is Archie, not Gem. In these final sentences, then, the intimate voice is paired with the vision of Gem's father. The effect is as if Gem is looking at her father, who is looking. Archie is once again someone who has to leave a thing of plenty behind. On the other hand, he himself is the creator of this fullness. So, in the end, his lack is soothed. In the very last phrases, Gem is no longer the addressee. The primary focalization is shared by the narrator and Gem, whose voices seem to overlap. Very subtly, Gem's newfound capacity to look in a more detached way, ready to explore laws, desires, and prohibitions, is linked to the suggestion of her readiness to speak for herself. She is ready to speak and to look for herself, to look at people in the adult world and offer her own comments.

Difference: The Creole Context

We can now trace how *Morning Sky* uses the tensions between Creole and Standard English to create a sensual universe that is, paradoxically, unveiled as the product of an often male or colonial desire at the very moment of its installation. The novel's play with the oral is very different from *Angel*'s, as I'll show—it doesn't resist postcolonial theorizing, and it doesn't claim an oral or performative aesthetics. Yet, if one reads *Morning Sky* with an eager ear for its oral and Creole orientation, one will discern a specificity that exceeds postcolonial theorizing. I'll show this by retracing the narrative. Then it will become clear that this specificity results from the central position of the Creole community.

Gem takes her place in the pattern in which *Morning Sky* links focalization and the themes of sensuality, orality, lack, and looking, themes that are always related to Creole or Standard English. The process that installs lack, and by which a child becomes an adult member of society, is represented as a process by which one learns to manipulate one's gaze. This process is described in relation to the Creole community: the theme of looking helps to indicate the position of the protagonists (as border dwellers) in relation to the Creole community. This in itself is already a significant choice: it is not the imperial center that functions as the focal point, or the inevitable site to address, but the decolonizing nation-to-be. What's more, this new focal point is imagined not as a unequivocal center one might belong to but as an ambivalent and complex site to refer to.

The act of looking, then, always implies a certain distance between subject and object of the look, most often the Creole community. This distance to Creole is linked to a certain closeness to Standard English. For Nichols, there is nothing unbearably tragic about the lack implied in the privileging and isolation of the gaze that is associated with the dominant language. If this novel is about split subjects, or about subjects in the process of splitting, it emphasizes that this split is partly inevitable. The entry into Standard English is also enabling. In addition, quite in line with psychoanalytic notions, it is related to the organization of desire. Standard English is reinvented as a potentially sensual, radical speech. In itself, this is not a highly innovative move. As Belinda Edmondson argues, even Brathwaite, the Caribbean advocate of Creole as nation language, defends the need for "standard" English literary forms as a means to convey a better picture of the Caribbean condition (Edmondson 1994). More generally, then, this linguistic and cultural alienation is seen to also hold the promise of a wider context of identification in which not all of the sensual or political aspects of orality need to be abandoned. What is innovative in *Morning Sky* is its refusal to situate Standard English outside the realm of address and sensuality, thus implicitly criticizing Ashcroft's proposal to differentiate the ideal norm of Standard English from the englishes of the colonies. One of the crucial aspects *Morning Sky* wishes to retain is the capacity to open oneself to be addressed by people, discourses, or events (as Ward also underlines). It is a talent that prevents people from surrendering to alienation and lack, as Dinah and even Archie show. The text takes the risk that it will eventually land them outside the sphere of Creole. *Angel,* in contrast, associates this openness to be addressed exclusively in relation to the centripetal forces of the community.

 Morning Sky's nuanced perspective on orality and Creole does not, of course, result in a specific oral aesthetics, which would claim a radical difference from the kind of postcolonial writing favored by postcolonial theory. Nichols's text establishes an aesthetics formed by different elements, of which some are borrowed from oral practices of which several are discussed above: the pleasure in the pure play of language that is inherent to oral or Creole performances is extended to Standard English; the text enjoys presenting strings of anecdotes and interludes rather than one strong linear development; it emphasizes the appeal and potential of convincing address (and in its interludes it also uses interesting structures of address itself). And finally, it grants not only focalization but also the visual an important place. This interest in the visual might be connected to its sympathetic relation to orality. Certain styles of narration in oral contexts can be characterized by an abundance of imagery. Ramchand explains that dialects in Caribbean novels display certain common features: "These are: improvisation in syntax and lexis; direct and pithy expression; a strong tendency towards the use of image, especially of the personification type; and various kinds of repetition of syntactic structure and lexis combining with the spoken voice to produce highly rhythmic effects" (1983: 107). In *Morning Sky*, the use of images occurring in Creole is extended to a general sensitivity for meaningful images and a taste for the visual, too. The narrator's Standard English, which makes ample use of visual descriptions, testifies to this preference.[9] The abundance of visual (and other sensual) descriptions also serves to create a sensual image of the Creole community in Standard English, as if from outside. This strategy differs strikingly from *Angel*'s descriptions of the oral community. The Grenadian community is hardly described in objectifying looks. It takes care of its own looking and resists any purely aesthetic discourse.

This specific manipulation of the visual and its appropriation of central stereotypes in colonial discourse, notably the stereotyped associations of Creole with sensuality and sexuality, falls within the scope of postcolonial theory (with its emphasis on mimicry and ambivalent appropriation).[10] Most important, the novel often focalizes upon the Creole world by means of a tortured eye, driven by lack. This choice intensifies the sensation of Creole as a sphere and a speech of fullness and sensuality. So, where Creole refers to the body itself, Standard English stands for the desire for the body. It is important to see that the text does not use Creole as such to establish a language of sensuality; it does not aim to broaden the scope of Creole in that way. But it explains, subtly and implicitly, that the outsider's notion of a desired, fulfilling sensual Creole sphere is the gendered and ethnic construction of either a colonial gaze, or the gaze of the many others, who, sadly, realize they do not belong. The sensuality lies in the eyes of the beholder, not in the Creole sphere itself. Here one could read a subtle critique of both colonial and nationalist stereotype.[11]

Morning Sky plays with the linguistic multiplicity of the Caribbean, and with the tensions between Creole and Standard English. Its relaxed refusal to restrict itself to Creole oral genres as its main source of inspiration may be linked to its focus on conflict: Brathwaite states, for example, that these genres (such as calypso, reggae, yard talk) fail in conveying the sense of alienation and chaos that in his eyes is the essence of the Caribbean experience (Edmondson 1994). To explore this chaos, then, *Morning Sky* plays with some speakerly conventions, as well as some readerly ones; it plays with the position of the outsider, restaging the pained voyeurism (of colonizers, middle-class men, and, perhaps, migrants) to intensify the sensuality of the Creole universe, thereby laying bare and mocking old stereotypes of the sensuality of Creole. But the novel also eagerly uses this stereotype to create a wonderfully sensual story that brings both the Creole and the (wrongly) assumedly untouchable Standard English into its orbit. Its play of appropriating, mimicking, criticizing, and subverting can well be analyzed within postcolonial theory. But it differs in its structure of address. It doesn't address the imperial center, nor does it only address colonial discourses about, say, the sensuality of Creole. For ultimately, it shares with *Angel* a firm refusal of a romantic view of the Creole community.

This can be seen in the approach to violence in both novels. They take different positions in the crucial theme of violence in Caribbean experience. Indeed, Caribbean societies are characterized by their highly multiform and hybrid nature; the Caribbean is eminently capable of incorporating and integrating widely different peoples, cultures, and views. But in the Caribbean, conflict takes on a more violent form than, for example, Ward's view allows. Both novels illustrate the fact. In both texts, we find large-scale imperialist violence paired with government or oppositional violence, as well as with revolutionary force and violence. In *Angel* this national violence is part of communal (post)colonial life. Even within families beatings occur regularly. In *Morning Sky*, however, where conflict abounds too, violence marks the very border of social and relational life.[12] It marks the end of reason, and above all the end of sensuality. I insert a last quote to illustrate this important point. A few years after their marriage, Archie recognizes that his passionate feelings for his wife are mixed with pain and jealousy.

"What would you do if I was to hit you, eh?" For he badly wanted to hit her. To slap her cheeks hard. To slap her for her own lovely childhood and his hard empty one. To slap her for the pain and jealousy she was already arousing in him.

They sat there staring at each other for a while, man and woman sizing each other up, testing each other. Different emotions chased across her face, but when her voice came it was very calm, "Make sure that whenever you hit me you do a very good job of it," she said. "Make sure that you don't leave an ounce of strength in my body. Make sure that I can't get up again, you hear."

Archie knew she meant it. (20)[13]

Clara makes very clear that violence is not acceptable. She does not want to be addressed by it, and she does not want to address it; rather, she prefers to be ended by it. Violence exceeds speech. It is incompatible with communication, to the degree that she cannot comprehend it. When the killing and battering of people in the street commences, she is not prepared for it, and she ("protectress of human life that she was") cannot accept or comprehend it (139). Archie does accept this violence, and he thinks Clara naive for her incapability to come to terms with it. Apparently, accepting violence as a part of human nature is obvious to people from the working class (Archie's background), whereas the middle class recoils from it. Archie, for example, has had to take recourse to violence himself to end the cruelties his classmates committed against him. As *Angel* is situated right at the heart of the working class, violence is acknowledged as a part of everyday exchange, even if it is a brutal part. It is not applauded, but it is acknowledged as a collective reality. The novel *Morning Sky* as a whole treats violence much more uneasily. It is always focalized through one of the characters, who does not observe the violent scenes to their end. The sensuality of contrasting descriptions comes to a definitive halt where violence is concerned. The aesthetics of the Guyanese novel bases itself on a (sometimes playful) distancing from the oral community and from violence. *Angel,* as well as *Morning Sky*, offers the opinion that violence and orality are quite compatible, thus implicitly opposing the more romantic idea of orality as closed communal harmony. In the Caribbean, the community can never be closed—not against violent foreign intrusion, which more often than not will also attack from within. This very sharp representation of the Creole community as a politically, socially, and culturally torn reality, which is far removed from its nostalgic projections, demands a more specific approach than a general postcolonial theory has to offer.

Writing for Listeners

In both *Angel* and *Morning Sky*, we find a twofold strategy: on the one hand, they employ oral strategies, or varied references to orality or Creole;

on the other hand, their linguistic strategies deconstruct colonial discourse. After our examination of their strategies, what have we learned about the way we should understand orality in this Caribbean migrant writing?

We have seen that in *Angel* orality is the medium that explores the diversity within the community. But it doesn't do so only by using creoles as the primary language. Orality is more than just using local speeches. The text does more than just *represent* speech; instead, one should speak of an oral aesthetics organizing the text as open and dialogical, addressing the oral, multilingual community of Grenada. However, *Angel*'s orality doesn't refer to an existing communality. Rather, it creates it: it creates a *we* that in the outside world doesn't exist in exactly the same way as in the novel. This new *we* is a diverse nation, divided by many conflicts but unified by the diverse, varied spoken language that also embraces the written language of, for example, family letters. In other words, *Angel* is oriented less toward representation than toward its performative effect—nation building.

We can contextualize this definition of orality as performance by referring to Gates's notion of the speakerly text: the Africans in the Americas began to write to show they were human, and they wrote their own speech to show they were different, trying to let the text escape its white scriptorial character. This kind of orality is not just imitation or representation either. It is an act of survival and has to be understood as such. Compare this to the work of Cameroonese writer Werewere Liking, who writes to explode language, to find new words through which she can speak a new human race into being. Her search for the essential words, invested with a unique vital power shows that she, too, wants her text to perform instead of to represent. There is a relevant example by John Berger (quoted in Bhabha 1990: 315–16) that shows how much language changes in postcolonial times. Berger states sarcastically that words are endowed with different meanings when spoken by a migrant. If a migrant man says "girl," this is misunderstood as if he were a sex maniac, lusting after "our women." If a stranger speaks the word, "girl" means a trespass, the insolence of crossing into "our" territory. As soon as you begin to utter it, language has unforeseen effects. Fixed meanings pale by the destructive, multiplying effects of power-infested colonial and racist structures of address. But postcolonial writers can use these same mechanisms to effectuate the sharpest critiques of these same structures.

A brilliant example is a short story by Dutch Surinamese writer Ellen

Ombre ("Mijmering van een autochtoon"—"Reverie of an autochthon"), which very convincingly quotes the spoken discourse of a working-class woman of Amsterdam (Ombre 1994). Remarkably, the story presents itself not as a short naturalistic sketch of an Amsterdam working-class woman's life but as the monologue of an *"autochtoon."* This term, used to designate the white Dutch, immediately invokes its much more frequently used counterpart, "allochtoon," which literally means "born elsewhere" but is usually reserved for the nonwhite Dutch. In this way, the title itself already thematizes the relation between those who, by right of birth, belong, and those who don't.[14] The rest of the story also focuses on the theme of migration; and the rest of the collection of short stories reinforces this theme as well. The juicy monologue, however, reveals that the assumed authochthon wasn't born in Amsterdam after all: she is an economic refugee from the poor, prewar Southern Netherlands. Paradoxically, the narrated *history*[15] pleads for naturalizing migration as an aspect of Dutch and Amsterdam identity, whereas the narrator's *text* refuses this naturalization and wishes to see migration as a sign of otherness. Race, of course, is the decisive but unspoken factor. Merely by mimicking this familiar (and in Dutch naturalist literature often celebrated) kind of speaking, by repeating it and slightly exaggerating it, the narrative lays bare the paradoxical nature of the Dutch discourse on nationality and belonging. At the same time, it calls upon the readers to witness and to testify to the irrationality and exclusionary violence of this kind of speech. Ombre's story teaches us several things: First, orality is *not* the absolute cultural difference Western oral theory often thinks it is; for this woman's talk, this easy, everyday flow of words, is the voice of a familiar Western metropole. Second, this orality is both specific (for it is linked to Amsterdam, just as *Angel* and *Morning Sky* are specifically oriented toward Grenada and Guyana) and general (for it represents a broader anticolonial strategy of the critical destruction of a broader colonial discourse). Third, this orality doesn't function as representation only, but it works because it calls on its readers to recognize its ironic strategy of deconstruction. Again, orality should first and foremost be understood as performance.

Orality, then, can be theorized as postcolonial, but it also exceeds postcolonial theory. It can be read within this context because it is often aimed at a critique of colonial discourse. But it resists the appropriation by postcolonial theory by not wishing to be interpreted within the context of

Western scriptocentrism. Postcolonial theory can often be said to favor scriptocentric readings. For example, it tends to read writing as a self-reflexive discourse, a discourse evaluating itself while expressing itself. This in itself is no reason for a stern critique: this reading is also relevant for non-Western forms of writing. To remind you of one example: the act of writing had, as Gates has shown, enormous implications. In addition, the African continent alone offers a wealth of theories on language and writing, such as the Bambara epic about the Guardian of the Word (the Sunjata epic). These theories may be referred to, or be reimagined or played with, in African writing or in the writings of the African diaspora. On the other hand, the postcolonial theoretical tendency to follow poststructuralist theories of language and subjectivity to read the body as text, and the text as body, is problematic when it comes to texts that do not wish to be read as texts alone. Texts that extend in a vivid performance, texts that wish to move their readers and to heal their communities, that want to address their readers and call upon them as witnesses, these texts do not want to be read as a scriptorial aesthetics or to be understood as an allegory of the bodily character of the text. Postcolonial theory may help us to understand the resisting, critical complexity of oral strategies in Caribbean migrants' writing, but by the writing's performative energies it evades the obstacles of a theory taking writing as its point of departure.

Let us, in conclusion, listen to the voices of the many Black women authors who articulate their own practice as an auditory art, not as the scriptorial visual art. Speaking of the position they take in relation to their community to find the medium for their writing, they depict themselves as eager, sometimes shamelessly secretive *listening* members of the oral community. The shift from *Morning Sky* to these writers is a shift from the universe of the eye to the universe of the ear. These writers relate the vernacular to the often female collective in which they were born and bred. Maya Angelou says tersely, "I write because I am a Black woman, listening attentively to her talking people" (Evans 1984: 4). And Toni Cade Bambara remembers: "[I w]ould linger recklessly in doorways, hallways, basements, soaking up overheards to convert in radio scripts I'd one day send out" (Evans 1984: 41). Note that Bambara speaks not about writing but about creating texts to be listened to instead of read. These women speak of listening and speaking when referring to their writing practice, instead of using more scriptoral notions. As writers, they declare themselves close kin to storytellers, theater performers, dub poets, griots, calypsonians, and jazz singers. This series is extended by Carolyn Cooper, who adds (with Lorna Goodison and, implicitly, Alice Walker) weavers. Cooper's comparison, however, brings textuality back in as the dominant art form to be deconstructed. But as I have argued, it is not necessary to approach orality as a critique of writing. Ghanaian writer Ama Ata Aidoo helps us to find an apt description for the oral passion toward the arts. Aidoo said in the course of an interview, "We don't always have to write for readers, we can write for *listeners*" (James 1990: 23).

Writing for listeners: offering them a Creole community and a revolutionary view on their own nation; upgrading their own language and their own favorite arts by presenting them as poetry and prose to themselves and to a world audience;[16] seducing them with language play; catching all gendered, social, and sexual dimensions of experience in revitalized versions of their marginalized languages; expressing the full scope of their linguistic inheritance; articulating marginalized theories of language, agency, culture.

Theorizing as listeners: studying the intertextual relationships between the different oral and written art forms;[17] entering a structure of address, and responding; hearing the difference, the non-Western and Black and hybrid theories of language and subjectivity, the theories of agency; recognizing that not all language play is postmodern (Tapping 1989: 91); recognizing that language experiment may be driven by a hardly reversible or deconstructible concern: survival, which is the ethical moment Kwame Appiah points out as the difference between postmodernism and postcolonialism (1991). And finally, reading talk as a specific performance for a specific (if multiple) audience, first and for all.

6

Jamaica Kincaid Is Getting Angry

How to Name a Silent Voice

I hear the silent voice; it stands opposite the blackness and yet it does not oppose the blackness, for conflict is not a part of its nature. I shrug off my mantle of hatred. In love I move toward the silent voice. . . . Within the silent voice, no mysterious depths separate me; no vision is so distant that longing is stirred up in me. . . . Living in the silent voice, I am no longer "I." Living in the silent voice, I am at last at peace [.] Living in the silent voice, I am at last erased.

—Jamaica Kincaid (1984: 52)

Regarding "voice," here is a remarkable one: a luring, tempting silent voice that promises peace, and the end of difference, separation, conflict, and desire. It appears in the first collection of short stories, *At the Bottom of the River*, by Antiguan writer Jamaica Kincaid.[1] The sweet murmur of the narrator, who talks of her longing for this lure of nothingness, does not distract her reader from the undesirable character of this beloved voice. Surely, one cannot exist as "I" in a fully undifferentiated and quiet atmosphere, which is in itself irreconcilable with life. This silent voice, this notorious paradox, is no novelty in literature. In the West, it occurs in modernist as well as postmodern literary texts. In the latter, silence surfaces in the gaps and pauses, questioning the self-evidence of significations. It renders the absence of fixed meanings suddenly audible. A silent voice embodies a postmodern accentuation of the gap between signified and signifier.

But in this fragment the silent voice is opposed to "blackness." The blackness, too, erases significance:

The blackness is not my blood, though it flows through my veins. The blackness enters my many-tiered spaces and soon the significant word and event recede and eventually vanish: in this way I am annihilated and my form becomes formless and I am absorbed into a vastness of free-flowing matter. In the blackness, then, I have been erased. I can no longer say my own name. I can no longer point to myself and say "I." In the blackness my voice is silent. First, then, I have been my individual self, carefully banishing randomness from my existence, then I am swallowed up in the blackness so that I am one with it. (Kincaid 1984: 46–47)

Blackness has the same property of engulfing the speaker and her voice, and of erasing meaning. But the "blackness" is not welcomed as the "silent voice" is, toward which the narrator moves lovingly. The blackness takes possession of the narrator as an unwelcome alienation that nevertheless belongs to her: "The blackness cannot be separated from me but often I can stand outside it" (46). The blackness is as overdetermined a concept as the silent voice. Within the context of recent African-American literary criticism, "blackness" cannot but refer to "race" too, and in consequence, to postcolonial, and/or black cultural practices.[2] Indeed, a reluctance to mean is often considered a feature of a postcolonial aesthetics.

In their discussion of the constituting features of postcolonial texts, Ashcroft and his coauthors refer at a general critical distance to the dominant, authoritarian language of power in postcolonial writing, and thus, sometimes, to a "silence" that shows that "neither the language nor the means of communication have been fully appropriated" (Ashcroft, Griffiths, and Tiffin 1989: 7–8, 84). Can one then read the fragments above as if they oppose a (silent) ("black") postcolonial voice to a ("silent") postmodern voice? And should the texts be read as the sad narrative of a Caribbean girl's surrender to the silence of a postmodern discourse that does not speak her reality?

As a first step in tackling the issue that is central to this chapter, I suggest the possibility of such an approach: if one wants to understand the process by which Kincaid creates her voice as a Caribbean woman writer in New York, is it adequate to situate her writing in the intersecting fields of postmodernism and postcolonialism? I will first discuss some of the efforts critics have undertaken to label Kincaid's work; feminist approaches disturb the neat symmetry of the dichotomy of postmodernism and postcolonialism I took as a starting point. In the sections that follow, I will consider the work that can be understood as a turning point in her writing career and that redirects her writing by explicitly addressing the issues of colonialism and postcolonialism: *A Small Place*. The means and the mood by which Kincaid effectuates this turn is "anger." After a discussion of the narrative devices Kincaid uses to articulate and vent her anger, I will consider possible ways to situate this "anger" within postmodernism and postcolonialism. I will then also come to speak about Kincaid's presumed aestheticism, which seems to oppose her anger and which so disturbingly complicates an understanding of her postcolonialism. Once I start to complicate things, I will proceed to bring in other aspects of Kincaid's work, which necessitate other approaches and which upset the original two-poled scheme that I set up as the original framework for my interpretation.[3]

Instances of Labeling

My consideration of the way critics have been applying labels to Kincaid's work concentrates on those characterizing it as (qualified) postmodern and (qualified) postcolonial. Some critics endow Kincaid's writing with the epithet "postmodern." They concentrate on the "silent voice" and do not differentiate it from "blackness." Thus, in an essay on *At the Bottom of the River* and *Annie John*, critic Giovanna Covi argues that Kincaid deserves acclaim for her position as a *radically* postmodern author who may be contrasted to the postmodern authors from the north operating within a narrow Eurocentric context (Covi 1990: 346). Kincaid is declared a postmodernist for the ambivalence, silences, and rejection of unambiguous meanings in the text; her writing subverts Western concepts of time and history. Covi mobilizes Derrida, Kristeva, Irigaray, and in passing Einstein, Heidegger, Wittgenstein, and Nietzsche to read Kincaid's texts. She also tentatively puts the texts within the context of a Black aesthetics, but her primary frame of reference is a Western canon of (post)modern and/or feminist philosophers. Her approach serves the purpose of subverting definitions and canons. According to Covi, Kincaid's postmodernism is radical. Thus, Covi defines a text from the periphery as a superior example in a Western tradition. Her addition of the adverb "radically" represents a critique of narrow concepts of postmodernism as well as an upgrading of Kincaid's work by situating it within (a supposedly prestigious) postmodernism.

However, the epithet "radically" shows the unease in the use of the term *postmodern*. The ultimate form of postmodernism would be a postmodernism that distances itself critically from its dominant definition as a Western cosmopolitan practice. Covi's rewriting of the concept of postmodernism by applying it to Kincaid's work sheds some light on the problems of defining texts that are written in the contact zones.[4] The following statement by Kincaid gets to the heart of the problem, as it offers a direct comment on Covi's perilous categorizing:

The New York Times said that the book [*A Small Place*] didn't have the "charm" of *Annie John*. Really, when people say you're charming you are in deep trouble. I realized in writing that book that the first step to claiming yourself is anger. You get mad. And you can't do anything before you get angry. And I recommend getting very angry to everyone, anyone. . . . I can see that *At the Bottom of the River* was, for instance, a very unangry, decent, civilized book and it represents sort of this successful attempt by English people to make their version of a human being or their version of a person out of me. (Perry 1990: 498–99)

In this interview with Donna Perry, Kincaid does not deem her early (presumed) postmodernism so very radical. The lack of anger and the decent conformity of her first publication is most visible in the reluctance to give meaning, or in other words the text's "silent voice." With the concept of the silent voice I refer both to the text's reticent style of narrating and to the silent voice that explicitly appears as a major theme. Kincaid now localizes this postmodern attitude: it represents an "English" attempt, an "English" concept of being.

This interpretation of Kincaid's alleged radical postmodernism brings one to understand Kincaid's writing as situated and, in that respect, postcolonial rather than postmodern: her texts evoke the pains and contradictions of a girl's life in a colonized location. Indeed, even the "decent" *At the Bottom of the River* pictures the struggle for identity in the colonial context of a Caribbean island. One of Kincaid's later texts, *A Small Place* (1988), makes the effects of colonialism on her native island an explicit theme. This text—which is shaped as a long essay—suggests that Kincaid's writing is more deeply engaged in a critique of colonial discourses and practices than one would suppose upon a first reading of her early texts. And if a critique of colonialism is more prominent in Kincaid's writing than a critique of Western humanist thought, then her texts should be understood as postcolonial rather than postmodern.

Nevertheless, there is a problem in labeling Kincaid's work postcolonial. To begin, there is of course Davies's strong argument (discussed in the introduction) that Black women's writing should not be subsumed under the denominator of postcolonialism. However, this is not the argument I want to present here. I will look back at an earlier debate and discuss the different arguments that have led critics to evaluate Kincaid's work as (qualified) postcolonial or (qualified) postmodern, with the dual purpose of highlighting some aspects of the debate on the relation between postcolonialism and feminism and the development of Kincaid's writing. Second, then, I want to point out that there is already a problem in differentiating postcolonialism from postmodernism. Heated arguments take place about the implications of seeing both as basically identical. The postmodern, some argue, originated in the United States *and* Latin America. Postcolonial and postmodern literary texts are closely related, so much so that the same texts may be defined as postmodern in one context and as postcolonial in the other.[5] Salman Rushdie is a case in point. However, postmodernism, as a concept that functions primarily within a Western theoretical discourse, does not adequately refer to the specific character of non-Western texts. A certain consensus has been reached on the points of difference between postmodern and postcolonial texts. The centrality of a critique of colonialism in these texts, referred to above, is one of these. Many critics subscribe to another general rule of thumb to differentiate between the two, namely, that postcolonial texts in some regard harbor a positive point. They will often display aspects of irreducible "otherness," references to a counterdiscourse or a counterculture,[6] or "a theory of agency and social change" (Hutcheon 1991: 183).[7] This is said to be one of its differences with postmodernism. Postcolonial texts, many postcolonial critics argue, may be dedicated to a deconstruction of dominant discourses and an exploration of plurality, as postmodern texts are, but only up to a certain point; they also show a tendency to represent a positive self (Kubayanda 1987: 123). This assumed positive character of postcolonial texts is sometimes opposed to the aesthetic and negative character of postmodern texts in which all meaning is deferred. In this context, Cynthia Ward speaks about an "oral antiaesthetics," a concept I have discussed in the preceding chapter (Ward 1990). In his introduction to a special issue of *Modern Fiction Studies* on "minority discourses" (in which postcolonial texts are included), Timothy Brennan signals an "aesthetic of the antiliterary itself:

a kind of counterfiction, a poetry without metaphor, a narrative without irony" (Brennan 1989: 5).

This way of opposing postcolonial texts (as positive and antiaesthetic) to postmodern texts (as negative and aesthetic) seems very problematic to me. For example, one might wonder if certain postmodernist texts do not also function positively, albeit unwittingly perhaps, in their reinforcement of the centrality of Westernness. Kincaid comments that she dislikes certain forms of northern American postmodern writing for its constant unglossed references to U.S. brand names, which has the effect of underlining the U.S. status as the obvious center of all cultural knowledge (Cudjoe 1990b: 221).[8] Moreover, there are texts written in the so-called postcolonial world in which the positive or constructive element is hard to find. *A Small Place* is one of these. Here lies one of the reasons why it is hard to label the text unambiguously as postcolonial. The characterization of postcolonial texts as antiaesthetic calls forth a series of dichotomies, two of which this chapter will question: aesthetics versus antiaesthetics; postmodern versus postcolonial. My discussion of Kincaid's writing will work through a critique of these dichotomies.

Before engaging in textual analysis, I want to point out another way of situating Kincaid's concept of the "silent voice." If one studies the concept of silence within the context of African-American women's writing, Kincaid's critique of her own former "decency" is clarified. For example, bell hooks reports that she was taught as a young girl that silence is "the right speech of womanhood" (hooks 1986/87: 124). She had to learn "to talk a talk that was in itself a silence" (125). This reluctance to signify, then, is the prescribed mode of expression for women from the South. Indeed, there are many readings that place Kincaid's texts within a tradition of women's writing or within a female problematics.[9] It is a common approach to her work. Covi discusses this aspect, too. In a recent essay, postcolonial critic Helen Tiffin has offered an exemplary analysis in which she highlights a feminist tradition of writing about the body within a postcolonial context. She wishes to illuminate the impact of colonialism on women's bodies, and she situates Kincaid's writing within the female experience of (post)colonialism (Tiffin 1993). Tiffin thus places Kincaid's texts within a qualified postcolonial literary context.

A combined approach to Kincaid's work is common, and perfectly defensible. Yet it is not easy to decide about the exact nature of such an approach. In her analysis of the multiple vision in Kincaid's *Annie John*, Laura Niesen de Abruña adopts the "crossroads" model another Caribbean critic, Evelyn O'Callaghan, proposes for the analysis of writings by women in the South (Niesen de Abruña 1991: 278). According to this model, women's texts are not placed within a general feminist tradition but situated "at a point of intersection of other concerns with race, class, or Creole cultural forms unique to the region" (278). The crossroads model, which stays open to the possible relevance of other critical approaches, will inspire the framing of my readings, too. However, I want to set limits to its ecclecticist nature by making some qualifications.

First, I understand the use of the word *concerns* to transcend the thematic level. My main interest will be in the narrative and discursive strategies used to carve out a position of speech. Second, I have my reservations about the image of the crossroads. Approaches may meet and overlap there, but often one approach cannot easily be combined with another. Some approaches even rule each other out. Crossroads, as is well known, are often the scene of road accidents and traffic jams. In this chapter, I will examine how a postmodern approach relates to a postcolonial approach, to a feminist approach, and even to an approach that places Kincaid's writing within the context of a Caribbean modernism.[10] Some of these are simply not compatible. The mere choice for a model that combines approaches, then, does not present an easy solution to the problem of situating Kincaid's writing. Instead, it marks the site of methodological reflection, and that, I contend, is useful enough.

Third and finally, a crossroads model might be used to comply to elements deemed present in the text. But, as I suggested above, postmodernism and postcolonialism can often primarily be seen as reading positions. This does not mean that readers are completely free in their choice of a critical approach; they will always be led by elements in the text, too. But the reader who shows some autonomy, or even disobedience in following the directions the text explicitly takes, has the advantage of seeing interesting intertextual connections.

Take the case of *A Small Place*. It does not allow its reader much freedom. The reader is directly addressed as one complicit in (neo)colonial practices. The text explicitly posits itself as postcolonial (in the sense of continuously deconstructing colonialism). But refraining from endowing this label has its advantages. For in spite of the postcolonial positioning of the text, Kincaid uses devices that also occur in *At the Bottom of the River* and are deemed postmodern in that context. In *A Small Place* they are applied in a slightly different way, with a definite decolonizing effect. Still, they retain some of their postmodern character. In addition, gender hardly seems prominent in *A Small Place*, whereas Kincaid's two earlier works, *At the Bottom of the River* and *Annie John*, are structured around female concerns. In the fourth section of this chapter, however, it will become clear that *A Small Place* is nevertheless based on a highly specific concept of gender. If one decides to read the essay as a gender-neutral postcolonial text, contrasting it to the female, postmodern writing in the first two texts, one misses the complicated links between them. And only through an understanding of these relations can one grasp the complex process by which Kincaid negotiates postmodern, postcolonial, modernist, and feminist aesthetics to construct a female Caribbean position of speech. *A Small Place* is a crucial step in the construction of that voice. This voice is not merely a female voice, or a Caribbean voice. It is a voice in which the complex, hybrid, and plural identity of a Caribbean migrant woman is expressed. It is not an exemplary voice, any more or less than the voices Collins and Nichols offer. The voice in *A Small Place* testifies to the difficult negotiation between discourses and dichotomies through which Caribbean women create a position for themselves as speaking subjects.

Devastating Dialogues

To explain the complex connections between the concerns addressed and the devices used in *At the Bottom of the River* and *A Small Place*, I will disentangle some of them—notably, anger and aestheticism—and discuss the ways they can be labeled. The central part of my argument is an examination of the relations between the two texts. I regard *A Small Place* to be a turning point in the trajectory of Kincaid's authorship. It represents a radical break with the obedient inward directed attitude of her two earlier works. Anger and satire make their entry, and aesthetics plays a different role.

A clearly visible difference between the texts lies in their different structures of address. *At the Bottom of the River* does not address itself to a reader; *A Small Place* does, in a complex and innovative way. The first part of the essay is straightforward enough. The narrator directly addresses the tourist, descendant of the colonists, as responsible for slavery and (neo)-colonialism. In the second part, however, the structure of address is complicated. The narrator positions both a "we" and a "them/they" (both referring to the Antiguans) as partners in her dialogue. Let us first consider the blunt identification of the first and second person. At the beginning of the story, "I" directly addresses the tourist, positioning herself as one of the people the tourist encounters on Antigua:

If you go to Antigua as a tourist, this is what you will see. If you come by aeroplane, you will land at the V. C. Bird International Airport. Vere Cornwall (V. C.) Bird is the Prime Minister of Antigua. You may be the sort of tourist who would wonder why a Prime Minister would want an airport not some great public monument? You are a tourist and you have not yet seen a school in Antigua, you have not seen the hospital in Antigua, you have not yet seen a public monument in Antigua. (3)

After this ominous beginning, in which the "I" reminds the tourist of his restricted perception and the presence of some hidden reality, she increasingly takes the guise of a fury, staging the narrative of the tourist, and demanding him to witness the effects of colonialism on his holiday resort and on himself:

An ugly thing, that is what you are when you become a tourist, an ugly, empty thing, a stupid thing, a piece of rubbish pausing here and there to gaze at this and taste that, and it will never occur to you that the people who inhabit the place in which you have just paused cannot stand you. (8)

The narrator fulminates, and she continues to sum up and to describe the miserable situation of present-day, postcolonial Antigua, which is still suffering the effects of North American neocolonialism.[11] She adds to this fulmination references to the crimes of former colonials and slave traders.

As an external narrator, "I" controls the tourist's text, ever following and defining his focalization. She also indicates the limits of his knowledge. The structure of address is remarkably unshakable: unflinchingly and implacably the "I" positions herself opposite this "you" she has tied down to his position as an addressee, witness, and accused. *A Small Place* is in fact an angry exercise in identification.

Above, I quoted Kincaid's remark on the importance of anger. I argued that her anger was a necessary step in her authorial project. Now I can relate this perspective on the function of anger to the issue of identification.

Audre Lorde, in a well-known essay, speaks about anger as a reaction to racism (Lorde 1984b). She argues that Black women are often angry, but they do not direct their anger to the persons they are in fact angry with. If they do so, then their anger becomes "a powerful source of energy serving progress and change" (Lorde 1984b: 127). She continues: "anger expressed and translated into action in the service of our vision and our future is a liberating and strengthening act of clarification, for it is in the painful process of this translation that we identify who are our allies with whom we have grave differences, and who are our genuine enemies" (Lorde 1984b: 127). Anger should be used to obtain a clear view of the positions of all concerned. It should lead to explicitness, that is, for Lorde it should give a direction to an undirected, powerless, inarticulated anger, whereas for Kincaid it will be used to break open the "decent" speech that calls for implicitness and silence. Thus, becoming angry and identifying who is friend and who is foe are part of the same process. This angry identification is aimed at the assigning of (political) positions. Lorde does not explain this identification as the revelation of an undivided, authentic self, nor as the construction of a position of "moral authority" (132). Her argument is constructed precisely to open up the possibility of recognizing racial, class, and sexual differences between women. To overcome the fear of these differences, she encourages Black and white women to discuss and "alter those distortions which history has created around our difference. . . . And we must ask ourselves: Who profits from all this?" (129) Kincaid is much less concerned with the reconciliation Lorde strives for, but she is driven by the same question: who profits from all this? This is the question that structures *A Small Place* in different ways. The centrality of the effort of identification is one of the most dramatic differences with *At the Bottom of the River*.

Two different techniques are used to clarify these positions. The first consists in the asking of questions to identify responsible parties behind criminal acts, and the hidden causes and interests that lie behind the abuses the narrator observes dryly. Here, *A Small Place* seems to follow Lorde's dictum about the function of the articulation of anger. The second device is its structure of address, in which, in the beginning, addressing "I" and addressed "you" are fixed in their positions. "I" and "you" do not display consistent characteristics, though. Both are labeled (or label themselves) within different discourses. The "I" identifies herself first as an inhabitant of the island of Antigua (which is the "small place" in the title), second, as a migrant who returned temporarily to her motherland but has obtained a different perspective on the place where she was born, and, third, a migrant who sometimes identifies herself as one among millions of victims of slavery and colonization. This multiple "I" addresses a "you" who is sometimes a tourist, sometimes a representative of the colonists and slavers. Thus, the "I" and the "you" are placed within different historical and political frameworks; at different moments they are positioned within different discourses. Nevertheless, the pronouns bind them to their fixed positions as opponents.

Anger clarifies syntax, then. But it does not install an opposite truth. This anger does not lead to a radically opposed discourse. Far from adopting, for example, a nationalist Caribbean discourse, *A Small Place* stays unsettlingly close to colonial discourse. It is, in fact, written in the "language of the criminal." If the narrator of *A Small Place* often uses an English that is very close to a dominant, colonial discourse, this means that she identifies the positions within the colonial tragedy in terms of the dominant discourse of the people she chastises. This kinship is visible in such statements as "people like me will never understand the notion of rule by law, people like me cannot really think in abstractions" (36), in which the narrator repeats some of the prejudices held against her "people," only substituting the personal pronoun ("me" for "you"). It can also be seen in the mimicking of the colonial terms *children* and *girls*, both used in reference to adults. In this way, *A Small Place* represents the standpoint that colonialism has corrupted the colonized completely and irrevocably. They are definitely and completely caught within the discourse of the European colonial power: "I met the world through England, and if the world wanted to meet me it would have to do so through England" (33). Thus, the narrator places herself within an English cultural context, an English discourse. It is the only vehicle for obtaining knowledge about herself as a (post)colonial subject. Elsewhere she asks sarcastically: "For isn't it odd that the only language I have in which to speak of this crime is the language of the criminal who committed the crime?" (31). Conscious of its provenance, she defines this criminal discourse correspondingly—accusingly and insultingly, unhampered by her dependence upon it.

Quite in contrast to many other Caribbean and African-American writers, Kincaid does not find comfort in the thought of an autonomous, uncontaminated past: "As for what we were like before we met you, I no longer care. No periods of time over which my ancestors held sway, no documentation of complex civilisations, is any comfort to me. Even if I really came from people who were living like monkeys in trees, it was better to be that than what happened to me, what I became after I met you" (37). In this statement, the narrator even rejects the whole discourse about origins, which carried special significance for colonists and slave traders. She does not explicitly protest the European racist argument about her origins. She flaunts her willingness to adopt this caricature, thus reinforcing her statement that references to another time outside of the period marked by (neo)colonialism are irrelevant to her criticism of neocolonialism as a destructive force.

The declaration of the irrelevance of the colonial discourse about origins, as well as of the criminal character of colonial discourse, does not entail that there be another discourse in which the narrator engages. In *A Small Place* there is no point whatsoever outside the colonial discourse where the colonized or the narrator herself could find a starting point for the articulation of a counterdiscourse. Benita Parry, discussing the debates on colonial discourse at the end of the 1980s, would consider this perspective an undervaluation of the anticolonial struggle. Inspired by Frantz Fanon, she points at counterdiscourses that have taken form in the complex interaction between dominant powers and the marginalized subjects who resist hegemony (1987). In contrast, listen to the following denial of the Caribbean ability to create a counterdiscourse: "The people in a small place [the Antiguans] cannot give an exact account, a complete account, of themselves" (53). Or, even more strongly put, "I look at this place (Antigua), I look at these people (Antiguans), and I cannot tell whether I was brought up by, and so come from, children, eternal innocents, or artists who have not yet found eminence in a world too stupid to understand, or lunatics who have made their own lunatic asylum, or an exquisite combination of all three" (57). This criticism of the Antiguans reminds one that *A Small Place* is not only an anticolonial text but also an antipostcolonial text, if we understand the postcolonial here as the postindependence continuation of colonialism, rather than its critical working through. The tirade against the tourist, regardless of how curiously challenging it may be for theorists from the same cultural and economical background as he (and I am among them), is not the crucial part of the book, as several theorists have emphatically pointed out to me.[12] Rather, this outburst is to be understood as an introduction to the critique of Antigua's postcolonial condition. In the second part of the essay, then, the narrator's anger is explicitly directed at the corrupt government of the small place. Now, a great many instances of corruption and crime are summed up, soberingly, and greatly incriminatingly. Here, the real addressee of the essay becomes visible. Notably, these new criminals are not addressed as "you." The narrator talks about them as third persons; in a crucial passage she presents the governing corrupt even more indirectly as the third persons in a discourse by other third persons (they, the Antiguans, talking about them, the government). In this passage, we can study the entanglement of the subject positions of the first and third person. Here, the narrator quotes the Antiguans in a torrent of words that takes pages and pages (57–68), so that one forgets she is quoting and takes this to be her own voice:

For it is in a voice that suggests all three [that the Antiguans are children, artists, or lunatics] that they say: "That big new hotel is a haven for drug dealing. The hotel has its own port of entry, so boats bearing their drug cargo can come and go as they please. . . . I have a friend who just came back from Switzerland. . . . She was in such a rhapsodic state about the Swiss, and the superior life they lead, that it was hard for me not to bring up how they must pay for this superior life they lead. For almost not a day goes by that I don't hear about some dictator . . . who has robbed his country's treasury . . . and placed it in his own personal and secret Swiss bank account. (57–60)

Then, at the end, the reader is reminded that the Antiguans were speaking here:

The ministers, the people who govern the island of Antigua, who are also citizens of Antigua, are legal residents of the United States, a place they visit frequently.
    And it is in that strange voice, then—the voice that suggests innocence, art, lunacy—that they say these things. (68)[13]

The choice of words and the narrative style of the narrator and the Antiguans are almost indistinguishable. The narrator takes over the Antiguans' voice with such self-assurance, such fluency, her (temporal) identification being so complete that she easily skips to the use of "I." Strictly speaking, this "I" is impossible here. The narrator gives an account of what "they" say. Of course, it would be quite possible that one of "them" would give some personal account; but, if so, this personal account cannot be differentiated from the personal accounts by the narrator herself in other parts of the text. This shift of focus from the tourist to the Antiguan government and people complicates the original twofold structure of address to such an extent that a radical ambiguity is introduced: the space in which a critical, ambiguous postcolonial voice can develop. Under this second aspect of the text's structure of address, the Antiguans are hardly represented as able speaking subjects. They form the unstable third instance in this structure: "them." The Antiguans are referred to as "them," "they," "the natives," "the slaves," and "the enslaved but noble and exalted human beings from Africa." The use of the third person relates intimately to the third person that in ethnographic discourse is used for the anthropological object. This is quite coherent with the dominant colonial discourse in *A Small Place*, which constructs the other as an object. Sometimes, however, the narrator identifies with "them," and then she uses "we," or she adds a phrase such as "(not unlike me)" (47). But even if the narrator chooses to side with the Antiguans, which allows her to adorn herself with a rather indefinite "we," in other moments she distances herself from her kin, in bewilderment and puzzlement.

Homi Bhabha states that new social movements, and the radical subjectivities related to them, stem from the ambivalent switching between the third person and first person (1997: 434). The third person is the objectified other created in other discourses (that dub one "Muslim" or "queer"). If one becomes aware to be thus (not) addressed, one may engage in political activism, by assuming already constructed subject positions ("so I'm queer, huh? I'll show you"). But it is only by confronting this third person to one's complex and conflicting experiences and sensations as a first person ("I") that a new, ambivalent subjectivity begins to be articulated. Kincaid's strategy of mingling and differentiating "I," "we," and "them" is highlighting this very space from which new subjectivities might stem. If Lorde has pointed toward the importance of sharp identification in the expression of anger, Bhabha explores the unresolvable dynamics from where inevitably ambiguous subjectivities come to grips with their anger. Lorde helps to understand the neat pattern of address in the first part of the essay; Bhabha allows us to understand the ambivalences of the second part. Both parts are needed for the establishment of a voice. Kincaid's wavering between "I," "we," and "they/them" is effective because it allows her to speak simultaneously as an insider and an outsider; it grants her the authority of the inside voice and the distance needed for harsh critiques.

To be able to shift between persons, the narrator has to adopt specific discursive strategies. As we have seen, she hardly strives to be labeled as a speaking subject. She assumes labels, even if they objectify her and the Antiguans, and then shows their absurdity, insignificance, and irrelevance. She rejects the idea of an alternative speech or "true-true" name.[14] Instead, she accepts and emphasizes the irreversibility of history, which shows the extent of both the colonial and the postcolonial crime and justifies her anger. She makes a laconic use of the grammar of colonial discourse, which labels the Antiguans and herself as objects. A discussion of her subversive narrative strategies from within colonial discourse will help to understand the subtle differences with her earlier (qualified) postmodernism.

These narrative strategies are predicative to the text's primary dependency on the dominant colonial discourse to such an extent that the text is constantly (if ironically) citing this discourse. There are few writers for whom citing is such a structural device as for Kincaid; she assumes languages, discourses, voices, statements, and labels. Mary Louise Pratt offers a suitable expression when she speaks of the "assuming of the label." In a discussion of a specific postcolonial text, she discerns the tactics[15] "not to reject the label . . . but to assume it, and speak from the position of speech it denotes. This taking of voice is a familiar gesture in emergent writing, which often carves out a position of speech by recoding the very images that have been used to exclude or silence its subjects" (Pratt 1993: 863). Kincaid shares these tactics with many others, as Pratt also suggests; an abundant intertextuality is a characteristic of postcolonial as well as postmodern texts. Some wish to see this tactic of assuming labels as a feminine strategy too; dominant voices may be used to express a feminine subtext, which becomes audible only in the gaps and silences in the dominant discourse.[16]

Kincaid's diabolic "assuming of a discourse" can be understood as a specific form of irony. Linda Hutcheon explains the nature of irony, which is frequently used in postmodern as well as postcolonial writing: "the use of the trope of irony . . . as a double-talking, forked-tongued mode of address . . . becomes a popular rhetorical strategy for working within existing discourses and contesting them at the same time" (Hutcheon 1991: 170–71). Postcolonial texts, however, will be specifically (though not exclusively) geared against colonial language and discourse, and also against the uses an opportunist postcolonial administration makes of this discourse. Hutcheon discusses the workings of irony in postcolonial writing with the help of a quotation by another postcolonial critic, William New, who offers almost the same definition as Pratt for the "assuming of the label": "the challenge is to use the existing language, even if it is the voice of a dominant language . . . and yet speak through it: to disrupt . . . the codes and forms of the dominant language in order to reclaim speech for itself" (Hutcheon 1991: 177). Kincaid might talk not about a "challenge" but rather about a necessity caused by a crime. Apart from this point, this observation explains quite well that Kincaid's tendency to assume voices and labels can be understood in connection to the centrality of irony in her writing. Kincaid disrupts not only one dominant discourse in this manner; in *A Small Place*, postmodern, modernist, colonial, and postcolonial forms and voices are all used ironically.

Hutcheon elaborates her argument about irony with the following statement: "irony allows a text to work within the constraints of the dominant while placing those constraints *as constraints* in the foreground and thus undermining their power" (177). Kincaid's strategy of unveiling the limits of colonial perspectives can be studied in many instances. The narrator often criticizes the discourse by suddenly inserting a completely different speech and using terms of quite a different kind. For example, here she again addresses the tourist, qualifying him as "a person marvelling at the harmony (ordinarily, what you would say is the backwardness) and the union these other people (and they are other people) have with nature. And you look at the things they can do with a piece of ordinary cloth, the things they fashion out of cheap, vulgarly colored (to you) twine" (Kincaid 1988: 16). The main text uses stereotypical Western statements about persons living in the South; they live in harmony with nature, they are excellent craftsmen. These, apparently, are the tourist's judgments. At the same time, however, the text disturbs these statements by inserting comments between parentheses that annoyingly comment on the tourist's terms or characterizations. Thus, the subtext unmasks the terms of the modern form of colonial discourse as euphemisms; the term *harmony* is denounced as a euphemism for the rude term *backwardness*. This strategy consists of the citing, exaggerating, and disturbing of colonial speech. These disturbances testify to the difference of "you," who have a specific, imperfect, restricted view ("they are other people," "to you"). In this aspect, the text acknowledges the existence of a different, noncolonial perspective, even if it cannot be opposed as a coherent, anticolonial discourse to the dominant colonial discourse. Yet, it exposes the narrow limits and the inadequacy of colonial discourse.

It is even possible to extrapolate a recognizable manner of speech from this noncolonial, Antiguan perspective, a discourse of sorts: "Our perception of this Antigua—the perception we had of this place ruled by these bad-minded people—was not a political perception. The English were ill-mannered, not racists; . . . the doctor was crazy, . . . not a racist; the people at the Mill Reef Club were puzzling, . . . not racists" (34). The text disqualifies the behavior of colonists with terms such as "bad-minded" and "ill-mannered." Elsewhere, we find kindred qualifications such as "badly behaved," "un-Christian-like" and "ugly." Puzzlement and the need for absolute distance can take priority: "funny," "puzzling," "crazy." The qualifications may also develop into "a bit below human standards," and even to "animals" and "pigs." Terms like *racist*, which would stem from an anticolonial discourse, do not fit into this Antiguan articulation of their critique of the English. It is not a politically rooted or Black, antiracist critique of objectionable behavior. Instead, it can be understood as the kind of "colonial mimicry" that is employed by the colonized (Bhabha 1984a: introduction and chapter 5, the analysis of Ombre). The manner of speech ascribed to the Antiguans is largely an imitation of a (presumed) English discourse of decency. To use Bhabha's phrase, it is "almost the same, but not quite"—the possibility of an adequate imitation being foreclosed, like the English discourse it imitates, is ultimately illusory. It can be deduced from novels and stories, perhaps, but it certainly cannot be observed in the manners and speech of English colonials. I will call this Antiguan manner of speech the discourse of the weak. The weak hold high norms of (Christian) decency, politeness, and respect simply because they cannot afford to oppose those in power openly (30). Deviance from these norms of decency is judged unmannered or crazy.

The discourse of the weak cannot be seen as a coherent counterdiscourse. Whether the colonial discourse is used or the discourse of the weak, both are *cited*. In the furious context of *A Small Place*, in which crimes are berated, the discourse of the weak can hardly be presented as the "right" or even the adequate articulation of the (neo)colonial situation. Likewise, I have already shown that the colonial discourse is used only as a speech to subvert. The narrator always keeps a certain distance from the words she utters. She never fully appropriates them.

One might argue that this will not hold for the very harsh critique of colonialism and slavery the narrator also gives. In that context, she calls the former slaves "noble and exalted," whereas the tourists and colonials are cursed as "criminals." She then follows a simple scheme of good against bad, "noble and exalted human beings" against "human rubbish" and "criminals," decency against indecency, grace against ugly gracelessness. One might be tempted to see here the postcolonial element of positivity mentioned above. Hutcheon, too, argues that "the postcolonial cannot *stop* at irony" (1991: 183). But even if it is true that Kincaid's text exceeds irony, the transgression does not lead into a realist representation of a counter-discourse or into a stable definition of her fellow Antiguans as worthy and different (except those in power, of course). First, the contrast between good and bad people introduced in the text is also deconstructed. This happens at that moment in the text when the narrator devotes herself to a devastating criticism of the postcolonial situation on Antigua, which is castigated as criminal and corrupt, too. At first sight, there would be no more reason to differentiate between good Blacks and evil whites. All would live within the confines of the same (neo/post)colonial discourse. Second, however, this essential unity of formerly colonized and former colonizer is also questioned in its turn, not by the content of the words but by the structure of address. Read the last sentences of *A Small Place*:

Of course, the whole thing is, once you cease to be a master, once you throw off your master's yoke, you are no longer human rubbish, you are just a human being, and all the things that adds up to. So, too, with the slaves. Once they are no longer slaves, once they are free, they are no longer noble and exalted; they are just human beings. (81)

One might wish to read here the soothing statement that "we" are all just human beings, if history only allowed us to dispense with the roles we have been playing. But that is not what the text actually says. This fragment is not about "us." There is a sting in these consoling words, and it is located in the structure of address. Even when the narrator deconstructs the opposition between slave and master and shows that both are only human beings in the end, she clings to the opposition "they"/"you" for the opposition "slaves"/"masters" she apparently wants to erase. The quotation shows how unshakably the text fixes the protagonists in their positions, even if it erases the qualifications that were responsible for their positions. If *A Small Place* exceeds its irony, it is in the moment of its anger, which is located in a choice of syntax, and not in an argument that would oblige it to give up its negativity and absoluteness.

This anger might be understood as part of the decolonization of discourse. According to Fanon, decolonization needs to be grounded in a practice of violent discursive resistance (Fanon, quoted in Slemon 1991: 5). Kincaid's anger, then, is part of a decolonization process—the process of chastising "English" discourse. Kincaid's anger reinforces her argument, that colonialism has been utterly destructive and still is. The violence of this opposition seems to me to be the characteristic of Kincaid's postcolonialism that can hardly be called constructive or counterdiscursive. From this violence stems the impossibility of a straightforward "we" and the necessity of the inconclusive manipulation of personal pronouns, which doesn't evolve into a collective new subjectivity. But this manipulating does produce a very strong voice.

If this text is read as a part of the large project by which Caribbean (migrant) women define their subjectivity, then its primary statement seems to be that this subjectivity can be articulated only in a difficult, indirect way, by inscribing it into the colonial discourse that denies it. Here I find a point in which this text differentiates itself from many postmodern texts through adopting a postcolonial perspective. Postmodernist writing dedicates itself to a rethinking of the subject through the many dialogic structures within which it positions itself (see, e.g., Hutcheon 1988: 84–85). Kincaid's essay discloses the colonial dialogue, through which she reconsiders subjectivity, as a destructive fake. Her anger can be seen as the savage statement that "your" dialogue has completely erased "me," the colonized subject.

A Small Place thus offers a radical comment on the postmodern concept of the dialogically situated subject. It differs from *At the Bottom of the River* not in that it uses a radically non-English, noncolonial counterdiscourse but in that *A Small Place* uses the master's voice in a satanical way, disturbing it by means of the colonized's speech, and identifying crimes, criminals, and victims in the process of subverting it. Its structure of address, together with its ironic appropriation of a criminal discourse, are the main instruments of this subversion.

My reading of the above fragments shows that Kincaid bases her angry critique of colonial discourse on the possibility of a noncolonized position, while refusing to represent a coherent, Antiguan nationalist discourse.

She rejects realism, but she also strives to identify the voices of criminals and victims, to expose their limits and show their interests and aims. A realist depiction of the (post)colonial situation, however, would undermine her critique of nationalism. She also uses other maneuvers to keep appropriating discourses, such as the nationalist discourses of a corrupted nation, at bay.

Beauty in the Service of Anger

Kincaid's first publication, *At the Bottom of the River*, was highly praised for its eccentricity and its visionary quality. It has a certain aesthetic quality that at first seems to be radically shattered to pieces by *A Small Place*'s angry intervention. The new narrative energy of the fury of that later text represents a dramatic shift away from the aesthetic quality of the early texts, as the text is interested no longer in ambivalence and changeability as such but only in the context of these phenomena. Yet, the later text does not offer a coherent, convincing argument or a realist description of this context. Instead of a rational or political argument, references to beauty and elegance orient the text. One might understand this orientation as a mark of Kincaid's postmodernism. But I will decline the opportunity to sketch postmodernist traces in an otherwise postcolonial *oeuvre* (or the other way round) to look instead into another effort to situate this aspect of Kincaid's writing.

Kincaid's writing must be placed not only in a general postcolonial, postmodern, or feminist context but also in a more explicit Caribbean context. To do so, I will now turn to a telling exchange between the writer and a well-known Caribbean critic, Selwyn Cudjoe. The interview concerns Kincaid's early writing. The passages I consider here relate to the issue of situating Kincaid's aesthetics of ambivalence and multivoicedness. Cudjoe opens the possibility of placing Kincaid's writing in the context of a Caribbean modernism, which is partly a critical reaction to European (colonial) modernism. Caribbean modernism can be seen as the Caribbean cultural movement, which opposes colonial discourses and finds its own forms through creolization, often by means of the transforming powers inherent in Afro-Caribbean popular culture. Scholar Simon Gikandi, who has written an extensive study about modernism and Caribbean literature, situates it in the space between colonialism and nationalism (Gikandi 1992).[17]

If I follow Kincaid's severe judgment of her own early work, I conclude that she rebukes the writing for its muddled sense of self. Where it should have claimed an identity of its own, it surrenders to a prescribed Englishness. Nevertheless, it is also true that her early narratives have a very distinctive, personal tone. The text's identity can be considered as torn between a (supposedly) English reluctance to speak and a very personal voice, which also uses Caribbean words and images. This split, understandable as the condition of speaking in several discourses, in several modes at the same time, might be associated with the modernist experience of an inner dichotomy. Moreover, if modernism is also characterized by a condition of uncertainty and changeability, then *At the Bottom of the River* is in that sense a modernist text. Selwyn Cudjoe follows this association when he characterizes Kincaid as a modernist in an interview (see below). Cudjoe carefully differentiates a European modernism from a specifically (general) American or Caribbean modernism. However, his endeavor to situate Kincaid in a modernist context does not fully succeed.

Talking about her grandmother, who was an obeah woman and through whom Kincaid as a girl came into contact with matters she did not understand, Kincaid says:

For a while, I lived in utter fear when I was little, of just not being sure that anything I saw was itself.
     Cudjoe: That's the modernist project, isn't it?
     Kincaid: Yes, and I think that's why it confused me. In fact it is quite primitive. When I read these modernists I think, "This is great! This is like my reality!" I mean, the first time I saw modern art, I really got into it. (Cudjoe 1990b: 226–27)

In this exchange, Kincaid takes up Cudjoe's definition of modernism, but only to show how the qualification of her experience as modernist does not help her in understanding the significance of her experience; it confused her. She may have been confused to find that there was an artistic movement expressing an experience she considered highly personal. She then introduces the problematic term *primitive*, and with it she characterizes her grandmother's conception of life, in which obeah played a central role. Using the term *primitive* is an instance of "assuming," and Kincaid's "assuming" of the label allows her a complex movement that is characteristic of her writing. The term occurs in different discourses, both in Western ethnocentric and in modernist discourses. In a modernist context, the term *primitive* has the connotation of "aesthetic." Kwame Appiah argues that Westerners often give the modernist label "aesthetic" to non-Western art

(Appiah 1991: 356). Kincaid uses the label too, but for different reasons. An aesthetic approach to the Afro-Caribbean experience that once caused her great anxiety allows her to distance herself from it; she does not romanticize it as other expatriots may do. Yet, she still keeps it available as an alternative aesthetical structure, as a possible source for her writing.

However, the term *primitive* is problematic. In the late 1980s and early 1990s, during the time the interview was held, this word inevitably bore the raw connotations of ethnocentrism. Kincaid's use of the term does not dismiss its blander connotations but even seems to acknowledge them. But its ethnocentric charge is not merely activated to offend or shock. The sheer force of the immodesty of the term *primitive* allows the speaker to free a space for a counterdiscourse and to insist on the non-Western character of a concept of life that is defined as Western. In this disrespectful manner, Kincaid reinforces the importance of non-Western influences in the emergence of modernism and thus reappropriates the concept of modernism. Instead of understanding the modernist anguish as the alienation and split identity connected to collective Western epistemological doubts, and instead of linking it to the Caribbean modernist urge to move away from colonial thought, she links it to the anguish of an African-Caribbean understanding of life, obeah. To her, then, this modernism is not a Western import, nor is it an anxiety caused by colonialism or the multiplicity of Creole. Her understanding of it connects it to a non-Western experience.

In his reaction to Kincaid's remark, Cudjoe elaborates on her alternative definition of modernism: "we have our own understanding of the subject that you don't have to go to Europe to discover. . . . We do have our own perception of that 'otherness.' In other words, your work—perhaps even more than you may realize—is within the form of the modernist project because you're doing the things that strike at the physical core of the entire Americas" (227). To this rather paternalistic critical intervention, Kincaid answers vaguely, "Well, yes, I mean, at one point in my life I never knew whether the ground would hold, whether the thing next to me was real or not. You see, in West Indian culture, things change so rapidly" (227). She does not say that she agrees with Cudjoe's interpretation, but returns to her personal experience, repeating a former statement, which she then contextualizes as West Indian. She evades Cudjoe's characterization of a (plural, general) American modernism.

This is not the only instance of her evading proposed definitions and

labels.[18] Kincaid often answers Cudjoe's tentative positionings with coun-
terdefinitions, evasive responses, and references to her very personal positions and attitudes. I cite some of her reactions:

How do you see your works fitting into the contemporary emphasis on feminist
writings?

    Kincaid: I don't really see it, but that's only because I don't really see myself
in any school . . . belonging to a group of anything, an "army" of anything, is
deeply disturbing to me. (221)

    Well, I'm not conscious of it. . . . (222)

    Well, I don't think I was trying to compare them, but if I were a person who
did compare these things. . . . (225)

    Well, until you mentioned it, I never thought it had any particular role. (229)

    Well, again, to be honest I don't really think I make these distinctions. (230)

In spite of her denials and evasions, Kincaid is quite willing to assume the
position her interviewer proposes: "if I *were* a person who did compare . . . "
(my emphasis). But at the same time, she distances herself from this fixed
position. On the whole, she politely takes on the proposed names, questioning them simultaneously. She seems to insist on her role as an author,
that is, on her right to idiosyncrasy. Thus, she opposes a generalizing critical
discourse. If she adopts it momentarily, she also subverts, evades, contradicts
it. This tactic is exemplary of the narrative strategies we find in some of her
writing: the assuming of labels.

    Nevertheless, it is quite useful to situate Kincaid's work within a Ca-
ribbean (and even a European) modernism. It shows the complicated site
of her authorship. As Gikandi suggests, Caribbean modernist literature is
formed through its violent or ambivalent dialogue with both colonialism
and nationalism, which can be seen as a modern Caribbean discourse (1992:
ix). Kincaid apparently rejects both. There are aspects of European modernism that appeal to her, first because they speak of her own experience of
uncertainty and unreality and second because they offer her a perspective
on Caribbean discourses and experiences that enables her to keep her distance from them without altogether giving them up.

    If Kincaid uses modernist images, devices, and moods in her own
writing—such as her device of describing people and behavior in terms of
beauty or ugliness—she disengages them from their usual contexts. She
connects them neither to a coherent Caribbean nationalist discourse nor to
aspects of a Western or modernist experience. Her view on Western mo-

dernity is rather bland. In *A Small Place*, when addressing the tourist, she viciously speaks of "that nice blob just sitting like a boob in your amniotic sac of the modern experience" (16). Only by partly and ironically adopting modernist or postmodernist forms is Kincaid able to keep her critical distance from repressive modern discourses such as nationalism. I see in Kincaid's presumed "aestheticism" one of the main modernist forms by which she disentangles her work from appropriating discourses. It serves the same purpose as her postmodern angle. It is a means of avoiding realism—which is "part of the tactic of nationalist legitimation" (Appiah 1991: 349). As I'll show below, Kincaid's aestheticism can be understood as a part of her maneuvering for a voice.

One of the most striking aspects of the narrative strategy in *A Small Place* I have considered above is the interference of the narrating voice with other voices. The narrator borrows other voices, or colors them, and lets go of them again. The interference is particularly visible in the enumerations. In *At the Bottom of the River*, the enumerations are one of many devices that also occur in modernist and postmodernist texts. But in *A Small Place*, they get quite a different signification, especially from the role interference plays in this text. This comparison will illuminate the difference between the nature of aestheticism in those texts.

In the following quotation from *A Small Place*, a series of statements about the beauty of Antigua's old library suddenly takes an unexpected turn:

But if you saw the old library, situated as it was, in a big, old wooden building painted a shade of yellow that is beautiful to people like me, with its wide veranda, its big, always open windows, its rows and rows of shelves filled with books, its beautiful wooden tables and chairs for sitting and reading, if you could hear the sound of its quietness (for the quiet in this library was a sound in itself), the smell of the sea (which was a stone's throw away), the heat of the sun (no building could protect us from that), the beauty of us sitting there like communicants at an altar, taking in, again and again, the fairy tale of how we met you, your right to do the things you did, how beautiful you were, are, and always will be. (42)

The enumeration shows that the library, which was to the narrator (as a colonized subject) an object of love, a site of a special quiet sensuality, was also the product of an alienating and appropriating colonialism. Suddenly, the narrating voice parodies the outrageous implicit statement of the colonizer. It does so in a very sudden interference, embodying the text's strategy of assuming labels while subverting them. The fragment criticizes the colonial past without giving up the naive, loving perspective of the formerly colonized. The reader is invited to identify with this love of an instrument of colonization and then is suddenly exposed to its alienating function, which, let us be clear, does *not* erase the loveliness.

The rhetorical device of the enumeration is not new in Kincaid's work. It already informs the structure of *At the Bottom of the River*. Here, questions, repetitions, and enumerations abound. They are dominant devices. But if one takes a closer look at them, the difference from *A Small Place* is very clear:

> My hands, brown on this side, pink on this side, now indiscriminately dangerous, now vagabond and prodigal, now cruel and careless, now without remorse or forgiveness, but now innocently slipping into a dress with braided sleeves, now holding an ice-cream cone, now reaching up with longing, now clasped in prayer, now feeling for reassurance, now pleading my desires, now pleasing, and now, even now, so still in bed, in sleep. (1984: 28)

Here, the hands are portrayed in many aspects. As a whole, the enumeration gives a multiple image of two parts of the body which seem to be independent from the narrator herself. This is a common theme in this text, where doubts about one's identity are often expressed in an alienating description of the uncontrollability of one's own body, or in the evocation of the transformation into an animal. But the repetition in the syntax here forces any unique or dominant signification into the background. The enumeration offers multiple aspects of the narrator's hands, all of which bear their own connotations. These connotations, however, are not hierarchically ordered to culminate in any sudden and unexpected conclusion that then subverts original connotations. In this quotation, the description closes with the quietness and immobility that is the common final note in *At the Bottom of the River*. The later text uses the same device, but instead of offering a silent ending it ends on a sudden and shocking subversion. To attain this effect, Kincaid needs to create the illusion of a beautiful, unpolitical colonial universe first. Only then is she able to disturb it violently and to shock the reader into an awareness of the harsh reality masked by colonial discourse.

The text appeals to the reader's fluctuating sense of a postmodernist, or modernist aestheticism, to lure the reader into a rhetorical structure that will suddenly be subverted; only in this way is the desired shock effect attained. This interpretation holds true not only for *A Small Place*. If one reads *At the Bottom of the River after* the later text, one wonders if it cannot also be read as the representation of a (post)colonial position. Here, it is its very postmodern rhetoric that refers to its ambivalent site on the borders of an imperial center, in which (post)colonial subjects are supposed to adopt the discourses of the center. Kincaid's texts are written in a contact zone in which the labels of postmodernism and modernism, postcolonialism and feminism apply. They use devices and images from texts from different strands, and they play on the reader's expectations of the function of these devices.

If a modernist aesthetics (or a postmodern "antiaesthetics") is used for postcolonial purposes, however, then it is also true that Kincaid uses these same aesthetics to integrate a remarkable Caribbean discourse in her writing in a very critical, subverting way. In fact, this curious Caribbean discourse is linked to the reticent voice in the first text. This is one of the ways in which *At the Bottom of the River* and *A Small Place* are related. One could consider *Annie John* as the bridge between them. If the essay consists largely in the assigning of positions to all engaged in the colonial practice, *Annie John* has initiated this practice of identification: it presents a narrating "I" by the name of Annie John, who can easily be identified as the nameless narrating "I" in *At the Bottom of the River*. *Annie John* adds a speaker to the earlier monological text, and thus it situates its cryptic speech. *Annie John* can be seen as a superior narrative level in which the first text could be embedded as if it were a protagonist's text. The essay takes its situating and identifying strategy from *Annie John* and makes it its central preoccupation.

However, if the later texts situate and frame the Caribbean discourse of the first text, they do not obliterate it. The Caribbean discourse returns in *A Small Place*. To add to an understanding of the role of aestheticism in the essay, I will now consider the concepts of time and space of the persistent Caribbean discourse that keeps informing Kincaid's narratives.

An important part of *A Small Place* is dedicated to a sketch of the Antiguans' opinions on history, time, and space, opinions the narrator considers highly remarkable: "I look at this place (Antigua), I look at these people (Antiguans), and I cannot tell whether I was brought up by, and so come from, children, eternal innocents, or artists who have not yet found eminence in a world too stupid to understand, or lunatics who have made their own lunatic asylum, or an exquisite combination of all three" (57). In this quotation, which I presented earlier, the narrator uses the worst colonial stereotypes for her compatriots, without excuses or mitigation. I have shown that this characterization also holds for her own narrating style, which makes use of the artistic right to idiosyncrasy and childish bluntness. The narrator characterizes this—partly her own—speech with the help of colonial discourse. She questions Antiguans' opinion about the narrative aspects she finds they neglect, that is, their vision of time and space:

> To the people in a small place, the division of Time into the Past, the Present, and the Future does not exist. . . . Then they speak of emancipation itself as if it happened just the other day, not over one hundred and fifty years ago. . . . In Antigua, people cannot see a relationship between their obsession with slavery and emancipation and the fact that they are governed by corrupt men. (55)

The narrator connects the Antiguans' lack of knowledge of their own history to the fact that they inhabit such a small island. The lack of space narrows their focalization. They are not capable of witnessing the larger context of events, and they are unable to order time into past, present, and future and to see causal links.[19] Again the narrator repeats an exotic stereotype that she puts in the mouth of the tourist at the beginning of her narrative. He thinks that the Antiguans are imputed with an imperfect sense of time because of the size of their island, "but perhaps in a world that is twelve miles long and nine miles wide (the size of Antigua) twelve years and twelve minutes and twelve days are all the same" (9).[20] Their "strange, unusual perception of time" (9) is seen to relate to the small place they inhabit and thus is considered a cultural (if not ethnic) characteristic. In the quotation above, the narrator repeats this argument in an absurdly literal way. She advocates another concept of time. To her, understanding time and obtaining a voice are closely connected. The Antiguans, however, do not push their semiotic efforts beyond the mere act of linking loose events, which keep referring to each other in the continuous movement of unlimited semiosis. The narrator believes that the Antiguans thus stay defenseless victims of isolated events, which to them just happen. In the essay, they play the role the narrator of *At the Bottom of the River* plays in the earlier text: the girl, like the Antiguans, refused to enter the adult symbolic order and went on indulging in strings of associative images. In *A Small Place*, the narrator condemns this attitude. This specific sense of time is connected to a paralyzing lack of (political, social, and historical) knowledge. The text mirrors the Foucauldian view that "[h]istory is both a discourse of knowledge and a discourse of power" (Mudimbe 1988: 188). The Antiguans lack both.

In a chapter about Michelle Cliff, Gikandi quotes Fredric Jameson to explain how Cliff portrays one of her main protagonists as a schizophrenic (Gikandi 1992). By doing so, Cliff pictures a postcolonial situation in which an individual may be placed within several cultural and linguistic discourses at the same time. In the very different context of a treatise about language and schizophrenia, Jameson says this about the schizophrenic:

he or she does not have our experience of temporal continuity either, but is condemned to live a perpetual present with which the various moments of his or her past have little connection and for which there is no conceivable future on the horizon. In other words, schizophrenic experience is an experience of isolated, disconnected, discontinuous material signifiers which fail to link up into a coherent sequence. (Jameson, quoted in Gikandi 1992: 250)

It is interesting that Gikandi connects this analysis to Cliff's representation of a lightly colored, exiled young woman who is torn between the multiple aspects of her origin. Kincaid, in contrast, applies the same concept to the Antiguans, who, after the Middle Passage, were never exiled but have since become immovably rooted within the confines of their modest birthplace.

The negative effects of the Antiguans' immobility are very serious. Gikandi explains that Cliff interprets the postcolonial schizophrenic position first and foremost as a language problem: "a key element in Cliff's narrative method is her portrayal of Clare as a schizophrenic who has failed to accede fully to the realm of speech and language" (249). For Kincaid, the condition of *not* being exiled is an impediment to the entry into language and history. It causes sheer (though interesting, according to Kincaid) madness. Frantz Fanon has spoken about the neurotic condition of the colonized (Fanon 1952). Kincaid seems to go a step further than Fanon and (Gikandi's) Cliff. For her, those colonized by neocolonialism are hopelessly psychotic. Kincaid's analysis is at odds with any nationalist endeavors. And insofar as modernism is implied in nationalism, Kincaid's representation of the nation refutes all efforts to read her as a straightforwardly modernist writer.

There is, however, a certain beauty in this schizophrenia. Kincaid does not shy away from it but looks it in the eye. She appreciates the spectacle, concentrating on its aesthetic and dramatic value. Her fascination with the aesthetic value of this schizophrenia is the starting point of her writing. It already forms the very subject matter of *At the Bottom of the River*. In her readiness to confront rather than transcend this split consciousness, she is close to Cliff, to whom the next chapter of my study is dedicated.[21] The connection between a schizophrenic sense of time and a paralyzing lack of knowledge is already suggested in Kincaid's first text. But even if that text is governed by a desire for silence and quietness, it also, in some instances, breaks through this paralysis. Quite fittingly for a story about the quest for a voice, even if it is a silent one, this breakthrough occurs most explicitly at the end: "And as I see these things in the light of the lamp, all perishable and transient, how bound up I know I am to all that is human endeavor, to all that is past and to all that shall be, to all that shall be lost and leave no trace. I claim these things then—mine—and now feel myself grow solid and complete, my name filling up my mouth" (1984: 82). The narrator recognizes the transience of the objects around her, and she acknowledges her own transience. Only the realization that she, like all existing things, is perishable gives her the feeling of stability that she needs to assert her identity and to find a voice of her own. It is precisely, and maybe exclusively, through the condition of fluidity and instability that she finds solidity. Only in that condition can her unruly, changeable body be reconciled to a stable, defining language.

I understand the narrator's newly won insight into the nature of time as being intricately bound to her own identity as a mortal. She finds her identity through a realization of the nature of time. Knowledge of one's identity means knowledge of one's position as a child, as the product of procreation, of sexuality. This insight into procreation and sexuality is in fact knowledge of time; time as the condition of transience and mortality, and thus as the condition of the passing of old generations and the creation of new generations. Some critics wish to understand Kincaid's deconstruction of linear time as a (radically) postmodern trait (Covi 1990). In contrast, I would argue that Kincaid's critique of her early work shows that the Antiguan concept of time and that of *At the Bottom of the River* should be interpreted not unambiguously as an effective cultural critique but rather as an obstacle to an insight into (neo)colonial relations. The narrator of the essay can manifest herself as a strong and critical speaking subject at the moment she dissociates herself from the schizophrenic atemporal and anticausal discourse of the Antiguans and of the earlier text. This is why the essay does not offer any Antiguan counterdiscourse. Antiguans are not supposed to speak, because they lack insight into the historical and political context of their lives. The narrator in the early text needed this insight to find the voice "filling up her mouth," and thus her dissociation from the Antiguans became unavoidable. In a later novel (*The Autobiography of My Mother*, 1996) Kincaid presents an even harsher analysis of colonial time, which is then considered as an inescapable present.

Later in this chapter I will argue that her analysis can well be read within the context of postcolonial theory. For the mere fact of its mad *beauty*, the force of the politicized voice is in large part based on this inadequate, weak Antiguan speech. However, it can be said that some aspects of the early voice are included in the narrator's effective multiple voice of *A Small Place*. This voice doesn't break away completely from its predecessor. Instead, it offers a deconstruction of some central notions in the earlier text. Although this text does not offer the liberated voice of an Antiguan woman, the essay gives us the elusive strategy of the woman migrant who freely uses colonial and anticolonial discourses but who never commits herself to one discourse or to one position. For she is interested less in rational, conveyable truth than in the beauty of marginality.

In the following section, I will discuss the role of gender in *A Small Place*, which, especially in the light of Kincaid's earlier texts in which the mother holds center stage, seems to be an ungendered text. Even if one examines the discourse of the weak, one may discern the influence of a mother's voice. This voice is bound up not with the discourse of the Antiguans of today but with the Antiguans of colonial times. Yet it is undeniably an Antiguan discourse.

Female Body, Ungendered Flesh, and a Good "She"

In the very beginnings of her book-length study of Kincaid's work, Moira Ferguson points out that motherhood, maternity, and colonialism are constantly interwoven in Kincaid's writing (Ferguson 1994: 1 ff). Discussions of colonialism will necessarily be gendered, even if this isn't always immediately clear. The gender-specificity of *A Small Place* cannot always be read in the explicit text but rather in the text's presumptions. I'll explain this statement with the help of a scrutiny of the narrative strategies. Kincaid's narrator speaks by carving "out a position of speech by recoding the very images that have been used to exclude or silence its subjects" (Pratt 1993: 863). The "recoding" of oppressive images comes down to an exposition of their absurdity and irrelevance. Indeed, the essay rests to a considerable degree on the assumption that readers will be able to recognize that absurdity without it being spelled out for them. This assumption is included in the main narrative strategy in the text, that is, the use of irony. Irony is easily reconcilable with the silence specific to Kincaid's earlier texts. Hutcheon even calls irony "the trope of the unsaid" (1991: 178). Thus, an underlying subtext can be suggested in which the truth about the oppressed's life does not have to be spelled out so that no dangerous information will be unveiled to those in power.

However, Kincaid's use of irony differs from that discussed by Hutcheon in that Kincaid also forcefully transgresses this unwritten rule of the oppressed not to reveal anything about their own situation. In an interview, Kincaid reports that Antiguans have commented on her publication of *A Small Place*, asking: "It's true, but did she have to say it?" (Perry 1990: 499). Other writers may feel a tension between the need to speak out and a fear of betraying the demand for loyalty; Kincaid seems to have discarded the norm of loyalty and to feel free to speak even the harshest insults of the people she claims to belong to. This does not mean that she claims to bring to light the whole suppressed and scandalous truth. On the contrary, the narrator postulates rather than unveils a certain truth that everybody knows, oppressors and oppressed, but that is usually not made public. Kincaid's indirect references are nevertheless shockingly blunt.

In the text, the narrator constantly refers to this unuttered truth without apologies or explanations: "The thing you have always suspected about yourself the minute you become a tourist is true: A tourist is an ugly human being" (14). The tourist is supposed to be in the know about this implicit knowledge: he has always suspected it. There is no gap between what the native knows and what the tourist (really) knows, or should know. The narrator constantly uses phrases like "You must not wonder" (13–14), "That thought never actually occurs to you. Still, you feel a little uneasy" (17). The tourist apparently has to suppress certain insights to maintain his position as a privileged tourist. This blindness characterizes the tourist also at those moments he is not a tourist, but at home and an "ordinary person"; "and really, as an ordinary person you are not well equipped to look too far inward" (16). This assumption about the shared knowledge of tourist and native again refers to the supposed unity between colonizing and colonized subject. But it also refers to a specific discourse that has little to do with the relationship between colonizer and colonized.

These constant references to certainties that are above questioning and are at the root of proper behavior speak of, and with, a gender-specific authority. I associate them with the mother's voice in Kincaid's texts. In her interview with Selwyn Cudjoe, Kincaid muses:

When I write, in some things I use my mother's voice, because I like my mother's voice. I like the way she sees things. In that way, I suppose that if you wanted to say it was feminist, it can only be true. I feel I would have no creative life or no real interest in art without my mother. It's really my "fertile soil." (Cudjoe 1990b: 222)

Reading through Kincaid's earlier texts, I find the voice of a strong motherly authority in some key passages, most apparently of course in the first fragment in *At the Bottom of the River*: "always eat your food in such a way that it won't turn somebody else's stomach; on Sundays try to walk like a lady and not like the slut you are so bent on becoming" (3). This is the voice of decency. This mother always refers to accepted, indisputable norms of behavior. She does not explain them, but she transmits them, expecting her child to accept them without questioning. They are deemed to be self-evident, a shared, collective common knowledge. I hear strong echoes between this maternal voice and the discourse of the weak, in which pleas for decency and strong criticism of bad behavior abound. Hence, the discourse of the weak does not seem ungendered: it is connected to the maternal voice that is omnipresent in Kincaid's earlier work. In *A Small Place*, the narrator adopts an attitude of astonished distance from the colonist's un-Christian behavior and an unambiguous belief in the universal validity of her mother's norms of decency. In the context of the history of global imperialism, this is rather a naive position, contrasting sharply with the clear insight into the criminal nature of colonialism articulated elsewhere. Again, the narrator appears to *cite* this voice instead of appropriating it wholly. She employs this mother's voice to tune the discourse of the weak, which constantly interferes with the colonial discourse.

On the other hand, the narrator sometimes uses the sort of speech a child might use. In doing so, she applies literal childlike innocence or naïveté to obtain the same effect of a naive, decent, self-evident speech, in which an underlying truth is made explicit: "(I once stood in hot sun for

hours so that I could see a putty-faced Princess from England disappear behind these walls. I was seven years old at the time, and I thought, She has a
putty face.)" (25). Note the parentheses: this statement is made in the margins of the story, and its self-conscious marginality reinforces its significance. The telling character of this observation results from the bluntness
and self-evidence of all statements made by an *enfant terrible.* The narrator
has characterized the voice of the Antiguans as the voice of "children, artists
or lunatics." All three kinds of people are situated outside the normal, adult
order. But this voice is also connected to the mother. I do not think that it
would be illuminating to state, metaphorically, that the mother should be
equated to a child (or to an artist or lunatic), but I do think that one should
consider a metonymical link here and see the child as her mother's daughter. In her independent observation of the Princess's ugliness, she shows
that she knows how to apply norms for grace and decency and to utter her
judgments harshly and without excuse. In this fragment, the child borrows
the mother's authority to make an evaluation that is independent of colonial standards.[22] She positions herself as a child and uses a voice in which
the voices of mother and child mingle.

A later fragment shows that the narrator's critiques may echo the
bluntness of a child's observation while also using a parent's voice to complain, in this case, about today's youth: "What surprised me most about
them [young Antiguans] was not how familiar they were with the rubbish
of North America—compared to the young people of my generation, who
were familiar with the rubbish of England—but, unlike my generation,
how stupid they seemed" (44). The topic of this sentence is not the evil of
Anglo-American cultural imperialism. The term *rubbish* is used in a much
too matter-of-fact and self-evident way. The structure of the sentence itself
makes it difficult to react to the implicit, underlying evaluation of imported culture as "rubbish." The real topic, the statement that might be
discussed, is the fact that the teenagers are so "stupid." The rest is deemed
shared knowledge, that is, shared knowledge to the generation of her
mother and those who identify with her. For there is a difference between
the colonized Antiguan subject during colonization and the colonist subject after independence. The first saw through the colonist and called him
"ill-mannered" and a "pig." The second does not make use of this knowledge. The narrator, of course, presents herself as a representative of the
first, better-informed group; she criticizes the members of the second

group as "stupid." In the above quotation, her judgment is as absolutely devastating as it is irrefutable.

Hence, the narrator positions herself in the margins as if she were her mother's child, borrowing her mother's voice, which is at the same time strongly connected to the voice of the marginalized Antiguans. Nevertheless, this futile voice is all the stronger because it does not employ a discourse that is unambiguously rooted in any recognizable political or ideological conviction (except, maybe, a commonsense Christianity). Therefore, it cannot be contradicted or refuted from a stable position within another ideologically founded discourse. It is as self-evident as all implicit, commonsense knowledge is. The narrator makes a clever use of this invulnerable discourse. Even when she offers an analysis that is informed by political notions, she uses the "naive" formulations of the colonized. She may give a theory of projection to explain racism, or speak of the language problem of the colonized, or she may offer a critique of Enlightenment; her arguments are in all these cases all the more powerful because they are *not* put into political terms. This way of speaking eludes the rational objections an explicitly political position would invite. But even in this aspect, I would say that this speech is a mother's discourse; in the eyes of a child, the mother's words hold a neutral and irrefutable authority and cannot be connected to one particular social position.

The speech strategy in *A Small Place* can be called gender-specific in the moments when it employs the mother's voice. It is difficult to find other traces of gender in the way *A Small Place* presents voices and speakers. One could understand this reluctance to endow them with gender as an indication of the fact that the gender of both tourist or colonizer and slaves do not really matter. The text implies that Northern men and women are all engaged in similar ways in this global exploitation of the South, or, if there are differences, these are not relevant to those in the South.

Except for the leading politicians staged in the essay, the gender of the Antiguans is not defined either. Only the narrator could be identified as a woman, if one were to be led by the references to the maternal voice in Kincaid's earlier work; the narrator would be a mother's daughter. But first and foremost the narrator is one of the "people like me," one of "us." She makes clear that the gender identity of "people like me" has been jeopardized by colonialism and slavery: "Do you know why people like me are shy about being capitalists? Well, it's because we, for as long as we have known you, *were* capital, like bales of cotton and sacks of sugar" (37–38). If one is treated as capital, as an object, then it becomes harder to claim a human subjectivity, let alone a female or male identity, as Hortense J. Spillers's analysis of female identity within the context of slavery has shown too; here "one is neither female, nor male, as both subjects are taken into 'account' as *quantities*" (Spillers 1987: 72). Spillers differentiates "flesh" from "body," and she defines "that distinction as the central one between captive and liberated subject-positions. In that sense, before the 'body' there is the 'flesh,' that zero degree of social conceptualization that does not escape concealment under the brush of discourse, or the reflexes of iconography" (67). The flesh, then, can be ungendered. Under slavery it is sold, tortured, and marked disregarding its gender. The flesh is completely objectified; it is appropriated not only for labor but also for medical experiments. Like Kincaid, Spillers roots her understanding of this ungendered aspect of female identity in slavery and colonization, rather than considering a yet uncontaminated African past as the foundation of Afro-Caribbean identity. Like Spillers, Kincaid's text implies that gender is less relevant than the status of colonized and slave. In the context of slavery gender is subordinated to the characters' identity as an object.

Nevertheless, the mother utters a statement that bridges the (post)-colonial strategy of objectifying and the colonized's needs for a subjectivity that is based on undisputed, shared commonsense truths:

my mother was putting up her party's posters on a lamppost just outside the house of the Minister of Culture. When the minister, hearing a great hubbub (my mother would only do this with a great hubbub) came outside and saw it was my mother, he said, perhaps to the air, "What is *she* doing here?" And to this my mother replied, "I may be a she, but I am a good she. Not someone who steals stamps from Redonda." . . . it made the minister turn and go back inside his house without a reply. (50)

The minister does not address the campaigning mother directly; she is not thought worthy of being his addressee. In this instance, her gender is not denied but accentuated to add to the insult of his refusal of addressing her directly. The mother reacts to the insult of the reference to her gender and shows that she has understood that the minister gave her the status of object: "I may be *a* she," she responds, thus rightly interpreting the minister's use of the personal pronoun as the use of a noun. Like her daughter she accepts the label, uncovering its full implications as a strategy that aims at objectifying. Then she appropriates it by adding, "I am a *good* she." The accusation that closes her utterance is a reverse act of negating her addressee's individuality; he is that "someone" who stole stamps from Redonda.

This strategy has great effect: not only does the minister stop criticizing her, but he also accepts her criticism of his behavior by not gainsaying it. On top of that, he loses his position as a speaking subject, at least for the duration of the fragment. The minister was doomed to lose this argument. The narrator had already given the mother, if not the advantage of being the first and primary speaking subject in this exchange, then surely the privilege of being the "hubbubbing" subject. And in Kincaid's semiotics, racketing and hubbubbing have the special value of invulnerability to rational arguments and are thus, in a certain respect, privileged over a speech that depends on reasoning or subtle colonial discursive strategies. The mother is quite unable to keep any thoughts she has about anything—and she has many thoughts on almost everything—to herself (50). The mother herself is not decent and quiet. Yet, she is not a speaking subject mastering her discourse. Instead, speech masters her—the sheer energy of her need to speak out drives her to her actions. The minister's retreat is the logical outcome of the setup of the fragment in which the mother is already the winner.

In Kincaid's writing, the body counters the objectifying strategies of colonialism by claiming the right to speak *as an object*. Thus, the tensions between speaking as first person and third person are ironically solved. I speak as "them," and I speak as "it," literally. This position freely takes over and identifies with pejorative labels that are assigned by dominant people while subverting these labels with the help of the self-certainty of the righteous. This righteous voice is connected to the mother. That is, it is a mother's voice with the authority it would have if seen through the daughter's eyes. In *A Small Place*, then, Kincaid sometimes occupies the position of a daughter borrowing her idea of her mother's voice to utter her devastating critique of colonial discourse.

At this point, I want to return to the issue of the female body once more, to situate Kincaid's anger more explicitly within the context of postcolonial women's writing. In postcolonial women's texts, the body may figure as a central image. Critics and writers share a concern to reinscribe the Black female body, which was, and is, erased by colonial practice (see, e.g., Spillers 1987). Helen Tiffin argues that "Anglo-European textuality and its authoritative institutionalisation not only captured the Afro-Caribbean body within Euro-representation, but severed body from soul" (1993: 911). She traces the account of this erasure and the retrieval of the erased body in texts by Erna Brodber and Jamaica Kincaid. The public recitation of English texts in school, Tiffin argues, can be seen as "metonymic of the wider processes of colonialist interpellation, in the reproduction, at the colonial site, of the locally embodied yet paradoxically disembodied imperial 'voice'" (914).

In *Lucy*, the novel Kincaid published after *A Small Place*, this "disembodiment" is undone by the assessment of sexuality as the experience of the protagonist's own female autonomy and power. At the end of the essay, Tiffin notes a very strong resistance to the written word, with its connotations of an authoritative, dominant, immobilizing discourse. When Lucy tries to write in a notebook that was given to her, she cries until the tears erase her text. "Lucy's body," Tiffin explains, "has erased a final act of scriptorial obedience" (920). This erasure could be read as a comment on the privileging of writing over speech in postmodernism, and thus as an indication of the resistance of Kincaid's writing to a definition as postmodern. Yet, in her writing strategy Kincaid shows her scriptorial inclination. The African-American and Caribbean strategy of introducing vernacular or other aspects of orality or orature in written texts just does not inspire her. She sings the praises of libraries and reading instead (1988: 42). She uses hardly any Creole or patois in her text. She writes about the body and its materiality, impropriety, and sensuality, but she does not have her writing disturbed by the vernacular voice by which the Caribbean woman's body would make itself heard. That, in contrast, is a strategy followed by, for example, Merle Collins.

Even if Kincaid decides to keep references to Caribbean orality at bay (maybe for their nationalist connotations), she still opts for a comparable strategy of disturbing the dominant discourse. Her anger disturbs because it is nonrational, unapologetic, absolute, negative, and improper. It cannot be appropriated, as it resists rational arguments; it installs a disturbing, inappropriate element in the heart of colonial discourse. Its nature as an inappropriate/d force connects it to Trinh Min-ha's description of postcolonial women's writing, according to which the retrieval of the body is a central aspect. Kincaid's anger is more ruthlessly critical than any use of Creole could be, because it is negation and resistance itself. In the end, however, Kincaid's anger is very close to Creole in that it introduces a disturbing element in the text that, like the body, opposes dominant discourse. In this way, Kincaid's angry texts can be situated in a series of postcolonial women's texts that posit the body as the disturbing element. For Kincaid, it is the mother's body that in the first place introduces anger, loudness, and nonrationality, a sign for the big hubbub. But in *A Small Place*, this anger becomes hers, so much so that it opens the possibility for the sustained, critical, discursive anger of her following novels, *Lucy* and *The Autobiography of My Mother*.

A Small Place is not an ungendered text. Its anticolonialism is formed by the text's affinity to the hubbubbing subject with a nonrational motherly authority. Moreover, by its insistence on the importance of the body, the text relates to a main concern in other postcolonial women's writing, even though it focuses not on the body itself or on Creole but on anger as a kindred disturbing force. The issue of gender, then, is never absent in Kincaid's texts, even if they appear to be about quite different things. I would even say that the essay's recurrent refusal to differentiate between female and male positions among colonizers and tourists offers telling insights into, for example, the complicity of white women in neocolonial practices. The feminist readings discussed in this section do indeed show that Kincaid's writing is never gender-neutrally postcolonial, not even in its most straightforward anticolonial moments.

The Usefulness of Labeling

This chapter opened with a reflection on the uses of labels. Is it illuminating to understand two of Kincaid's early texts as situated between postmodernism and postcolonialism? I stated that *At the Bottom of the River* and *A Small Place* share many characteristics: the rhetorical devices of the enumeration and the repetition; the centrality of beauty; the use of Standard English; the presence of an ironic marginal discourse about time and history; and the importance of the mother's voice and/or body. The essay, however, sheds the "silent voice" coveted in the earlier text and opens up in an angry address of colonial agents, tartly identifying victims and offenders, "you," "me," "us," "them," and even "it." I argued that this anger leads neither to an essentialist definition of the otherness produced by colonialism nor to a nationalist discourse. *A Small Place* is a parody without

counterdiscourse. Its anger combined with the absence of a realist posi-
tivism, leading to a coherent argument, is deeply disturbing to some readers, as the following quotation shows: "However satisfying it may be for
the writer, rage seems an ill-chosen idiom for the expression of anything
one really wants to make understood—like the letters that one writes but
should never send" (Fonseca 1989: 30). This review by a critic in the *Times
Literary Supplement* amounts to the flat refusal of a letter. Rage, she argues,
cannot represent adequately; this letter is not realist, not "illuminating," it
is not true, so it should not seek out an addressee (and certainly not me).

I quote Fonseca because her statement illustrates tellingly that anger
and realist discourse are often incompatible. And indeed, Kincaid's rage
does not aim at a realist description of colonial and postcolonial crimes.
Knowledge of these crimes is thought to be generally shared, even if it is
suppressed by those who do not dare to acknowledge it. The text expresses
a sentiment—rage—instead of offering a coherent argument. But if this
rage is catapulted into the world, Kincaid is doing nothing but "talking
back." It was not she who started the unwished-for destructive dialogue
with England. Nor does she feel obliged to be silent about the disastrous
postcolonial situation.

If the *Times* critic criticizes Kincaid's text for its lack of realism, she
situates herself within a discussion about the function of realism in postcolonial literature. Following the opinion that postcolonial texts insist on
the representation of their "otherness," some hold that they opt for a certain form of realism. But in the case of Kincaid's essay I have argued that
this generalizing observation poses some problems. Kincaid's anticolonially
motivated anger is incompatible with realism to such an extent that the reality of Antigua itself is explicitly questioned:

Antigua is beautiful. Antigua is too beautiful. Sometimes the beauty of it seems
unreal. Sometimes the beauty of it seems as if it were stage sets for a play, for no
real sunset could look like that; no real seawater could strike that many shades of
blue at once . . . all of this is so beautiful, all of this is not real like any other real
thing that there is. (77–79)

Antigua's beauty places it outside history, outside the strings of events that
happen elsewhere in the world and are not comparable to Antigua's intensity. Yet, in Kincaid's poetics, such beauty is a crucial point of reference.
Kincaid needs beauty to express her anger; she has to summon up beauty to

transmit the pain of its destruction, as in the case of her enumerations. She chooses an "aesthetical" device as a starting point to destabilize it, to interrupt it, and to show the contrasts with the harshness of its colonial context.

Ultimately, Kincaid shows that this beauty is unreal. That opinion is foremost a critique of the real: apparently, the real (colonial, corrupt) world does not allow for such beauty. However, she does not long for this beauty herself either, even if she does appreciate it. Her rejection of a discourse about (beautiful) origins reveals the absence of such a longing. Kincaid's references to beauty are not meant to suggest the possibility of an alternative discourse or reality; her social criticism based on this sense of beauty is unsentimentally futile. But that, of course, does not mean that she is wrong.

Kincaid's narrative is critical of realism. I argued above that this distrust is connected to her critique of nationalism, which, for example, is illustrated by her very harsh depiction of present-day Antigua. Like the African novels written after the late 1960s, as Kwame Appiah argues in a subtle essay on postcolonialism and postmodernism referred to already, Kincaid's writing might be seen to identify "the realist novel as part of the tactic of nationalist legitimation" (Appiah 1991: 349). Kincaid's refusal of nationalism is candid and explicit. This refusal of realism might be misunderstood as a postmodernist stance. However, Kincaid's refusal is not a turning away from politics toward a negative aestheticism but rather a politically motivated aestheticism. Kincaid's writing is aesthetical because it questions legitimacy—the legitimacy of modernity, colonialism, rationality, and nationalism. Appiah, however, decides not to use the term *postmodernism* for this project of multiple delegitimization. Instead, he argues that such a project "is grounded in an appeal to an ethical universal" (353).

This appeal is quite visible in *A Small Place*. It is there in its direct address, in its assumption about the shared knowledge of the criminal character of colonialism, and in its equation of beauty to goodness and ugliness to evil, which stresses the self-evidence of Kincaid's judgments and their indisputable, universal value. In addition, one finds very clear traces of a general, outspoken but imprecise ethic in those instances where the narrator insists that slaves are always noble and exalted and the masters criminals. This ethical attitude is visible in the very last phrases, which I have already quoted above, and in which Kincaid's narrator declares that all participants in colonialism are ultimately nothing more or less than human beings. If this poetic position can be situated in relation to postmodernism and postcolonialism, it must certainly be connected to women's writing too, as the voice of righteousness so central to it is clearly connected to the mother.

The often frustrated efforts to endow Kincaid's work with unambiguous labels teaches us that her texts partly resist important characteristics of several (postcolonial, postmodern, modernist, women's) bodies of writing, while, often ironically, appropriating other elements. It is clarifying to situate her work not between postmodernism and postcolonialism—her writing does not inhabit a binary scheme—but in a zone where modernisms, postmodernisms, postcolonialisms, and feminisms collide and overlap, and it picks its own itinerary through all of these. It is the process of labeling that illuminates the hybrid and plural nature of the site of her writing. Not discussing the ambivalent site Kincaid's writing occupies within present-day literature would come down to a counterproductive definition of "uniqueness" that would miss the point of Kincaid's kinship to the discursive and thematic struggles of other Caribbean (women) writers who often opt for solutions different from Kincaid's.

Refusing the Future: A Postcolonial Reading

Kincaid's texts may be situated between cultural discourses and aesthetical traditions, but one is not always obliged to read the uttermost plurality in her texts. In this last section, I will argue for a specific postcolonial reading of one of her later texts, with the explicit aim of finding insights to help me articulate a theoretical perspective. Such a perspective should acknowledge Kincaid's specific, gendered postcoloniality and her difference, and from there it should be open enough to understand the difference of other Caribbean women writers.

Kincaid's anger seems to reach its peak in *The Autobiography of My Mother* (1996). This eruption of rage is tempered in the following book (*My Brother*, 1998), in which there is bitterness and sadness but also more detachment in the condemnation of the mother, and a firmer awareness of having escaped, of having carved out a no longer threatened different existence, a different subjectivity. *The Autobiography of My Mother* appears as the provisional highlight of Kincaid's literary project of the unleashing of rage. Even if the novel was deemed an almost unbearable, inhuman text, it can be read as a forceful and deeply insightful gendered postcolonial critique, effectuated through an utterly radical presentation of the body. In this section, then, my reading brings together the crucial themes from the preceding sections: the mother, the mother's voice, anger, time and history, the anticolonial, the antipostcolonial, and the postcolonial strands in Kincaid's writing, and, most visibly, the body. This enables me to argue, finally, that a reading of Kincaid's work as postcolonial is productive.

In 1996, reviewers responded with a curious mixture of feelings to Kincaid's latest: both admiration and harsh dismissal. "it is . . . inhuman, and unapologetically so"; "disturbing . . . almost unbearable" (Schine 1996), "its anger is so violent and accusing . . . you feel . . . excluded, as a reader" (Donkers 1997), "a literary massacre" (Breure 1997). On the other hand, the text was judged very well written: "elegantly and delicately composed," "the most beautiful prose we are likely to find in contemporary fiction" (Schine 1996, and this, of course, went into the blurb). But since the text's beauty was judged cold and inhuman, the final judgment of the book was hardly positive. The body is irresistibly revived, "with the smell of menstrual blood and the stick of sweat smeared across the pages" (Schine 1996), but its sensuality does not offer any possibility for positive identification. Indeed, the text's rich sensuality creates a naked, dead-ended but significant present, which dismisses the comfort of narrative and language. It is by this very strategy that this uncompromising text reveals so much about our position within postcoloniality. I'll begin my argument in favor of this statement by asking, how can we theorize the body in the postcolonial?

Even if, nowadays, we have little patience for binary pairs such as text/body, at least as points of departure for analysis, and we think it much more productive to analyze subjectivity as both physical and psychological, as shaping itself through perception, sensational experience, and language simultaneously (Silverman 1996), many postcolonial texts are structured around the rhetorics of body versus text. Helen Tiffin, for example, signals in the essay discussed above that colonialism's apparatuses (such as writing) obliterate "the colonised (specifically female) body," and she points to the "counter-colonial strategies by which this 'lost' body might be reclaimed" (1993: 909). She is not the only one to do so. Within postcolonial practice, the text is made to bear many burdens: to be the site of colonialism, of Eurocentric dominance, of passive, elite intellectualism. The body is then mobilized to disturb or shatter the dominance of writing. On closer scrutiny, one finds that this disturbance is only relative: it occurs as text, in the text, and it leaves the text relatively intact. Tiffin's analysis is a case in point. She reads the passage in which Kincaid's protagonist, Lucy, is crying over her own cliché writing as a redeeming act of the body, coming "to her rescue in obliterating the re-production of the already-written" (1993: 920). But this analysis implies that the body is able to act on the textual if, and only if, it is theorized in terms of textuality. In this passage, it is the body's fluidity that is able to erase the fluidity of the ink in which the text was written. Tears function as the neat counterpart of ink. In criticism like Tiffin's, the body is modeled on the text, and it is only as such that it is able to interfere with the textual.

Indeed, the general practice of postcolonial criticism is focused on the textual, expressing itself steadily in the metaphors of text and writing. The concept of the body may be used to root theory into materiality—but it is often Black women's bodies that are evoked, often by white men's and women's apparently disembodied writing. Black women's bodies are then appropriated to articulate a white postmodern or postcolonial perspective (Homans 1994). The complex agency of these bodies is erased, and they are reduced to a rhetorical device.

But the body is a much more complex and irresistible site of critique. Within postcolonial writing, it keeps surfacing on different levels, in its different aspects, challenging the dominance of the (colonial) text, and of (colonial and postcolonial) theory *on its own terms*. When the body is thus evoked, it is often in vague yet significant terms such as "otherness" (Davies 1994) or "a certain kind of way" (Benítez-Rojo 1992)—terms that try to escape discourses and to make the presence of a living, antagonistic body felt through the evocation of, for example, its rhythm. One of the strategies through which the difference of postcolonial and Black writing is articulated is the dismissal of writing as the privileged practice for obtaining knowledge. Black and postcolonial theorists turn away from the study of writing altogether, and they study orality as an autonomous form of expression rather than as a disturbance of writing. Orality is then theorized as performance, not as a specific form of narrative; it is analyzed not in terms of writing but in terms of the body. Carolyn Cooper's work on orality demonstrates that the insistence on the body is related to a different, critical form of knowledge production (1993). In postcolonial theory, such a critical practice is developed by referring to the ways of knowing through other senses, for example, through hearing: music and dance are fine examples (Baker, Gates, Brathwaite, Benítez-Rojo). Rhythm is a highly appropriate model to study both dance (as an exemplary body art), music, and text. For written texts can be perceived as a rhythmic art too, when they are studied within the frame of, say, orality studies. This refusal to study the body as text, or even the text as text, is comparable to the efforts to theorize the text as performance and event instead of as reference.

The most productive moments in theorizing occur when the body is not represented in terms of the text, that is, as the text's disturbing counterpart, but when it is theorized in different terms altogether. I'm less interested in analyses of tears, mother's milk, and sperm as the bodily counterparts of ink. It is more promising to focus on the efforts to criticize Eurocentric forms of theorizing through representations of the body in terms of smells and taste—senses that do not easily translate into terms of textuality.

This is what Jamaica Kincaid's novel has to offer: a sense of the body that is wildly at odds with the tidiness of the text. Smashing conventions in writing on postcolonial identity and in writing about one's mother, Kincaid evokes the uneasy, loud, hard, tactile and smelly presence of a self-conscious woman, Xuela, the "my mother" in the title. Her body functions not as spectacle but as the fragmented site of a sensual communication with the self, often opening itself to sexual pleasures induced by others. The text's presentation of the body succeeds in sucking me into its harsh tactility. A woman who will not stop touching her genitals when in private, then smelling her fingers constantly when in public, a woman enjoying the rotten smell of her old menstrual blood, a man eating the wax of his ears when contemplating the sea. When reading, I was reminded of a reader's response to another Caribbean book, this one by Surinamese writer Astrid Roemer.[23] Several Surinamese woman readers agreed that the book was just too smelly to read—belying Barthes's statement that even shit, when written, has no odor (Barthes, quoted in Anderson 1995: 669). Apparently, the book invites reading positions that do not interpret the written body as text, but that consist in a strong physical reaction to the text. From sheer disgust, the reader's body even stopped the text altogether. As speech act, then, this text is both an offense and a challenging claim to a scandalous self.

Kincaid has been soliciting the fierce reactions to her text. After having been praised for the postmodern charm of her earlier work (e.g., *At the Bottom of the River*), she declared in a 1990 interview "I'm not very interested in that sort of expression anymore. Now, for instance, I've become very interested in writing about sex, or smells. I'm interested in being not a decent person" (Perry 1990: 499). Kincaid's inappropriate success in making the text "smell" is also a success in challenging colonialism, and with it, the theoretical discourses still related to colonial discourse and to the narrow postcolonial discourses she loathes. Here is an opportunity, for students of postcoloniality to deepen or transform their practices of theorizing. In choosing a text, one can study the occurrence of nontextual models of knowledge *in a text*, and as such perhaps articulate the possibility of opening up one's theoretical texts to these nontextuals models, too. If theory is etymologically related to seeing, what kind of knowledge will be produced when sight is challenged by taste and smell?

Kincaid's text seems to suggest that colonial discourse excludes the formerly colonized in the Caribbean from knowledge. The narrator states, "Everything about us [the colonized] is held in doubt and we the defeated define all that is unreal, all that is not human, all that is without love, all that is without mercy. Our experience cannot be interpreted by us; we do not know the truth of it" (37). Against this colonial denial, the text argues that, in contrast, the colonized are eminently equipped for a search for insight. True, it has often been suggested that oppression dulls the senses, as if oppression closes the oppressed off from knowledge. But this is not so with Kincaid's heroines. Here, oppression causes a very acute sense of one's surroundings—a sharp, deep, real knowledge. "Those who have lost are never hardened—they feel it deeply, always" (193). Those, of course, are the colonized. It is only "the callous, the cynical, the unbeliever" who "will say . . . life is a game" (192). This deep, continuous, painful experience renders one vulnerable and susceptible. In this way, the defeated are privileged; they are not closed off from life's sensual though painful reality. But the truth they, and Xuela, are capable of grasping, is not a textual truth. Early in the story, it is already stated that "[t]he words she [her foster-mother] used were without meaning . . . they did not hurt me, for I did not love her" (9). Textual meaning is predicated upon love. When there is no love, there cannot be meaning either. The absence of love is the result of the death of Xuela's mother, who sadly died at her daughter's birth. Her death is the decisive moment with which the narrative opens. Xuela's experience of meaninglessness is caused by the traumatic shock of losing her mother—one might read this as the shock of the loss of the mother country in slavery. As Geoffrey Hartmann states, such a trauma may result in the dissociation of the phenomenal and representation. The process of healing that split will have to go through reestablishing contact with the body (Hartmann 1995). This is Xuela's way. Dismissing the possibilities and opportunities of representation, she focuses on the body as the only way to full subjectivity. The partly orphaned Xuela is endowed with a heightened awareness of taste, smell, touch, sight, and hearing, but her tastes, smells, and sights are spoilt. Loveliness has left them, and tastes have soured.

Even if visual impressions are strong, in general the text plays down the importance of the visual as superior sense. There is a sound reason for this. Sight exposes the glaring racial otherness in the features of the colonized: both children and adults were taught to mistrust anyone looking like themselves (48). The colonized are taught to loathe not only their own appearances but also their own faculty of sight. In addition, they learn to distrust their eyes; their visions of presumed supernatural events are deemed superstitious hallucinations. This loathing causes the community to split, and it isolates its people, but it also binds them in an inescapable, destructive mirroring.

Because for the colonized, then, looking is no longer a privileged sense, other senses are brought into play: hearing, for example. Xuela's careful listening to distinct sounds offers important insights into the nature of reality and unreality (42). But the most remarkable textual move is the privileging of smell. The impact of Kincaid's emphasis on smell is high, since smell is one of the senses with a scandalous prestige. In the slow development of a Western hierarchy of the senses, the visual has been put on the higher part of the scale, and smell on the lowest (Classen, Howes, Synnott 1993). Nevertheless, both smell and sight were mobilized in the colonizing strategies of othering. Smell is seen as the savage way of knowing, producing a very basic, physical knowledge. The association to savagery has been institutionalized in the process of colonization: colonial peoples were judged dirty, smelly; they were imagined as disgustingly open, polluted and polluting bodies, in dire need of cleansing. Thus, colonial strategies have very literally focused on the hygienic reform of the people in the colonies (e.g., the Philippines; see Anderson 1995). Kincaid appropriates smell as one of her privileged ways of experiencing and knowing the world and one's self. Colonialism dismissed smell as a route to knowledge altogether, even if it employed smell in its creation of a glaring, shameful difference. Kincaid acknowledges the intertwining of sight and smell and exposes it by focusing on smell as a route to knowledge of the self. Xuela uses smell to give herself a sense of self; she likes touching her genitals and does so often, always eagerly smelling her own strong intimate smell on her fingers. One might read the insistence on scandalous, sexual smell as a provocation. I also see a daring act of a claiming of self. Kincaid is writing about people who have been deeply, deeply shamed. Colonial discourse has declared them as physical, smelly, shameful; and shame, an unbearable emotion, silences, immobilizes, freezes. There is something magnificent about the way Kincaid appropriates the most shameful of bodily aspects, the smell, as the foundation of the knowledge of self and others. This is not just because she insists on proprioceptivity as her strategy for identification (and therefore on the autonomy of self-definition). To the contrary, smell is significant because *others* know you by it; so, when Xuela smells herself, she smells herself as if a scandalized other might smell it. Identification cannot occur without the interference of an Other. Identification is the process in which one's own experience of one's body and the others' gaze come together; and as the text clearly demonstrates, the others' gaze is also a cultural gaze, implying cultural norms and values (Silverman 1996). But in the detour from genitals to nose, Xuela subverts the colonial judgment into her own automatically positive evaluation: "Whatever I was told to hate I loved and loved the most" (32). Xuela's self-identification consists of the appropriation of the degrading images offered to her by colonialism by means of the elegantly simple gesture of inversion. Smell produces a knowledge that cannot be doubted.[24] Scents and smells form the rock bottom of Xuela's experience and therefore the foundations of her knowledge of the world—not because it is a direct, unambiguous sensual knowledge, but because colonialism declared it the most debased form of knowledge, which therefore, by the text's simple logic of reversal, must be the colonized's ideal route to knowledge.

The key word here is *appropriation.* The notion of appropriation helps us to gain insight into the text's postcoloniality—and into its radically postcolonial definition of sensuality as a route to knowledge. From a consideration of the narrative level of the text, I now turn to the speech act performed by the text. For it is less the narrative itself than the textual act that enrages its readers so. Moreover, the text's postcoloniality is primarily located in its performative aspects. According to one reviewer, Marnel Breure, the text is nothing less than a literary massacre, and it is. It is the daughter's killing of the mother, who is also guilty of murder, as, in the text's curious paradox, this mother denies her children life. But it is at the same time a rehabilitation of both murderers and, consequently, a quest for identity.

Here is the key passage that forms the starting point of my discussion. In this horrifyingly picturesque passage, situated after her first abortion, Xuela narrates how she will refuse being a mother:

I would bear children, but I would never be a mother to them. I would bear them in abundance; they would emerge from my head, from my armpits, from between my legs; I would bear children, they would hang from me like fruit from a vine, but I would destroy them with the carelessness of a god. I would bear children in the morning, I would bathe them at noon in a water that came from myself, and I would eat them at night, swallowing them whole, all at once. . . . I would walk them to the edge of a precipice. I would not push them over; I would not have to; the sweet voices of unusual pleasures would call to them from its bottom; they would not rest until they became one with these sounds. I would cover their bodies with diseases, embellish skins with thinly crusted sores, the sores sometimes oozing a thick pus for which they would thirst, a thirst that could never be quenched. (97)

and on and on, until the mention of the boxes in which she will bury them. What strikes me in this passage is the boundless sensual richness of the destruction. This is an open, plural body, sprouting edible children in mythological and organic ways, pissing over them, opening up their bodies, too. This body extends itself to bring these eerie babies to the edge of life, to the edge of a luring universe of sounds. The babies lust for these sounds of death and the taste of the rot afflicted by their mother.

This murderous mother is not unlike the anonymous African mothers in slavery who killed their children to save them the hardships of slavery (see for example Toni Morrison and Ama Ata Aidoo); she also kills her children partly because she is unable to see a life that is not corrupted by colonialism. On the other hand, the children are not innocent either; their lust for death and corruption makes them kin to the spirit-children described by such writers as Ben Okri and Amos Tutuola. For example, in the Igbo and Yoruba cultures, spirit-children (called "ogbanje" in Igbo and "abiku" in Yoruba) are children who die soon after their birth. Parents assume that they will return to be born again, and to die again, to pester their grieving parents. This childish greed for death and corruption clears the mother's guilt. She has not really killed them; they killed themselves already. Nevertheless, this is a gruesome passage, vivid with violent accusation. Keeping in mind that this is a daughter's account of her mother's life (Kincaid writing her fictional mother's autobiography), this passage exposes a terrible murderous mother who neglects her children cruelly but magnificently. The text screams its passionate outrage at such a mother while at the same time glorifying and absolving her. For the outraged daughter is among the spirit-children, thirsting for the wounds afflicted by the mother, as this pain is the only intimacy to be had from her. As a spirit-child, she admits desiring death too, a death that is both emancipation from the mother and a return to the mother, who, in this text, is always closely associated to death.

Sixteen years before the publication of this book, Kincaid said, "the way I became a writer was that my mother wrote my life for me and told it to me" (Perry 1990: 248). Now, turning the tables and grasping her mother's discursive authority, Kincaid writes her mother's life for *her*, in a discourse originally taken from her. In fact, this is as much a narrative of identification as it is a narrative of, to use a both psychoanalytical and Caribbean (post)colonial notion, cannibalism. The daughter allowed her mother to devour her, thus (to use Silverman's evocation of Scheler's terms) identifying heteropathically with the mother, who has swollen into her ideal ego. The same heteropathic identification can be observed in Kincaid's, the daughter's, continuous literary strategy to let herself be devoured by colonial discourse. She does not just speak English, but she surrenders completely; in her literary career she has developed a very effective strategy of *quoting* this discourse. The mother's dismissal of colonial discourse as lies and hypocrisy is strong, much stronger than Kincaid's. Yet, the mother, too, employs aspects of colonial discourse (e.g., the notion of the lack of history in Caribbean people, her crude description of her physical self, her emphasis on truth). She has taken colonial discourse in her mouth, but on her own terms. Thus, she incorporated colonial discourse in the same manner as she devoured her daughter, that is, in an act of idiopathic identification, identifying the other as herself. Her proprioceptive subjectivity is so strong that at a certain exhilarating point in the story, when she sees a man who pleases her very much, she stands there ("enjoying completely the despair I felt of being myself," 165), looking at him, and begins shouting her own name, again and again. This is enough to attract him to her. This, to me, is Kincaid's provoking celebration of the splendor of unabashed idiopathic identification, a celebration of identification as a brutal act of cannibalism. The trope of cannibalism to indicate postcolonial processes of identification has not always been met with great enthusiasm. It is a bit of a dead-end strategy—let's face it—and it leaves little space for utopian musings about multicultural futures. Indeed, the devouring mother, Xuela, ultimately wishes to be devoured by death itself. Perhaps this was one of the reasons why some reviewers dismissed Kincaid's book as unethical. However, the reference to cannibalism also evokes vitality, sensuality, sexuality, and rebellion, as in the famous, outrageous calypso by Sparrow, in which cannibalism (as is often the case in calypso) is a metaphor for having sex, or, in this case, rape. The text lacks Sparrow's vitality, but sensuality and sexuality are paramount as the privileged routes to identity and knowledge. However, they are related to death, not life, to the present instead of to the future. The text's postcoloniality, then, is located both in its cannibalistic strategies of appropriation and in its curious temporality.

As I argued in the introduction, the concept of the postcolonial refers to (1) that which comes after the colonial, (2) that which opposes colonialism (anti), and (3) that which can be described as a *critical working through* of the colonial. Kincaid's text helps understand the complexity of the last definition in two different ways.

First, *the postcolonial inhabits the colonial.* My argument about cannibalism demonstrated just that. But there's more to it. If this narrative seems to be an account of endless acts of incorporation, it is because the outside (i.e., the colonial) is brought inside, just as much as the inside (Xuela's sensational self, her name) is brought into the open. In the end, everything is in the open. And this bare presence has the strength of truth, of real knowledge. The following passage will show what I mean:

a lady is a combination of elaborate fabrications, a collection of externals, facial arrangements, and body parts, distortions, lies, and empty effort. I was a woman and as that I had a brief definition: two breasts, a small opening between my legs, one womb; it never varies and they are always in the same place. . . . Such a description has at its core the act of self-possession" (159).

The truth contained in the focus on the bare force of life and sexuality is at the same time mastery over one's self. It is not in the first place a mimetic or representational truth, but it is primarily true as performative, that is, because it is effective, as it offers a basis on which Xuela can claim herself. Remarkably, this is very much a crude description *from outside.* The insistence on this bare, absolute truth functions as a strong critique of colonialism, which is here schematically defined as a layered system. The top layer consists of elaborate discourses about civilization, Christianization, cultivation, which the text defines as lies. The bottom layer consists of what the text may call crime, plunder, exploitation, murder. Knowledge consists of grasping the bottom layer, which is also a kind of "outside." It is the hidden part of colonialism, and as such it is defined as outside discourse. But this truth is also already contained within colonial discourse (the top layer) itself, especially in its unmitigatedly blunt racism and sexism, or in the moments when it ironically subverts itself. For this reason, Kincaid uses colonial terms to articulate the truth. For example, when Kincaid uses the term *lies* to define white speech, and the term *truth* for the pain felt by the colonized, she echoes Joseph Conrad's definitions, strengthening herself with a grand colonial tradition. So, curiously, truth lies at the heart of colonial discourse, which is also its material, embodied "outside." Outside itself is where it is most itself.[25] For here one finds the *effects* on the bodies of others. Against the endless discourses about the colonized, against the endless fabrics of words and lies, Kincaid opposes a strong, multiple concept of truth, that is, the material truth of colonialism, which consists of the colonizer's and the colonized's sensual and emotional experiences of pain, shame, and anger.

This is why the text's vehement "no" to colonial discourse is expressed through evoking the body. There is no rational critique of its arguments, as Kincaid's postcolonialism has appropriated colonial discourse lock, stock, and barrel. Its critique is harshly expressed in the shameless exposure of the gloriously degrading colonial truth. This "no" is so harsh and bitter that it is experienced as disgusting by its readers in a very physical way. The postcolonial has been defined as the impossible "no" to a structure that one critiques yet inhabits intimately (Spivak 1993b: 60). Following Silverman's insight into the nature of text as address instead of reference, postcolonial writing could be approached as the act of saying no, as a relative turning away. Here, however, one finds a much more intense gesture. We could try not just to acknowledge the critique implied in the presence of the physical, or the different mode of knowing evoked; we might also acknowledge the act contained in the representation of the body in the text. A text may be seen to kick up a blinding, deafening, physical row. Yet, it may not move outside the site and moment it is criticizing. And this is the second way in which we can understand the postcolonial as *a critical working through*. It can be seen as a continuous returning, as a refusal to move on.

The temporal aspect of postcoloniality is directly linked to the issue of identification. According to Silverman, succeeding in bringing together the sensational body and the (cultural) gaze results in a beneficial feeling of being in place, in time. We have seen how hard it is for the colonized to reconcile the dehumanizing colonial gaze to the sensational body (Silverman also points to this insight). Black identity has often been described as being displaced and, with Fanon's term, as being "belated." Xuela's continuous efforts to create a present for herself points to her unease with the disjunction of sensational body and cultural definition, or at least with the peculiar temporality resulting from it. Xuela's maternal efforts to resist reproduction can be read as a resistance to future and a desire to locate oneself in a stable present. By sending her children into death, the place where her own mother resides too, Xuela refuses not only a future but also her past, for she refuses her children to relive her own past. Cutting herself off from past and future, she compresses her life force in the present, which receives an incredible force. All identities are collapsed in a present enlarged by magnifying its sensual immediacy. Kincaid has stopped history.

This is the most literal way one could imagine the third definition of the postcolonial, as a continuous working through of the present. We can now read the insistence on sensuality as related to death as a postcolonial dismissal of both history and future. The issue of history is explicit in the book, if only because it is dedicated to Derek Walcott, Caribbean author and Nobel Prize winner, who has written extensively about the Caribbean need to escape history. Kincaid's text is very much about the death represented by colonial history. History is a grave, in a very literal sense (185). In the next, sudden, and unexpected passage all temporalities threaten to collapse: "This account of my life has been an account of my mother's life as much as it has been an account of mine, and even so, again it is an account of the life of the children I did not have, as it is their account of me. . . . This account is an account of the person who was never allowed to be and an account of the person I did not allow myself to become" (227–28). In this key passage the full implications of Kincaid's writing process become clear. The insistence on truth makes way for the acknowledgment that the narrative was written in an imperfect future tense. Until this passage, the text focused on the present as the perfect site, as the only place from where knowledge can spring. It was a celebration of the actual, to use Deleuze's happy term. "The present is always perfect. . . . The future I never long for—I am never in a state of anticipation" (205) and "oh, to be a part of anything that is outside history" (218). Now, the present is revealed to be conditional, virtual. At the same time, the text deplores its impotence to actualize this present; this present is the condition of a mother who has not been. It is only in the enthralling energy of the text itself, which addresses our senses, that time is fleetingly arrested. And we, too, are brought back to face the actual postcolonial pain and anger, so bitterly structuring a present we do not yet fully experience.

But can we translate this refusal of history to either a critique of dominant forms of knowledge production, of theory, or even a different notion of knowledge? I have defined the postcolonial as situated *inside* the colonial; and you might counter that definition by saying that this is an act of Eurocentric appropriation, submitting the postcolonial to the scriptocentric laws that structure many dominant Western theoretical discourses. But that is not my point. In general, if postcolonial writing inhabits colonial discourse, as a hybrid form of writing it also inhabits and evokes other discourses—for example, nationalist, Marxist discourses, Creole orature. It would even be possible to see a reference to African epistemologies in Kincaid's emphasis on sensational experience. It has been pointed out that one differing trait of African philosophy (in general) would be its emphasis on the empirical (Gyekye 1997: 26, 43n2). Kincaid's text is almost exaggerating the importance of the empirical, the sensually experienced. Instead of a mere reference to an (essentialist notion of an?) African epistemology, we find a critical reinvention of such an epistemology. It would not really enhance our understanding of the text if we tried to *explain* it from an assumed African epistemological background. But it is not necessary to seek such a vague, general concept to frame our interpretation of the text. As Jean Marie Makang, professor of philosophy, suggests, if the text testifies to a different (African, or Afro-Caribbean) epistemology, this is so because it is also rooted in the prephilosophical experience of racism and colonialism (Makang 1997). Such a perspective helps to interpret Kincaid's position. She offers a critique from the inside (by inhabiting colonial discourses), but her position as a speaker is firmly situated in extradiscursive moments, that is, in the pain and anger inflicted by colonialism. We need a theory of truth and text that understands Kincaid's rebelliously postcolonial text as a speech act, a loud, angry, accusing "no." As a Dutch reviewer (Jos de Roo) remarked, this act can even be understood within a Caribbean rhetoric of provocation. The body here is the sensual (tactile, smelly) mirror of Western stereotype and is thus cast back in Western faces. Kincaid's critics have understood her apparent desire to stop history as a megalomanic act of evading transcience and have dismissed it as a tyrannical desire for absolute mastery. This is true, perhaps. But this is also a familiar response to people expressing unwelcome emotions like unabashed anger. This is the challenge offered by Kincaid's indecent performance. How can theory respond to anger?

Much of postcolonial criticism is trying to open up a promising future in which anger will be clarified, fear acknowledged, pain recognized. Indeed, what would our work amount to if we weren't driven by the effort of moving beyond the atrocities of the past and the painful present? Kincaid, in contrast, brings us back to the terror and shows it to be fully operative in an unmovable present. She may be right in stating that we still have to linger before we have arrived. This present must still be acknowledged and actualized—among others things, by refusing to always conceptualize the body as text and to open up to the body's often disagreeable plural actuality.

7

A Dog with a Foaming Mouth: Michelle Cliff and the Dangers of the Interior

> And beneath that silence, there is a raw welter of cadence that tumbles
> and strains towards words and that makes the silence a blessing because
> it shushes easy speech. That cadence is home.
>
> —Dennis Lee (quoted in Ashcroft, Griffiths,
>   and Tiffin 1989: 141)

Silence, for Canadian critic Dennis Lee, is the blessed instrument for muting deceitful, alienating speech; silence is the condition that makes perceivable a meaningful rhythm—a cadence that may be the as yet inarticulated precondition of a "home language." But this silence is undermining too, and "[i]t saps our nerve." It is the disquieting element in what some would wish to be the orderly process of aiming for speech. Such a silence may seem to be a more general literary phenomenon. Indeed, silence has been extensively theorized from many perspectives. It has been scrutinized as an element of modernism, as an aspect of postmodernism. It has been hailed as the marker of difference in feminist fiction, and it has been called the "active characteristic linking all post-colonial texts" (Ashcroft, Griffiths, and Tiffin 1989: 187; see also Huggan 1990: 22). But in a postcolonial context it functions in a demonstrably specific way.

In their handbook about postcolonial theory and practice, Ashcroft, Griffiths, and Tiffin consider "silence" in connection with the problem of applying an imported, "alien" language to the different spaces of the settler colony. To writers in the colony, the language of the mother country seems "inauthentic" in the new context, and this inauthenticity cannot be solved by the adaptation of language to the new location. Writers seem rather to want to explore the tension between words and place. They advocate "the task to un-name," a task which, according to Ashcroft's reading of these writers, has to be performed against the primary background of the *silence* that is central to the (post)colonial linguistic experience.

Ashcroft, Griffiths, and Tiffin end their short paragraph about language, place, and theory in the settler colonies with another quote by Lee, in which he wonders whether the real task of the colonial writer is not "to fake a space of our own and write it up, but rather to find words for our space-lessness" (163, quoted in Ashcroft, Griffiths, and Tiffin 1989: 142). This wavering between silence as home and silence as space-lessness serves well to introduce the role of silence in several texts by Jamaican writer Michelle Cliff, who now lives in the United States.[1] From her writing, I conclude that Cliff would rather agree with the latter statement than with Lee's former suggestion that a "home" can be found in the sounds of that silence. As I will show below, Cliff is not attracted by a rhetorics in which the "home" functions as the natural closure. "Home" is for her a highly problematic notion.

Instead of being radically and superiorly "placeless," Caribbean women writers have different (desired and detested) homes and residences, and they will have to find words for their complicated plural position within, against, and between all those places. Women writers may want to articulate their specific relationship to such concepts of "home" and add concepts of their own. In the work of many of them, one can indeed discern a specific feminine position. This plurality is wrongly neglected by Ashcroft, Griffiths, and Tiffin, who deny gender-specificity by claiming too easily that their argument goes for "the" feminine position as well. It is telling that the collective of Lee's postcolonial writers is indicated by the pronoun "we" and that a "he" is used for each of its members, even when Margaret Atwood is mentioned as an example. What about the *Black* "she"? What about all the different women writers, with their different hybrid cultural, racial, ethnic, and sexual positions? On examining the works of Michelle Cliff, one sees that her specificity, for example, is to be found in the way the theme of sexuality is interwoven with that of postcolonial and Black language. For Cliff, sexuality is thematized as *lesbian* sexuality. It is an important aspect of her analysis of the complexities of home and race. Even if it has become difficult to maintain that a woman has no country, as Adrienne Rich has explained to Virginia Woolf, Cliff may hold that a lesbian may have no family, no home, no country, until she has found a way to speak her sexuality together with her race.

Cliff's struggle with language is part of the postcolonial struggle in that it consists, in part, of efforts to articulate the necessary distance to a deceitful language. But Cliff has to wage battle against two languages at the same time, the King's English and *patois*, both of which she needs to express different sides of her person. To find a speech to articulate the complexities of her exile, she takes recourse to a variety of Black and white genres and discourses. But her other task is to battle the heterosexual, masculine, and/or class assumptions of these identifying discourses. To do so, she uses language strategies of silence and indirect speech.

Silence, however, is not usually seen as a feminist strategy for women of color. Articles by African-American and Chicana writers often stress the lifesaving necessity of shattering silence. Chicana writer Anzaldúa, set upon acquiring her "serpent's tongue," cries out, "I will overcome the tradition of silence" (Anzaldúa 1987: 64). Audre Lorde, bell hooks, and many others side with this hard-won slogan. So does Jamaica Kincaid in her essay *A Small Place*, offering us an interestingly ambivalent postcolonial feminine perspective on silence (see Chapter 6). In her earliest work, Kincaid explores a "silent voice." In her next novels she radically dismisses her former celebration of silence, implicitness, and inwardness. In the preface to a collection of literary pieces, *The Land of Look Behind* (1985), Michelle Cliff seems to agree with Kincaid's literary statement about the necessity to learn to speak out explicitly, even angrily. Nevertheless, Cliff's desire to speak out openly herself did not result in an unequivocal, positive text. This seems to be the point Caribbean critics Mordecai and Wilson are making when they refer, somewhat irritatedly, to her aesthetics of alienation, which would place her within the literary tradition rather of "a 'francophone' than an anglophone consciousness" (xvii). Indeed, Cliff's speech seems to be structured by a certain implicitness, even in the texts that made her an uninhibited writer who "tore into the indoctrination of the colonizer" and who "surprised [herself] with the violence of [her] words" (16). It is one of the aims of this chapter to look into the background of her slightly contradictory strategy of speech.

Cliff testifies to a deep mistrust of language. She experiments with syntax, with prose and poetry, with hampered speech and stuttering to find a fuller means of expression. Cliff uses strong metaphors to formulate her understanding of speech and silence. For example, Cliff thematizes the idea of interiority, which is central to her writing, through beautiful metaphors like the garden. With the help of the Caribbean feminist/womanist literary concept of the *kumbla*, I can explicate the function of the trope of interiority in Cliff's work.

Cliff's silence can be studied as an object of representation. To do so, I examine the explicit, obvious discourses on silence and the metaphors that are used to point to it. But I will also examine the ways Cliff *uses* silence as a strategy of representation to tell her stories about silence. I'll frame my reading of her silence first in a Caribbean context, then in more general postcolonial and feminist contexts to offer an evaluation of the situated nature of this silence.

Plurality: Passing and Polyglotting

I was also, in those sections, laboring under the ancient taboos of the assimilated: don't tell outsiders anything real about yourself. Don't reveal *our* secrets to *them*.
—Michelle Cliff (1986: 16)

This silence is presented as something that belongs to the private sphere. Cliff, speaking as the reminiscing author herself in the preface to her collection *The Land of Look Behind*, describes silence as the weapon to defend *our* secret identity against outsiders. Silence, in Cliff's texts, has very much to do with the impossibility of pronouncing a straightforward "I" or "we." Cliff's text thematizes the complex position of the light-skinned Jamaican woman, taking the act of "passing" as its recurrent motive. Passing stands here for passing for white. For Cliff it is equally important to reflect on the act of passing for heterosexual, and to reflect on the condition of being "forced into male modes of thinking and argument" (1978: 7). When one is passing, the distinction between "we" and "they" necessarily becomes blurred, and the "we" becomes ambivalent. In *The Land of Look Behind*, silence is connected to passing, to hiding, to invisibility. The connection is stated clearly in a fragment called "Claiming an Identity They Told Me to Despise," in which Cliff feels that "my use of language and imagery had sometimes masked what I wanted to convey" (16). There one finds this: "Passing demands quiet. And from that quiet—silence" (22).

A useful concept in Caribbean feminist literary practice that captures this situation well is the *kumbla*. The term is derived from *calabash*, and in the novels of Jamaican writer Erna Brodber it is used to describe a closed space that serves as a treacherous protection for Black women (especially those who are from the middle class, especially those who are light-skinned) against a racist and sexist world. The kumbla represents strategies of adaptation, assimilation, and disguise.[2] If Cliff's texts are read through this image, we can see that they often center around a kumbla (even if it is never defined as such). Her kumbla has been formed by her mother's demands for her behavior as white, as straight. From this kumbla, however, Cliff has also learned a strategy of an ambivalent, plural use of pronouns, and this tool will help her in coming out. Indeed, the kumbla itself offers her the tools to break out of her kumbla. Second, Cliff's kumbla does not consist of employing the dominant discourse only. Cliff uses both dominant and nondominant discourses, as I will show. Third, Cliff thematizes the metaphor of the kumbla by exploring the threat present in voids and interiors, such as the womb. She will carry it through to the point of deconstructing the very notions of inside and outside, refusing all ideas of closed interiority.

I will discuss these three characteristics below. I begin by looking at the first point and examine the way Cliff's "we" is destabilized by the context of passing and hiding of her texts. Somewhere else in the collection, in a piece written much later, I find a citation from a letter from Addie Saffold, writing to her brother Captain Pinchback, the grandfather of Jean Toomer: "In all the wide world there is no safety for the Negro but Pink *we* are *not* Negroes" (86). After having cited the fragment, the narrator bursts into a rhythmic rhyme, slightly tinged by vernacular:

> Girl, what made you confuse your priorities so?
> Why do I care what you said a hundred years ago?
> Because you are lost to me, and I to you.
> We are—because of who we are—unsafe.
> And no amount of nonsense will protect you. (86)

"I," "you" and "we" are rather complex positions here. Their complexity could well be considered the main issue of the verse. This can be observed when one takes a closer look at the concept of the protecting "nonsense" in the last lines. They refer to Audre Lorde's famous saying "Your silence will not protect you." Significantly, "silence" is here replaced by "nonsense." Why? On the one hand, silence has an ambiguous function in Cliff's writing. She needs it to be able to break her silence. On the other hand, the inability to break her silence in a literal way is not her problem. Cliff, as she states in the preface, has since her adolescence been able to "speak fluently," "in eloquent linear prose"—her problem was rather that "I could speak fluently, but I could not reveal" (12). She could speak only in the guise of a European, a white woman. She has to break open this "nonsense" to address the things that really matter. One aspect of this nonsense is the nonsensical choice for a speaking position, for the way one situates oneself as a white "I" and a white European "we."

The most serious part of the nonsense, however, is the supposition that there is an unambiguous position, or even only one position to speak from. Hence, even when defending the opposite statement, namely that there is only the *Black* position from which lightly colored women can speak, the speaker takes up a double position. In the third line, the speaker acknowledges a shared position with the passing woman and thus distances her from those who find the case irrelevant. The speaker too has been a "white marble figure of no homeland" (85), "a Statue," as the title of the fragment indicates: "The Laughing Mulatto (Formerly a Statue) Speaks." *As* (formerly) passing women, acquainted with the ambivalence of their identity, the speaker and the spoken-to can meet only under the shared denominator of *Black*. The "We" of the fourth line refers to Saffold and the speaker as light-skinned women, but also to the collectivity of all Black women; and in the last line, the speaker borrows the speaking position of Audre Lorde to be able to speak as an (unambiguously, outspoken) *Black* woman to the sister with whom she shares her confusion.

Perhaps already in her use of orality (vernacular, rhythm, rhyme, questions), but especially in her choice of signifying upon a Black woman writer she speaks as a Black woman. However, in her address she poses as a woman with a lighter skin who still finds it most relevant to discuss the choices of lightly colored women in present and past. In this regard, speaking one's plurality means breaking the silence of the old taboo by pronouncing that one is *Black*, a statement that is meaningful only when heard together with the implicit declaration of being not-quite-Black, a mulatto, a former "passing woman."

The second characteristic of the kumbla in Cliff's writing is the strategy of quoting not only the dominant but also the nondominant practices. The necessity of a plural speech strategy is connected not only with the act of passing for white but also with the practice of passing for straight. In this section I will examine the question in terms of *language*. Here are two short statements about the function of *patois*. In the preface, Cliff states that in her new novel (*No Telephone to Heaven*, I suppose) she alternates "the King's English with *patois*, not only to show the class background of characters, but to show how Jamaicans operate within a split consciousness. It would be as dishonest to write the novel entirely in *patois* as to write entirely in the King's English" (14).[3] Later, in the "Fire"-piece, after her cousin Henry, who has been confronted with English racism, invites her to sleep with him, she takes refuge in *patois* to refuse without either confessing her lesbianism or hurting his already threatened Black manhood: "I pretend I am back home and start patois to show him somehow I am not afraid, not English, not white" (69). The Black cousin has shown his contempt for homosexuals earlier, so if she revealed her lesbianism to him she would distance herself from him. In this situation, declaring oneself a lesbian is declaring oneself white, and she desperately wants to be close to him and to repair the damage to his manhood racism has caused. *Patois* is the Black vernacular that differentiates its speaker from the colonizer; here, it is also the language of heterosexuality, specifically male sexuality. In Cliff's vision, difference in sexual orientation is erased within this discourse. Racial difference pushes aside difference of sexuality.

But even if Cliff doesn't find a way to speak this other difference in *patois*, she finds the means to say it in a more general *Black* speech:[4]

> Your best friend's a bulldagger
> That is very plain to see
> I say, your best friend's a bulldagger
> That is very plain to see
> Now that you been told it
> Can you tell them you love me? (88)

The subtle and sudden change of address resembles the one in another verse, even if it is less dramatic:

> Some of us part Indian
> And some of us part white
> Yes, sisters, some of us part Indian
> And some of us part white
> But we still call you sisters
> Even if you judge our skin too light. (89)

In both verses the narrator is able to play with the identification of herself, speaker, and addressee. Staying within the Black community, within Black orature, she can perform difference by subtly shifting speaking positions. The second verse seems clear to me. The "us" in the first lines embraces the whole community of Black women, whereas in the last lines this "us" is suddenly differentiated in a more specific "we" and "you."[5] The first verse may need some elaboration. In this verse, the speaker (an implicit "I") is first an anonymous other who rather harshly informs a "you" about the sexual identity of her best friend. But in the last two lines, this best friend in her turn addresses the "you" and the speaker(s) in the first lines are referred to as "them." The last "I," the lesbian, has others unmask herself in no unclear way; thereafter she can close the verse with a highly significant "me"—this "me" carries the burden of the pejorative name others bestowed upon it, but this "me" refers also to the loved one who had always figured in another discourse. It is no liberated, autonomous "me" that is claimed here; it is a "me" marked and soiled by others.

In other pieces in *The Land of Look Behind* there are other instances of the borrowing of tongues, but mostly from dominant discourses. In "A Visit from Mr. Botha" Cliff parodies "Gilbert and Sullivan because their work epitomizes salient aspects of the British Empire which remain vibrant" (14), in "I-tie-all-my-people-together" she uses incantations from a Yoruban hymn (117–19), publicity spots (98), but also "found poems" on the gravestones of two Africans who died in the United States at the beginning of the nineteenth century.

In fact, this ability to speak in many different voices is rooted in the strategy of passing, which necessitates the adoption of the voices of others. I have shown that Cliff reappropriates the strategy of passing by applying it to her endeavor of expressing her highly multiple identity. Cliff's texts often reflect on the possibility of using the strategy of passing (i.e., the kumbla) in a subversive way that is aimed at expressing the very identity the kumbla wishes to mask. But the multiplicity of this identity can never be articulated as a whole in one and the same voice. Therefore, Cliff's writings also consider the impossibility of an effective use of the strategies of the kumbla, and from there they ponder the inadequacies and even the danger and the evil inherent in the kumbla itself. This is the third aspect of Cliff's implicit use of the image of the kumbla, and I will need the rest of this chapter to consider this aspect.

The Void in the Expression of Plurality

You see—the whole business
is very complicated.

    —Cliff 1985: 68

Cliff is most aware of the need to articulate the different aspects of one's identity. She is also aware of the impossibility of this project. She even makes it the explicit object of her reflection in a fragment that occupies a key position in her work. It is Cliff's "angry" piece, and it functions in a way that is comparable to Kincaid's angry piece, *A Small Place*, as a necessary stage in the development of her voice. "That piece of writing led to other pieces" (17), Cliff reports. She wrote it after having read the novel in prose and poetry *Our Sister Killjoy* by Ghanaian writer Ama Ata Aidoo, by which "something was set loose in me, I directed rage outward rather than inward" (16).[6] "If I Could Write This in Fire, I Would Write This in Fire" analyzes the situation of Jamaican women in eighty-four short paragraphs. It is written as an autobiographical text, narrated by an identifiable "I," a girl/woman from the light-skinned Jamaican middle class, who often addresses "our" background and outlines the influence of the English on "our" sense of identity. The last paragraph reads as follows:

There is no ending to this piece of writing. There is no way to end it. As I read back over it, I see that we/they/I may become confused in the mind of the reader: but these pronouns have always co-existed in my mind. The Rastas talk of the "I and I"—a pronoun in which they combine themselves with Jah. Jah is a contraction of Jahweh and Jehova, but to me always sounds like the beginning of Jamaica. I and Jamaica is who I am. No matter how far I travel—how deep the ambivalence I feel about ever returning. And Jamaica is a place in which we/they/I connect and disconnect—change place. (75–76)

It is true that in "If I Could Write This in Fire," the pronouns "we" and "they" can alternately be interpreted as referring to light-skinned middle-class Jamaicans, all nonwhite Jamaicans, all Black Jamaicans, and maybe sometimes all Jamaicans. There is, however, a clear distinction between the Jamaicans and the English, who are definitely the enemy (72), even though whiteness is also described as a quality attained or attainable by light-skinned Jamaicans (72). This is a Caribbean articulation of the plurality, ambiguity, and fragmentation of identity. The Rastafarian concept of "I

and I" is evoked to show how the concept of the plurality of subjectivity itself is well rooted in Jamaican epistemology. Indeed, for many, the essence
of Caribbeanness is situated in plurality and hybridity. Benítez-Rojo even
talks about the mestizo-text of the Caribbean, in which contrasts are not
brought to synthesis. His argument would induce us to talk not of hybridity (with its connotation of breeding and synthesis, and its persistent reference to the binary logic it wishes to break with, as Robert Young has
pointed out, 1995) but rather of syncretism, a term referring to a constructed plurality that can never be dissolved in synthesis (Becquer and
Guatti 1991). Up to a certain point, I agree, and I even think syncretism a
better concept to designate Cliff's plurality than the more specifically located concept of creolization, because Cliff's work seems to posit (homo)-
sexuality as the resisting factor that can never be assimilated to the otherwise ethnic and racial plurality of identity. On the other hand, the ubiquity
of sexuality and the body in Cliff's work makes me appreciate the sexual
connotations in the concept of hybridity. I will therefore keep using this
term. Carole Boyce Davies proposes yet another term, "migratory subjectivity," to designate Caribbean women's shifting, plural identity (1994).
The term is well chosen in that it defines Caribbean plurality not as a fault
or abnormality but as a potentially positive and empowering capacity. However, Cliff's reflection focuses on the pain of this plurality, which makes me
hesitate to endow her specific fragmentation with a positive label. Cliff's
plurality is tempestuous, innerly contradictory, and replete with gaps and
voids, as I'll show.

The Void: Violence

The hybridity of Caribbean identity is no quiet harmony. Cliff, as I
have argued, has trouble in talking "as a mulatto." She wavers between the
speech of a Black woman and the veiled speech of the passing woman. She
is able to articulate plurality in juicy rhythmic pieces as an ideal, but her
texts are also torn by the impossibility of articulating the full complexity.
The complexity may be too violently contradictory to be uttered. Plurality, paramount in Caribbean culture, is not the kind of free heteroglossia
of carnival and marketplace celebrated by Bakhtin. There is strife and violence between the many tongues. Benítez-Rojo characterizes Caribbean
texts as "projects that communicate their own turbulence, their own clash,

and their own void" (27), and he interprets the void as the unspoken violence that for him is at the heart of Caribbean history and society. Indeed, racial plurality in itself is rooted in violence, in sexual violence: "Many of us became light-skinned very fast" (66), says Cliff, "Our mothers' rapes were the thing unspoken" (66). Hence, speaking about one's "race" implies speaking—or not speaking—about sexuality. Cliff does not elaborate upon "the thing unspoken." The mothers' rape is only mentioned, and named for what it was—then there is a blank.

For Cliff, speaking one's plurality necessarily entails expressing a silence in which speech has become impossible. The silences, breaks, and disruptions in Cliff's text might thus be interpreted as an articulation of the impossibility of putting the plurality into words. Cliff wants to say it all, including the impossibility of saying it all. As a result, she lingers on the brink of a void; she stresses ambiguity and the difficulties of speaking and thematizes complexity, interiority, disconnectedness, fog, and voids:

III

My grandmother: "Let us thank God for a fruitful place."
My grandfather: "Let us rescue the perishing world."

This evening on the road in western Massachusetts there are pockets of fog. Then clear spaces. Across from a pond a dog staggers in front of my headlights. I look closer and see that his mouth is foaming. He stumbles to the side of the road—I go to call the police.

I drive back to the house, radio playing "difficult" piano pieces. And I think about how I need to say all this. This is who I am. I am not what you allow me to be. Whatever you decide me to be. . . .

Encountering the void is nothing more nor less than understanding invisibility. Of being fogbound. (70–71)

These fragments follow after the story of the narrator's Jamaican cousin Henry visiting her in London, which leads to the painful clash of anti-racism and heterosexism mentioned earlier and an impression of Rastas and American hippies imitating them. They precede a consideration of passing and the dangers in hiding from one's real sources.

This is a key fragment in Cliff's writing, and I will propose an interpretation by discussing the text in minute detail. The text brings several concepts together: pockets of fog, a dog with a foaming mouth, the need to express the multiplicity of one's identity, the void, invisibility, the condition of being fogbound. All of these concepts together serve to create a specific view on the kumbla. Invisibility here refers to the act of passing (expressed by the concept of the kumbla), which is a strategy that makes one blend with one's surroundings and renders one invisible. Passing cannot be understood only as the linguistic and narrative strategy of keeping silent, and thus as associated to the sense of hearing. It can also be associated with focalization and the visual. In the fragment, understanding invisibility, that is, assessing the condition of passing, is linked to looking into a void. Being invisible is equated to being fogbound, which therefore means nothing less than being within a stifling kumbla. The fog, then, can be compared to the kumbla. But this kumbla is not merely an empty container. It harbors something dangerous.

The narrator did look into this kumbla. Driving through pockets of fog and clear spaces she looked, not to encounter nothingness in the void of its heart, but something dangerous as well as pathetic: a rabid dog. Entering the fog means assessing the kumbla of passing. But if one starts to study one's strategies of passing, one has to acknowledge the very reasons for this passing. These reasons are the painful secrets about oneself that cannot be uttered. These are the dangerous, harmful secrets that are well hidden in the voids and silences of one's life narrative. They are as dangerous as a dog with a foaming mouth. As I have argued above, Cliff's aesthetics does not allow for a direct revelation of these secrets. But it is possible to acknowledge the anger, madness, and illness caused by the need to hide the secrets. The rabid dog is an image that evokes all these sentiments.

Cliff vigorously denies the definition of the kumbla as a protecting device. As the kumbla exists by virtue of the hiding of one's secrets, it harbors a real, murderous threat. The dog in the parable does not confront the narrator, however, but stumbles aside. The narrator does not confront it either, wisely, I would think. She remains safely enclosed within her car, and she summons a regulating institution to deal with the danger. In a comparable way, literary strategies are called up to avert or to abate the dangers of violent confrontation and destructive insights: Cliff wants to take a close, difficult look at the dog without being killed by it. The indirectness of disciplined writing might be of more use than a personal, physical approach. The harmful secret has to be situated and isolated. Cliff's writing succeeds in isolating the secrets by surrounding them with silences and by refusing direct comment and direct elaboration. Rather, the texts ponder the strategies of speech themselves.

As in *Angel* (Collins) and *Whole of a Morning Sky* (Nichols), looking in itself is deemed a dangerous act. Angel's loss of sight in one eye in the fight against the American invaders, however, is also the mark of her initiation as an adult Grenadian woman. In the same vein, Gem's bitter lesson about the traumatizing effects of looking (at her friend's death in the fire) inaugurates her position as an adult who is capable of manipulating her gaze. Cliff's protagonists will often be torn by this same realization, that looking in itself may be harmful, or problematic, or futile. The fact that these Caribbean writers relate the gaze to pain and violence is not surprising, and not only because both Caribbean past and present harbor so many traumatizing events that all manners of acknowledging them are painful: speaking of them, feeling them, hearing about them, reimaging them. However, visual models especially will be problematic in a postcolonial context that is still defined by appearances. Color is still defining social status and privilege, and it divides the community. Cliff's struggle with the visual persists throughout her work. In her 1993 novel *Free Enterprise*, for example, she shows a keen mistrust of the visual, and of the gaze. Here the gaze is inevitably equated with appropriation. One of her protagonists is a photographer. This white woman feels estranged and unreal, and she tries, in vain, to bridge the gap between herself and the marginalized people she is interested in by photographing them. But pictures are lost, or they are too vague to be significant, or people refuse to let themselves be photographed. Pictures do not allow for interaction, and this is what the woman photographer really wants—to be part of life, to be part of the community in dialogue. One of the recurring motifs in the novel is the famous painting by Joseph Turner (*Slavers Throwing Overboard the Dead and Dying, Typhon Coming On*, 1840). The white company of art lovers suggests that, even if the represented event is horrible, the piece can be enjoyed for the sake of its art. The only Black woman present, however, explains that she cannot but focus on the narrative implicit in the drowning, fragmented Black bodies in the foreground (80). It is only the narrative that counts. A female alley dweller, a slave who escaped, refuses to let her picture be taken. Instead, she offers to tell the white photographer her life story. Cliff suggests that merely visual models are not very helpful in establishing the interaction needed to construct a multiracial Caribbean (or American) identity. Telling, not showing, then—once again, and this time the difference is made for very specific reasons, with very specific effects.

Even if Cliff decides to confront the dangerous insights by means of narrative, we see that this telling cannot but be indirect, too. Thus, instead of trying to express an inexpressible multiplicity, Cliff takes recourse to thematizing the painful impossibility of speech through the trope of the dangerous voids, the sites of unspeakable secrets. The awareness of these secrets—these rabid dogs—is central to her writing. The title of this chapter refers to that central issue. This study, however, does not share Cliff's narrator's predicaments or strategies. Therefore, I will work toward a closer understanding of the secrets in the voids.

The Void: Sexuality

In a fragment from her earlier work, *Claiming an Identity They Taught Me to Despise*, entitled "The Garden," Cliff also talks about a void: "Women gone mad from childlessness—the philosophers talk about unfulfilled purpose—stray uterus rampaging—burning, cutting, slicing—discarding. *Immanence* and *inner space*. Our universe—the black hole—the void within" (51). Not unlike a rabid dog, the womb starts to stray, rampage, destroy; it represents a deadly secret at the heart of one's identity. Whereas the secretive void in the first quote was associated with "passing for white," that is, with "race," it is here connected to female sexuality. A few lines above those quoted, the narrator declares, "I have no children and know I never will" (51). The obvious question is, why not? But the question is not posed and stays unanswered, thus producing a rather loud silence. In the fragment following the quote, the narrator recounts a dream in which she declines responsibility for the as yet unformed child delivered by her mother and sister, and thus the narrator causes its death. When read *after* the more recent pieces of *Look Behind*, the choice not to have children can be interpreted as a reference to the narrator's lesbianism, apparently a difficult aspect of sexuality to talk about.

But there is another aspect to this void, which brings us back again to the question of origin, family, class, and "race." The reference to the void quoted above occurs in a piece that is about both gardening and fertility, and from there, too, about the relationship to the narrator's mother. The narrator cites (probably) herself in a fragment enclosed by quotation marks, thus distancing the confession slightly—and inserting silence—when she is pondering her motives for gardening:

When I garden, which is almost daily, I think at least once of my mother's challenge that everything will probably die, and so it's my challenge to assure that everything lives—my difficulty in thinning, *sentimental obstacle.* This goes to a deep place; to being told I was unloving and unnurturing as a child (and adult). I feel the weeds in the garden encroaching as a personal threat to my ability to nurture. I also feel them as my mother and sister encroaching on my life; so the plants become a metaphor for my own life and the powerful weeds (which seem to be able to endure anything) my mother's and sister's demands. (48–49)

Her mother's accusation of not being loving and nurturing, not being able to let things grow, is a constant threat: "I have also felt as I walk to the garden (in the middle of a meadow) that I am threatened; that there is a snake or animal lurking somewhere—that someday I will see this creature, and the garden will be spoiled" (49).[7] So, here too there is the fear of encountering a monster in an interior. The narrator's mother, whose family had a sense of self as "just a flock of red people" (59), and who married a lighter-skinned man, made her daughter pass for white from an early age. Read in this context, the fear of the threat in the void also refers to the narrator's real fear of being unloved by her mother and thus losing her place in the family that binds her to Jamaica. However, the narrator finds it impossible to answer her mother's demands and gain her mother's love. She is caught in a paradox. If she did as her mother asks, she should "pass." But passing here would mean to pass for white, which would distance her from parts of her family, and her mother. It would also mean passing for straight and hiding her lesbianism. Apparently, the narrator has chosen otherwise. In theory, her refusal to pass for white would reconnect her to her family. In practice, it does not, as her refusal is incompatible with the family's values. The narrator's refusal to pass for straight has also estranged her from her mother and her family. Her mother now reproaches her for being autocratic, aloof, puritanical, willing to devote her life to "strangers" rather than to "family," deviant, and the like (49). Jamaica, however, is a place she can claim as *her* plurality only by means of her mother's family. For this family is firmly rooted within Jamaican society, whereas she herself is not. Her distancing from her family therefore threatens her very ethnic, racial, and cultural identity.

In the act of gardening the narrator finds a means to express a sense of her own identity as loving and nurturing, in defiance of her mother's curse. Yet, ultimately, she can establish her identity only through the reconciliation with her/a mother. In other words, as an exile she can return to Jamaica only through such a reconciliation. In another fragment she sighs to a Jamaican collectivity, not her mother: "I bear in mind that you with all your cruelties are the source of me, and like even the most angry mother draw me back" (1986: 103).

The narrator cannot just turn away from her mother, as her mother represents aspects of her identity she cannot afford to lose. Her endeavor to articulate her full identity is related to her desire to be acknowledged and loved by, primarily, her mother, as well as by those who are in the position of her mother by virtue of the quality of their "belonging." Therefore, she seeks ways to negotiate her fear of being rejected by her mother and her desire of loving and being loved without having to surrender her silences. In the image of the garden she has found a way to handle these needs and fears.

The void in the narrator's multiple identity makes it impossible to express that identity. But in the image of the garden Cliff has found the means to picture the void itself without touching the dangers at its heart. I have offered an interpretation of this void and the nature of the dangers it harbors. I understand Cliff's thematizing of this void as a strategy of imagining the unspeakable plurality of her identity. Yet she never fully abandons the project of articulating the suppressed secrets of sexuality and violence. The next sections are dedicated to Cliff's play with silence to speak about love and her indexical manner of speaking about violence.

Silence Speaks of Lost Loves

Cliff's narrator's difficult evocation of the theme of love is part of Cliff's general aesthetics of reluctance. I'll therefore approach it by first quickly considering some of the related narrative strategies Cliff uses to speak about the presence of the unspeakable without directly confronting it. One of the narrative strategies I wish to discuss is connected to the urge to keep intact the complexity that consists of positive statements *plus* silences. "I need to say all *this*," ponders the narrator in "If I Could Write This in Fire" (emphasis mine), accompanied by "difficult" (European classical? modern?) piano pieces—*This* is who I am, all eighty-four fragments of the piece, including blanks, pauses, skips. As the passage about the music suggests, this is a difficult topic, difficult to the point of being unspeakable, difficult because of the otherness involved (music instead of language, European instead of Caribbean, professional instead of amateur). Sometimes, the narrative states this difficulty more than once: "It is a complicated business" (12), "our situation was not that simple" (58), "You see—the whole business is very complicated" (68), "None of this is as simple as it may sound" (72), as if there are even more aspects to the situation than can be spelled out, aspects that are too subtle to make explicit.

Another strategy of abating the dangers of speech, and thus inserting gaps in her speech, is to be found in Cliff's technique of embedding narrative levels. The narrator does not say, "I need to say all this," but "And I think about how I need to say all this." She does not declare that she is angry but says instead, "And I have a hard time realizing that I am angry" (69). Thus, "as I write I realize that what I say may sound fabulous" (73). As a result, a split is created between the "I" observing and commenting on herself and the "I" who experiences emotional responses. Again, the suggestion is that unambiguous, direct identifications must be avoided.

A very literal way of inserting gaps is of course the organization of the text as a series of loosely connected fragments separated by blanks. The narrator does not link them explicitly. She may offer very direct comments and interpretations. She often abstains from comment.

Instead of having direct comments by a light-skinned narrator, Black women writers are sometimes mentioned as the frame of reference for the account of light-skinned experience. Thus it is contended that light-skinned experience is part of the Black experience. See, for example, "Those middle-class Jamaicans who could not pass for white managed differently—not unlike the Bajans in Paule Marshall's *Brown Girl, Brownstones*" (60); Toni Morrison's *Sula* evokes her own memories of a childhood friendship with a girl ("It was Zoe, and Zoe alone, I thought of," 63); Ama Ata Aidoo is mentioned on page 67; and Audre Lorde is referred to on page 86, and, moreover, the book as a whole is dedicated to her.

The principle of these devices is that the narrator often remains in the background and has things described and named by others. In this way she is able to write a multivoiced discourse, which is certainly incontestably Caribbean[8]—more so than if she would have used a light-skinned middle-class voice without the Jamaican "twang" (67)—and she is still able to suggest that her own truth is elsewhere, still somehow unspoken.

Cliff's play with silence to evoke the issue of (lesbian) love is connected to these strategies to create distance between narrator and utterances. However, this particular play with silence is much more complicated, in part because it implies a fundamental link between silence and sexuality. I will therefore discuss it at length. We have seen (in the preceding section) that the issue of the family brings together the categories of both sexuality and "race." If one's relation to these identifying categories is problematic, one's position in language is problematic too. I have suggested earlier that (lesbian) love, (brutal and lesbian) sexuality, and violence are at odds with speech: the sexual violence of the colonizer's rape cannot be *told*, only named; lesbianism cannot be stated within Caribbean discourses; lesbianism must remain the unspoken reason for the narrator's refusal of motherhood and family life. This kind of forced chastity would lead to an impotent silence, which is exactly what is expected of women, as Cliff shows in an earlier, autobiographical piece, "Notes on Speechlessness" (1978). Here she refers to Virginia Woolf's observations on the relation between sexuality and speech: "In the note she [Woolf] connects not-speaking with chastity: the transgression of both of these with 'shame.' She observes that these two admonitions enforce the patriarchal notion that a 'woman's mind and body shall be reserved for the use of one man and one only'" (7). It seems that things have not changed much, not through time, nor from one continent to another. Being silent about her sexuality, however, is no help to Cliff's narrating "I." For being a passing, silent lesbian makes her "a lady," an identity that divorces her from her family (49). What's more, her lesbianism is the very thing that links her to Jamaica, more than anything else. Her love for another girl, Zoe, made her feel a part of the Jamaican community. So Cliff does explore love, as giving up speaking of love and sexuality would divorce her from her family and country and would confine her to silence only. Under the (imprecise) battle cry "We got to love each other / That is what is known as the bottom line" (89), she embarks upon a complicated play of speech and silence in order to speak the unspeakable.

I will consider two instances of this play. The first example concerns the two-page piece that gave its title to the whole section of the collection: "Love in the Third World" (102–3). Again, different themes overlap. The piece consists of a statement of the complexity of love in the Third World, which is then favorably compared to the equally complicated love in the

First and Second Worlds and in all the planets of the solar system, beautifully enumerated and fitted with epithets, one after the other. This enumeration is followed by the report of two women living in wretched circumstances in Jamaica. A woman shows the picture she took of them. "At least, the photographer says, they have each other" (102). In the last three paragraphs, the narrator reflects on the poverty of their situation and her uneasy feeling of belonging with them:

I wonder if I will ever return—I light a cigarette to trap the fear of what returning would mean. And this is something I will admit only to you. I am afraid my place is at your side. I am afraid my place is in the hills. This is a killing ambivalence. I bear in mind that you with all your cruelties are the source of me, and like even the most angry mother draw me back. (103)

The "your," in "my place is at your side," in the fourth line, refers not only to the two women, but to a larger group of Jamaicans—"My people"—whom she has followed from her residences abroad. Yet "your" can be read as referring more significantly to the two women. They represent the crucial knot in this short story of national identity. The elaborate introduction to the theme of "love" seems to evaporate in the development of the story after the crucial scene of the two women living together. One expects more about this love, but the topic has already changed into something like "squalor in the Third World." The poem continues to picture the narrator's fascination with her Jamaican people.

The poem also emphasizes the issue of representation. Here, the issue is taken up in the enumeration of the ways in which the narrator kept track of "her people" by following their appearance in movies, advertisements, photographs, graffiti, apart from her own direct observation. The theme of the narrator's intense interest in representations of her fellow Jamaicans will be developed in connection with the issue of the representation of Jamaican lesbian love. The reader realizes that there is another love story to be read in the text, that is, the difficult love of the exiled middle-class narrator for her revoltingly poor, mostly lower-class "people." She values their pictures as if they were her loved ones.

The very important concluding declaration of the "I"'s love for the Jamaicans and identity as one of them, however, becomes possible only because of the earlier *representation* of love between women in Jamaica. There has been only one other account of love between women on Jamaica, and that was the warm evocation of the narrator's childhood friendship with the girl Zoe. But that friendship could not be represented as a love story. Now there is a photograph of a love between women, taken by a Jamaican woman visiting "home." This woman actually translates the picture into a love story. It has become possible to situate this more or less lesbian love story within a multileveled story of poverty, marginality, exile, and belonging. Only now can the narrator envision herself back "home." Only now can she reimagine her relationship with her/"the" mother and thus the possibilities of the representation of her own identity in a Jamaican "vernacular," even if she pictures her reconciliation with the angry mother not as a concrete option but rather as a "killing ambivalence." Thus, the possibility of representing lesbian sexuality or love between women as a part of the plurality of the Jamaican community looms on the horizon. But this can be done only by suppressing the theme of love, banishing it to the title and to the plea for the recognition of the complexity of Third World Love. Even so, this device makes the silence about the clamorously announced love a very visible absence, which almost eclipses the explicit text.[9]

The second example of the use of silence to talk about love is to be found in "The Laughing Mulatto (Formerly a Statue) Speaks," a piece I have discussed already. In this text, love is always lost, hidden, unspoken. Yet the speaker is motivated by a wish to talk to the dead. However, unlike Monique Wittig (in *Le Corps Lesbien*, 1973), and unlike Marlene Nourbese Philip (who I'll read in the next chapter), she doesn't call her lost dead back into life, to talk, touch, and make love to them again. She doesn't go underground, nor does she embark upon an endless journey into an almost inconceivably distant past, like Philip's Traveller hunting Livingstone. She just laments her loss. Then she says, "I am writing the story of my life as a statue. But no kiss set me free to speak" (85). Even Jean Toomer's great aunt, her passing sister, was addressed only to be told that she was lost to the speaker.

The Laughing Mulatto was not loved back into life, into speech. How then did she escape the paralyzing, mute condition of the passing woman? She does not tell. She did not find her way into speech by someone's love, even if that seems the only way to gain speech. Yet, she must have been revitalized, for she is now alive and laughing. But by lack of enough love, as the implicit reproach is, one could say, she did not find a way to open speech—she has found access only to a difficult, hampered speech. Instead of speaking freely, she writes reservedly. In this way she muses with a certain reticence about "three sisters" who gave her flowers and notes and more:

Come back now sisters. Now I can speak. But they are gone never to come back.

I am talking about three real women. One dead. Two living. Who chose to live as ghosts. And whom I understand. And whom I have tried to love. (86)

The three women here are conjured up in a suggestive, significant way: they are *real* women. By changing her address, the narrator earnestly warns her readers that they have stepped outside the parable. The intensity of this statement is telling. This must be a very significant passage. While positioning herself clearly on the positive side of the boundary between living and dead, real life and shadow life, present and past, the narrator still identifies with her lost loves, the silent women. She places their impossible love at the other side of the boundary, in the space of the unspeakable.

Death, however, does not have to be a boundary to writers who need to bring the past back into life. By not inviting these dead or mute women to participate in the narrative as speaking subjects, Cliff's texts sing of the importance of that boundary, which takes the guise of a veil behind which passing and loving women live like the dead.[10] In this way she reinforces and accentuates the veil. But by thematizing the boundary she also enables herself to install a silence that keeps referring to the forbidden, lost loves between women. She speaks some of this love, negotiates between race and sexuality, secrecy and privacy, and always inserts silence to allow for another qualification that would make it possible for her to escape one definition and at the same time open the possibility for yet another identification.

One might wonder whether one could not submit Cliff's reluctant text to a Machereyan or Eagletonian critique of ideology. This might help us to understand how the topic of lesbianism functions as a disturbing factor in the text, responsible for gaps and silences. But it is not really possible to maintain that this is the central disturbance, the main taboo. Cliff does not overwrite lesbianism with the discourse of heterosexuality; she can in places be open about her/her protagonist's sexual orientation. This is most apparent when she is writing in *Sinister Wisdom,* "A Journal of Words and Pictures for the Lesbian Imagination in All Women," of which she is an editor. In *Look Behind* she also speaks quite intimately about sexual pleasure: "I can come from having my nipples sucked. And this gives me pleasure but also makes me feel unreal. As if I have exchanged one purpose for another—unjustified" (96). This original purpose is the suckling of babies, and babies are important in the fragment from which this citation is taken, "The Crazy Teepee." In it, she describes the narrator's visit to a large store of used goods. Without babies or children with her, it seems as if she has "no need" for them (96)—"Except a need for the past?" (96) The used goods in the Crazy Teepee—old clothes, old books she knows, pornography, dirty tricks like fake vomit, trite mass-produced Indian pottery, carvings and utensils—offer her a revolting narrative of the past, shot through with racism and sexism. The musing about her displaced sexual pleasure is set within this context.

Thus, her sexuality is a deterritorialization of the breast, comparable to Deleuze's definition of language as a deterritorialization of the mouth, whose first function would be eating (Deleuze and Guattari 1991: 62). Her sexual pleasure also represents the displacement of motherhood and heterosexuality. This displacement, which prevents her from having babies, and the concrete need for the used goods alienate her from the "real." But that distance also enables her to understand the collection of goods as the representation of provoking racial and sexual violence of history.

Now I can clarify the function of Cliff's strategy of displacement and associating: she does not overwrite her (protagonist's) perverse sexuality with a more accepted sexual discourse, no more than she spells it out as a desire that is part of lesbian desires. Instead, she places it within a complex network of racism, sexism, the need for a past and its absence, the problems of deterritorialization, and, maybe, the need to dream and write to answer the need for history. She does not silence her lesbian identity, but she connects it in such a complicated way that it can never be the sole topic open to undiluted reactions. A negative reading according to the critique of ideology would obscure this positive strategy.

I would like to approach Cliff's writing as a project to "persevere in flight" (Benítez-Rojo 1992), an experiment in how one can insert silence into a text so that language is able to be loud and clear and yet open enough to admit plurality. In fact, according to Benítez-Rojo's view, Cliff is very much a Caribbean writer in her endeavor to convey her painful paradoxes, her refusal to be pinned down to one position, to have her "wings pinioned" (Cliff 1985: 46). Indeed, she speaks her silence, as if it is more important to indicate the boundaries of what may be said, to uncover the existence of the void itself, than to spell out what is at the bottom.

The strategy of displacement and association, which creates an ungraspable multiplicity, is not the only strategy Cliff uses to "persevere in flight." Another strategy allows her also (and perhaps more intensely) to confront the dangerous void and the rabid dogs and snakes at its heart in a safe way.

Talking about Trees

In a piece entitled "A Visit to the Secret Annex," Cliff describes a pilgrimage to the place where Anne Frank hid during the Second World War. The motto to the piece is by Bertold Brecht, "For Those Born Later":

> What kinds of times are these, when
> A talk about trees is almost a crime
> Because it implies a silence about so many
> horrors?

And Cliff's narrator/protagonist feels herself to be addressed.

> I was born later
> not into this world.
> The trees were not the same
> The horrors not exact—but similar. (104)

She then talks in short sentences about her visit. She is afraid to burst into tears. "Yes, my girl. I say this to myself. (Because part of me is a girl and part of me is a woman speaking to her.) Here is the heroine you once had and wondered about" (105). On the next page she begins to risk Brecht's crime:

> I hold a conversation with myself about trees.
> To see if she might have had a living tree as a companion—even
>   a tree in a churchyard—instead of one cut from colored
>   paper. (106)
>
>   . . .
>
> But she would never have seen her tree—the windows of the hid-
>   ing place were always shaded, covered with paper or painted
>   blue.
> To keep their existences secret safe.
>
> Had she cracked the pane to peek as her tree flowered, or shed its
>   fruit or leaves, she would have been killed.
> Sooner. (107)

Speaking this criminal silence is for Cliff a relevant way of speaking about the horrors. The nature of these horrors becomes most visible in the things rendered irrelevant by the horror, so one should describe the horror by describing the things it destroys. The horror is most explicitly felt in the fact of being cut off from trees. So, if one really wants to tell everything about the horror, one should speak its absence more than its presence, its silence more than its sounds.[11]

In *Look Behind,* Cliff tries to find different "negative" positions to speak the complexity of something. As I have argued recurrently above, her speech consists of the effort of articulating the complexity together with the impossibility of expressing it. This impossibility is related to the existence of sexual secrets or secrets of violence. In this context, it is the gruesome event of the unimaginable violence of the holocaust. In the manner of speech I describe as "talking about trees," the narrator avoids too much straightforwardness by speaking about a metonymically related subject. However, this subject was not chosen at random. It enables the narrator to adopt one of the other narrative strategies to evade directness, namely, the strategy to connect to other voices.

First, by talking about trees the narrator intertextually relates to Brecht's critical discourse, in which trees figure. Instead of speaking the horrors, the narrator inscribes herself into the discourse of a playwright and director who was known for his capacity of shocking his audience into awareness of the crimes and horrors presented on stage. The second point I want to make about Cliff's narrative strategy is related to the metonymical nature of the trope of the tree. In an essay about Dutch writer and artist Armando, Ernst van Alphen enters into the relevance of the metonym instead of the metaphor. Armando writes and paints about the issue of the Second World War without referring to specific places or events. For this reason his work is often seen as metaphorical. Van Alphen does not agree to such a reading. If one interprets the unspeakable horror of the Second World War as a metaphor for the human condition, one implies that this horror is not unique, that everybody shares in that experience, and that it is therefore representable. Van Alphen proposes another way to read Armando's work. Rather than stating that his writing is metonymical instead of metaphorical, he uses a concept from another semiotic discourse, that of C. S. Peirce: "*His language is radically indexical.* He 'encircles' the unspeakable of 'the war' by speaking, or representing, what is contiguous to it, what touches it" (Van Alphen 1993: 32). Thus, Armando writes with bitter resentment about the trees around Camp Amersfoort, which, as witnesses to and thus indexes of the presence of evil, would have turned evil themselves. This is precisely the strategy employed by Cliff too, not only in this poem but throughout her work. She *localizes* evil and speaks about that which surrounds it or is next to it: a void; the fog; a garden; or, in this case, the tree next to the secret annex. For Cliff as well as for Armando speaking about trees is a strategy of coming to terms with her anguished awareness of racist violence.

Cliff uses the trope of the tree indexically and (in terms from another discourse) metonymically.[12] By using metonyms instead of metaphors, other significations are not repressed; instead, they are relegated to adjacent spaces, where they stay within reach as alternatives to more central meanings. In fact, this preference for metonymy has the effect of supplying the text with implicit references to an otherness that cannot be expressed in the main discourse. This style of metonymical reference is one of the ways postcolonial writing establishes the notion of a specific otherness or unease that eludes expression in colonial discourses. This otherness cannot be said to be repressed or overwritten; it is often connected to marginalized non-colonial discourses.[13] Metonymy, then, can be understood as the trope that revolts against universalism and transcendence, notions that are at the heart of Western colonial discourse (Bhabha 1984a). Metonymy is the trope that situates, and that specifies positions. As such, it is crucial to postcolonial writing. Bhabha refers repeatedly to the potentials of a metonymical reading of postcolonial texts. Only in that way can the text be seen to refer to the nonliterary processes within which it situates itself.[14]

For Cliff, though, this otherness does not refer to something specifically Jamaican, that is, to a postcolonial specificity. In *Look Behind* it rather refers to sexuality and the body, which is often the disturbing factor in feminist postcolonial writing. In her poem about Anne Frank, obviously, the unsaid is related to the destructive evil of the Second World War. But it is imagined through the isolation and destruction of a girl's body, thematized primarily through the smaller event of the curtailing of her sensual perceptions.

In contrast to Armando, Cliff does not see the trees as witnesses to and indexes of the presence of evil that have turned evil themselves. For Cliff, the tree testifies not to evil but to something good. It refers to a nurturing form of vitality, which stands in close metonymic relation to the vitality of the enclosed girl. Part of the girl's predicament is that she and the tree are isolated from each other. Together, however, the girl and the tree refer to the nurturing identity the narrator herself is accused of lacking. Cliff's use of the trope of the tree serves two different functions: it offers her the possibility to negotiate her intense emotions about the holocaust in the manner explained by Van Alphen; second, it enables her to connect with an image of the loving warmth she would have liked others to recognize in her.

However, I argue that the narrator, even if she identifies with Anne Frank, does not somehow try to adopt the presumed nurturing vitality of the tree and the girl. On the contrary, she implicitly appropriates Anne's isolation by modeling it upon her own condition. For, in contrast to the poem's statement, Anne Frank *did* look at her tree. See, for example, the entry on February 23, 1944: "From my favorite spot on the floor I look up at the blue sky and the bare chestnut tree, on whose branches little raindrops shine, appearing like silver, and at the seagulls and the other birds as they glide on the wind. . . . We breathed the fresh air, looked outside, and both felt that the spell should not be broken by words" (Frank 1972: 142).[15] Of course, the families under cover had to look carefully and only under specific conditions (see, e.g., the entry for August 14, 1942; 1986: 241). But my point is that Anne did take the risk of looking outside and that her look strengthened, comforted, and inspired her. In Cliff's aesthetics closed interiors, invisibility, and the incapability of seeing are central. But her idiopathic identification with Anne Frank kept her from seeing Anne Frank other than cut off from the outside, blinded, entrapped.[16] In Cliff's writing, horrors are necessarily related to sealed interiors. Instead of losing herself in the alienation of identifying with others, Cliff's texts tend to appropriate other voices to speak for her, here as much as elsewhere in *Look Behind*. In spite of its recurrent use of metonymy, this text does not allow for another interpretation of Anne's confinement. The text appears to be unable to imagine the condition of looking out from within. The text does install the tree as an indexical sign, but the indexical movement itself, the act of connecting tree to girl is declared impossible. Anne's confinement cannot be but total. For the narrator, speaking about what is enclosed is virtually impossible—to the point that even mentioning Anne's name has become an impossibility. Indeed, the poem never mentions Anne Frank's name. Thus, the strategy of appropriating other voices, and thus denying other fears, desires, or strategies, may have the effect of bringing the narrator back into an abhorred predicament. It always encloses her in the confinement she fears most, and her own strategy prevents her from escaping.

In addition to all the text's efforts to associate itself to other discourses and to have other voices speak for the narrator, there is also an instance in which the narrator turns away from those others and engages in solitary identifying practices. Characteristically, the practice entails the creation of an "open inside," to be entered from without.

Evil in the Garden

The text presents an appealing, strong image of the open garden as an identifying practice, which has the connotation of an alternative sexuality that defies definition. I have shown that in "The Garden," gardening stands for a recuperation of a sense of loving and nurturing identity the narrator's mother denies her. As such, it is the anguished positioning of a woman in relation to her mother, who has to conquer an alternative definition of womanhood to her mother, while the latter denies her her own sexuality. The crucial trope of the garden helps us to evaluate the potentials of Cliff's aesthetics.

In several respects, the trope of the garden is a happy one. It permits the narrator to call up the image of an alternative fertility to heterosexual womanhood, that is, to open the possibility of lesbianism without having to spell it out, or to be obliged to enter the issue of lesbianism in terms of her parent's understanding of it, as deviance, maybe as pathology. It enables her, too, to situate herself within a tradition of Black and white women, writers, activists, and artists using the topos of the garden and also to connect herself to the images of gardening women painted by European men. It also relates to the Garden of Earthly Delight, the pristine state of humanity undivided —a situation that stands in stark contrast to the complexities the narrator actually suffers. Finally, it also relates to Jamaican market women, including her own grandmother. Gardening stands in an accepted artistic tradition for Black women, as Alice Walker has shown (1984).

Caren Kaplan has taken up Cliff's beautiful evocation of her open garden as the mapping of "a new terrain, a new location, in feminist poetics" (1987: 197). She sees it as an example of reterritorialization, but with a much better understanding of the conditions of deterritorialization than Deleuze and Guattari show themselves. For a discussion of Deleuze's and Kaplan's argument, I refer to Chapter 3. Cliff implicitly explains the notion of reterritorialization as a light, partial appropriation. Kaplan quotes Cliff's poetic description:

> Not a walled place—in fact, open on all sides.
> Not secret—but private.
> A private open space. (48)

She goes on:

> Not a room of one's own, not a fully public or collective self, not a domestic realm —it is a space in the imagination which allows for the inside, the outside, and the liminal elements of inbetween . . . Cliff's garden is the space where writing occurs without loss or separation . . . [such writing] points towards a rewriting of the connections between different parts of the self in order to make a world of possibilities out of the experience of displacement. (197–98)

Kaplan notices a very important aspect of Cliff's writing, namely, the refusal of the idea of a beneficial interiority. Refusing to endorse the kumbla of the passing her mother demands of her, she also refuses the womb, with all it signifies, like heterosexuality and motherhood, and with all the advantages it could bring. Yet she needs to imagine a maternal figure—even if it is an angry mother—to connect her to the land of her birth, and to her sense of self as a sensitive and creative woman. Instead of a womb or some other enclosing space, she chooses the open garden as a metaphor, which, as I have demonstrated, enables her to redefine radically unwelcome spatial concepts of interiority while still keeping the connection to the mother.

However, in my opinion this is by no means a space that offers the opportunity to write "without loss or separation," as Kaplan suggests. It is primarily a place of the painful assertion of a self against the denial by mother and sister, as I have shown above. Hence, separation is already inscribed in it, and the gardening/writing occurs to transform this separation into another conceptualization of fertility that would make her mother's definition of infertility irrelevant. The trope of the garden does not succeed, however, in removing the threat of the mother's discourse or in healing the separation. The snakes are still lurking in hidden corners. Nor does this poetics prepare for battle.

Cliff's garden is not a secret place, but it is private. One cannot keep a secret from begging to be discovered, as it is its nature to do so. A secret suggests an inside, in which it is hidden and into which others will want to force a passage to uncover it. Evading this discourse, Cliff announces that there is nothing shameful here, nothing to be conquered; yet she asks for a respectful distance. Privacy is the middle class's need. It is expected to be respected. It should not be defended; others should grant it. Yet this does not mean that it is not in need of defense. Cliff's narrator tells how a neighbor enters and damages her garden. Her reaction: "I could kill" (48). She could—but she does not. So, in choosing to accept violence from outside, but in refusing to attack this violence in turn, Cliff's texts form a vulnerable and painful, multiple, hybrid discourse, which doesn't offer easy ways out of the necessity of incessant negotiating, but which allows for raging, dreaming of killing and destruction (97), laughing, parodying, and always inserting silences as safety exits, and the possibility to retreat from senseless human violence. This vulnerable, subtle multiplicity is breathtaking and convincing (and it cuts painfully close to the bone of some of its—middle class—readers. Like me).

This pain is not necessarily caused by what one might feel to be the truth of Cliff's writing. Cliff's writing is also riddled with a more idiosyncratic and less inevitable pain. For there is a price to pay for one's withdrawal from the communication with humanity. This withdrawal is implied in Cliff's use of the trope of the garden. In "The Laughing Mulatto," watching nature is used as a symbol for the futility of human communication. Ultimately, then, the narrator's gardening gives her the opportunity to loosen herself from her sometimes counterproductive identifications with her ambivalent allies: "To garden is a solitary act" (52). But is it? Can it ever be?

Above I suggested that the trope of the garden is part of many different highly valued discourses in which the text happily inscribes itself. But it is important that it also functions in the very colonial discourses the text is geared against. In his study on "white writing," Coetzee states that the topos of the garden "is more extensive than the Judaeo-Christian myth of Eden" (1988: 3). The myth of Eden structured the discourse of the colonial conquest of South Africa, too. However, this topos took on a life of its own, and colonists testified to a fear that the land would degenerate into wilderness, and they themselves into "the idle and brutish state of the Hottentots." Coetzee continues: "Like Joseph Conrad after them, they were apprehensive that Africa might turn out to be not a Garden but an anti-Garden, a garden ruled over by the serpent, where the wilderness takes root once again in men's hearts. The remedy they prescribed against Africa's insidious corruptions was cheerful toil" (1988: 3). Cliff's rewriting of this topos implies a subversion. She has recreated it as an open garden, which means that she did not colonize it, did not brutally separate it from its surroundings. Also, she has trouble pulling out and destroying weeds, a mood in contrast to the cheerful battle against the wild creatures in the South African garden. Moreover, other imperialists break their way into Cliff's beloved space and corrupt and destroy it—the narrator identifies with the colonized rather than with the colonizer. Yet, in her evocation of the topos, echoes of the colonial perception linger. Cliff, too, takes recourse to maybe not cheerful but incessant toil to keep control over the place. Even if Cliff suggests desiring a solitary voice now, in speaking about the need for control she doubles a colonial voice. Cliff's choice of deploring instead of addressing the element of anxious appropriation and control in her gardening leaves her vulnerable to the violence of others, as the brutal intrusion of the neighbor shows.

Perhaps I am driving the matter rather far if I argue that an innocent act like gardening has its violent moments, through which it connects to the history of colonialism. There are, admittedly, other (critical) forms of gardening too, just as there is a way to appropriate writing and even colonial discourse itself for critical aims, as this study has often shown in the preceding chapters. Jamaica Kincaid has made some remarks to this extent. In one of her essays about gardening, Kincaid speaks of colonial and pre- or anticolonial ways of gardening and treating plants. Not surprisingly, after the argument presented in Chapter 6, she accentuates the nonpurposiveness of the noncolonial form, in which the beauty of flowers may be suddenly acknowledged but never sought out expressly. Plants are for use, and the visual pleasure they offer may be merely one of these uses. The colonial form of gardening, in contrast, is based on a violent act of renaming, stealing, transplanting, and transforming native plants (Kincaid 1992). It seems to me that any form of gardening relates to this history and thus enters into a difficult dialogue. The existence of alternative modes of gardening (as in "wild gardening") prove the fact, just as the circumstance that migrants may want to grow plants from "home" in their gardens in exile. However, all forms of gardening are necessarily forms of control and appropriation. Not acknowledging this aspect of the dialogical nature of gardening may well render one incapable of countering the violence of this history of appropriation. Obviously, if one were to acknowledge this history, one would enter into a direct confrontation with the "snakes" in the garden, and the fears and violence in the narrator's heart—and this, again, is at odds with Cliff's aesthetics of reluctance.

The topos of the open garden offers Cliff the opportunity to engage with a plurality of traditions of artistic expression and of appropriation. The issue of appropriation in itself is not addressed. The narrator claims the right to turn away from these discourses, to refuse collectivity and engage her own personal battle with definitions of fertility, sexuality, and origins. Even if in her later pieces she does situate herself within these traditions, by using different genres and parodying freely, she also creates, playfully, her own literary forms and silences. This strategy of borrowing other voices has its drawbacks, as I have argued. But Cliff does not strive for definitive solutions. Her writing accepts the imperfection of strategies and apparently aims at an incessant process of rewriting. As Cliff's work evolves, it becomes even more delicately balanced, sparse, and even more effective.

Conclusion

I have discussed a powerful strategy of using silence to establish a feminist postcolonial voice. Cliff's use of silence can be understood by connecting it to the concept of the kumbla, that protecting but also suffocating strategy of passing for white and for straight. Cliff borrows some of the strategies of the kumbla to break out of her silence and invisibility. Thus she can be seen to borrow other voices and to play with the pronouns of "we," "you," and "I" to express the different aspects of her racial and sexual identity—her Blackness and her not-quite-Blackness, her Jamaicanness and her not-quite-Jamaicanness, as well as her sexuality, which also signifies her not-quite-Jamaicanness, though it can be reconciled with her Blackness. Articulating this silence not as secrecy but as privacy, she creates the image of the garden as a counterpart to metaphors of interiority that stifle and silence radically. The image of the garden is beautiful and rich, perhaps all the more so because it does not lead away from the necessity of the painful acceptance of separation and violence connected with stranger as well as kin.

My reading of Cliff's writing leads me to conclude that she offers a splendid analysis of this violence while refraining from imagining the means to openly confront and combat it (as *Angel* does, for example). Cliff's writing is often rigorously indexical. Her silence about the violent or sexual issues she addresses functions as a boundary that cannot be transgressed. Her narrative strategies offer great advantages, as they allow one to trace the incredible complexity of the issue of postcolonial feminine identity. Moreover, these strategies resist seductive forms of closure that would "solve" or "heal" this complexity. In this sense, Cliff's writing might be called restricted—or, perhaps, postcolonial, in the sense of incessantly working through the colonial trauma. This position is related to the choice not to confront the destructive dangers in the interior, which renders one definitely incapable of overcoming the trauma they imply, and which has one remain within the anguish of colonialism, (hetero)sexism, and racism. Cliff's position fits in so well with postcolonial theoretical discourse that one might value her work as the last word on women within postcoloniality. Alongside Cliff, however, there are also those who decide to face the dog with the foaming mouth, for example, by re-memory or by looking for Livingstone. Caribbean women's writing is intensely varied, and it also offers us a feminist poetics that acknowledges the inescapability of the confrontation of violence without succumbing to nationalist discourse. So, in answer to Kaplan's (in itself appropriate) praise of Cliff's writing, I suggest we avoid haste in choosing our utopian dreams, or in interpreting those of others. There are yet other promising narratives, other utopias that testify to another kind of courage. One of these is the subject of the next chapter.

8

The Castration of Livingstone: Marlene Nourbese Philip's Successful Seduction of the Father of Silence

"A bon entendeur, silence."
"Let s/he who understands, keep silent."
Until Afro-Caribbeans write/right their own origins they will, like Ti-Jean, run the risk of staying in the belly of the beast. This they can only overcome by disregarding the Logos of the Father for the Silent Song of the Mother.
—Clarisse Zimra (1990: 156)

Like the veiling of women . . . silence can only be subversive when it frees itself from the male-defined context of Absence, Lack and Fear (as Feminist Essence). When it becomes a language of its own.
—T. Minh-ha Trinh (1986/87: 8)

Silence, Sex, and Self-Knowledge

"Did you know that female elephants send out mating calls to the males at frequencies so low humans can't hear?" I sensed him getting tense again. "Relax, Livingstone—this is not about sex, but just think, your Word, my Silence— matching frequencies so low, so precise only we could hear. Word and Silence— which of the two sent out the mating call, Livingstone, *your* Word or *my* Silence? Have you thought of that? Maybe this *is* about sex after all, Livingstone-I-presume—what do you think?"
—Marlene Nourbese Philip (1991: 73)

Turning history upside-down, translating the age-long process of col-onization into gender-specific terms of sexual aggression from the word to silence, inserting a very disrespectful and playful sexuality in a field as grave as the postcolonial deterritorialization of language, the Caribbean-born, Canada-bound African writer Marlene Nourbese Philip explores the question of silence. She writes as if she is the first historian of silence, its very first mythographer.

In this chapter I will argue that one cannot discuss silence without evoking sex. The preceding chapter has shown that silence may be needed to express an otherwise unspeakable painful complexity. That silence was connected to difficult issues of sexuality, too. Philip's treatment of the relationship between silence and sexuality is completely different. First, it is not connected to the fear of the discovery of a "shameful" sexual secret. When Philip's women characters engage in lesbian lovemaking, they do so openly and happily. But quite in agreement with Cliff, Philip refrains from adopting the most visible Black feminist strategy of speech, which is the unambiguous determination to break the silence. She sides with those who do not accept the definition of "voice" as presence, "political agency and empowerment," and the equation of silence with powerlessness. Christopher Miller, for one, would consider such definitions to be Western (1990: 248). He is one among a growing number of scholars who engage in the postcolonial discussion about the qualities of silence in literature. Some base their observations on African or Asian or general postcolonial discursive habits.[1] Some explore specific Black female traditions of using silence strategically.[2]

Marlene Nourbese Philip, a Tobagonian lawyer, writer, and poet who lives in Canada, has written two important publications in which she explores the nature of silence in both a Black feminist context and a postcolonial context. In 1988 *She Tries Her Tongue: Her Silence Softly Breaks* was awarded the prestigious Casa de las Americas Prize. In 1991 a narrative in poetry and prose was published: *Looking for Livingstone: An Odyssey of Silence.*[3] This last text, the unprecedentedly courageous, playful, and irresistible theorizing of the entanglement of silence, sexuality, knowledge, and (colonial and native) power, will be the focal point of this chapter. The first collection will be read alongside.

Odyssey is the story of a woman who, to Livingstone and her readers, wants to be known only as the Traveller. She pursues Livingstone through a gigantic time-space (the time "of our word"), which spans the age of the universe. She wants to find him because he may have found what she is searching for herself, something that she discovers to be Silence. During her quest, she is housed, helped, and tested by peoples whose names are anagrams of the word *silence*. These (almost exclusively) women help her by submitting her to tests (that take the form of initiation rites), which make her attain an ever deeper insight into the nature of Silence. When she finally meets Livingstone, she realizes that this Silence has always been with her and can be reached through an intense, maybe sexual contact with her colonial and sexual other. The Traveller's quest can be understood as a quest for self-knowledge. However, in contrast to the many Western narratives of the quest for self-knowledge through a contact with cultural and racial others, this narrative gladly and naturally adopts the position of the colonized.

Philip's texts articulate the process of developing an adequate voice for a Black woman's perspective. In Michelle Cliff's work, silence also plays a role in the mapping of the complexity of the postcolonial female experience. In her text, the silences are threatening—apart from the horror of the secrets they signify, they can also disturb a discourse that is needed to speak urgent truths, for example, for purposes of (Black, female) solidarity. Philip offers a different mood: her silences are the vitalizing element. Whereas other postcolonial writers may envision a path from silence or inauthentic speech, through an intermediary zone of madness, silence, or inarticulation, to full speech, Philip has her protagonist break loose from speech, to find her silence, the ultimate object of her desire. Silence is welcomed to disturb discourses as their disturbance will open up exhilarating possibilities of new kinds of speech. Even though Philip's texts are permeated with a sense of lack, it is not the lack of lack itself, which would doom her endeavor to stay within the male-defined context of Absence, Fear, and Lack evoked by Trinh in the quotation at the beginning of the chapter. Philip's aesthetics differs from Cliff's aesthetics of reluctance. When a devious apparition tempts Philip's heroine in *Odyssey* by offering her mastery over everything that surrounds her, she does not follow the biblical line of conduct of bringing the threat out of view: "but I didn't tell him to 'Get thee behind me, Satan.' I wanted him right up front where I could keep my eyes on him" (65). For her, averting one's eyes belongs to a Christian tradition; she, in contrast, wants to look the object of her distrust in the face.

Philip's version of the colonized's story is structured by the intense need to penetrate into the heart of the matter, quite in contrast to Cliff: "I will open a way to the interior or perish" (7). This desire is strongly connoted. The sexual aspect is accentuated, but so is the epistemological aspect. If one accepts the Freudian thesis that all desire for knowledge can be traced back to the desire for knowledge about sexuality, then the opposite will hold here, too. The wish to find a discourse that could articulate the (post)colonial female experience is as strong as the wish to know the other sexually. In this respect, it can hardly be a coincidence that African scholar Daniel P. Kunene also refers to Livingstone's famous utterance: "And I say, we, as Africans, deserve it all if we fail to rise to the occasion, to the challenge, and take the lead in affairs that affect us the most, and of which we have the most intimate knowledge: *We've got to get inside those languages and listen to what they say!—OR PERISH!*" (Kunene 1992: 14). Philip's use of the metaphor of the interior is close to Kunene's, and it is essentially different from Cliff's, for whom entering the interior is life-threatening. Philip makes grateful use of the sexual connotations that accompany the trope of "getting into the interior"; it is an aspect of its signification that is explicitly visible in colonial discourse, where Africa is likened to a female, virginal space, ready to be appropriated and penetrated. Philip reinforces this physical explanation. Knowledge must always be carnal knowledge too, and this ambivalence gives the journey of Philip's protagonist, "the Traveller," a sexual character, and it turns her meeting with Livingstone into a sexual confrontation. But this search is also a search for the self, a self that can be found only in its entanglement with its others.

The relation between self-knowledge and knowledge of the other is the central issue of this chapter. It leads to a discussion about two related topics: first, the status of hybridity in Philip's poetics; second, the relevance of the concept of narcissism to explain this relationship. As for the second question, one could well extend it to the larger question about the desirability of a Freudian or Lacanian psychoanalytic approach to postcolonial texts. I will defend the position that some of these psychoanalytical concepts can be of use. Philip's texts form a radical critique of patriarchal, imperialist culture, which includes a critique of certain Western psychoanalytical schemes and models, especially the myths of Narcissus and Oedipus. To show the extent of her critique, I will use the Freudian and/or Lacanian understanding of these myths through some postcolonial, Black, and feminist critiques of them. From such a suspended position, I can show that Philip uses other concepts that also function within psychoanalytical discourses (notably *womb* and *castration*). However, she prefers to endow them with the complex meanings they have attained within debates about race and ethnicity, coloniality, sexuality, and gender. The most interesting point is that Philip derives a certain narrative technique from each. So, in using concepts that refer to sexuality and gender, and also to coloniality and silence, Philip works hard to make silence "a language of its own" and to delineate a vital noncolonial, Black, gendered counterdiscourse.

Native and Woman

The native is silent. Homi Bhabha knows it, as he has studied the question of representation extensively. He reads to us from a book that informs us that the Africans "are deprived of the two fundamental signs of communication and exchange within Western society—words and money—both of which are monopolized by the European in the colonial context." They cannot represent themselves, they must be represented: "the discourse of Christian ideology . . . mediates the passive silences of the oppressed and gives them—between the lines—a stoicism and dignity" (Bhabha 1984a: 108–9). Many claim that the colonized do not possess a counterdiscourse.[4] Spivak is heard to say, "The subaltern cannot speak" (1988: 308; 1993a: 30). Africa is a continent that resonates with an overwhelming, threatening silence. Philip has Mary Livingstone complain about "the massive, impenetrable and continental silence" of Africa (29). Africans, the oppressed, the colonized, the subaltern—all these marginalized categories (which should not be collapsed) seem to be characterized by what can be summarized as their silence.

Philip, like Cliff in her fiction, and like many Caribbean writers, is a mythmaker, bent upon the creation of a (pre)history and a mythology in which there is only a history of things too horrible to remember, or memories eradicated, too sparse, too dim. Philip's *Odyssey* is rewriting the myth of the silent native. Philip enters it to turn it into quite an opposite myth, in a movement not unlike that of the writers of the *écriture féminine*, but more embracing and more daring, as it also has a bearing on "race" and colonization. So, natives have to be silent? Philip accepts the myth and inserts the "silent natives" and Silence itself as characters in her text.

But in doing so, she gives quite a different meaning to the notion of silence. First, she shows that this silence is not an original quality of the African; the concept of the African's silence was produced through and by colonialism: Stanley and Livingstone, who opened the continent to colonial abuse, are said to be the white fathers not only of the continent but also "Of Silence" (7). This first move, of accepting the colonial fiction about Africa's silence, is no less than an ironically literal acceptance of historical truth. Philip stresses the fact that imperialist geopolitical power-relations created silence by defining African languages as such and by muting Africans. Her insistence is the audible articulation of an implicit statement in Conrad, remarked upon by JanMohamed, suggesting that "darkness, both as a metaphor and as the practice emblematized by slavery, comes with colonial occupation" (JanMohamed 1986: 89). Thus, she gives a loud voice to dim traces of colonial self-critique.

Philip's second, unexpected deconstructive move is to refuse the dominant definition of this silence as negativity. Yes, the native is silent, and what a rich and wonderful quality her silence is! This unexpected revaluation of silence should be seen not just as a playful reversal of Western hierarchical notions of silence and speech. In non-Western traditions, one may discern different epistemologies wherein silence is highly esteemed. Miller states, "While orality is perceived in Western metaphysics as the immediacy of the voice, in the Malinké tradition orality is already a duplicitous betrayal of *silence*" (Miller 1986: 297).[5]

Philip reinstalls several (sometimes conflicting) narratives of silence as authenticity and as counterdiscourse, associated with the maternal womb, whereas the word is presented as dominant, (sexually) aggressive, violent, male (as in 1991: 13). For instance, silence is sometimes characterized as something that others can take from you: "And so their ancestors . . . mounted armies of words to colonise the many and various silences of the peoples round about" (12), "they had gorged themselves, grew fat over the centuries on our silence" (57); "upon it *their* speech, *their* language, *and their* talk was built—solid as the punning Petros upon which the early church, harbinger of silence, had been erected" (58). Indeed, silence can be put in "the Museum of Silence," as an act of intimidation of those it was stolen from (57). But in other places, silence is presented as the deepest personal point of authenticity: "It is the only thing I have that is not contaminated. My Silence—my very own Silence" (65). "That was all I had—*my* birth, *my* death, *my* silence" (43). It can even become a language, as with the people of the CESLIENS, who reverse the hierarchy of silence and speech and hold that "the word was but another sound—of silence" (35). Philip's second move creates the space for a counterdiscourse: "silence" functions as the irrepressible possibility of otherness.

However, it is not only the space for racial, ethnic, or cultural otherness that is opened here. *Odyssey* contains many narratives about the origin of silence and word that give an explicit gender-specific, sexual interpretation of both concepts. Sometimes they take the form of explicit myths of origin (11–12); sometimes they are found, more implicitly, in the poems. There, silence is placed within the interiority of the female body, in her womb:

The womb
Oasis of Silence

Blooms

as one poem ends (28), placing Silence within the womb, and another
begins:

In the beginning was—
nothing
could
would
be
without Silence
culture
nurturing the paradise
the parasite in word
with the upon of
hang
wait
depend
Word and Silence feed
the share
in need
wed
content
with the conspire
in symbiosis—
embryo word
clasped
clings to the surround in
Silence
divided by the Fall
in word into
silence minus word
wanting Silence
cleft
one
into two (30–31)

Here, the word is seen as the embryo within the womb. Silence is likened
to the womb that surrounds the embryo, or the womb is equated to the
surrounding aspect of Silence. There is the suggestion of a harmonious

symbiosis between the equal absolutes of Silence and Word, but it is soon overwritten by the original image of Silence nurturing the word (without capital). The unity of womb/embryo, Silence/word is split by the Fall. The biblical reference is explained as the Fall that is present *in* the word, which is an aspect of the word. It is also the activity of the word, the Fall (or falling) of the word that is responsible for the split. One understands the role of the word better if one remembers that the word, according to another (contradicted) myth, was created by the first sexual intercourse of man and woman, who had hitherto been living "happily together within this silence" (11). The word is male; that is, its male aspect is responsible for the split. The poem continues:

>   halved into twin
>   into split
>   severed
>   by the Lord in word
>   whole
>   original (31)

The unity with the mother is brutally disturbed by the intervention of the Lord, the father, who is present in the (apparently "Lord"-ly, domineering) word. He seems to be in possession of qualities like wholeness and originality, and he is indeed, according to the myth of the origin of Christianity. But *Odyssey* gives priority to other myths in other parts of the narrative. *Odyssey* defines silence in a strict and clear sense as a "native" and female quality. To understand the way this text treats these qualities in relation to their counterparts, another text must be consulted, in which she does not separate them so neatly.

The Mother Tongue

Philip's poem "Discourse on the Logic of Language," a four-page text from *She Tries Her Tongue* (1989) connects silence, language, gender, coloniality, and sexuality. The poem is well on its way to becoming a classic. In a stimulating defense of the paramount importance of the mother tongue for African writers, Ghanaian poet Kofi Anyidoho has chosen to study the poem as an eminent contribution to the discussion on the language question in Pan-African writing (Anyidoho 1992). Susheila Nasta, editor of

Motherlands, a collection of essays about Black women's writing, has chosen it as the preface to the collection (1991). For Nasta, the poem must have seemed significant in the light of the gender-specific subject of the collection; Anyidoho, however, pays no attention to matters of gender and sexuality in the poem. He also neglects some of the paradoxes in Philip's text to make his own point. I will instead concentrate on some of these paradoxes to make my own point about the complex intertwining of gender, sexuality, language, and coloniality.

Anyidoho could disregard some of the poem's complexity by using only selected quotes. I will repeat the poem in full:

DISCOURSE ON THE LOGIC OF LANGUAGE

English
is my mother tongue.
A mother tongue is not
not a foreign lan lan lang
language
l/anguish

—a foreign anguish.
English is
my father tongue.
A father tongue is
a foreign language,
therefore English is
a foreign language
not a mother tongue.

What is my mother
tongue
my mammy tongue
my mummy tongue
my momsy tongue
my modder tongue
my ma tongue?

I have no mother
tongue
no mother to tongue
no tongue to mother
to mother
tongue
me

I must therefore be tongue
dumb
dumb-tongued
dub-tongued
damn dumb
tongue
but I have
a dumb tongue
tongue dumb
father tongue
and english is
my mother tongue
is
my father tongue
is a foreign lan lan lang
language
l/anguish
anguish
a foreign anguish
is english—
another tongue
my mother
mammy
mummy
moder
mater
macer
moder
tongue
mothertongue

tongue mother
tongue me
mothertongue me
mother me
touch me
with the tongue of your
lan lan lang
language
l/anguish
anguish
english
is a foreign anguish

To the left of this text there is another text, vertically printed:

WHEN IT WAS BORN, THE MOTHER HELD HER NEWBORN CHILD CLOSE; SHE BEGAN
THEN TO LICK IT ALL OVER. THE CHILD WHIMPERED A LITTLE, BUT AS THE MOTHER'S
TONGUE MOVED FASTER AND STRONGER OVER ITS BODY, IT GREW SILENT—THE
MOTHER TURNING IT THIS WAY AND THAT UNDER HER TONGUE, UNTIL SHE HAD
TONGUED IT CLEAN OF THE CREAMY WHITE SUBSTANCE COVERING ITS BODY.

Under it, on the next page, a second text, also vertically printed:

THE MOTHER THEN PUT HER FINGERS INTO HER CHILD'S MOUTH—GENTLY FORC-
ING IT OPEN; SHE TOUCHES HER TONGUE TO THE CHILD'S TONGUE, AND HOLDING
THE TINY MOUTH OPEN, SHE BLOWS INTO IT—HARD. SHE WAS BLOWING WORDS—
HER WORDS, HER MOTHER'S WORDS, THOSE OF HER MOTHER'S MOTHER, AND ALL
THEIR MOTHERS BEFORE—INTO HER DAUGHTER'S MOUTH.

To the right of the poem there are also two texts, printed horizontally, in
short sentences.

> Edict I
> Every owner of
> slaves shall,
> wherever possible,
> ensure that his slaves
> belong to as many ethno-
> linguistic groups as
> possible. If they can-
> not speak to each other,
> they cannot then foment
> rebellion and revolution.
>
> Edict II
> Every slave caught speak-
> ing his native language
> shall be severely pun-
> ished. Where necessary,
> removal of the tongue is
> recommended. The of-
> fending organ, when re-
> moved, should be hung
> on high in a central place,
> so that all may see and
> tremble.

On the opposite page of the first part of the poem there is a short treatise on the racist and sexist insights of two nineteenth-century brain doctors. On the page opposite the last part, there are four multiple choice questions about the tongue and speech.

Anyidoho reads in the central text of the poem a repudiation of the "violator's language," labeling it as "a father tongue . . . a foreign language / not a mother tongue" (59). The last stanzas are seen as "a fervent prayer for rebirth and deliverance from her historical anguish" (60), motivated by "the absence of any retrievable mother tongue" (59). Anyidoho stresses the foreign, alienating quality of the poet's E/english, and the poet's urge to abandon it. But to reach this conclusion, Anyidoho, while citing the last three stanzas, omits the part after "dumb-tongued" and before "tongue mother / tongue me / mothertongue me"; this is just the part where the poet expresses the *ambivalent* character of the English/english she has to use: "and english is / my mother tongue / is / my father tongue /"; and thus, the impossibility of abandoning the father tongue altogether. Whereas Anyidoho emphasizes Philip's view that speaking English is connected to lack and alienation, with the purpose of encouraging African writers to give up the use of the colonial language in favor of their mother tongues, Philip makes clear that she cannot just turn her back on English/english, as it is the only language she has: mother tongue and foreign tongue are one. There is no easy way out.

Anyidoho speaks of a "prayer for rebirth," which ends the poem. This expression is apt, as the metaphor of birth is very pertinent in Philip's poetics, even more so in *Odyssey*. I am not so sure about the aptness of "prayer," though. The poet calls upon someone to "tongue" and touch her "with the tongue of your / lan lan lang / language." I do not interpret this as a request for divine intervention, at least not for a disembodied intervention. The reference to the Pentecostal mystery is relevant. In this miracle, the apostles were touched by the Holy Spirit to burst into a torrential speaking in tongues (one finds it too in *She Tries Her Tongue*). However, I think one should downplay the connotation of the divine and rather emphasize the reference to the mother in the subtext, who licked / tongued her baby clean and blew words into the mouth of her child. In other instances in Philip's texts, there are even clearer indications of a refusal of the divine. At the very end of *Odyssey*, the Traveller protests at Livingstone's reference to God as the final signifier: "'Oh, Livingstone-I-presume, you would have to go and complicate matters further with God, wouldn't you?'" (74) She seems to indicate that there is no need for anything more metaphysical than Word and Silence. Elsewhere, earlier in the same scene, the Traveller asks Livingstone for a kiss "to seal this unholy pact of ours: your Word, my Silence" (72). Again, the answer is to be found not in the realm of the divine but rather in the realm of the physical, which is in itself significant and spiritual enough.[6]

In "Logic," the poet's passionate request to be licked is addressed to someone of a more physical inclination than a God, to someone who, indeed, speaks this two-faced english: "touch me / with the tongue of your / . . . english / is a foreign anguish." This fragment can be read as the desperate impossibility of being touched by the mother tongue: in the midst of the act of being touched, the tongue changes and appears to be (also) the tormenting stranger, the "anguish." I do endorse the interpretation of english as a foreign tongue, like Anyidoho proposes. Still, there is the request to be touched by the mother/father language, and even if the wish is expressed as the wish for the mother's tongue, it necessarily has to include the wish for the father's tongue. The two cannot be separated. If I read the poem closely, I have to acknowledge Philip's formulation as the need for rebirth by means of very close, sensual contact with (a speaker of) the *foreign* language, or the foreign aspects of english. This is, in short, the plot of *Odyssey* too. When she has finally found the English-speaking Scot, the Traveller asks to be "licked," to be kissed, by him (72).

In fact, Anyidoho is as impressed as I am by Philip's evocation of the intimacy and sensuality of the conveyance of the mother's words to her baby. He did not remark, however, first, the fact that this sensuality is also connected to the foreign language; second, the intense sensuality of the description; and third, the fact that the child was gendered by the reception of the words as a *daughter*, not a son. However, these aspects of gender and sexuality are crucial to the understanding of Philip's concept of language. Philip tackles the paradox by inviting the father tongue to take the mother's place—not by replacing her desire for the mother with the desire for the paternal phallus, far from it—but by asking him to adopt the maternal logic of care without lack. I agree with Anyidoho that the poet laments a loss, rather than proposing a way out. She does not offer a promising strategy here; it is rather that she is trapped into inviting the father tongue by the impossibility to talk about the mother tongue without also evoking the father tongue.

Philip's need for rebirth can be compared to the need to return to the native island, as Aimé Césaire has put it, to the body of the defiled mother (see Chapter 3).[7] But language compels the poet to envisage a reconciliation with both mother and father. Both are defiled; the mother because colonization has corrupted her; the father because he is the corrupter unmasked. The poem needs both father and mother and exiled, desiring child to create the setting for its plot. Philip seems to be bent upon speaking her "serpent's tongue," a tongue that is in an even more literal way than Anzaldúa's, a split tongue, a double tongue (Anzaldúa 1991: 207). I discern in this endeavor the painful acceptance of hybridity, a hybridity that can become the signifier of identity only if it passes through the structures of desire, and if it becomes the object of sexual desire. To be able to desire it, *Odyssey* will separate the different (maternal and paternal) aspects and explore the possibility of an erotic investment in each.

How to Desire the Mother: Instructions for the Understanding of the Symbolic as Maternal

The desire of the mother comes easily to those in *Odyssey*. It is the desire of the father that poses a problem. For a solution to this problem, Philip looks at the circumstance of the intertwining of both. As I have shown, her mother tongue is her father tongue, too. This means that her most intimate, authentic self, her silence, is to be found in the interior of all her intimate ones, be they woman or man, Black or white, kin or enemy; in them she can touch it. This is the way one can understand how a quest for an authentic language is connected to the desire for the other. Philip's aesthetics makes hybridity the focal point. Her story about a search for self-knowledge, for her own, inalienable identity, thus takes the shape of the sexual pursuit of the other, the hostile element in her hybrid identity. Her quest for self culminates in the realization, to a degree, of her identity (in the literal sense of sameness) to *him*, her opposite, her shadow, her nemesis (61).

Having said all this, it is important to emphasize that her desire for this white man cannot be placed within the context of something like a "natural" heterosexuality: nothing could be less sexually attractive to the Traveller (who, by the way, clearly prefers women) than this sick, gaunt, old, prim white man (61). What kind of desire is this, then?[8]

My discussion of the nature of desire in Philip's texts lands me within the context of psychoanalysis. However, in the act of reading Philip's texts, I am relating primarily to the cultural periphery, a sphere structured by African and Caribbean desires as much as by imperialistic ones. In contrast, the Freudian and Lacanian schools of psychoanalysis, to which I will refer here, are disciplines of the West. They narrate the neuroses of the West, explain its literary dreams of dark African rainwoods and deep hot caves in India, and its sexual fantasies about Black women and men. But what do they have to say about those who are not raised within the nuclear family? What of that Other of whom the West dreams so feverishly?

In spite of the problems involved in the use of psychoanalysis in the South or in the African diaspora, much work has been done in this area. Frantz Fanon has done pioneering work in this respect. In the 1950s, he started to theorize the relation between colonized and colonizer with the help of the concept of the Oedipal relationship. He assumed a symmetrically oppositional, Manichean relationship between self (colonized) and other (colonizer) and analyzed the violence involved. Many postcolonial theorists draw on his work; one can find assessments of the Fanonist legacy in the work of scholars like JanMohamed, Spivak, Said, and Bhabha and in essays by Parry (1987), Gates (1991), Prasad (1992). The way postcolonial authors like JanMohamed developed Fanon's line of thought has been criticized for its essentialism (Prasad 1992: 76) and for its reification of the relation between self and other (Chow 1992: 363). I will return to JanMohamed below, as I think that his rather neat model is nevertheless useful for the interpretation of Philip's play with dualism.

Others, however, plead for a broader concept of the colonized's subjectivity. Such a concept can be found in nonpsychoanalytic theories that account for the production of plural postcolonial subjects by (geographically and historically) different specific economical, sexual, and political practices. Indeed, this dimension can also be found in Fanon's later work. Several important Black women theorists emphasize the need for a materialist analysis, which would inquire into the workings of the category of race, instead of considering one's individual racial identity or position (Abel 1997: 114, mentions Valerie Smith and Hazel Carby). It has been argued, and with reason, that it is especially white readers who tend to privilege psychological over political approaches (Abel 1997: 106). A materialist approach, favored by a considerable group of Black theorists and critics, would lead away from psychoanalysis, and this is exactly what they wish. Scholars like Iginla argue that psychoanalytical theory has nothing to offer Black feminists. Iginla's main argument is that psychoanalysis is too much of a universalist discipline, which looks for the same psychological patterns in all cultures, sexes, and historical periods (31–33). The same would hold for the notion of "oedipalization-as-colonization"; the character of the myth of Oedipus as a master ("and therefore universalist") narrative would hinder a plural, historical, and political understanding of (female) subjectivity (32).

Indeed, Oedipus lands most of us in deep trouble. All women suffer from the dominant centrality of this myth. The way it is formulated normatively as the necessary structure of the process of obtaining identity makes it hard for them to complete their passage through the Oedipal phase and win the prize—the entry into the Symbolic order, which would bring them social and cultural advantages. They will always run the risk of being stuck in the realm of the Imaginary. The same would apply to the "native," as Spivak explains (1993a: 17).

There are, however, psychoanalytical approaches that try to account for the structure of subjectivity without taking recourse to those elements in Freudian and Lacanian thinking that insist on the primacy of the phallus and the paramount centrality of Oedipus. Deleuze and Guattari developed the idea of "face" instead of the phallus, which would be of more relevance to a discussion of racism. One may think of the work of Melanie Klein, in which the importance of the Oedipus complex is played down, and which offers another understanding of the pre-Oedipal relation between mother and child. There are also many explicitly white feminist proposals. One may remember Luce Irigaray's refusal of the phallus as central signifier and her project of basing a feminine aesthetics on the self-sufficiency of the female sex. Elisabeth Bronfen proposes to concentrate on the less gender-specific navel instead of the phallus as the anatomical sign of lack, and Mieke Bal explores the possibilities of the navel as an aspect of an antiphallic semiotics. The most radical innovation to date might be Kaja Silverman's theorizing of the negative Oedipus complex, which makes it possible to place the girl's desire for the mother within the symbolic; this approach will come in useful at the end of this section in the discussion of Philip's views of the desire for the mother. Another relevant contribution from a postcolonial feminist perspective is to be found in a recent article by Spivak, who in a discussion of the figure of Echo in the myth of Narcissus reconsiders the hierarchical relation of Symbolic and Imaginary order.[9] Most recently, a pathbreaking collection of essays appeared that was based on the conference Psychoanalysis in African American contexts in Santa Cruz, 1992 (Abel, Christian, and Moglen 1997). Hortense Spillers, in this collection, answers Iginla by stating firmly that "the psychoanalytic object, subject, and subjectivity constitute the missing layer of hermeneutic and interpretive projects of an entire generation of Black intellectuals now at work" (Spillers 1997: 136), and she adds that "[t]here are genuine costs as a result," resulting in, as she suggests, "occasional lapses of ethical practice in social relations among black intellectuals themselves" (136). I would add that the exclusion of psychoanalysis from white readings of Black or/and postcolonial texts may also produce an inadmissibly and stereotypically reduced understanding of these texts, which would appear as shallower than white and/or Euro-American texts. The efforts of all the scholars I've mentioned to create concepts that are not based on the centrality of the West and of masculinity open a new space for the discussion of desire.

In using some of these insights in my discussion of Philip's narrative about postcolonial and Black female identity, I hope to show that creative and critical psychoanalytical notions cannot be missed if one aims at an understanding of the intimate dynamics of subjectivity, language, and desire within a Black and postcolonial context. My choice links me to the kind of literary criticism found in *Out of the Kumbla*; there one finds many brief references to (especially) Lacanian concepts. In contrast to most of these authors, I will not "use" those concepts, instead I will concentrate on the question that moved the authors in Abel, Christian, and Moglen 1997: in what ways can psychoanalysis be made to bear on issues of race *and* gender?

In *She Tries Her Tongue*, as well as in *Odyssey*, Philip refers to Western myths—even if she does not explicitly mention those of Oedipus and Narcissus, she does displace the myth of Proserpine, putting it in a wonderful vernacular Caribbean context (1989: 28), and she even takes the epigraph to the title poem in *She Tries Her Tongue* from Ovid (84). She upsets Christian rituals and phrases and invents other myths, parodying the classical and Christian ones. She juxtaposes all of these with all kinds of normative (real or imagined) *Practical Guides*, lessons, meditations, definitions, exercises of grammar and semantics. If I read in her texts some implicit, structural references to the master narratives of Oedipus and Narcissus, I will treat these not as a superior framework within which to explain textual structures, but as imperialist narratives, among other normative and oppressive narratives, which she rewrites. Her rewriting begins with the deconstruction of that crucial signifier: the phallus.

If Philip's treatment of desire can be seen as a critique of traditional Western psychoanalysis, as I propose, it becomes particularly acute in her play with the difference and similarities between phallus and tongue. Within Western schools of psychoanalysis, the phallus is of paramount importance for the child's entry into the symbolic order. In the poem "Logic," however, the tongue takes the place the phallus has in much Western thought. That is, it is—tentatively—equated to the penis. This equation is prepared in the first multiple choice question of the four that end the poem:

A tapering, blunt-tipped, muscular, soft and fleshy organ describes
(a) the penis.
(b) the tongue.
(c) neither of the above.
(d) both of the above. (59)

The nature of the tongue as a central signifier for ethnic, racial, and gender difference is elaborated in other parts of the poem. I will come back to this. If in my reading I take into account the signification given to the penis within phallocentric systems of thought (such as Lacanian psychoanalysis), this equation is telling. You might say that the poem robs the phallus of its uniqueness and absolute dominance: the tongue shares its properties. The tongue is raised to the dominant position to which the phallus lays claim. At the same time, the phallus is inscribed with some of the qualities of the tongue, for example, with the tongue's potency to denote cultural, if not racial, specificity through its association with speech and language. Thus, the poem accentuates the advantage the tongue has over the phallus, namely, that both sexes possess, lack, and desire it—in both its physical and metaphorical sense.

In other fragments of the poem the relation between the two fleshy organs is carried through until the hierarchy between them is reversed. For what is desired is not the "phallus," but rather the "tongue," that is, the mother tongue. Indeed, the mother tongue functions here, as "the signifier of (the subject's) alienation in signification" (which is the first part of

Silverman's definition of the phallus, and a quote from Lacan; 1984: 183). The tongue can hardly be understood as the "signifier for the cultural and positive values which define male subjectivity within patriarchal society" (which would be the second part of the definition of the phallus; Silverman 1984: 183), but it mirrors this description exactly to make it fit Philip's African woman's situation. Therefore, it signifies those values that define female subjectivity within a female, maternal society outside the scope of imperialism.

This is why the child is gendered as a *girl* upon entering the maternal symbolic order. If I follow the Lacanian narrative but replace the crucial terms, I can describe this entry in the following way: the girl enters this symbolic order by means of the alienating mother's tongue, but she knows that, as a girl, she will grow up as a woman who will be in full possession of this tongue, which holds promises of fullness and gratification. Whereas within the patriarchal order, the female subject lacks the lack of the phallus (Silverman 1984: 186), she is seriously lacking in Philip's order, where she lacks the mother tongue, she lacks silence. So, the Traveller necessarily has to be a woman, for only as a woman can she be the acting, desiring subject whose subjectivity is structured by this positive lack.

But this alternative staging of Oedipus is not only about femininity. It is just as much about the colonized subject; for just as "the cultural primacy of the phallus can be established and maintained" (Silverman 1988: 189) only if the mother desires it (and, in consequence, lacks it), colonial relations can be maintained only if the colonized desires the phallus-as-Name-of-the-Colonial-Father. Of course, this desire is what the Traveller refuses. Her refusal of the Colonial Phallic Word is in itself already a threat to coloniality. The tongue, then, is clearly inscribed with notions of culture as well as with notions of sexuality, and hence, gender. The tongue is the site of the erotic as well as of culture and "race" (which coincides with culture here).

In the fragment of the poem about the mother licking her baby, I read an alternative narrative about the child's entry into the symbolic. The mother tongue functions as a language that does not exclude the body, but envelopes and articulates it as an object and as a subject of desire. The mother tongue licks the infant's body, first to seduce it into whimpering (which I would interpret as the sign of its experience of its difference from the mother at the same time as its connectedness to her) and then into silent approval; after that, it blows her words into its mouth. Thus, the mother tongue teaches the child difference and pleasure without lack.

This concept of language might bring us close to Luce Irigaray's fantasy of a woman's language that is based not on the absent phallus but on a notion of self-fulfilled, female sexuality. Indeed, the name of Irigaray is mentioned on the back of Philip's novel as a predecessor, along with that of French "écriture féminine" writer Monique Wittig. Irigaray has been criticized for her ethnocentrism, though. Ann Rosalind Jones argues, for example, that the concept of the "jouissance" of ever-touching, ever-embracing lips may be of minor relevance in a context of clitoridectomy (Silverman 1988: 146). I agree wholeheartedly with Jones's critical exposure of the limited appropriateness of such a notion of "jouissance." Yet dooming women from the South automatically to a lack of pleasure amounts to a reduction of women to victims, and this is a definition rightly criticized by Mohanty (1988). Philip does examine the potentials of pleasure in the process of finding a position for the female subject of a full, plural voice.

The Traveller wants to be desired by the mother: she wants to be "licked" by her. In the narrative, she is initiated again and again into a deeper insight into the nature of silence. In fact, the episodes of initiation mirror the first scene in the poem, in which the mother licked the infant until it was ready to receive her words. Each time anew, the Traveller is received by maternal figures, who treat her roughly but also with loving care. She is licked by these women—in both meanings of the word. At the end of the story, she asks to be licked/kissed by Livingstone. The father, then, is asked to become the mother—the logic of the desire for the mother is supplanted to the relation to the father. This is in striking contrast to Western Oedipal logic. According to those Oedipal norms, the desire for the mother, produced in the course of the child's entry into the symbolic order, and its subsequent loss of the mother, should be replaced by the required desire for the fatherly phallus. In *Odyssey*, it is not. The stories of the Traveller and of Livingstone are *both* governed by the dream of the mother's seduction—and this is, as Silverman explains, the girl's dream of the *negative* Oedipus complex. According to Silverman, the negative Oedipus complex, and thus the girl's desire for the mother, is firmly rooted within the symbolic.

As for Livingstone, his desire for the mother is much more ambiva-

lent. He desires the Supreme British Phallic Mother, the Queen; this much
is clear. And this desire makes him a dutiful British son. His longing for
fame, a Name, a place in History can be read as a (proper) desire for the
paternal phallus. Phallic Mother and Paternal Phallus come together in this
utterance: "I want all the glory for myself, my God and my Queen" (24).
But the significance of a claim to the phallus depends on the existence of
phallocracy, a system that is under attack in the text and has lost its influence. Hence, Livingstone's desire for maternal silence would be of more
consequence than his desire for the phallus. The text suggests, however,
that the explorer is hardly aware of the nature of his desire for the maternal
sphere. This desire has to be deduced from the remarks of others (the Traveller, Mary Livingstone). He never articulates it directly. Yet, it is an essential, though repressed, element of his identity. The text uses two devices to
create its alternative view on language: it replaces the phallus with the
tongue, and it places the girl's desire for the mother within the symbolic.
Both moves provide a background to understand the statement *Odyssey*
wants to make: the mother tongue, silence, is a language. This statement
gainsays the colonial theory that the "native" stays trapped within the order of the imaginary (Spivak 1993a: 17). And that, precisely, is the myth
Philip's text upsets.

How to Desire the Father: The Castration of Livingstone

Now I shift my attention to that other looming presence in the text,
the father. If desire is restricted to the maternal symbolic, how can one explain the desire for the colonial father, which, after all, structures the narrative as a pursuit of the symbol of white dominance?[10] I have shown that
in *She Tries Her Tongue* the desire for the mother tongue is often expressed
as an ambivalent or double desire; the mother tongue is father tongue too,
and the white father hides in his bosom the quality of the maternal.
Odyssey separates the intertwined elements of mother and father to redefine each separately as well as the relationship between them. This is done
by acts of (unorthodox) "parsing," which become clear in the poetic parts
of the text, and it is done by the elaboration and problematization of the
dualisms between silence and word, womb and phallus, woman and man,
Black and white, Traveller and Livingstone. Apart from revaluating the ma-

ternal as a symbolic sphere, the text rather brutally reconsiders the position of the male, too. This is done through the characterization of Livingstone.

On the first page of the story, he is already designated as the one who "fathered" silence. The discourse of conception, pregnancy, and sexuality that is announced here is first taken up in parables of birth as in the image of a woman/I swallowing with difficulty the both strange and kindred kernels of silence, taking them into the womb, and then giving birth to the fruit (8–9). Then, in large capitals, which occur only in the two fragments from which the following fragment is taken, one is confronted with the image of a white man copulating violently with a Black woman:

HE—LIVINGSTONE—AND I COPULATE LIKE TWO BEASTS—HE RIDES ME—HIS WORD SLIPPING IN AND OUT OF THE WET MOIST SPACES OF MY SILENCE—I TAKE HIS WORD—STRONG AND THRUSTING—THAT WILL NOT REST, WILL NOT BE DENIED IN ITS SEARCH TO FILL EVERY CREVICE OF MY SILENCE—I TAKE IT INTO THE SILENCE OF MY MOUTH—AND IN A CLEARING IN A FOREST HE SITS AND WEEPS AS STANLEY COMFORTS HIM—

"I SAY, OLD CHAP, WHAT'S THE MATTER?"

"MY WORD, MY WORD IS IMPOTENT—" (25)

Picturing the brutal confrontation between European colonizer and African in sexual terms as well as in terms of language, Philip avoids calling it rape. On the contrary, the aggressor is robbed of his dominance, and the woman who appears to be victim changes the act of copulation into an act of fellatio, which enables her to reclaim control over the situation and even cause the invader's impotence.

Rather than a history of rape, this is the story of a castration. This story is a rigorous rewriting of a history of victimism. According to many, the dis-membering of woman lies at the base of Caribbean history (Johnson 1990: 113). Now, the rapist is castrated; but he is not victimized in turn —it is a wholesome castration. Philip uses the familiar rhetoric of the accepted historic approach (the sexual metaphors to picture the colonial confrontation as rape; the gendering of Africa; the bringing of the word; Africa's silence) to structure a different discourse. In Lacanian terms, castration anxiety motivates the male child to leave the imaginary and to enter the symbolic, through which he also has to suffer loss. In Philip's phantasmic mirror-world, Livingstone is castrated by his entry into the mother's symbolic, silence: in taking his male organ in her mouth, the Traveller lets him enter her silence, and as a result, he becomes impotent. If one follows Lacan's explanation of castration as the term referring "to alienation in signification" (Lacan, quoted in Silverman 1984: 183), one can say that Livingstone, like every male subject, had to undergo castration to be able to enter into the symbolic. But his narrative has doubled itself. Apart from his successful entry into the imperialistic, patriarchal Symbolic—by which he gained power in the form of fame, a Name, and phallic keys to cities—there is his awkward entry into the maternal symbolic.

However, his entry is shown only as a possibility. By his castration, Livingstone has turned from Oedipal colonial father into narcissistic boy-child—sulking "like a little boy" (63), unmanly selfish (24), and child-like in his need to boast about his deeds (62, 69). As a child, he can no longer lay claim to his possession of the phallus. He is just another child suffering the separation from his mother, just like the Traveller. He has now won the promise of the reunion with the mother. But this is not the Imperialist Queen Mother, who can be seen as the cause of a former castration and his apparently haunting sense of lack.

According to Lacan, the primordial lack of castration is also the result of the child's separation from the plenitude of the mother's body, that is pushing the child away or is otherwise absent. In Philip's alternative image of the maternal sphere, one finds a different mother. As I have argued, the entry into the Symbolic is effectuated by the loving firmness of a present mother, who acknowledges difference but does not deny continuity. For the Africans outside the reach of imperialism, the real separation from the mother came only after, with the advent of the colonial father, who caused the loss.

Before his castration, Livingstone could give himself a place in this patriarchal, imperialist order. Now he has the possibility of a reintegration into the fullness of the maternal. However, Livingstone never even enters the historical symbolic universe "of our word," the space structured by maternal patterns more than by paternal ones, and in which the Traveller roams freely. Livingstone's entry is precarious and provisional, just as is the girl's entry into the phallic symbolic order. As a matter of fact, *Odyssey* never fully realizes his entry. Instead, the text invents another semiotic space where the two protagonists meet.

This place is outside both traditions of history and time presented in *Odyssey* (either "of our word" or "of our Lord"). It is very much governed by silence. It is called "Somewhere in Africa," and the time is a near but only possible future—except in the ambivalent ending of the story, to which I will revert in the last section. In this literary maternal space, Livingstone's own cultural views are no longer valid. This demise of his views is exemplified by the refusal of the Traveller to give him her name; she prefers not to be signified within his discourse. She also knows, that names are appropriated, changed, and forgotten (such as Mosioatunya, the name of the falls Livingstone renamed as Victoria Falls). On the contrary, she proposes to rename *him* according to her own historic views: "I myself prefer 'thin edge of the wedge' as a title to describe you" (66).

But despite her critique of him, this is the place where the Traveller can recognize his relationship to silence. Even if he does not, she acknowledges the presence of the maternal Silence in his person. She recognizes his desire, and wishes to be recognized and desired in turn. That is how the father can be desired without succumbing to the logic of a destructive phallogocentrism: by castrating him, making him the subject of the same desire as herself, the Traveller can undo the violence of their Oedipal relation. Now, she can desire his recognition of her and his desire for her; a desire that has become possible only because she is as much in possession of the maternal silence as he is, and she lacks it as much as he does.

Philip uses two main devices to structure her narrative. One of these techniques is related to her idea of castration. Philip herself thematizes the relation between parsing, dismembering, castration, and rape in a poem in *She Tries Her Tongue*: in a section entitled "Universal Grammar" one finds among many entries this one: "*Parsing*—the exercise of dis-membering language into fragmentary cells that forget to re-member" (66). At the bottom of the same page, on which only the above sentence is printed, is a grammatical analysis of the word "rape." The opposite page, which is the last of the section, consists of a poem in which the memory faculty of cells occurs anew, followed by the next fragment:

Slip mouth over the syllable; moisten with tongue the word.
Suck Slide Play Caress Blow—Love it, but if the word gags, does not nourish, bite it off—at its source—
Spit it out
Start again

From *Mother's Recipes on How to Make a Language Yours or How Not to Get Raped.* (67)

This short piece tells us a lot about the castration scene in *Odyssey*. Castration, then, is a way of defending oneself against the rape by a foreign language. This dis-membering annihilates that language's power. The same occurs in the exercise of parsing, which becomes visible mainly in the poetry: if words and sentences are parsed into the elements of which they are composed, and even further, then only ungrammatical elements remain. Thus, words are stripped of their usual meaning—they forget where they have been, unlike Bakhtin's words—and the suggestion of other, new meanings springs up.

Even though I will contrast the castrating device of parsing to the one based on the interior of the womb, in these parsing poems the writer is led by the trope of interior, too. Incessantly she reduces verbs to qualities that are located *within* substantives. In the poems cited above there are many examples of this technique. By this parsing, and the splitting open of grammaticality, the relations between words and concepts change. In a way, the text lets their meanings explode; Philip's aesthetics loves explosions, implosions, catharsis.

Not surprisingly, one finds several references to scientific theories and metaphors like the atom. There is a predominantly negative attitude toward calculation and measuring ("these maps are utterly unreliable," 32, and see the fragment about the irrelevance of the measuring of the circle, 36–37), but the texts do use the comparable device of parsing to track the traces of the joints of composite words. According to Mark Taylor, who reads Derrida, "Language is constituted by *not saying* the trace" (1990: 4). Philip's poetry gets as close to the saying of the trace as is possible, and this brings her to the very brink of collapse. For if she would say the trace, she would speak the Silence, and that would mean a larger surrendering than this narrative can contain:

> How parse the punish
>
>   in Silence
>   —Noun
>   —Verb
>
>   absent a Grammar
>   how surrender to within
>   that without
>   remains

Silence
>> demands the break
> the die
>> in release
> in life (59)

To the returning question in *Odyssey* of whether it is possible to parse Silence, the answer is no—one cannot castrate, dismember Silence. It is ungrammatical, whole, undividable. One can enter it only by a complete surrender. It seems that this is a radical, maybe even violent step, in which one has to stake one's life. The nature of Silence is absolute. However, the narrative is attached to its symbolic, hybrid nature, which is, after all, the condition of narrativity. So, apart from her parsing poetry, *Odyssey* presents juicy pieces of prose in which the trace is happily neglected. In this, Philip does not follow the second option of Deleuze and Guattari: "opt for the German language of Prague as it is and in its very poverty. Go always farther in the direction of deterritorialization, to the point of sobriety. Since the language is arid, make it vibrate with a new intensity" (Deleuze and Guattari 1991: 61). She sets out to deterritorialize, but she knows too that the end of such an endeavor will be an impotent silence; that is not what she seeks. So, she accepts hybridity and plurality (that is, of narrating techniques) to develop her story as a rich narrative, that passes through lively dialogues and intimacy to end in a kind of mute catharsis. Parsing, then, is only one of her techniques. It is balanced by narrative strategies that are derived from other images.

Above I have explained how Philip's writing shows how those living in the postcolonial world can desire the mother as well as the father. The text makes these desires possible by creating a symbolic sphere in which not the phallus but the tongue is the central signifier. Men as well as women, Blacks as well as whites, desire the mother tongue—silence—as much as they lack it. Not only does Philip make this radical transformation her main theme; she also creates this different symbolic sphere on the level of the text itself, by disturbing a rational, linear form of writing. Her inspiration for this linguistic strategy comes from the notion of dis-membering, of castration. However, a more direct path to her different symbolic sphere is conceivable. For her texts have already been imagining this maternal symbolic; it exists in the mouth receiving the phallic word, and it exists in the womb. Indeed, Philip is not the first to associate a maternal semiotic sphere to the notion of the womb. But her imagination of these notions cannot be merely equated to other theories or fictions—Philip's perception offers specific, new insights. A closer consideration of Philip's reading of the womb will allow me to articulate a precise and detailed interpretation of Philip's vision of the maternal Symbolic.

The Womb: The Chora and the Kumbla

The concept of the womb in *Odyssey* might best be discussed in relation to two kindred concepts: the *chora* and the kumbla. Finally, it will be possible to discern a specific kind of writing connected to the metaphor of the womb, a writing based on the notions of the circle and the spiral.

Both the chora and the kumbla are associated with the womb, and both imply a specific modality of signification. The concept of the *chora* links the womb explicitly to a nondominant modality of the signifying process. The concept of the kumbla, however, does not establish such a direct link. It can be argued that it implies such a link, as I will show. But the relevance of the concept of the kumbla for my discussion of Philip's texts lies primarily in its function of elucidating the difficult position of marginalized Black women who are trapped between alienating white, dominant discourses and stigmatized Black discourses—which is precisely Philip's topic. Before proceeding with my comparison of the concepts of the womb in *Odyssey*, the chora and the kumbla, I will use some lines to discuss each of these concepts in some depth.

At first sight, Julia Kristeva's concept of the chora seems to be of exquisite relevance to the discussion of the domain of articulate female sexuality. Kristeva borrows the concept from Plato (*Timeus*), who used the term *chora* (of which the main literal meaning is "space") to indicate an assumed, logically derived, but unnameable space that must be seen as a "receptacle" and that stands in opposition to reason and reality. Kristeva understands the chora as something outside spatiality and temporality and outside discourse itself. She sees in Plato's description of the chora already the suggestion of its being both a "thing" and a mode of language (Kristeva 1974: 23, note 15), and she develops this suggestion into her own reading of the concept, for she describes the chora primarily as a modality of language. Kristeva also stresses Plato's comparison of the chora to a mother, as the chora is in the position of the one who receives, which is by Plato's definition the maternal position. In the following terse description of Plato's chora, Kristeva brings all of these elements together: "Plato's *Timeus* speaks of a *chora* . . . receptacle . . . unnamable, improbable, hybrid, anterior to naming, to the One, to the father, and consequently, maternally connoted" (Kristeva 1980: 133). Kristeva then relates the chora to one of the two modalities of language, that is, the semiotic, a signifying disposition she opposes to the symbolic. The semiotic disposition is not governed by a transcendental ego. It is characterized by a heterogeneity of meaning, as it can be observed in the rhythms and intonations babies utter before they start to speak. It also appears in poetic language, in the "'musical' but also nonsense effects that destroy not only accepted beliefs and significations, but, in radical experiments, syntax itself, that guarantee of thetic consciousness" (Kristeva 1980: 133). This disruptive, nongrammatical language use belongs to the nondominant sphere of the mother. Kristeva's description seems to bring us close to Philip's exploration of silence as the nongrammatical mother tongue.

In a critical examination of Kristeva's understanding of the chora, Kaja Silverman offers a description that highlights even more clearly the very aspects in the chora that are crucial to Philip's understanding of the postcolonial feminine position within language. Silverman states that according to Kristeva the choric fantasy refers to "the image of the child wrapped in the sonorous envelope of the maternal voice" (101), which is "not only a fantasy about pre-Oedipal existence, the entry into language, and the inauguration of subjectivity; it is also a fantasy about biological 'beginnings,' intra-uterine life, and what she [Kristeva] calls the 'homosexual-maternal facet'" (Silverman 1988: 101). The chora stays with the subject through adult life, even if he or she moves away from it; the subject can turn back and find itself once again within the chora (106). The main issues in Philip's writing return in this notion: the definition of this maternal sphere in the process of signification as opposed to the father, the fact that the maternal sphere is voiced, the fact that this sphere is accessible throughout life, its status as a fantasy, its nature as a fantasy about origin, and finally the reference to homosexuality (the desire of the mother, of women).

However, there are serious disadvantages to adopting Kristeva's discourse for the understanding of Philip's images of the interior and the womb. First, Kristeva's chora is associated with the disturbance of syntax and signification; it is connected to a modality that disturbs and threatens the Symbolic. In Philip's texts, this disturbing function is attributed to the poetic technique of "parsing," a mode derived from the idea of castration. As such, I have placed it in opposition to (and not associated it with) the mode of the womb. Silverman's critique of Kristeva's treatment of the subject offers a second argument. Silverman argues that Kristeva's concept of the chora is riddled with a negative view of the mother as an obstacle to the child's entry into the symbolic, and with a negation of her discursive role. In Philip's early aesthetics, as I have argued, the mother is plainly the one who initiates her child into speech. Philip presents a Caribbean or Black view of the mother, who is, to mention only one point, seen as the transmitter of culture, whereas the figure of the mother Kristeva talks about is at odds with culture. Philip's conceptualization of the maternal silence of the womb shows that this maternal sphere is a significant symbolic system as well. Both *She Tries Her Tongue* and *Odyssey* are indeed explorations of the semiotics (by which I do *not* mean Kristeva's confusing term) of otherness. Using a concept that would confine this maternal, "other" sphere outside the Symbolic would mean a premature dismissal of this project.

There is another concept that is closely associated with the womb and that also implies a modality of signification: the kumbla. This concept may be more pertinent to my discussion than Kristeva's chora, as the concept of the kumbla is clearly situated *within* the symbolic. The concept of the kumbla has been introduced into the field of literature by Erna Brodber's novels *Jane and Louisa Will Soon Come Home* (1988a) and *Myal* (1988b). In Caribbean womanist/feminist literary practice, the concept has been developed to indicate a specific language strategy by which marginalized women and men survive by adapting to dominant white norms of speech and behaviour.[11] Brodber's first novel contains a chapter entitled "The Kumbla." I quote:

A kumbla is like a beach ball. It bounces with the sea but never goes down. . . . But the kumbla is not just a beach ball. The kumbla is an egg shell. . . . It does not crack if it is hit. . . . Your kumbla will not open unless you rip its seams open. It is a round seamless calabash that protects you without caring.

Your kumbla is a parachute. . . . Your kumbla is a helicopter. . . . A comic

strip space ship. . . . And inside is soft carpeted foam, like the womb and with an oxygen tent. Safe, protective time capsule. Fed simply by breathing!
    They usually come in white. (Brodber 1988a: 123)

The metaphor appears to be rich in connotations. As for its literal meaning and etymology, Carolyn Cooper shows (quoting a scholar in the field of Jamaican speech) that the term *kumbla* is derived from *coobla*, which is "probably a reduction of *calabash*, which is what it means" (Cassidy, quoted in Cooper 1991: 284). The kumbla, as can be learned from the above quotation, has come to refer to an ambivalently connoted closed space. But it can also refer to linguistic and discursive practices.

    Rhonda Cobham refers to the narrative function the kumbla can have; she states how in a certain Anansi trickster story (in Brodber's text), the story of the kumbla functions as "a protective but disfiguring narrative device" (Cobham 1993: 49). Cooper, referring to the same type of story, expands on this aspect. Following Cassidy, the above-mentioned scholar of Jamaican speech, she says that the process of nicknaming and reducing a word, by which the word *kumbla* has been formed, is a general speech habit, a "playful disguise, characteristic of the Jamaican Creole lexicon. . . . The shaping of the *kumbla*, an act of creativity, is also the art of subterfuge, a flowering of the spirit of the morally ambivalent Anansi" (Cooper 1991: 284). Here one may have found a Caribbean (and/or eminently female) counterpart to Gates's trope of signifying, derived from Esu-Elegbara, who appears as a trickster figure (like Anansi) in folklore. But the speech strategy of the kumbla differs from the strategy of signifying, as the concept implies in the first place that the disguise it entails may suffocate and arrest growth: "But the trouble with the kumbla is the getting out of the kumbla" (Brodber 1988a: 130). Cobham defines the kumbla as a social and interdiscursive rather than a narrative strategy, that is, as "a symbol for the manifold strategies by which Black women throughout the ages have ensured their own survival and that of the race" (Cobham 1993: 49). Before anything else, these strategies imply adaptation to white, dominant culture. By "their complicity within it," women have acquired the power to challenge these strategies of adaptation, as Cobham formulates it (51). At the same time, however, they risk getting caught within these strategies. Many novels in which a kind of kumbla is created also narrate ways to escape, or failures to escape, from the kumbla.

    The editors of *Out of the Kumbla*, Carole Boyce Davies and Elaine

Savory Fido, explain the ambivalent nature of the kumbla in the following way: "The closed space has the potential of functioning both nega-
tively and positively—but positively only if it is used as cocoon (cf. our
titular *kumbla* metaphor) from which growth eventually comes" (Davies
and Fido 1990: 26). An earlier remark emphasizes that the kumbla can be
valued positively only if it is understood as a point of departure: "'Out of
the Kumbla' then signifies for us movement from confinement to visibility, articulation, process . . . a sign for departure from constricting and restricting spaces" (19). Michelle Cliff gives us a perfect example of the
alienating effects of such a kumbla in her description of her situation as a
student in London. Then, she was fluent in "eloquent linear prose," writing about "intellectual game-playing in the Italian Renaissance" (1985:
11–12). For a young Jamaican woman, this talent testifies to an excellent
capacity of adapting; in Cliff's eyes, this must have been her kumbla.
Elsewhere, Cliff introduces her view of the A-beng as a means to be addressed from outside such a kumbla, and thus, implicitly, to escape from
it. The connection between A-beng and kumbla has been made in a somewhat opaque remark by Pamela Mordecai in her preface to *Out of the
Kumbla*. Mordecai emphasizes the aspects of transformation and confusion of the kumbla, here in connection to the way the concept is used in
different essays in *Out of the Kumbla*: "'Kumbla' becomes the calabash . . .
'l'espace clos' . . . and 'A-beng.' The metamorphosis is unintended but
evident. A thing turns into something else and at the same time retains
its identity and intactness. The association-in-disparity and capacity-for-
being-confounded both signify" (Mordecai, in Davies and Fido 1990: viii).
Mordecai's interpretation of the A-beng as a kumbla (as in Brodber) poses
some problems. *Abeng* is the title of one of Cliff's novels, which is the subject of a densely written essay by Lemuel Johnson. He shows how the
novel uses the concept of the A-beng as a means of remembering Caribbean (pre)history and thus as a possibility for Caribbean women to find a
new kind of female consciousness in relation to the history of sexual and
racial violence between many cultures. Literally, the A-beng is the name
for "the conch-shell passing messages *for and against* enslavers" (121). Johnson adds, "when the conch shell sounds, it invariably calls up(on) the slave
and the maroon, at once invoking and bridging the Middle Passage" (125).
So, the A-beng signifies a hybrid language, a hybrid address, to and from
conflicting historical positions, which it at once connects and separates.

From these descriptions, one learns that the A-beng is certainly not a space or container, as the kumbla is. Apart from their similar shape, the A-beng can be compared to the kumbla only if one stresses the kumbla's narrative and discursive aspect: the A-beng, just like the kumbla, is a means to disguise (here, messages) and it is also provided with a voice. It seems to me that, contrary to the kumbla, it is not a discursive strategy that one can use as one's own voice. The A-beng is primarily a call to answer. As it calls upon the different aspects of one's identity, it can be a means of acknowledging plurality, and so, a means of breaking out of one's kumbla. The A-beng seems to be an antidote to the kumbla, just as myal is to obeah in Brodber's novel.

The comparison between A-beng and kumbla is useful, if only because it shows that there are common aspects to the different metaphors Caribbean women writers use to imagine aspects of the processes of undoing and reconstructing Caribbean women's subjectivity. Transformation, disguise, ambivalence, strategy of survival, and strategy of speech are key words in the concept of the kumbla; being addressed by the past/those connected to the past, remembering, and mythmaking are key words in the concept of escape from the kumbla.

These notions are also present in Philip's writing. I will now elaborate on the central, recurring metaphor of the womb before relating it to kumbla and chora. In *Odyssey*, the womb takes many forms. It functions always as the place where the rites of passage are to be undergone. One finds it echoed in the description of a magic circle within a circle, one is trapped within it like a fetus, and one cannot escape but by retiring to its interior. Its radius can be measured by means of a cord, which is a snake as well as an umbilical cord (36–38). In another passage, the womblike space is a sweat lodge; there one loses all words save the three most essential ones ("birth," "death," "silence"); one is reduced to crying weakness, "curled in the fetal position on the floor" (45). In yet another passage, it is a huge room at the deep end of a long corridor, "ablaze with coloured fabric and yarn" (51); there one is locked up in loneliness to come to an understanding of the nature of one's own Silence. It is in all cases a place of transformation and the attaining of a deeper insight. Within this womb, one lives through an initiation rite that makes transformation and growth possible. Before anything else, the womb is the site of possibilities. As the ending of the poem says, in the beginning was

                             not

word

      but Silence
      and a future rampant

                             with possibility

and Word (40)

Silence is the site of a promising future, which also holds the Word (the purified word), as concreteness and realization. But the narrative accentuates potentiality and possibility, and modes of promising uncertainty instead. This is why the puns on Stanley's famous but unhappy dictum ("Dr. Livingstone, I presume?") proliferate. "I presume" becomes the sign for the mode of possibility, and thus for the denial of the forceful nature of actual history, of reality. During one of her many tests by a people she visits, the Traveller is confronted with a skill-testing question: what were Stanley's first words to the doctor when they met? Not only is the historic utterance a ludicrously wrong answer, but even the thought of the possibility of Stanley's saying this brings the people to a raucous hilarity, and to an explosion of feasting and dancing, with bursts of shouting: "I presume!": "We presume, we presume, oh, how we presume! Long live I presume! Long live Dr. Livingstone, Stanley and Silence!" (21). Later, when the Traveller and Livingstone finally meet, she consequently calls him Livingstone-I-presume ("and

I don't know why I call you Livingstone-I-presume—you look like Livingstone-I-presume, I suppose," 66).

First, I hear the celebration of the wish that history had not happened in this way. In fact, a party is thrown on the festive occasion of the rewriting of real, violent, catastrophic history into a hilarious myth. At the same time, possibilities of other imaginations of history are opened. The mode of the future tense is installed; the desire for narrating is inaugurated. Postcolonial writers receive their working space, their playing field. Second, Livingstone himself is named as a possibility. He is not accepted as real by the Traveller; he is a phantasm, a possibility. Of course, on the very first level of the enunciation, he is the invention of the I/writer, as he is a character in her narrative; but he is also someone who is full of potential, and the ability to transform. He, too, can escape from the rigid discourse of history, from his role of the imperialist pioneer. On the other hand, he might not have existed. Whereas "facts" are established by those who have power, as the Traveller explains (67–68), it is possible to conceive of another history of facts, decided by others, who would not think Livingstone's visit to Africa, or even his mere existence, a fact worthy of mention.

In *Odyssey*, this mode of potentiality is connected to the womb. The womb, the maternal space, offers the possibility of a mode of otherness, where desire, the transforming power of Utopia, is acknowledged as a real power of transformation. The playful use of the colonizer's masque is another aspect of the narrative mode of the womb: *Odyssey* often parodies British colonial speech, which at the end of the story also informs the Traveller's actions and thoughts as one of the possible discourses she can adopt. The occurrence of this parodied speech opens the possibility of juicy dialogue and other kinds of narrative contrast (in which caricature has its place). These are at the base of the story's sass, which balances its deep seriousness.

Now I can clarify how Philip's *womb* implicitly reinterprets the concept of the kumbla and thereby offers a comment on the challenges of Caribbean women's writing. In fact, Philip creates her own concept of the womb by appropriating aspects of both the kumbla and the chora. The womb can be seen as a kumbla in that it is the very place of interior transformation. But it is not an adaptation to white, Western norms—on the contrary, it is a return to the *otherness* of one's self. Indeed, Philip's womb is thoroughly hybrid. The dominant discourse is always present, even in one's deepest inner self: in the form of the tape measure/snake/birth cord; in the sweat lodge, where (english) language receives new importance; in the room where the fabric of Silence has to be sewn with the help of the stitches of the word. The womb teaches Silence (as a language), but also the necessity of the word; that is the strategy of speech *Odyssey* proposes. The womb, then, is not a confining, stifling kumbla, as it shows the inevitability of hybridity. Neither is the womb an alienating kumbla. However, like the kumbla, it is the enclosed spot of transformation and growth. Indeed, like other theorists of the kumbla, Philip relates the kumbla to the strategy of masking (and the adoption of dominant discourses). But, as I have explained above, in Philip's case this masquerade is a vigorous, vital game. It seems that Philip persistently refuses to understand the womb or the maternal in a negative way, even when she shapes these as a kumbla.

This interpretation shows the specificity of Philip's vision. Her text testifies to the necessity of embracing and appropriating colonial languages and discourses as much as the mother tongue. Philip introduces the notion of desire in her narrative to evoke the emotional and intensely physical challenge of the need to come to terms with the alienating and oppressive discourses. In this aspect, then, she can be said to take recourse to the concept of the chora. Like Kristeva's concept, and unlike the Caribbean concepts of the kumbla, Philip's womb is the place where desire is installed. As I have shown, Philip holds that this is an ambivalent, double desire.

Above, I suggested that two main techniques are used to structure the narrative of *Odyssey*. I argued that the first technique can be related to Philip's understanding of castration. In *Odyssey* one also discerns a second mode of writing, which is connected to the womb. The story of the pursuit of the other is accountable for one of the ways *Odyssey* is structured. In spite of the linear line according to which time is propelled forward, chronologically but at a more than dizzy speed, the text is structured as a circular, inwardly directed motion: every episode repeats the preceding, in which the Traveller makes another step toward an insight into her inner self, her Silence. Every trial brings her to a still deeper insight, but each time she resumes her journey in a new pursuit of her aim. At every new trial, the story gains in intensity and narrative richness. A helpful but ignorant, nameless, and toothless old woman of the second people visited by the Traveller (15) is replaced with named characters in the next episodes, who assume the same role as guideswoman and initiator, while the trials are described in ever more detail and become more and more drastic and painful. Finally, this actantial position is taken by a lovingly and intimately characterized woman: "I could picture her—straight, proud back, beautifully black face as profound as a midnight sky—walking away with the keys jangling at her waist—a smile on her pointed, pixie face" (51). This woman, named Ar-whal, becomes the Traveller's lover.

Here, the story shows great narrative complexity, with retrospects and embedded narratives, sometimes functioning as prospects and *mises-en-abyme*, and with a deviant chronology. The love affair between Arwhal and the Traveller is described cursorily but in sensual detail. In addition, the technique of using color to characterize the silence and intensity of the interior is applied again. When the fourth group of people (of the six that are explicitly named) is visited, the deep colors of the landscape at sunset are accentuated. Especially the color red is endowed with the significance of the sacred ("a red rain that kept the earth under its branches sacred," 36). During the last visit, the space of enclosure is "ablaze with coloured fabric and yarn" (51). The more one approaches the zero point of the narrative ("the end of time," 60), the more colorful and narratively interesting it becomes, whereas the fixed development of the episodes remains unaltered.

Livingstone is situated in the heart of this inwardly directed spiral. In a certain sense, he is the rabid dog Cliff encountered in the heart of the fog. He is also an alter ego. Cliff's alter ego took the shape of the silent African, appearing as if in a vision, who went up in smoke before she could address him (117–19). Philip, however, is able to look into the face of what she encounters at the core. The inwardly spiraling movement of the text leads to this: the essential, mythical meeting of these crucial others. And, as Philip wants to heal the alienation of the body, she wishes to understand knowledge as carnal knowledge, too. So, the meeting cannot but have the character of a sexual confrontation—it is a meeting within the womb.

On the Other Side of the Mirror

The womb where the Traveller and Livingstone meet could, perhaps, be understood as Philip's definite image of a maternal symbolic sphere. If it could be seen in that way, then Philip's presentation of the womb might give us an idea of what the "otherness" of Caribbean women's writing would amount to. For this reason, I will now discuss the time-space of this ultimate confrontation. For if I have been bold enough to call the female African universe in which the Traveller moves a maternal symbolic,[12] I cannot be certain that the space in which both protagonists meet is a maternal symbolic too—or maybe even the full-blown version of such a Symbolic.

To enter into the impossible but necessary dialogue within the womb, Philip has the time topple over into an equally impossible time that is not mythical as it was before. In *Odyssey* the "mode of the possible" described above is made visible in the ungrammatical treatment of time in the story. History is rewritten on a cosmic scale. The story begins somewhere near the beginning of the universe, as the date on the first page suggests:

THE FIRST AND LAST DAY OF THE MONTH OF NEW MOONS (OTHERWISE KNOWN AS THE LAST AND FIRST MONTH) IN THE FIRST YEAR OF OUR WORD

0300 hours(7)

This date announces the respectable scope of the narrated time, which indeed spans the lifetime of the universe (or even more, as Philip, contrary to scientists, puts it down at eighteen billion years, 61). All events in the narrative take enormous amounts of time: one travels easily for five million years to get from one place to another (19), an initiation rite will demand an incarceration of at least seven hundred years (54), and at the very end of the story, when movement seems to have slowed down even more, a moment of silence can take one hundred thousand years (74).

But the recorded date above is also an impossible time, as it is described as last and first at the same time. It is also the time of a very specific universe, which is described as "our word." This expression also occurs in the famous Malinké epic of Sunjata. Guinean author Camara Laye, who has written down the narrative as told him by the griot Babu Condé, reports that Condé taught him that Malinké history is ordered in the following way:

—KUMA LAFOLO KUMA, the history of the great Sundiata, the son of the buffalo-panther woman and of the lion, the first emperor of Mali, or the History of the First Word;
—KUMA KORO, the history of the men before our era, or Ancient Word; [and so on]. (Laye 1980: 30)

Philip gladly appropriates this African notion of the Word to indicate a large time-span. Simultaneously, by imagining "our word" as an incredibly expanded time, she emphasizes the immensity of African history. In this African discourse, then, time is defined as a language, a discourse. This formulation indicates the possibility of other eras, other histories. And indeed, the ending of the narrative is dated:

THE FIRST AND LAST DAY OF THE MONTH OF NEW MOONS (OTHERWISE KNOWN AS THE FIRST AND LAST MONTH) IN THE EIGHTEEN BILLIONTH YEAR OF OUR WORD, WHICH IS THE SAME AS THE END OF TIME, WHICH IS THE SAME AS THE FIFTEENTH DAY OF JUNE, NINETEEN HUNDRED AND EIGHTY SEVEN IN THE YEAR OF OUR LORD SOMEWHERE, AFRICA

0000 HOURS (60)

This specification shows us that this universe of the word, this shadow universe, is an alternative time-order to the well-known Christian chronology, where the years are dedicated to the Lord. The next dates, however, show that there is yet another time: it starts out with the 1st–15th June, then goes through 20th–30th June, then continues further into the impossible 31st day of June, a space of time where the hours tick away lustily until they count twenty-eight instead of the prescribed twenty-four. One has moved out of historical time and finds oneself in the time when the alternative meeting between Livingstone and his pursuer takes place.

Not only has the history of the universe been rewritten as a myth of grand dimensions in which the relationship between colonizer and colonized is reimagined, but also, this treatment of time is opening up a space for a mythic future time: the Utopia of what will happen if the return to the defiled father is realized. At the same time, this dream-time is firmly rooted in historical time. The fact that Livingstone has died long ago, for example, is acknowledged. The time is seen as a narrative between parentheses, as an aside, or as an offshoot of the main stem of history. But it is also the narrative's climax, and as such it has supreme significance. One is here more than ever in the time of I-presume; it is the time of the womb, as is suggested by the repeated statement that this meeting takes place in a time-space that is closely embraced by silence: "And all around was Silence . . . waiting patient content willing to enfold embrace everything the Word, even" (74). The Traveller and Livingstone are enveloped by Silence, which acts as background as well as character: "Finally (silence) Dr. Livingstone, I presume? (silence) we meet (silence) he and I (silence) in a clearing (silence) in a forest (silence) somewhere (silence) in time (silence) it doesn't matter (silence). . . . He (silence) and I (silence) and my silence (silence)—his discovery (silence)" (60–61) and again, on page 61: "he and I . . . and Silence . . . my silence."

The womb, then, is also the place of Utopia, the place of reconciliation and rebirth. But it appears that everybody possesses the womb, as it is equated with the ever-present Silence; the Traveller can enter Livingstone's silence, and he can enter hers. This mutual embrace places both protagonists inside the alternative Symbolic, which is the only place where reconciliation can take place.

Yet there are some problems in defining this time-space as an alternative Symbolic. I will consider possible reasons for doing so or not doing so in relation to the issue of narcissism. "I'm off to the interior or perish, but I seem to be following you—in your footsteps—or is it you who follows me—each becoming a mirage to the other" (27). Considering the space of mutuality and mirroring evoked above, which seems to lead to the disappearance of both protagonists, one may well wonder about the symbolic nature of this maternal, "native" sphere. Should one side with Livingstone, just for the sake of argument, and have a serious look at the Hegelian judgment that the "native" is caught within the Imaginary? As a matter of fact, it is possible to argue that the Traveller's pursuit of Livingstone is the hunt for an "other" who would mirror her own identity; disregarding the references to their racial and gender differences, one can stress aspects of sameness.

The Traveller suspects Livingstone of desiring the same thing she does (silence), and she stresses their similarity as old and tired explorers, possessed and driven by their addiction to discovering; Livingstone is clearly presented as her alter ego. Originally, this other's project is defined in a clearer way than the Traveller's. It is assumed that he knows what he is looking for; the Traveller does not. At the beginning of the story, Livingstone seems to be a mirror-image with more substance and stability than she, just like the mirror-image the child identifies with in his or her process of obtaining a self. "I would see myself as a shadow, a dark ghost— . . . haunting you in your sleepless nights down throughout the ages," she says (73).

Note, however, that Livingstone is not recognized as a cultural, normative Other, transcendent, the "absolute pole of the address," as would be the definition of the Other in Lacan's association of the Other to the Symbolic. *Odyssey* does not accept (neo)colonial dominance. Livingstone will not be acknowledged as "Other"—he is allowed to be "other." As an "other," he can be approached and be engaged in a play of desire, at some distance to the cultural imperatives embodied in the superego. Cocky, bragging, sulking Livingstone and the stubborn Traveller who tries to seduce him are literally caught in a game of "seduction, exhibitionism or despotism"; as two rivals identifying in "an Imaginary duplication," as the description for the imaginary relationship has it (Boons-Grafé 1992: 297). It seems that the "native" Traveller mirrors herself in her colonial other. That would mean, indeed, that at least in her relationship to Livingstone the Traveller is stuck in the mirror-stage, in the logic of narcissism.

I might argue that the Traveller and Livingstone form a pair similar to the Manichean couple of colonizer and colonized analyzed by Abdul R. JanMohamed. In JanMohamed's view, the colonizer is caught in the projection of his own fears and desires for the colonized other, which cannot be recognized in his or her own right. JanMohamed uses this notion to differentiate between types of colonial literary texts. To a certain extent, it is also relevant to the understanding of those postcolonial writers who use the language of the other to find a unified image of themselves; at the same time, however, their relation to this other is marked by their consciousness of their difference, and their experience of being colonized, negated, and excluded by this mastering other. It is an exemplary instance of a harmfully alienating identification. But this is not quite the position of the Traveller. The main difference is that Philip unambivalently chooses the perspective of the colonized: the protagonist's desire is projected upon the colonizer; *her* desire becomes *his* desire, even as he is originally seen as her "truer" self. Later in the story, the Traveller even rephrases his desires in her own terms. She rejects his own observations about his motives, wishes, and experiences.

Nevertheless, to accept the hypothesis of narcissism as the main principle according to which the narrative has been constructed would mean a severe reduction of the tale. For that could mean that the story imagines the meeting between colonizer and colonized as a regression. Fortunately, one does not have to accept inherited notions of narcissism to understand the mirror-relationship between the two protagonists. It is not inevitable that one accepts narcissism as a dead-end, as an obstacle to the entry into the Symbolic, no more than "woman" and "mother" have to be defined as outside the Symbolic. Gayatri Spivak offers an original rereading of the myth of Narcissus, which is in large part dedicated to the female figure of Echo, which could offer an ethics for the bourgeois feminist of color who wishes to express her relationship to her subaltern sisters in her scholarly and political work (Spivak 1993a). What interests me here is that Spivak chooses to reflect on Echo in order to question the habit of seeing the passage from the Imaginary to the Symbolic as a progression:

Who can deny that, in the construction of the subject's history, the driving force of the symbolic is a desire for self-knowledge, although full self-knowledge would mean an end to symbolicity? Why, in spite of so many hard lessons to the contrary —not the least from the vicissitudes of many cultural and gender-inscriptions— do we still cling to the rotarian epistemology of *advancing* from the Imaginary to the Symbolic? (Spivak 1993a: 35)

One can understand this better if one reconsiders the relationship between Narcissus and knowledge. "[T]he tale of Narcissus," Spivak claims, "is a tale of the aporia between self-knowledge and knowledge for others" (19). Philip, as I have argued, situates her story at the same point of intersection. In her narrative, knowledge of oneself must necessarily be knowledge of the other, too. It is possible to read the Traveller's quest as a search for knowledge of her self in the other, the other in her self. Let me propose such a reading. I will then discuss the implications of my reading for an understanding of Philip's critical rewriting of the notions of the symbolic and imaginary spheres.

In the beginning of *Odyssey*, a pursuit is staged: recognizing their sameness, one protagonist sets out to pursue the other; the woman is driven by a desire for the (m)other as well as by a desire for her self. As the story develops, the object of her pursuit appears to take on narcissistic traits. As an absolutely self-centered man, Livingstone refuses to share his project with others (that is, Stanley), he cannot maintain the dialogism of a relationship to his wife, and he refuses to acknowledge the otherness of African discourses. In the final part of the narrative, when the protagonists finally meet, the narrative identifies the Traveller's project clearly, although ironically, with Livingstone's, or rather, with that of his British, male counterpart, Stanley. She muses about the right words to use at their meeting: "'Well, fancy meeting you here'; 'Good to see you, you old bugger,'—they all sounded forced. Would I be cool enough to give him a first rate black hand shake and say, 'Yo there, Livi baby, my man, my main man!'?" (60).

And she thinks about ways of recording their meeting for posterity. She settles, though, for the radical, postcolonial statement, asserting the African perspective: "You're new here, aren't you?" by which she redefines the priority between the discourses. If this is about mirroring, one sees now that it will not be the Traveller who will mirror the discourse of the Explorer. The ensuing hampering dialogue does not lead to a narratively satisfying enlightenment of Livingstone—he does have his insights, but according to the Traveller, they are quite beside the point.

But then, the story is about the Traveller's quest for self-knowledge, not about Livingstone's. He plays a role in *her* final grasp of insight—but in spite of himself. When the Traveller becomes aware of how much she and her other are surrounded and riddled with silence, during her implacable critique of Livingstone's discursive claims, their conversation stalls, and the light starts to fail. Visibility declines. The Traveller starts to see Livingstone in fragments; she hears his voice without seeing him; she gropes for his hand and touches it without feeling or seeing the rest of his body. They both seem to take part in a game of fragmentation, not unlike that of the child before the mirror stage who experiences its body as fragmentation, contrary to the unified image of the other in the mirror before him at the mirror stage. It is as if the Traveller experiences Livingstone as if he were her *self*, not her image; Livingstone is no longer her other—he becomes her self, without her losing her sense of self. The story ends when the Traveller surrenders "to the silence within," that is, surrenders to the silence she discerns in the pluralized, fragmented self that consists of Livingstone as well as herself. This is the ultimate answer to her quest for self-knowledge. The consequent effacement of characters and events signifies the provisional end of the story.

At this point in my argument I can conclude that the Traveller's quest for self-knowledge through knowledge of her alter ego is structured by narcissism. Nevertheless, it is not easy to see the outcome of the narrative as a counterdiscursive celebration of a specific kind of narcissism as the means of entering into a new, maternal Symbolic, and of identifying oneself as an independent Black female subject. By the end of the story, the elements of the story about the attainment of self-knowledge that situate the quest within the Symbolic have dissolved in a narrative of the Imaginary. This might seem unsatisfactory in the light of my wish to criticize the ethnocentric devaluation of the "native" as narcissistic. For now I will have to answer the question I asked at the beginning of this section—is the womb a maternal Symbolic?—in the negative.

However, Spivak's question about the inevitability to proscribe a progressive motion from Imaginary to Symbolic suggests that there is another solution. As a prelude to that question, she asks (and I quote her again): "Who can deny that, in the construction of the subject's history, the driving force of the symbolic is a desire for self-knowledge, although full self-knowledge would mean an end to symbolicity?" (Spivak 1993a: 35). Surely, full self-knowledge means a full apprehension of the self. It would be (but can never be, for those who believe that the self cannot be anything but dialogic) the final gaze that does not need a mirror and collapses fragmentary self and unified self. It would mean a surrendering to "the silence within." Here one finds the possibility of another evaluation of the Symbolic and the Imaginary: the Symbolic ceases to be the final goal of one's development as a knowing subject—there are spaces beyond the symbolic sphere, which can be seen as worthier goals. These spaces could perhaps be the sites from where the seeds of another kind of Symbolic might spring— who knows? They are beyond representation.

It seems to me that Philip's narrative underwrites this statement wholeheartedly. *Odyssey* is highly critical of the Symbolic as the only possible space for gaining subjectivity, insofar as it is Livingstone's Symbolic, which is structured by the Word of the Colonial Father. The subject positions offered by this symbolic order are false, repressive, and therefore precarious. Here, *Odyssey* links to other Black theoretical projects, which redefine the symbolic order as historical, trying to measure "the ways that the Symbolic engages and refuses history" (Abel, Christian, and Moglen 1997: 10). Helene Moglen even speaks of the "shared psychosis of the culturally Symbolic," and she proposes to escape from this doomed order by claiming the Real as a new point of departure for self-formation (Moglen 1997: 203–4).

Both colonizer and colonized, man and woman, can really gain a position as a subject only by renouncing the tortuous symbolic sphere (unmasked as a historically and culturally specific formation by Moglen, Spillers, and others) and entering into another one—a Symbolic governed by the silence and word of both mother and father. In such a Symbolic, the self would not be white and male, nor would the other be Black and female. However, such an entry is not yet possible, as such a Symbolic cannot even be imagined. But the courageous exploration of the sameness of self and other in a narcissistic space is presented as an inevitable move toward the possibility of the Symbolic of the hybrid self/other. *Odyssey* offers its own interpretation of the narrative of narcissism, as it dismisses the evolutionary account of narcissism as a regression. Narcissism brings a deep, physical knowledge of the intertwining of racial and sexual self and other, and this knowledge is the precondition of the imagination of another Symbolic.

For theorists such as Moglen and Spillers, the Real might be a better sphere in which to find new beginnings for the shaping of an undistorted self. Spillers states clearly that "the politics and reality of race" should be situated in "a different relation to the 'Real'" (Spillers 1997: 150). And indeed, one might argue that Philip's Silence resembles the Real, being ungrammatical, whole, and undividable. Spillers reminds us, through Borch-Jacobsen's reading of Lacan, that the Real, too, is "'pure and simple,' 'undifferentiated,' 'non-human,' 'without fissure'" (Spillers 1997: 150). But there are differences between Philip's trajectory and that proposed by Moglen and Spillers. First, Philip defines her Silence emphatically as a language (which the Real is not). Second, Philip doesn't shy away from the Imaginary as the dead-end game of oppositional logics. For her, the Imaginary is a necessary phase in the path to knowledge and self, and if it is organized within the context of a racialized and gendered culture, it can still be traversed and overcome if it is conceived as the site of unparalleled intimacy. The scholar may accept my interpretation of the text's appropriation of the notion of the Symbolic to suggest the possibility of the construction of a self in a maternal symbolic sphere. The reader, however, may not be quite so content. For she or he is confronted with an unsatisfactory ending to Philip's story, as it ends with absence: of time, voice, and identity. The last section will ponder the implications of the multiple, open ending of the narrative.

Conclusion: The End

The preceding section has provided me with an answer to the ethnocentrist view that purports to place the postcolonial in a regressive narcissism. However, one is still left with the nagging question of how one should interpret the story's solution into silence—which, for the reader, amounts to nothingness. One could read it as the statement of the impossibility to speak without the word, that is, without the father tongue. The disappearance of Livingstone, the champion of the word, is immediately followed by the disappearance of the Traveller, the champion of silence. This would amount to an acceptance of the necessity of hybridity to express the Black female experience within the Symbolic. A pure, autonomous Black female voice would not exist.

However, there is yet another possible reading. The story shows, with Spivak, that ultimate self-knowledge ends symbolicity. The answer to the one supreme question about the nature of one's self seems to be stated clearly: surrender to the silence within. But this is not the nihilistic end of the story. There is an afterword that discusses the different copies of the Traveller's diary on which the printed edition (*Odyssey*) is supposed to be based. There are conflicting stories about the existence of an original version, which would be kept by the only people who had successfully guarded their silence. Even as the story cannot be told without the father tongue, there is again the assertion of the existence of another symbolic sphere, in which the story is told in the mother tongue, silence. *Odyssey* ends on the note of a hopeful reference to the unattainable, always invigorating possibility of otherness, which will always stay out of the grasp of dominant discourses. This open ending is more than a plea for the use of nation languages. It is a vigorous reminder of the permanent need to acknowledge otherness, postcolonial and racial as well as sexual.

Perhaps this is also the point at which Philip's narrative resists a psychoanalytical reading. Above, in my discussion with Anyidoho, I have dismissed a spiritual reading of Philip's "Discourse on the Logic of Language" in favor of a more embodied interpretation. But *Odyssey* has a spiritual dimension that feeds the narrative from the beginning onward. The Traveller's quest is spiritual too; her passages through the many initiation rites always bring her closer to a both spiritual and physical, sacred and sexual, universal and individual knowledge that comes close to (a certain) enlightenment. Philip's deconstruction of Freudian and Lacanian categories led me to a critical psychoanalytical reading, but one might wish to begin reading her anew and relate her writing to the spiritual strands in other Black women writers' works (Moglen, Hull, Shaw, and Christian in Abel, Christian, and Moglen 1997). This chapter argues that a spiritual reading need not oppose (as Black versus white) psychoanalytical readings. As our racial and cultural identities are shaped by each other, as Philip maintains, we will need to read our narratives from a hybrid perspective, informed by both dominant and less dominant discourses.

In the two chapters of the section "Silence" I have discussed two writers struggling with rabid dogs, mothers, or fathers; two women hungry for privacy or silence. Something is still unattainable for Caribbean women writers and their readers; something must still be the subject for eager, difficult, painful writing and reading, which always risks slipping away into silence. This something—full identity, healing, a voice—can be won only in a relentlessly open, ongoing dialogue. Cliff, in spite of all her differences, ends like Philip, speaking about (but, characteristically, not *to*) her (male) other:

> I need him
> The fingers of his right hand wrap around his staff.
> He has come a long way to find me.
>
> I feel an immense quiet around us.
> There is not one sound. We have moved out of sound.
> We are not in this house. Something holds us. We are not in this time. We are caught somewhere. At this instant there is nothing but us.
>
> Stillness.
> I can see by his eyes that he knows me.
> That he has come all this way to tell me.
>
> The street sounds   he is gone.
>
> —Michelle Cliff (1985: 119)

Silence: the place for dreams, visions, writing.

9

Conclusion: On the Hybridity
of Cross-Cultural Dialogue

Seven chapters explored the issues addressed by Caribbean women writers in exile who are creating their literary voices. I have argued that the issue of "place" is addressed in a critique of dominant narratives that insist on understanding the (Caribbean) female body as space. This issue is also addressed in narratives that develop the tropes of sea and moisture into feminine discourses of bound travel. I showed how the issue of "voice" is understood both as counterdiscourse and as a complex of strategies of mimicry and subversion of colonial discourse. The issue is central to Collins's Caribbean feminist efforts to shape the Creole language into both a national and a women's language. The issue is also taken up in Nichols's rhetorics in which some of the aspects of Creole (sensuality, performance, and specularity) are isolated and developed in a coming-of-age narrative of young Caribbean sisters. In addition, it is addressed in the elusive work of Kincaid, in which she installs a motherly voice as a subversive form of colonial mimicry. I demonstrated finally that the issue of silence is explored in Cliff's efforts to simultaneously express and refrain from expressing her multiple identity, and in Philip's victorious tale that centers on the irreducible and radical otherness of a Black feminine discourse.

My readings, however, were not merely intended to articulate the aesthetics of Caribbean migrant women's writing. When I introduced the main concerns of this study in the introduction, I presented a second set of questions to be addressed alongside those elaborated upon above. They concern the nature of the dialogue established through the writings discussed, and the manner in which non-Caribbean, non-African European readers are also involved in this dialogue. The seven preceding chapters have taken up these questions too, often by engaging themselves explicitly in a critical, postcolonial, and cross-cultural dialogue. This postlude is dedicated to a few concluding remarks about this dialogue and about this study's position.

David Livingstone, the antihero of Philip's narrative, had to be displaced, haunted, and castrated before an intercultural, interracial, postcolonial dialogue could take place. Indeed, the Black Traveller has done more than her best to establish that miraculous dialogue. In fact, even if it doesn't address white readers in the first place, her story could be read as a challenge to white readers too: how do you manipulate this deadly, dominant tongue to enable yourself to enter this dialogue? Indeed, the capacity of addressing several audiences at the same time has been a continuous characteristic of Black women's writing (e.g., Henderson 1990). It is perhaps only in the last decades that Black Caribbean writers have been able to explicitly write in the service of the building of a Black or Caribbean community and thus focus more strictly on a Black or Caribbean audience, or the Black diaspora. Today's Afro-Caribbean or Black feminist criticism privileges this last focus, advocating a well-argued strategic essentialism. This position is elaborated in Carole Boyce Davies's pioneering work, and, most recently, exemplified by Miriam Chancy's book on Caribbean women's writing in exile. Here, she defines Black feminist criticism (of which Afro-Caribbean diasporic feminism would be a modified form) as "a critical method serving the needs of Black women scholars cross-culturally and cross-nationally" (Chancy 1997: 13). Such a criticism is urgently needed, indeed, and it is already developing into a forceful, vital counterdiscourse (as in the work of Davies).

However, it seems to me that much of the migrant Caribbean women's writing discussed above addresses a more hybrid and diverse audience, while thematizing and criticizing essentialist efforts at community building. I am thinking of Michelle Cliff most prominently, but also of Jamaica Kincaid, while the writings of Marlene Nourbese Philip also imply an appeal to white readers. Even if their work addresses Black Caribbean women (primarily or also), its structure of address appears to be ambivalent and plural. However, if a non-Black, non-Caribbean audience is (also) addressed, this doesn't happen by referring to any traditional, liberal, transcendental notion of intercultural dialogue, such as has been celebrated in concepts like "Commonwealth literature." This writing clearly breaks with a notion of dialogue that implies a set of autonomous subjects engaged in a free exchange. Instead, it offers a completely different analysis of the intercultural dialogue and, in consequence, of the hybridity of today's cultural identities.

These writers' analysis relates to those I have pointed to during the course of this study: Nawal El Saadawi could be heard to describe the intercultural dialogue as a violent form of intertextuality, instead of a free exchange. George Lamming confessed his desire not to be known by others. He spoke primarily about the people on the island of his birth, and on other Caribbean islands, but his remark can be extended to bear on a highly reluctant position within an intercultural exchange. We could go on and discuss other well-known writers on the issue, such as Nigerian writer Buchi Emecheta, who, in her first novel, *Second-Class Citizen*, reflected on the racial and cultural outsider's bitter need to adapt to dominant white discourse and manipulate it (Hoving 1995). Her unsentimental approach is aimed at survival, not (yet) on community building. Some twenty years ago, white South African writer Nadine Gordimer still offered a pessimistic view of the intercultural dialogue; in her novel *July's People* (1981) she declares the self-deceiving white liberal to be incapable of engaging in such a dialogue. In her other novels, though, she points at white revolutionary action and at interracial heterosexual practices as ways to enter the dialogue (Gordimer 1979, 1987). Like Gordimer, white Canadian writer Margaret Laurence struggles to define the obstacles hindering white Europeans from interrelating with Africans. Her own strategy of overcoming these obstacles is a constant critical self-reflection (Hoving 1995).

These notions do not sit happily with the celebratory rhetoric of multiplicity, multivoicedness, and heteroglossia that nowadays abounds in Western cultural scholarship. This rhetoric is often seen as a promising break away from unproductive oppositional schemes for the interpretation of power relations. However, it does not miraculously dispose of all political, social, or cultural antagonisms, nor does it disseminate positions of power. In theorizing, it may be useful to oppose notions such as "authenticity" or "purity" to the more sustainable argument that all aspects of culture are formed through contact with others and are therefore hybrid. However, just like this celebrated notion of multivoicedness and heterogeneity, hybridity can also be understood in its violent aspects. Bakhtinian notions of dialogism and heteroglossia can be confronted with models that assume a more violent network of colliding and appropriating voices among whom power is unevenly distributed. As Shohat and Stam have it, hybridity or syncretism are "not a game but a sublimated form of historical pain" (Shohat and Stam 1994: 43).[1] The concept of the postcolonial situation as a violently hybrid field that is riddled by shifting but fierce antagonisms (dictated by, e.g., "race," class, and gender differences) is explored in the works of Kincaid, Cliff, and Philip, and it shapes their structure of address. If the notion of hybridity is understood in this way, and if it were developed into a politicized and differentiated discourse of the postcolonial condition, postcolonial theory would be transformed in such a way that Western views would no longer be self-evident and central. Bhabha's and Harris's theorizing are already indicative of this possible consequence.

Bhabha speaks of the situation in which "the words of the master become the site of hybridity" (1984b: 104), thus characterizing hybridity as the subversion effectuated by the native. Wilson Harris's interpretation of the Carib bone flute as a model of cross-cultural dialogue can be evoked to push this understanding of hybridity a bit further, beyond its soothing limits until it changes into a highly unpleasant spectacle to European eyes. The bone flutes were made by Carib Indians from the bones of the Spanish invaders they had slain during the struggles following the Spanish aggressions. The Carib are said to have eaten the Spanish flesh and kept the bones. By playing these flutes, the Carib are reported to enter the aggressor's spirit to find out about the nature of their violent disposition. Rephrasing Bhabha, one can say that "the bones of the invader become the site of hybridity." As a model for interculturality and hybridity, this image is indeed far removed from a liberal vision of happy, colorful multiculturalism. Read in a certain way, it refutes the liberal academic opinion that all win by the embrace of the rhetoric of hybridity. More important still, it disavows the notion that the rules for hybridity are set by the center (Harris 1970, 1985; Maes-Jelinek 1991; Spivak 1993b: 194).

In this study, in addition to my effort to outline a Caribbean women writers' aesthetics, I have tried to answer the appeal to white and/or European readers implicit in Caribbean migrant women's writing (even if white and/or European readers were clearly only a secondary audience) by responding to two challenges: (1) to acknowledge the violent history my discipline is implicated in and reflect upon both the political and the theoretical aspects of this implication, and (2) to denaturalize and decenter its apparently self-evident Western/European conceptual framework and learn about other concepts and frameworks. To do this, this study couldn't but be a dialogic enterprise, relating to noninstitutionalized voices and theories rather than only, or primarily, institutionalized discourses.

Surely, from the vantage point of today's Afro-Caribbean or Black feminisms (characterized by strategic essentialism), any claim to a rightful readership must be defended and negotiated. Critics will often be the "them" reading "us," and the position of "them" will inevitably disqualify, to some extent, their outsiders' readings. In answer, I have tried to be as transparent as possible in my claims to adequate and productive interpretations. In this, I have been inspired by my observation that Caribbean women's writing creates many different "we's." Chancy describes Afro-Caribbean women's writing in exile as a search for safe spaces, and her rhetoric of a long-awaited homecoming is supported by many (as Collins and Cobham pointed out in Chapter 2). But Michelle Cliff, for one, has written about the different and complementary need to deconstruct and leave homes if these are ethnically or sexually restrictive and reductive, even when no other home is available. Just as Black and migrant women writers often speak about themselves as homeless, or suspicious of houses, or as ambivalently housed, white, antiracist feminists are constructing a tradition of leaving homes: twenty years ago Minnie Pratt had already analyzed this necessity to give up the white racial home. Caribbean migrant women's writing can be seen to entice white women to leave their confining cultural and racial homes, and, perhaps, to help create less exclusive, less violent spaces and contact zones: sites of new coalitions and communities.

Let me end on an optimistic note. This study followed Ngcobo's hopeful pronouncements and tried to contribute to such doubly liberating listening, effectuating both speaker and listener, not by denying violence or difference but by acknowledging a shared need for a less violent and less exclusive world. This study sides with El Saadawi in its conviction that some forms of criticism and reading must be violently dismissed. Finally, it turns back to the forceful writing of the young Emecheta to learn anew that writing and reading, for all of us, are acts of survival.

REFERENCE MATTER

Notes

1. For a discussion of the difference between postcolonial criticism and post-colonial theory see Moore-Gilbert 1997.

2. Barbara Bush even argues that women acted as "primary agents in the emancipation of the slave community" (quoted in Cudjoe 1990a: 7). Cudjoe himself is not so sure (10).

3. Even at the time of the first slave narratives, the intertwining of Caribbean social conditions and Caribbean literary expression can be observed. In this early period, Caribbean literature already appears to be a transnational event, not unlike the different internationally inspired Caribbean itineraries toward independence themselves. Haiti fought for its independence and gained it in 1804, inspired by the ideas of the French Revolution; this momentous feat in its turn inspired other communities in the Caribbean to fight for independence, and it also energized the antislavery movement in England.

4. I add the "anti" because I want to highlight the critical or polemical dimension in postcolonialism, which is certainly often there.

5. Western scholars may have yet another interest in embracing notions of multiple subjectivity. Within the postcolonial context, these scholars may wish to use a liberal notion of multiplicity to displace a painful and guilt-provoking scheme in which master and slave, colonizer and colonist, white and black are violently opposed. This displacement allows those at the dominant side of the opposition to dismiss this antagonism as an essentialist construction. It makes possible the evasion of the inescapable workings of opposed interests, political antagonisms, and the necessity to construct collectivities for strategic reasons. Scholars of postcoloniality, however, will wish to resist these two forms of closure: both the appropriation of Black women's multiple subjectivity to Eurocentric discussions and the celebration of a liberal multiplicity, a celebration that might well be motivated by the relief of evading the issue of (political) responsibility.

6. Spivak raised the relevant issue of the precise relation between the migrant and the postcolonial, and of the function of the migrant as the paradigm of the

postcolonial (1993b: 221–22, 235, 243, 250, 252). Spivak sees migrancy and the post-colonial as radically different, often even opposed. As I will show in Chapter 2, the Caribbean situation is different in that Caribbean identity *implies* exile or migra-tion. One could even defend the statement that, in a Caribbean context, one has to migrate to enter postcoloniality, as Kincaid suggests (chapter 6). The centrality of migration to the Caribbean identity has led me to focus on Caribbean women's *migrant* writing as a crucial form of writing within postcoloniality (and not neces-sarily as a form of postcolonial writing).

7. Sometimes it primarily offers a preparation for such a move. A serious dia-logue with the less accessible, less published national and regional approaches sometimes demands more space than allowed for by this study, which is first and foremost an exploration of the strategies women writers choose to negotiate the odds they come up against. Yet, this study does explore the *difference* in the texts under scrutiny.

8. There are other arguments in the critique of postcolonialism mentioned by Hall that cannot be answered here; they will form a constant point of reflection throughout this study. These critiques run as follows: postcolonialism fails to an-alyze the development of the global capitalist market, in which the transformation from traditional colonialism into other economical and political power relations take shape. Postcolonialism contends itself by looking at texts only, neglecting eco-nomic and political aspects. Hall makes this serious point productive by referring to Foucault's insight into the interwovenness of power and knowledge. The post-colonial is both a power structure and a system of knowledge and representation (and this is why the critical and epistemological dimensions of the concept cannot be separated). This insight is especially relevant in the Caribbean. As Simon Gi-kandi points out in the introduction to his book on Caribbean literature and mo-dernity, key concepts in Caribbean culture can have both a political and a theo-retical dimension, like the notion of creolization. The concept can be found in the discourses of José Martí, the leader of the Cuban struggle for independence (1868–78), who "would posit cultural syncretism as the fundamental code for ex-plaining Caribbean culture"; and in that of Toussaint l'Ouverture, who gained Haitian independence. In addition, however, the concept of creolization also func-tions as an aspect of modernist theory (Gikandi 1992: 16–17). This perspective of-fers a starting point for every scholar of postcoloniality. I'll answer it by counter-balancing my focus on identity and voice as a literary construct with my effort to show how Caribbean migrant women's writing *exceeds* the purely literary, where it offers its own concepts and discourses, and how it resists institutionalized differ-entiations and hierarchizations of the cultural and the political.

9. This study does not offer an overview of the complex processes by which these practices ambiguously link with or disengage from each other. Valuable and much-needed elements of such an impossible project may be found in Appiah 1991 (postmodernism—postcolonialism); Hutcheon 1991 (postmodernism—postcolo-

nialism) and 1988: 141–68 (postmodernism—feminism); Adam and Tiffin 1991 (postcolonialism—postmodernism); Ashcroft, Griffiths, and Tiffin 1989: 161–65 (postmodernism—postcolonialism) and 174–77 (postcolonialism—feminism); Bhabha 1994 (postcolonialism—psychoanalysis); Davies 1994; Spivak 1986, 1988, 1993a, 1993b; Gandhi 1998: 81–101; Loomba 1998: 215–31 (postcolonialism—feminism); and in other general handbooks such as Boehmer 1995 and Chrisman and Williams 1994. This study restricts itself to pointing out some of the connections, tensions, and gaps that are most crucial to my sketch of the three issues "place," "voice," and "silence."

10. Indeed, these issues are already the topic of postcolonial debate. Moreover, within cultural analysis too these very issues have been explored extensively. Therefore, the choice of these issues allows me to approach the issues of postcoloniality through cultural analysis. The advantages of this approach will be elaborated below.

11. See, e.g., Miller 1993: 6; Bhabha 1994: 3.

12. In postmodernism, too, women (or rather "woman") can be observed to appear as a (theoretical) site (Donaldson 1992: 125).

13. These discourses need not be "new," modern, or postmodern at all. Spivak, for example, points to the work of an Algerian writer, Marie-Aimée Hélie-Lucas, who speaks about women in exogamous societies: "a woman's home is radical exile, fixed by her male owner." In this area, Spivak continues, one finds a "critique that *can* be mobilized against all essentialist notions of the home as base of identity" (Spivak 1993b: 162).

14. See, e.g., Ganguly 1992 (Chapter 2).

15. Michelle Cliff writes about an open garden; Jamaica Kincaid speaks in passing about her kitchen; most strikingly, there are the escapes and alliances of Mama King in Beryl Gilroy's *Frangipani House* (Chapter 3).

16. Ashcroft, Griffiths, and Tiffin 1989; Nightingale 1986.

17. Within cultural studies, this shift can be observed in the work of scholars like Michel de Certeau. See Chapter 3.

18. See Clifford 1992; Fabian 1983, 1991; Gupta and Ferguson 1992.

19. Cobham and Collins 1987; Grewal et al. 1988.

20. Anyidoho 1992; Ngugi wa Thiong'o 1986; Chinweizu, Jemie, and Madubuike 1980; and Chinweizu 1988 advocate this approach.

21. My use of the term *colonial discourse* refers to a discourse that took shape during the centuries of colonization and that persists today in the imperial centers of the world. Peter Hulme defines colonial discourse as "an ensemble of linguistically-based practices unified by their common deployment in the management of colonial relationships." He adds:

> Underlying the idea of colonial discourse . . . is the presumption that during the colonial period large parts of the non-European world were *pro-*

duced for Europe through a discourse that imbricated sets of questions and assumptions, methods of procedure and analysis, and kinds of writing and imagery, normally separated out into the discrete areas of military strategy, political order, social reform, imaginative literature, personal memoir, and so on. (Hulme 1986: 2)

In this study I broadly follow Hulme's definition of colonial discourse as a discourse connected to political and economic colonial practices, and as a discourse producing the colonial subject. In his own study of colonial discourse, Hulme concentrates on different key tropes and narratives, without claiming to delineate the main elements of colonial discourse. He defends his reserve by pointing out that the study of colonial discourse has not yet advanced sufficiently to offer grounds for such claims. In this, too, my study is connected to Hulme's. With Hulme, finally, I refer to Edward Said 1991 for a groundbreaking introduction into the nature of colonial discourse.

22. William Shakespeare, *The Tempest,* act 1, scene 2.

23. This mode brings to light the deep ambivalence of this discourse. The ambivalence results from a contradictorily double perspective on the colonized as both appropriate and inappropriate (Bhabha 1984b: 126). This means that the colonized is seen as both identical to the colonist (hence the colonial right to govern and appropriate) and different from the colonist (hence the colonial right to dominate, as the colonized are not themselves capable of governing themselves). Colonial mimicry is the strategy that represents the Other as "almost the same, but not quite," or as Bhabha also says, "almost the same, but not white" (Bhabha 1984b; see also Ashcroft, Griffiths, and Tiffin 1989: 103). Bhabha differentiates colonial mimicry from the colonized's narcissistic identification with the white colonizer as described by Fanon (Bhabha 1984b: 129). He discusses mimicry primarily as the weak spot in colonial discourse, as it points to the ambivalence that threatens the authority of colonial discourse. Like other well-known scholars of colonial discourse, such as Gayatri Chakravorty Spivak and Abdul R. JanMohamed, Bhabha concentrates predominantly on the analysis of the domineering colonial discourse, not on the less visible discourses of non-Western people, colonized or noncolonized.

24. Indeed, it may be necessary to point out with some emphasis that this study assumes a basic difference between two positions colonial subjectivity may take: it differentiates between colonizer (usually white) and colonized (usually Black). This is not to defend a symmetrical scheme of opposed positions, or to dismiss the poststructuralist observation that coloniality lives at the heart of the postcolonial, and the postcolonial at the heart of the former colonial powers. Contrary to an approach like that in Ashcroft, Griffiths, and Tiffin 1989, I think it necessary to keep referring to the difference between (white) settlers, the native inhabitants of the colonies, and the African and Asian population who arrived by sheer force or from economic necessity in, say, Africa and the New World. This difference per-

sists while at the same time it is taking on new forms. Such differentiations are, alas, by no means self-evident.

25. Gates's theory of signifyin(g) acknowledges the important role nondominant discourses and strategies can play, while avoiding a too symmetrical relation between dominant and nondominant discourse. This African-American strategy can be understood as a specific form of a general postcolonial ironic subversion of colonial and other dominant discourses.

26. There also exist quite different approaches to postcolonial writing, which hold that this is "literature without irony" (Brennan 1989; Kubayanda 1987). In Chapter 6 I argue that this statement is untenable.

27. See, e.g., Mohanty 1988: 61, where she criticizes the "discursive or political suppression of the heterogeneity of the subject(s) in question" implied in colonization. She then concentrates on the "production of the 'Third World Woman' as a singular monolithic subject in some recent (Western) feminist texts."

28. *Carnegie Hall.*

29. Such practices are also current in Women's Studies. Margaret Homans published a valuable, thought-provoking essay in which she elaborates on Valerie Smith's critique of white feminist poststructuralists for appropriating Black women's experience and Black women's writing "to rematerialize the subject of their theoretical positions." Homans argues that white feminists (Haraway, Butler, Fuss) reduce the ambiguity in Black women's representation of the embodied self to construct an argument for their own antiessentialist positions. Thus, they efface Black women's (pragmatical) recourse to (an ambivalent) essentialism (Smith 1989; Homans 1994).

30. Bhabha privileges the latter approach, and he reads Fanon primarily for his psychoanalytical insights, undervaluing his later texts in which other approaches were developed (Gates 1991).

31. Introduced in the writing of Jamaican author Erna Brodber (1988a, 1988b).

CHAPTER 2

1. *Annie John* (1985). For more information about Jamaica Kincaid, see Chapter 6, "Jamaica Kincaid Is Getting Angry."

2. The rumor goes that the story is based on an autobiographical event in which the statement referred to the ruder and more debasing fact of the great man's inability to shit when need made itself felt (Perry 1990: 497). Even so, the published, censored version is more poetic and in a way more significant, as it concerns Columbus's (and the other patriarch's) mobility, which might be seen as the essence of his identity as prototypical traveler—as *the* traveler.

3. See Lemaire 1986. See also Todorov 1984; Gikandi 1992.

4. See, e.g., Deleuze 1977; Deleuze and Guattari 1980; Clifford 1989, 1992; Said 1983.

5. In the debates about modernity, reference is also made to its gendered na-

ture. The modern can be seen as an anguished rejection of femininity too, as Christel van Boheemen convincingly argues (1990: 277–80). In Western dominant discourses, the fear of women and the fear of non-Western people may be intertwined. For instance, non-Western areas are often depicted as if they were female. Chapter 8 will consider such a discourse in more detail.

6. See Wilson Harris 1983 for an extreme formulation of this view; see also Ashcroft, Griffiths, and Tiffin 1989: 156–61.

7. I would have liked Gikandi to be more precise in his use of the terms *modern, modernism, modernity*, etc. He relies on Anderson's discussion of these concepts (Anderson 1988) but does not state explicitly whether he follows Anderson's descriptions consistently. To me, it seems he implies a problematic continuity between modernism (as the historical epoch heralded by Columbus's journeys, i.e., the period following the Middle Ages), the modernism of Enlightenment, modernism as the cultural and literary movements on both sides of the ocean at the beginning of the twentieth century, and maybe even postmodernism.

8. See Deleuze 1977; Deleuze and Guattari 1980; and Kaplan 1987: 188.

9. A comparable point is made by James Clifford (1992, see especially page 108).

10. I have been thinking about this "us." At first, I was tempted to criticize it, as it seemed to me it was rather elitist and excluding: for many of us, i.e., for Black people and people from outside the European community and the United States, traveling is not only exhausting, tedious, and difficult; for "us," the world is rapidly becoming an array of places one can *not* visit, and of places where one cannot stay. To some, it may even appear as a network of frontiers where one probably will be arrested, interrogated, ill treated, imprisoned, and/or sent back to places where one cannot live either. However, on second thought, I realized that the "us" reading Culler's book may well be the elite for whom Culler's statement holds true. And that, exactly, leads to the challenge students of interculturality need to face. I articulate this challenge in the main text.

11. See, for example, the hilarious account of a tourist's visit to the Caribbean by an African-European woman in *Tap-Taps to Trinidad* by Zelda Longmore, 1990.

12. Culler states, "to condemn tourism may be morally satisfying, but to do so is also, I fear, to rely on the naive postulate of an escape from semiosis and to cut oneself off from the possibility of exploring semiotic mechanisms which prove persistent and ubiquitous, central to any culture or social order" (1998b: 167). However, I do not want to push my comparison too far. Scholars are, of course, before anything else writers, and it would often be more appropriate to see them as improvising musicians, being inspired by other pieces and borrowing and appropriating these as a matter of course (see for example Gates 1989: xxx). On the other hand, scholars are answerable to their strategies of quoting and appropriating in a definitely different way. Interestingly, Gates, who uses the metaphor of the musician to describe his own art, is often quite concerned with acknowledging the context from which he takes his concepts. He is, certainly, when discussing the trope

of the signifying monkey. He is much less when referring to the Russian concept of *"skaz"* to develop his notion of the speakerly text.

13. I do not want to imply that Gikandi excludes women writers, for he does not: three of the seven chapters of his book are dedicated to female authors. But it is true that he discusses their works *after* his initial sketches of Caribbean literature in exile, which he bases upon men's writing. For a more balanced account of the history of Caribbean literature, see my account in the introduction.

14. Dutch poet Ankie Peypers wrote a poem on the very subject of the women's names of Columbus's ships, called "Na Columbus" ("After Columbus"). The poem reappropriates this practice of naming by relating it to the present-day feminist journeys of discovery by which women discover each other and themselves (Peypers 1982: 50).

15. See, e.g., Rosi Braidotti's compelling feminist rhetoric of nomadism (Braidotti 1993). However, also see Boer 1996, which critiques Braidotti's view.

16. In fact, tropes of travel are so common that they are to be found in almost every novel, as Bakhtin has remarked (Bakhtin 1988b), and that they are widely used as metaphors for life itself. It is therefore difficult to condemn all discourses of travel as a matter of principle.

17. Like Anzaldúa's borderlands, a notion Wolff mentions favorably, among others, disappointingly without uncovering its provenance (Anzaldúa 1987).

18. In the main argument of her study, however, Davies demonstrates convincingly that Black women's writing can be studied as an autonomous literary field, which despite its plurality is structured by continuities. My critique in this essay is directed at the few moments in which she emphasizes the "negative" aspects of Black women's writing.

19. In fact, this scholarly attitude will sound as ridiculously self-evident to many of my readers as it sounds to me. However, many cases of postcolonial analysis still prefer to depart from Western concepts exclusively, and to discuss non-Western texts within the framework of Western theories only.

20. In Chapter 7, I will discuss the work of Michelle Cliff, in which one finds a comparable wish to express irreducible complexities as well as make unambiguous political statements.

21. One might read this reference to a "deepest self" as a form of essentialism. Instead of criticizing this essentialism, however, I would argue for studying its merits. Indeed, (a strategic) essentialism can be indispensable at times, e.g., in the political struggle.

22. Pratt describes contact zones as the "social spaces where disparate cultures meet, clash, and grapple with each other, often in highly asymmetrical relations of domination and subordination—like colonialism, slavery, or their aftermaths as they are lived out across the globe today" (Pratt 1992: 4).

23. This goes also for other heroines in Riley's texts. For example, in her fourth novel, *A Kindness to the Children* (1992), one of the main protagonists, Jean, regu-

larly surrenders to casual, almost anonymous sex. But if she does, she is mainly a victim of an act she considers debasing. She is soiled and destroyed by it; she sinks into madness and finally dies in the street, a mad woman.

24. It is the father's repeated, unsupportive warning against white racism that keeps Hyacinth from seeking outside help (30, 51, 64, 67, 69, 95). The way he warns her is terrifying instead of strengthening. It is also his behavior (verbal and nonverbal) that models her negative perception of Black people.

25. She is kept moving, as she is ordered around to do household chores (40, 61). At one point in the story, she turns to aimless wandering to stay outside her dreary home (96). Unlike the protagonist in Ellison's famous *Invisible Man* (1947), who is kept running by the racist institution, she is kept running by male authority and cruelty.

26. Riley herself made remarks to this extent (at the conference *Motherlands*, which was dedicated to Black and Third World Women's Writing, in London, September 1991).

27. Riley published the following novels after *The Unbelonging* (1985): *Waiting in the Twilight* (1987), *Romance* (1988), and *A Kindness to the Children* (1992), all published by The Women's Press, London.

28. The term "innocent anthropologists" is taken from the hilarious, honestly Eurocentric accounts by Nigel Barley (1987). *The Innocent Anthropologist: Notes from a Mud Hut* (1986) and *A Plague of Caterpillars: A Return to the African Bush* (1987).

29. The interest in political aspects often plays an important role in Caribbean novels by women writers in exile. In *Timepiece*, e.g., a novel published in 1986, Janice Shinebourne uses her protagonist's return to the vanished village of her youth as the occasion for a flashback to her development into a politically aware person. See also the more elaborate discussion in Nichols 1986; Collins 1987; Cliff 1985; and Kincaid 1988, which will be discussed in chapter 6.

30. See also Benítez-Rojo 1992.

CHAPTER 3

1. *Frangipani House* is Beryl Gilroy's first novel for adults. Besides her children's books (Macmillan, 1970–75) she has published her autobiography, *Black Teacher* (London: Cassell, 1976); *Boy-Sandwich* (Oxford, England: Heinemann, 1989); a collection of poetry, *Echoes and Voices (Open-Heart Poetry)* (New York: Vantage Press, 1991); a tale of historical fiction; *Stedman and Joanna—A Love in Bondage: Dedicated Love in the Eighteenth Century* (New York: Vantage Press, 1992); and *Sunlight on Sweet Water* (1994), *In Praise of Love and Children* (1996), *Gather the Faces* (1996), and *Inkle and Yarico* (1996), all with Peepal Tree Press, Leeds, England. Her *In for a Penny* won the GLC Creative Writing Minorities Prize in 1982 and was published by Holt Saunders. *Frangipani House* won a prize in the GLC Black Literature Competition.

2. Ashcroft, Griffiths, and Tiffin 1989; Rutgers 1986, 1994; Ramchand 1983.

3. This is also an observation by Wim Rutgers, the author of a study on Dutch Caribbean literature (Rutgers 1986: 21). I agree with him that the metaphor of the house for "identity" can hardly be called specifically Caribbean or even postcolonial. This metaphor can be found, e.g., throughout Dutch and English literature, if not in all literatures. Even so, within different literary traditions one can distinguish different treatments of that trope, just as the problematics of identity always takes on a specific form, and like Rutgers, I too discern a specifically Caribbean approach.

4. Minnie Pratt wrote a personal essay on the construction of the notion of home in her North American white family, in which racist, classist, sexist, and heterosexist discourses were engaged (Pratt 1984; for an appreciation, see Martin and Mohanty 1986). Black men and women, Black and white lesbians had to be eliminated to make this home possible. This violence in homemaking is, then, not only endemic to the Caribbean. I would like to stress that the dominant party using this violence for its own practices of identification cannot just renounce these practices without renouncing its desired identity. Often, even, one cannot speak of unambiguously opposed interests (though the interests will probably differ widely). In a critique of both Gilbert and Gubar's and Spivak's reading of *Jane Eyre*, Laura E. Donaldson argues that Jane Eyre's apparent emancipation consists in a large part of resistance to patriarchy, and in this she is close to her Caribbean counterpart, Bertha Mason, whose final, fatal acts can be read as self-destruction as much as a form of protest and resistance (1992: 20–31). According to Donaldson, Jane does not kill Bertha. Such an analysis suggests that there is no easy way out of the violent condition of homemaking.

5. Joan Riley should be mentioned as the chronicler *par excellence* of Black women's oppressive accommodation: in her novels, she depicts these depressing housing conditions in ruthless detail.

6. In my use of the terms *strategy* and *tactics*, I would have liked to follow more closely Michel de Certeau, who understands tactics as the strategy of those who do not possess a territory in which to situate their acts, and therefore must undertake their critical enterprises on the territory of other, dominant groups. However, as the term *tactics* is rather unusual, I will as a rule use the word *strategy* for both terms.

7. Lillian Smith has written about this topic in *Killers of the Dream* (1963). She also speaks, importantly, about the complicity of white women.

8. What comes to mind here is Kincaid's domestic strategy of appropriating the "outside," which I discussed in the preceding chapter.

9. But compare Spillers, who pictures women's space on the slave ships as comparable to that of the men (Spillers 1987); see below.

10. Chapter 8 is about this dichotomy between womb and phallus, the signification of the interior, and the role of psychoanalysis.

11. See their introduction to a 1992 issue of *Cultural Anthropology*, which is dedicated to the discussion of space, identity, and difference.

12. I have discussed the gendered and Eurocentric nature of certain concepts of free travel in the preceding chapter.

13. Clifford also comments on the twofold nature of localizing, which is always "spatio*temporal*" (Clifford 1992: III, note 2).

14. According to Fabian (1983) this would be so in an evolutionist notion of time: "In the study of 'unchanging' primitive culture, temporal relations can be disregarded in favor of spatial relations" (18).

15. There are different opinions about the difference between the terms *space* and *place*. I will follow Mieke Bal's definitions (Bal 1985), which come close to the approach of Michel de Certeau, a scholar of whom I will come to speak. Often, however, the difference between place and space is articulated in quite an opposite way. Gupta and Ferguson state that "a space achieves a distinctive *identity* as a place. . . . The identity of a place emerges by the intersection of its specific involvement in a system of hierarchically organized spaces with its cultural construction as a community or locality" (1992: 8). In their view, place is derived from a more abstract space; it is space endowed with meaning. As I am working out a literary approach, I will continue to employ the literary definitions.

16. His definition reverses the usual relation between place and space, which considers place as a structured space (Morris 1992: 3; see too Yi-Fu Tuan, quoted in Baker 1991: 72). But it comes quite close to the narratological approach of Bal, who situates space on the level of the story of the literary text, not on the level of the fabula.

17. One of these potentials is to define the intertwining of "home" (or "space") and "journey" in a more rigorous manner. James Clifford uses the concept of practice to relate "place" (or "space") to travel in the following way: "A focus on comparative travel raises the question of dwelling, seen not as a ground or starting place, but as an artificial, constrained practice of fixation" (Clifford 1992: 114). According to him, place is as much a practice as movement is.

18. A comparable argument (but differently directed) can be found in Bhabha (1994). Bhabha's work repeatedly argues that the temporality of modernity is ambivalent, inwardly contradictory. In a discussion of his notion of "cognitive mapping," Fredric Jameson stresses that modernity's plurality is not spatial, but it consists of different incommensurable temporalities. Therefore, this plurality can not be represented, or even imagined (Bhabha 1994: 218–19, also 231, 238, 239).

19. This is true even if he does not take into account the important role gender plays. For a gender-specific approach to the chronotope, one could consult O'Connor 1990.

20. I will speak in detail about this very important trope in Chapters 7 and 8.

21. But of course Toni Morrison is right when she points at the generality of the image of the woman at the window. However, when a certain trope is very

general, it appears in different guises and with different implications in different texts; and this also goes for *Frangipani House.*

22. A wonderful example is Njau 1975.

23. It is the same kind of raving that occurs in the nightmarish delivery-episode in Emecheta's *Second-Class Citizen.* Just as in that instance, the scene in *Frangipani House* is set on the threshold between life and death: it is the situation of the rite of passage, even if in this case, it is the passage from life to death, and not the reverse journey of birth into life.

24. Kenyan scholar J. S. Mbiti has been severely criticized for his universalism in stating that African languages and African epistemological traditions are incapable of referring to the future. See Kimmerle 1995.

25. See Bakhtin 1988b: 120 on the chronotope of the road.

26. Bakhtin 1988b: 206 ff and 224 ff.

27. Here, I differ with Giovanna Covi, who has written about time in the work of Jamaica Kincaid (Covi 1990). See Chapter 6.

28. See, e.g., John Sinclair, editor in chief, *Collins COBUILD English Language Dictionary.* London and Glasgow: Collins; Stuttgart: Klett, 1987: 1194.

29. I choose the term *landscape* here, though it is often used in quite an opposite way, i.e., as a décor, a setting for action, as, e.g., in Bakhtin 1988b: 217: "then nature itself ceased to be a living participant in the events of life. Then nature became, by and large, a 'setting for action,' its backdrop; it was turned into landscape." I do not wish to use the term *nature* as it is too compulsorily opposed to *culture*, an opposition not pertinent here. Therefore, I follow Maxwell's definition, quoted below, in the main text.

30. In the definition of *understanding* in Collins's *COBUILD*: 1589.

31. Here Bakhtin's understanding of language and texts as outwardly directed comes to mind: "Discourse lives, as it were, beyond itself, in a living impulse . . . toward the object" (Bakhtin 1988a: 292). Indeed, Bakhtin's perception of literature as a living, dialogical speech practice is much closer to postcolonial perceptions of the literary text than formalist or structuralist approaches to literature as an autonomous, closed system. Significantly, Bakhtin speaks of the *taste* of a certain word, indicating a need to develop a multisensual understanding of language.

32. Following Maxwell, many others studied the significations of landscape in postcolonial writing. It appears to be a rich theme. In one train of writing—the tradition of Joseph Conrad's *Heart of Darkness*—the colonizer's fear of the "dark other" is worked out in the theme of the landscape (Pratt 1986, 1992; Coetzee 1988). In another, landscape is the theme by which cultural traditions, or the colonial tensions that threaten these traditions, can be explored (Ibitokun 1991).

33. This evaluation of the centrality of the spatial in postcolonial literary criticism is based on several studies, among which is that of Guyanese author Wilson Harris (1983).

34. Quoted in Gooneratne 1986: 15.

35. Such endeavors to always relate a place to persons living in that place could be connected to yet another way of defending non-Western societies against imperialist appropriation: the effort of countering the trope of the "empty land." Mary Louise Pratt, among others, has written about the tendency of colonists to imagine populated areas as uninhabited, to be able to "discover" and "cultivate" these areas as if they had been unpopulated (Pratt 1986).

36. As in this passage: "The shaft of light streaked across the bed, its phallic form touching all that was vital in her—magically reconstituting and reawakening her—making her whole again" (79). The novel refers here to the "male-centered" aesthetics of the sun, which can be read in Brathwaite's writing. Bev Brown criticizes this aesthetics as a foundation for a more general theory of creolization, because it cannot offer an adequate approach to Caribbean women's writing (Brown 1985).

37. The metaphor of the wind is not elaborated in the novel. Still, I will remark on it in passing. The suggestion that the wind is a very relevant trope in Caribbean women's writing is offered in Pamela Mordecai's introduction to *Out of the Kumbla* (Davies and Fido 1990). I subsume it under the common denominator of the trope of the landscape. In this context, the representation of the wind supports my argument to understand the landscape as a semiotic "text" that is richer than a text that can only be seen and read. However, the text of the landscape can be equally destructive.

38. See Chapter 7.

39. For a structural study of rites of passage, see the work of Victor Turner (Turner 1967, 1969).

40. In the next part of this book, I will present a frame for analysis and interpretation based on orality and Creole studies.

41. Representation as an object is not the same thing as representation as space. It is quite possible that women are not put in the position of objects but are a "representation of a space that is protected from reification, different from and other than the market place" (O'Connor 1990: 140).

42. Compare Covi (1990: 352) on a comparable desire to stay outside the house (as an institution of the patriarchal order) in Jamaica Kincaid's *Annie John*.

43. See the collection *Motherlands*, edited by Susheila Nasta (1991).

44. Like the early African-American women writers, who caused Houston Baker to describe their literary practice as "the Daughters' Departure" (1991: 88).

45. I emphasize the desertion by the daughters, not only because this, to me, seems a more central theme in *Frangipani House*, but also because this aspect links the novel to those other semiotic endeavors to pair movement and gender. This said, I must hastily add that Beryl Gilroy's second novel is specifically about the role sons may play in this pattern of displacements. *Boy-Sandwich* (1989) explores ways that (grand)sons can share in caring, their position toward the return to the homeland, toward their grandparents, within the large theme of age, generations, and gender.

46. And this is exactly what happens in *Boy-Sandwich*, where the son refuses to continue sexist patterns of behavior.

47. Austin 1962.

CHAPTER 4

1. With a lowercase e, "english" is differentiated from "standard" British English, with a capital E, and refers to the language used in postcolonial countries.

2. Brathwaite explains that nation language is the English spoken by those brought to the Caribbean (if he had read Ashcroft, Griffiths, and Tiffin 1989, he might have used the term *english*). The concept of "nation language" must be understood in contrast to "dialect," a concept that "carries very pejorative overtones" and "is thought of as 'bad English'. . . . Nation language, on the other hand, is the *submerged* area of that dialect which is much more closely allied to the African aspect of experience in the Caribbean" (1984: 13). Brathwaite takes recourse to an essay by Edouard Glissant to explain more clearly what this still scarcely researched concept means: "nation language is a strategy . . . to disguise his [the slave's, IH] personality and to retain his culture" (16). Brathwaite adds that the "connection . . . betwe[e]n native musical structures and the native language" is most important in understanding the concept. He therefore pays much attention to the specific rhythm structure of nation language poems, which differs from the European pentameter.

3. See, e.g., Edwards and Sienkewicz 1990: 6; Finnegan 1988: 56 ff; Scharlau and Münzel 1986.

4. See, e.g., Ramchand 1983: 90; Ashcroft, Griffiths, and Tiffin 1989: 44 ff; D'Costa 1983.

5. E.g., women are said to be the champions of the spoken word, the guardians of the oral tradition, and/or as the illiterate. Yet, Caribbean women writers not only speak but also use literary devices to create their alternative voices.

6. Among Collins's publications we find a collection of short stories, *Rain Darling* (1990); a book of poems, *Rotten Pomerack* (1992); and her novel *The Colour of Forgetting* (1995), published with Virago in London.

7. Latin America Bureau, *Grenada: Whose Freedom?* (1984).

8. One might even consider taking up Kenneth Ramchand's suggestion to read this Standard English as West Indian Standard, i.e., by "hearing" it as a voice that is closer to Caribbean dialects than to British English (Ramchand 1983: 97).

9. This is a characteristic of many oral genres. The theme of a text is an event the audience is acquainted with. E.g., the narrative function of the song is less important than the lyrical, parodying function. The result is that the narrative structure loses its linear form and seems to circle around an emptiness. Sometimes the history is told backwards. Or the text itself may remain very short. As Maria Chona phrases it in an epigraph to an essay by Cynthia Ward, "The song is very short because we understand so much" (Ward 1989: 121).

10. One argument to sustain this assumption lies in the researchers' practice of recording oral narratives in a much reduced form. Thus, Europeans know (say) African oral narratives only as short and bald abstracts. Nigerian critic Chinweizu offers an illuminating example of this simplifying method of transcription (Chinweizu and Madubuike 1983: 36–59).

11. It is remarkable that there is hardly any emphasis on ethnic differences, quite in contrast to *Whole of a Morning Sky*, where the tensions between African-Caribbean and Indian-Caribbean people are an important subtheme (unfortunately also taken up in a rather ungraceful portrayal of an Indian neighbor, Mrs. Lall). It is true that the population of Guyana is ethnically much more diverse than that of Grenada: in Guyana, more than half of the population is Asian (especially Indian), whereas about 40 percent is African (1986). The small remaining part of the population consists of Amerindians, Europeans, and others. Grenada's population is overwhelmingly African. In 1970, only 20 percent were Indian, European, or other.

12. This is an important point in a sociological or political approach to Caribbean texts by women. Mordecai and Wilson have said, for example, that "[i]f one considers that politics can constitute an uneasy presence in the works of writers as experienced as Lamming and Naipaul . . . the accomplishment of women at a stage when they are relative newcomers to the genre becomes more evident" (Mordecai and Wilson 1990: xii). The reader might bear their caution in mind as a background of my analysis of the precise ways that Collins and Nichols treat the subject of politics.

13. According to the glossary in *Angel* (293), eat up your food (Jamaican).

14. Ward cites Ivan Illich to sustain her argument about the nature of orality. She connects orality and regional vernaculars with a cultural space, which exists outside the public area of the economy of the capitalist market. Following Illich, who uses terms from Roman jurisdiction, she opposes the public and the private sphere.

15. The dichotomy between public and private has come under serious attack from the side of Women's Studies. It supposes wrongly that there would be a well-defined, closed private sphere in which no paid labor is done. But many women do earn a living by working within their homes: home labor is very extended; many women trade from their homes or prepare goods or food they then sell on the road or in their yards, etc.

16. The exceptional, military violence of the U.S. invasion is the end of communal strife—but this destructive machine is considered to be outrageously alien to Grenadian communal scuffling and quarreling.

17. Chinua Achebe did speak of the writer as a teacher (Achebe 1975), but this is not the only option for the African, Black, and/or postcolonial writer. Other relationships exist between audience and artist. The notion that the artist has the task to educate the masses may rest on an artificially constructed opposition between ignorant passive masses and well-informed artists from a higher class (Trinh 1989: 11–15). In fact, Cooper criticizes the Sistren collective precisely for its hierar-

chic organization, where a higher-class individual edited and directed the words and performances of the working-class members of the collective.

18. The model of the Creole continuum shows that, even if Creole and Standard English are linked in an antagonistic colonial relation, they cannot just be imagined as opposite poles in a two-language context. The relation between these language codes is fluent. The author of a well-known pioneering study of Caribbean literature, Kenneth Ramchand, argues that "[i]n the twentieth century we have to give up the notion of separate languages (Creole English and Standard English) and we have to envisage a scale." He adds that "in West Indian fiction the two voices (Standard English and dialect) no longer reflect mutually exclusive social worlds" (Ramchand 1983: 90, 97). The quotation from *Angel* with which I began this chapter is an illustration of the Caribbean language situation as explained by Ramchand; there are different Creoles that are (ambiguously) connected to different social and cultural positions. Jamaican writer Jean D'Costa explains that the West Indian situation is very complicated. She opposes those who think that "[t]he continuum [of language registers, IH] would possess a magical one-to-one correspondence with the whole range of life, generating without doubt or conflict all of the registers relating to any given social context" (D'Costa 1983: 255). This is not the case; e.g., the tense, power-infested relationship between Standard English and Creole, which address different audiences, obligates the writer to mediate carefully between the need to communicate simultaneously with several audiences of different status and class who do not share the same linguistic, cultural, and communicative skills (D'Costa 1983).

19. In Western Europe, understanding language as "practice" is one of the important shifts effectuated by Cultural Studies (see, e.g., During 1993: 2).

20. Cooper is not the only one to experiment with the demands of twentieth-century criticism and a desire to represent oral critical expressions. Cynthia Ward has also published an essay in which she first presents an oral narrative of native Canadians and then continues to have the narrative discussed by the native Canadians in their hut themselves—however, she has them use academic discourse (Ward 1989).

21. Sure, male Creole speakers do not refrain from talking sex in Creole, as is readily apparent from the many calypsos about the subject. Sparrow's song in Nichols's novel is a good example (see the next chapter). However, this kind of talk has a function different from the one I refer to: the male talk is a form of "boasting" (Edward and Sienkewicz 1990: 100 ff), whereas I am looking for a Creole of a more intimate character.

CHAPTER 5

1. Which is different from the claim of verisimilitude of the narrator. I am referring here to the futile search for the origin of narratives in oral traditions so often practiced in the West.

2. Besides, *Angel* offers a Creole saying to express the same sentiment in a subtitle on page 270: "It have more ting is [*sic*] dis world dan what we know about."

3. The ambiguously distant relation to "my people" is discussed in relation to an overseer in Lamming 1987: 18–19.

4. Sam Selvon made the following remark in connection to the issue of orthography: "People love to hear me read, but I am not very much concerned with that. My concern is that they read the book as a reader, and that they use the senses of a reader rather than those of a listener to interpret the language and once they can interpret it as readers that is the main thing to me" (Selvon, quoted in Mair 1991: 145). Like Selvon, Nichols is interested in wedding the potentials of writing and reading to the semiotics and politics of Creole oral practices. She approaches "reading" as a potentially empowering practice.

5. This political education is common to the younger Caribbean generations that (especially in the 1970s) went abroad to study.

6. Indeed, a *red* star. But I prefer to read the color red not merely as a reference to communism. That would be an insulting simplification of the always nuanced and implicit rhetorics of the novel. No, the star is "reddish," and where red can stand for love, blood, communism, and many other things, the plurality of these alternating connotations, which present themselves tentatively, should not be reduced.

7. Between 1962 and 1964 Guyana went through a period of general strikes, arson attacks, and other sorts of violence. Spring 1964 was the most atrocious time, in which the battering and killing of people (especially Asians) reached a peak. A general strike in 1963 was financed with U.S. funds.

8. It is striking that Angel looses the sight in one of her eyes in the course of her resistance against the U.S. invasion. She, too, bears the mark of having seen death in the eye. And like Gem, the damage to her (up to now) uncurtailed gaze is the sign of her coming of age.

9. This strategy of writing is not unusual in Caribbean literature. For example, Brathwaite signals it also in Mais's novel *Brother Man*, where he comments upon the strong visual and aural elements in Mais's narrator's style (Brathwaite 1974: xiii), which become necessary parts of a structure that also relies on the alternation of Standard English and Creole.

10. The novel specifically views the mechanisms of appropriation. If *Angel* appropriates "writing," *Morning Sky* appropriates Standard English as a possibly emancipating, liberating speech. To appropriate it, however, one has to "read" it in a careful, anticolonial way, just like Dinah. Moreover, one has to take it from the mouth of an intermediary (such as Hartley). And his use of Standard English can already be understood as an oral practice, characterized and situated by other speakers in the multilingual community.

11. There are a few moments in which the novel as a whole plays with the temptation to become an oral performance, a direct address itself. I refer to the interludes in which the narrator addresses Gem with an intimate "you." Here, the novel

seems to play a trick with the reader. The use of "you" in these intermittent pieces fleetingly places the reader into the position of a marginal listener, maybe even a voyeur. But as this "you" is clearly Gem only, absorbed in her own intense observations, the text expels the reader from its narration at the same time. Thus, the reader occupies the position of a voyeur and eavesdropper, locked in the same ambiguous position as Archie in relation to his wife's sensual sphere. Again, focalization becomes a theme, this time involving the reader, who is suddenly part of the novel's aesthetics. But as I have said, this is but a joke: the novel continues and the reader is comforted with the readerly conventions of the following parts of the novel.

12. In Guyana, then, there is a different political situation: imperialist violence came from within, through infiltration, and this intervention was one of the main causes of communal violence.

13. A similar scene occurs in Michelle Cliff's *Abeng* (1984). However, there the roles are reversed. See Lemuel Johnson 1990.

14. Even if in the Netherlands one's citizenship is legally decided by one's passport—a passport one might (in some well-specified cases, with lots of luck) obtain as a migrant or refugee—the nation's tenacious ethnocentric discourse has long reserved, and is often still reserving, Dutch citizenship for white people who are born in the country. It is only with the ethnographic changes of the last decade, and with, for example, the sports successes of many young Black Dutch, that things are beginning to change.

15. I'm using the narratological term (Bal 1985).

16. A more oral approach to publicizing calypso would be the feat performed by calypsonians The Roaring Lion and Atilla the Hun, who in 1934 sang calypso on the North American radio. Famous singer Harry Belafonte, too, has been called the ambassador of calypso (even in calypso), though his music is often seen as somewhat removed from what, in the Caribbean, is understood as calypso.

17. In the case of Caribbean women's writing, a nonscriptocentric approach will take into account the often tense relations between the recent novels and the rather sexist and sexually loaded genre of calypso. For if calypso is an important Creole art form in which the history of the people is commented upon (in the form of calypso known as "social comment"), it consists also in a range of very popular, very misogynist "party songs." As such, calypsos continue their tradition as an aggressively virile Caribbean carnival genre, probably derived from the songs accompanying stick fights in West Africa before the Middle Passage. Women are now taking up calypso too, and Calypso Rose won the title of Calypso Monarch in 1963, thereby breaking the male hegemony. Yet there is still a strong need for critical examinations of the images of women in calypso as has been published recently (Davies 1990; Mohammed 1992). This misogynist aspect of Creole culture is also present in *Morning Sky* and *Angel*, even if in these cases, too, calypso refers to communal collectivity and physicality. In the following quotation the sexual threat implied in calypso is effectively pictured:

> Doodsie was silent for a while. Angel sang quietly:
> "All day all night Mary Ann
> Down by the seaside siftin sand . . . "
> "Angel, what stupid ole calypso you singing dey?"
> "Dat is not a calypso, non, Mammie!"
> "What it is, den?"
> "Is a calypso, yes," shouted Simon from outside.
> "Hush you mout, boy. You don know nutting!" (100)

The nursery rhyme about Mary Ann also exists as a "very bawdy calypso" recorded in a chaste version on a record from 1987 (Charly Records Ltd.). And Naipaul's *Miguel Street* (1977 (1959)) quotes on page 166:

> All day and all night Miss Mary Ann
> Down by the river-side she taking man.

Which goes to show that calypsos are also very much on the interpreting end of intertextual relations between colonial and Caribbean oral arts. Calypso's appropriation is as much anticolonial as utterly sexist. *Angel* opposes several other genres of singing, which are often women's songs, to these calypsos. These are not only the hymns sung by Doodsie and even by Angel but also the many belligerent political songs.

CHAPTER 6

1. Jamaica Kincaid was born as Elaine Potter Richardson in 1949 on Antigua, a small Caribbean island. She currently lives and works in the United States. She has published several collections of literary pieces, many of which were first published in the *New Yorker*: *At the Bottom of the River* (1984), *Annie John* (1985), *A Small Place* (1988), *Lucy* (1991), *The Autobiography of My Mother* (1996), and *My Brother* (1998). In addition, she has written other texts, such as stories for the *Paris Review* and *Rolling Stone*, the text to a series of lithographs by Eric Fischl (1989), and in the early 1990s a series of essays on gardening in the *New Yorker* (see Chapter 7).

2. See Henry Louis Gates Jr., "The 'Blackness of Blackness': A Critique of the Sign and the Signifying Monkey," in Gates 1987a: 235–76. See also Morrison 1992.

3. I take my inspiration for this approach from Jonathan Culler, who described his own course in another context with the following words:

> In mapping contemporary criticism as a struggle between New Critics, structuralists, and then post-structuralists, one would find it hard to do justice to feminist criticism, which has had a greater effect on the literary canon than any other critical movement. . . . To discuss feminist criticism adequately, one would need a different framework where the notion of post-structuralism was a product rather than a given. (Culler 1983: 30)

4. Pratt describes contact zones as the "social spaces where disparate cultures meet" (Pratt 1992: 4). See Chapter 2, note 22, for a more elaborate definition.

5. Helen Tiffin argues that labels such as postmodernism and postcolonialism are very much the product of *reading* (Adam and Tiffin 1991: vii). Of course, this goes for the definition of all literary texts. However, in the case of postmodern and postcolonial writing it is all the more conspicuous that the corresponding characteristics are not somehow intrinsic to the texts themselves but are produced through a specific reading, as it happens so often that the same texts are considered now exemplary postmodern, then exemplary postcolonial (or, of course, not post- at all, but Black, or Caribbean).

6. Paul Gilroy differentiates counterculture from counterdiscourse (Gilroy 1990/91: 11).

7. See also Slemon 1991; Gikandi 1992; Kubayanda 1987; Cobham 1990.

8. Kincaid probably refers to a kind of writing described as "dirty realism" or "minimalist fiction," or to the books of the "brat pack." These writings are often understood as a particular form of postmodernism—though some prefer to contrast them to postmodern writing. I am grateful to Arie Altena for teaching me these nuances.

9. E.g., Morris and Dunn 1991; Murdoch 1990; Niesen de Abruña 1991; Wilentz 1992.

10. This critique goes for all those approaches are based on the image of multiplicity and dialogism. See, e.g., Benítez-Rojo 1992: 27, and Miller 1990: 26–28, which both criticize Bakhtin's neutral understanding of dialogism and heteroglossia.

11. I consider the narrating "I" a woman for reasons I will explain later. My interpretation of the tourist's gender is more ambiguous, but I will also come back to that.

12. And for this valuable lesson, I am in debt to Carole Boyce Davies and Basker Vashee. The same statement is to be found in Ferguson 1994. This different emphasis in reading sheds light on the debates surrounding postcolonialism, for I began my analysis by assuming the reading position of the Western-European who considers all literature from former colonies by definition as critical responses to the West, as if the West is still domineering all aspects of their cultures. The word for this attitude, of course, is Eurocentrism, and postcolonial criticism should avoid it.

13. Apparently the lack of closing quotation marks causes some confusion: in the Dutch translation, the quotation of the Antiguan's voice is closed after the very first sentence. This solution makes the closing remark ("And it is in that strange voice . . . ") incomprehensible, as it follows after many pages of narrator's text. But it is also understandable: it is clear that the narrator's voice takes over in what should be the reported speech attributed to the Antiguans.

14. Mordecai and Wilson 1990: viii.

15. See Chapter 3, note 6; the term *tactics* is borrowed from de Certeau and refers to the strategy of those who do not possess a territory to situate their acts and therefore must undertake their critical enterprises on the territory of other, dominant groups. Again, as the term *tactics* is rather unusual, I will as a rule employ the term *strategy* for both terms.

16. Kincaid's eagerness to quote and thus "inhabit" a variety of discourses is connected to Kincaid's own spatial metaphor of domesticity. This metaphor has feminine connotations (see Chapter 3). It is possible to see in Kincaid's writing an evasion of labels (Covi 1990). I hold that this evading can be understood only if it is related to Kincaid's choice for the strategy of the domestic person she says she is (Perry 1990). Her use of irony and parody allows her to inhabit a discourse she loathes and loves, just as she loathes and loves Antigua's colonial library. Her ironic attitude allows her to inhabit it anyway. It gives her space for a very sharp, very gripping, inappropriate critique. I do think that Kincaid's strategy of quoting colonial discourse is gendered too, but in a very specific way. I discuss this in the fourth section.

17. For a discussion of Caribbean modernism, see Gikandi 1992. He bases his approach to a large extent on Houston Baker's writing about modernism in his work on the Harlem Renaissance (Baker 1987). Wilson Harris, who is discussed by Ashcroft, Griffiths, and Tiffin as one of the major Caribbean postcolonial critics, is mentioned as the most self-conscious Caribbean modernist. The two qualifications are compatible; a postcolonial critic can be a (critical) modernist, too. I do think that an understanding of the modernist context of Harris's work helps considerably in coming to terms with his complicated writings.

18. There is an instance when sheds a telling light on the awkward nature of the exchange between Cudjoe and Kincaid: Cudjoe's remark about the "charm" of Kincaid's first book. In the interview with Donna Perry, which was conducted later, Kincaid comments on the term *charming*. However, I do not mean to disqualify Cudjoe's efforts to endow Kincaid's refractory work with a literary context. The tensions in their exchange to a certain degree are due to the very difficult position of the criticism that tries to account for the literature written within postcoloniality.

19. Kincaid's description of the Antiguans' sense of time and history is surprisingly (or perhaps unsurprisingly, by now) close to Hegel's observation about the Africans, as quoted by James Snead: "*In this main portion of Africa there can really be no history. There is a succession of accidents and surprises*" (Snead 1991: 215).

20. See Lamming 1987: 16, 17, 23, 25, where in a description of Caribbean life one also finds a play with the equation of numbers: "*Three, thirty, three hundred.*"

21. This strategy is already suggested by Gikandi when he refers to a creative schizophrenia: the writer can *use* his or her hybridity to speak with a voice that breaks away from binary oppositions (Gikandi 1992: 13).

22. This is not the only instance in which she does so: in Chapter 2 I have dis-

cussed how she borrows her mother's judgment on her mother's father to free herself from the authority of Columbus.

23. This happened during an intercultural reading group organized and moderated by cultural theorist Roline Redmond.

24. When Xuela, looking back, remembers how one of her lovers-to-be entered her nightly bedroom for the first time, she hesitatingly reports how he must have looked, what he must have said. All this is uncertain. One thing only she is sure of: his smell (149).

25. D. A. Masolo, professor of philosophy, defines postcolonialism as "a critique of the verisimilitude yet ideologically bloated Eurocentric representation of Others" (Masolo 1997: 294). I do not think such a definition exhaustive (e.g., why a critique of verisimilitude, and not of the effects intended or realized? Why only representation of Others?), but it is very relevant here. Kincaid's text is very much about issues of truth.

CHAPTER 7

1. Michelle Cliff was born in 1946 in Jamaica and spent part of her youth there and part in New York. She has lived in the United Kingdom and in the United States, where she is now a resident. She has published several books and collections of short stories, for example, *Claiming an Identity They Taught Me to Despise* (1981), *Abeng* (1984), *The Land of Look Behind* (1985), *No Telephone to Heaven* (1988), *Bodies of Water* (1990), *Free Enterprise* (1993), and *The Store of a Million Items* (1998). Her work has received high critical acclaim.

2. These are connected to the strategic masquerades of Ellison's *Invisible Man* (1947) and of the ambivalence and indirectness of signifying, explored by Henry Louis Gates. This strategy of speech can be a means of survival: if you don't say anything about yourself, you will not be caught out, and you will be able to move around freely and even laugh at those whom you are cheating.

3. This is not a strategy for the mulatto or light-skinned Caribbean only, as some might argue. Marlene Philip argues for the same, a Creole strategy of hybridity, in the introduction to her *She Tries Her Tongue: Her Silence Softly Breaks*.

4. However, others have redefined Creole as the language of Caribbean mothers. See Chapter 4 on Merle Collins.

5. We can recognize this same strategy in a later novel, *Free Enterprise*. Here, in picturing a wide community of outcasts, both the marginalized and the privileged, she addresses her readers: within this multitude of voices, which are our cultural history, will you listen to me and address me? She doesn't ask for direct recognition of her difference. Instead, as in the poem, she reimagines the community ("us") as essentially varied and structured by difference; making difference the norm allows her to claim her own difference and demand to be acknowledged as one of "us."

6. Curiously, Aidoo's otherwise original, inspiring, and daring text has its mo-

ments of homophobia. That Aidoo's narrative was nevertheless the very text that broke Cliff's kumbla testifies to the paradoxical nature of Cliff's condition.

7. For the notion of gruesomely hidden animals also see 19, 56.

8. And sometimes American, in the broad sense (in which the Caribbean is part of the Americas), but then explicitly Black American; sometimes, Cliff's context is all of the African diaspora.

9. I should add that the theme of love is not the only theme in the poem. For "the hills," where the narrator fears to belong, are the site of the Jamaican guerrilla fighters. The theme of the need for political resistance, then, is another suppressed theme in the poem (see Schwartz 1993: 600).

10. The speaker is no necromancer; and if it seems strange to formulate this as a deviant position, it is useful to realize that in many novels by Caribbean women writers some kind of necromancy is used to reactualize the past and to be able to find a voice. Even writing itself may be in essence a kind of necromancy, a talking to the dead.

11. We find this strategy also in "Europe Becomes Blacker," in which she extensively talks about what she is not talking about (108 ff).

12. In postcolonial discourse one does speak of metonymy. For the sake of coherence, I will return to that discourse, even if I think Van Alphen's argument in favor of Peirce's terminology convincing (1993: 31).

13. In this statement I follow Benita Parry (1987) rather than Bhabha and Spivak, for example, who seem to argue that postcolonial otherness cannot express itself. I will come back to their point of view. In my study, I tend to follow Parry's opinion. My following is mediated, however, by Moore-Gilbert's formulation of Spivak's suggestion that "the idea of a 'pure' (and accessible) subaltern consciousness is a necessary 'theoretical fiction' which enables a critique of the dominant models of colonial and national-bourgeois historiography to be begun" (Moore-Gilbert 1997: 88). Acknowledging the discernible *difference* of (if not the subaltern) the varied marginalized people in the Caribbean, and keeping open the possibility of their articulated difference, seems to me at least an act of courtesy.

14. Another example: in his essay on the role of mimicry in the constitution of the colonial subject, Bhabha discusses the colonial strategy of mimicry as "the representation of identity and meaning [which] is rearticulated along the axis of metonymy" (Bhabha 1984a: 131). The threatening nature of mimicry (to colonial eyes) rests in the fact that it consists of "conflictual, fantastic, discriminatory 'identity effects'" (131), offering a charged, partial resemblance. See also Ashcroft, Griffiths, and Tiffin for a discussion of metonymy, especially in connection to language variance (1989: 51 ff).

15. "Vanuit mijn lievelingsplekje op de grond kijk ik naar de blauwe hemel, naar de kale kastanjeboom aan wiens takken kleine druppeltjes schitteren, naar de meeuwen en de andere vogels, die in hun scheervlucht wel van zilver lijken . . . we

ademden de lucht in, keken naar buiten en voelden, dat dit iets was om niet met woorden te onderbreken" (Frank 1986: 514).

16. Kaja Silverman differentiates idiopathic identification from heteropathic identification: "Heteropathic identification is the obverse of idiopathic identification; whereas the latter conforms to an incorporative model, constituting the self at the expense of the other who is in effect 'swallowed,' the former subscribes to an exteriorizing logic, and locates the self at the site of the other" (Silverman 1992: 205).

CHAPTER 8

1. Miller 1990; Huggan 1990; Pattanaik 1991; see also Hoving 1987.

2. Seej, e.g., Delamotte 1993; Rosello 1993; Zimra 1990; Trinh 1986/87.

3. *She Tries her Tongue* is Philip's third collection of poems. It was published after *Thorns* and *Salmon Courage*. In 1990 the novel *Harriet's Daughter* followed. She has also published *Frontiers: Essays and Writings on Racism and Culture* (Stratford, Ontario: Mercury Press, 1992) and *A Genealogy of Resistance and Other Essays* (Toronto: Mercury Press, 1997).

4. See Parry 1987 for an overview and a critique.

5. See, for another example, Pattanaik 1991.

6. This is not to say that the text is not also about spirituality. However, this spiritually is very intimately located in the body. I will come back to the position of spirituality below.

7. Of course, one could also understand the need for rebirth as the desire to return to the lost continent, Mother Africa. However, I prefer to place Philip within a Caribbean tradition and so use images and metaphors from the Caribbean.

8. My question links to that posed by Miriam Chancy in her analysis of Philip's text. Chancy also wonders about the representation of sexual desire in Philip, but she criticizes the author for not representing the lesbianism of her character more explicitly (1997: 116–17). I do not agree with her critique. First, in contrast to Chancy, I was agreeably struck by the very warm, obvious, open, and explicitly lesbian atmosphere of the text as a whole, which is structured by (Black) women's multiple desire for (Black) women, of which sexuality is an integrated aspect. By the way, an explicit love story *is* part of the narrative. Second, *Odyssey* is not *about* lesbianism; it is written *from* a self-evident lesbian perspective, both for the refreshing sake of it and because of its wish to write within the context of a different, African/women's symbolic. *Odyssey*, then, is about the intertwining of sexuality and knowledge, in the context of the painful history of race and colonialism. One of the reasons for my deep love for this text is its unparalleled undogmatic and positive analysis of the role of sexuality as an omnipresent, capricious, and, by virtue of its capriciousness, potentially healing force in our lives. My analysis hopes to convince my readers of this specific brilliance of this generous text.

9. See, e.g., Deleuze and Guattari 1980; Irigaray 1984; Bronfen 1989, 1991; Bal 1991: 20–24; Silverman 1988, esp. 101–40; Spivak 1993a.

10. It is illuminating to compare Philip's writing with the wonderful work of the young poet Jennifer Rahim from Trinidad, who also explores the potencies of silence (Rahim 1992). The two poets relate differently to the figures of the father and the mother. Rahim occupies the position of the daughter who has the courage of questioning the dominance of her mother and of expressing her need for her father. Philip's desire of the father is much less self-evident, as I will show in this section.

11. Cooper 1991; Cobham 1993; Davies and Fido 1990; and Mordecai and Wilson 1990.

12. Of course, this is not to say that Philip's universe would really be *the* essential universe of all African femininity. It is one of Philip's playful inventions, on the one hand a parody of all those universalist concepts productive in colonial discourse, and on the other hand the serious proposal to accept an otherness that is as heavy and complete as Western concepts of self.

CHAPTER 9

1. See also Young 1995; Papastergiadis 1997; and Becquer and Guatti 1991 for an analysis of the concept of hybridity.

Works Cited

Abel, Elizabeth. 1997. "Black Writing, White Reading: Race and the Politics of Feminist Interpretation." In Elizabeth Abel, Barbara Christian, Helene Moglen, eds., *Female Subjects in Black and White: Race, Psychoanalysis, Feminism.* Berkeley and Los Angeles: University of California Press, pp. 102–31.

Abel, Elizabeth, Barbara Christian, and Helene Moglen, eds. 1997. *Female Subjects in Black and White: Race, Psychoanalysis, Feminism.* Berkeley and Los Angeles: University of California Press.

Achebe, Chinua. 1975. *Morning Yet on Creation Day.* London: Heinemann.

Adam, Ian, and Helen Tiffin, eds. 1991. *Past the Last Post: Theorizing Post-Colonialism and Post-Modernism.* New York: Harvester Wheatsheaf.

Alleyne, Mervyn. 1989. *Roots of Jamaican Culture.* London: Pluto Press.

Alphen, Ernst van. 1993. "Touching Death." In Sarah Webster Goodwin and Elisabeth Bronfen, eds., *Death and Representation.* Baltimore: Johns Hopkins University Press, pp. 29–50.

Anderson, Perry. 1988. "Modernity and Revolution." In Lawrence Grossberg and Cary Nelson, eds., *Marxism and the Interpretation of Culture.* Urbana: University of Illinois Press, pp. 317–38.

Anderson, Warwick. 1995. "Excremental Colonialism: Public Health and the Poetics of Pollution." *Critical Inquiry* 21, no. 3: 640–69.

Anyidoho, Kofi. 1992. "Language and Development Strategy in Pan-African Literary Experience." *Research in African Literatures* 23, no. 1: 45–63.

Anzaldúa, Gloria. 1987. *Borderlands/La Frontera: The New Mestiza.* San Francisco: Spinsters/Aunt Lute.

———. 1991. "How to Tame a Wild Tongue." In *Out There: Marginalization and Contemporary Cultures,* ed. Russell Ferguson, Martha Gever, Trinh T. Minh-ha, and Cornel West. Cambridge, Mass.: MIT Press, 203–11.

Appiah, Kwame Anthony. 1991. "Is the Post- in Postmodernism the Post- in Postcolonial?" *Critical Inquiry* 17: 336–57.

Arnold, A. James. 1994. "The Erotics of Colonialism in Contemporary French West Indian Literary Culture." *New West Indian Guide/Nieuwe West-Indische Gids* 68, no. 1–2: 5–22.

Ashcroft, Bill, Gareth Griffiths, and Helen Tiffin. 1989. *The Empire Writes Back: Theory and Practice in Post-Colonial Literatures.* London: Routledge.

Austin, J. L. 1962. *How to Do Things with Words.* Cambridge: Harvard University Press.

Baker, Houston A., Jr. 1987. "In Dubious Battle." *New Literary History* 18, no. 2: 363–69.

———. 1991. *Workings of the Spirit: The Poetics of Afro-American Women's Writing.* Chicago: University of Chicago Press.

Bakhtin, M. M. 1988a. *The Dialogic Imagination.* Ed. Michael Holquist. Austin: University of Texas Press.

———. 1988b. "Forms of Time and of the Chronotope in the Novel." In Michael Holquist, ed., *The Dialogic Imagination.* Austin: University of Texas Press, pp. 84–258.

Bal, Mieke. 1985. *Narratology: Introduction to the Theory of Narrative.* Trans. Christine van Boheemen. Toronto: University of Toronto Press.

———. 1991. *Reading 'Rembrandt': Beyond the Word-Image Opposition.* Cambridge: Cambridge University Press.

Barley, Nigel. 1986. *The Innocent Anthropologist: Notes from a Mud Hut.* Harmondsworth, England: Penguin.

———. 1987. *A Plague of Caterpillars: A Return to the African Bush.* Harmondsworth, England: Penguin.

Becquer, Marcos, and Jose Guatti. 1991. "Elements of Vogue." *Third Text* 16/17: 65–81.

Benítez-Rojo, Antonio. 1992. *The Repeating Island: The Caribbean and the Postmodern Perspective.* Trans. James Maraniss. Durham, N.C.: Duke University Press.

Bhabha, Homi. 1984a. "Of Mimicry and Man: The Ambivalence of Colonial Discourse." *October* 28: 125–33.

———. 1984b. "Representation and the Colonial Text: Some Forms of Mimeticism." In Frank Gloversmith, ed., *The Theory of Reading.* Sussex: Harvester Press, pp. 93–122.

———. 1990. "DissemiNation: Time, Narrative, and the Margins of the Modern Nation." In Homi Bhabha, *Nation and Narration.* London: Routledge, pp. 291–322.

———. 1994. *The Location of Culture.* London: Routledge.

———. 1997. "Editor's Introduction: Minority Maneuvers and Unsettled Negotiations." *Critical Inquiry* 23: 431–59.

Boehmer, Elleke. 1995. *Colonial and Postcolonial Literature: Migrant Metaphors.* Oxford: Oxford University Press.

Boer, Inge E. 1996. "The World Beyond Our Windows: Nomads, Travelling Theories, and the Function of Boundaries." *Parallax: A Journal of Metadiscursive Theory and Cultural Practices* 3: 7–26.

Boheemen, Christel van. 1990. "Postmodernisme en ethiek: ras, geslacht en het primaat van de taal." *De Gids* 153, no. 4: 275–88.

Boons-Grafé. 1992. "Other/other." In Elizabeth Wright, ed., *Feminism and Psychoanalysis: A Critical Dictionary.* Cambridge, Mass.: Blackwell, pp. 296–99.

Braidotti, Rosi. 1993. "Nomads in a Transformed Europe: Figurations for an Alternative Consciousness." In Ria Lavrijsen, ed., *Cultural Diversity in the Arts.* Amsterdam: Royal Tropical Institute, pp. 31–44.

Brathwaite, Edward. 1974. "Introduction." In Roger Mais, *Brother Man.* London: Heinemann, pp. v–xxi.

Brathwaite, Edward Kamau. 1984. *History of the Voice: The Development of Nation Language in Anglophone Caribbean Poetry.* London: New Beacon.

Brennan, Timothy. 1989. "Preface." *Modern Fiction Studies* 35, no. 1: 3–8.

Breure, Marnel. 1997. *De Groene* (Amsterdam), 12 February 1997.

Brodber, Erna. 1988a (1980). *Jane and Louisa Will Soon Come Home.* London: New Beacon Books.

———. 1988b. *Myal.* London: New Beacon Books.

Bronfen, Elisabeth. 1989. "The Lady Vanishes: Sophie Freud and 'Beyond the Pleasure Principle.'" *South Atlantic Quarterly* 88, no. 4: 961–91.

———. 1991. "Death: The Navel of the Image." In Mieke Bal and Inge Boer, eds., *The Point of Theory: Practices of Cultural Analysis.* Amsterdam: Amsterdam University Press, pp. 79–90.

Brontë, Charlotte. 1847. *Jane Eyre.* London.

Brown, Bev E. L. 1985. "Mansong and Matrix: A Radical Experiment." *Kunapipi* 7, no. 2–3: 68–79.

Certeau, Michel de. 1984. *The Practice of Everyday Life.* Berkeley: University of California Press.

Césaire, Aimé. 1971. *Return to My Native Land.* Paris: Présence Africaine.

Chancy, Myriam J. A. 1997. *Searching for Safe Spaces: Afro-Caribbean Women Writers in Exile.* Philadelphia: Temple University Press.

Chinweizu, ed. 1988. *Voices from Twentieth-Century Africa: Griots and Town-Criers.* London: Faber and Faber.

Chinweizu, Onwuchekwa Jemie, and Ihechukwu Madubuike. 1983. *Toward the Decolonization of African Literature.* Washington, D.C.: Howard University Press.

Chow, Rey. 1992. "Race/Imperialism." In Elizabeth Wright, ed., *Feminism and Psychoanalysis: A Critical Dictionary.* Cambridge, Mass.: Blackwell, pp. 361–64.

Chowdhury, Kanishka. 1991. "Theoretical Confrontations in the Study of Postcolonial Literatures." *Modern Fiction Studies* 37: 609–15.

Chrisman, Laura, and Patrick Williams, eds. 1994. *Colonial Discourse and Post-Colonial Theory: A Reader.* New York: Harvester Wheatsheaf.

Christian, Barbara. 1990. "The Highs and the Lows of Black Feminist Criticism". In Henry Louis Gates Jr., ed., *Reading Black, Reading Feminist: A Critical Anthology.* New York: Meridian/Penguin, pp. 44–51.

Classen, Constance, David Howes, and Anthony Synnott. 1993. *Aroma: The Cultural History of Smell.* New York: Routledge.

Cliff, Michelle. 1978. "Notes on Speechlessness." *Sinister Wisdom* 5: 5–9.

———. 1980. *Claiming an Identity They Taught Me to Despise.* Watertown, Mass.: Persephone Press.

———. 1984. *Abeng.* Trumansburg, N.Y.: Crossing Press.

———. 1985. *The Land of Look Behind.* Ithaca, N.Y.: Firebrand Books.

———. 1988. *No Telephone to Heaven.* London: Methuen.

Clifford, James. 1989. "Notes on Travel and Theory." *Inscriptions* 5: 177–88.

———. 1992. "Traveling Cultures." In Lawrence Grossberg, Cary Nelson, and Paula A. Treichler, eds., *Cultural Studies. New York: Routledge,* pp. 96–116.

Cobham, Rhonda. 1990. "Women of the Islands." *The Women's Review of Books* 7 (July): 31.

———. 1993. "Revisioning Our Kumblas: Transforming Feminist and Nationalist Agendas in Three Caribbean Women's Texts." *Callaloo* 16, no. 1: 44–64.

Cobham, Rhonda, and Merle Collins, eds. 1987. *Watchers and Seekers: Creative Writing by Black Women in Britain.* London: Women's Press.

Coetzee, J. M. 1988. *White Writing: On the Culture of Letters in South Africa.* New Haven, Conn.: Yale University Press.

Collins, Merle. 1987. *Angel.* London: Women's Press.

Colomina, Beatriz, ed. 1992. *Sexuality and Space.* New York: Princeton Architectural Press.

Condé, Maryse. 1979. *La Parole des femmes: essai sur des romancières des Antilles de langue française.* Paris: L'Harmattan.

Cooper, Carolyn. 1989. "Writing Oral History: Sistren Theatre Collective's *Lionheart Gal.*" *Kunapipi* 11, no. 1: 49–57.

———. 1991. "'Something Ancestral Recaptured': Spirit Possession as Trope in Selected Feminist Fictions of the African Diaspora." In Susheila Nasta, ed., *Motherlands: Black Women's Writing from Africa, the Caribbean, and South Asia.* London: Women's Press, pp. 64–87.

———. 1993. *Noises in the Blood: Orality, Gender and the "Vulgar" Body of Jamaican Popular Culture.* London: Macmillan Caribbean.

Covi, Giovanna. 1990. "Jamaica Kincaid and the Resistance to Canons." In Carole Boyce Davies and Elaine Savory Fido, eds., *Out of the Kumbla: Caribbean Women and Literature.* Trenton: Africa World Press, pp. 345–54.

Cudjoe, Selwyn R., ed. 1990a. *Caribbean Women Writers: Essays from the First International Conference.* Wellesley, Mass.: Calaloux Publications.

———. 1990b. "Jamaica Kincaid and the Modernist Project: An Interview." In Selwyn R. Cudjoe, ed., *Caribbean Women Writers: Essays from the First International Conference.* Wellesley, Mass.: Calaloux Publications, pp. 215–32.

Culler, Jonathan. 1983. *On Deconstruction: Theory and Criticism After Structuralism.* London: Routledge & Kegan Paul.

————. 1988. "The Semiotics of Tourism." In Jonathan Culler, *Framing the Sign: Criticism and Its Institutions.* Cambridge, Mass.: Basil Blackwell, pp. 153–67.

Dalphinis, Morgan. 1985. *Caribbean and African Languages: Social History, Language, Literature, and Education.* London: Karia.

Dash, Michael. 1989. "In Search of the Lost Body: Redefining the Subject in Caribbean Literature" *Kunapipi* 9, no. 1: 17–26.

Davies, Carole Boyce. 1990. "'Woman Is a Nation . . .' Women in Caribbean Oral Literature." In Carole Boyce Davies and Elaine Savory Fido, eds., *Out of the Kumbla: Caribbean Women and Literature.* Trenton, N.J.: Africa World Press, pp. 165–93.

————. 1994. *Black Women, Writing, and Identity: Migrations of the Subject.* London: Routledge.

————. 1998. *A Place in the Sun? Women Writers in Twentieth-Century Cuba.* London: Zed Books.

Davies, Carole Boyce, and Elaine Savory Fido, eds. 1990. *Out of the Kumbla: Caribbean Women and Literature.* Trenton, N.J.: Africa World Press.

D'Costa, Jean. 1983. "The West Indian Novelist and Language: A Search for a Literary Medium." In Lawrence D. Carrington, ed., *Studies in Caribbean Language.* St. Augustine, Trinidad: Society for Caribbean Linguistics, pp. 252–65.

DelaMotte, Eugenia. 1993. "Women, Silence, and History in *The Chosen Place, The Timeless People.*" *Callaloo* 16, no. 1: 227–42.

Deleuze, Gilles. 1977. "Nomad Thought." In David Allison, ed., *The New Nietzsche.* New York: Delta, pp. 142–49.

Deleuze, Giles, and Félix Guattari. 1980. *Mille Plateaux: capitalisme et schizophrénie.* Paris: Editions de Minuit.

————. 1991. "What Is a Minor Literature?" In Russell Ferguson, Martha Gever, T. Minh-ha Trinh, and Cornel West, eds., *Out There: Marginalization and Contemporary Cultures.* Cambridge: MIT Press, pp. 59–69.

Derrida, Jacques. 1976. *Of Grammatology.* Trans. Gayatri Chakravorty Spivak. Baltimore: Johns Hopkins University Press.

Donaldson, Laura E. 1992. *Decolonizing Feminisms: Race, Gender, and Empire-Building.* London: Routledge.

Donkers, Jan. 1997. *NRC* (Amsterdam), 7 January 1997.

During, Simon. 1991. "Waiting for the Post: Some Relations Between Modernity, Colonization, and Writing." In Ian Adam and Helen Tiffin, eds., *Past the Last Post: Theorizing Post-Colonialism and Post-Modernism.* New York: Harvester Wheatsheaf, pp. 23–45.

————, ed. 1993. *The Cultural Studies Reader.* New York: Routledge.

Edmondson, Belinda. 1994. "Race, Tradition, and the Construction of the Caribbean Aesthetics." *New Literary History* 25, no. 1: 109–20.

Edwards, Viv, and Thomas J. Sienkewicz. 1990. *Oral Cultures Past and Present: Rappin' and Homer.* Cambridge, Mass.: Basil Blackwell.

Ellison, Ralph. 1947. *Invisible Man.* New York: New American Library.

Emecheta, Buchi. 1981 (1974). *Second-Class Citizen.* London: Fontana.

————. 1986. *Head Above Water.* London: Fontana, 1986.

Evans, Mari, ed. 1984. *Black Women Writers (1950–1980): A Critical Evaluation.* Garden City, N.Y.: Anchor Press/Doubleday.

Eze, Emmanuel Chukwudi, ed. 1997. *Postcolonial African Philosophy: A Critical Reader.* Cambridge, Mass.: Blackwell.

Fabian, Johannes. 1983. *Time and the Other: How Anthropology Makes Its Object.* New York: Columbia University Press.

————. 1991. *Time and the Work of Anthropology: Critical Essays 1971–1991.* Chur, Switzerland: Harwood Academic Publishers.

Fanon, Frantz. 1952. *Peau noire, masques blancs.* Paris: Editions du Seuil.

Ferguson, Moira. 1994. *Jamaica Kincaid: Where the Land Meets the Body.* Charlottesville: University Press of Virginia.

Finnegan, Ruth H. 1988. *Literacy and Orality: Studies in the Technology of Communication.* Cambridge, Mass.: Basil Blackwell.

Fonseca, Isabel. 1989. "Their Island Story." *Times Literary Supplement,* 13 January, 30.

Frank, Anne. 1972. *The Diary of a Young Girl.* Trans. B. M. Mooyaart-Doubleday. New York: Pocket Books.

————. 1986. *De dagboeken van Anne Frank.* Introduction by Harry Paape, Gerrold van der Stroom, and David Barnouw. Ed. David Barnouw and Gerrold van der Stroom. 's-Gravenhage: Staatsuitgeverij; Amsterdam: Bert Bakker.

Fuller, Vernella. 1992. *Going Back Home.* London: Women's Press.

Gandhi, Leela. 1998. *Postcolonial Theory: A Critical Introduction.* Edinburgh: Edinburgh University Press.

Ganguly, Keya. 1992. "Migrant Identities: Personal Memory and the Construction of Selfhood." *Cultural Studies* 6, no. 1: 27–50.

Gates, Henry Louis, Jr. 1983. "The 'Blackness of Blackness': A Critique of the Sign and the Signifying Monkey." *Critical Inquiry* 9: 685–723.

————. 1987a. *Figures in Black: Words, Signs, and the "Racial" Self.* New York: Oxford University Press.

————. 1987b. "'What's Love Got to Do with It?': Critical Theory, Integrity, and the Black Idiom." *New Literary History* 18, no. 2: 345–62.

————. 1988. *The Signifying Monkey: A Theory of Afro-American Literary Criticism.* New York: Oxford University Press.

————. 1991. "Critical Fanonism." *Critical Inquiry* 17: 457–70.

Gikandi, Simon. 1992. *Writing in Limbo: Modernism and Caribbean Literature.* Ithaca, N.Y.: Cornell University Press.

Gilbert, Sandra M., and Susan Gubar. 1979. *The Madwoman in the Attic: The Woman Writer and the Nineteenth Century Literary Imagination.* New Haven, Conn.: Yale University Press.

Gilroy, Beryl. 1986. *Frangipani House.* Oxford: Heinemann.

———. 1989. *Boy-Sandwich*. Oxford: Heinemann.

Gilroy, Paul. 1990/91. "It Ain't Where You're From, It's Where You're At . . . : The Dialectics of Diasporic Identification." *Third Text* 13: 3–16.

Glissant, Edouard. 1981. *Le Discours Antillais*. Paris: Editions du Seuil.

Goody, Jack. 1977. *The Domestication of the Savage Mind*. Cambridge: Cambridge University Press.

Gooneratne, Yasmine. 1986. "Place and Placelessness in the Criticism of the New Literatures in English." Peggy Nightingale, ed., *A Sense of Place in the New Literatures in English*. St. Lucia, Australia: University of Queensland Press, pp. 13–21.

Gordimer, Nadine. 1979. *Burger's Daughter*. London: Jonathan Cape.

———. 1981. *July's People*. London: Jonathan Cape.

———. 1987. *A Sport of Nature*. New York: Alfred Knopf.

Gorp, Hendrik van, et al. 1980. *Lexicon van literaire termen*. Groningen, Netherlands: Wolters-Noordhoff.

Grewal, Shabnam, Jackie Kay, Liliane Landor, Gail Lewis, and Pratibha Parmar, eds. 1988. *Charting the Journey: Writings by Black and Third World Women*. London: Sheba.

Gupta, Akhil, and James Ferguson. 1992. "Beyond 'Culture': Space, Identity, and the Politics of Difference." *Cultural Anthropology* 7, no. 1: 6–23.

Gyekye, Kwame. 1997. "Philosophy, Culture, and Technology in the Postcolonial." In Emmanuel Chukwudi Eze, ed., *Postcolonial African Philosophy: A Critical Reader*. Cambridge, Mass.: Blackwell, pp. 25–44.

Gyssels, Kathleen. 1996. *Filles de Solitude: Essai sur l'identité antillaise dans les (auto-)biographies fictives de Simone et André Schwarz-Bart*. Paris: L'Harmattan.

Hall, Stuart. 1996. "When Was 'the Post-Colonial'? Thinking at the Limit." In *The Post-Colonial Question: Common Skies, Divided Horizons*, ed. Iain Chambers and Lidia Curti. London: Routledge, pp. 242–60.

Haraway, Donna J. 1991. *Simians, Cyborgs, and Women: The Reinvention of Nature*. London: Free Association Books.

Harris, Wilson. 1970. *The Sleepers of Roraima: A Carib Trilogy*. London: Faber.

———. 1983. *The Womb of Space: The Cross-Cultural Imagination*. Westport, Conn.: Greenwood.

———. 1985. "On the Beach." *Landfall* 39, no. 3: 335–41.

Hartmann, Geoffrey. 1995. "On Traumatic Knowledge and Literary Studies." *New Literary History* 26, no. 3: 537–63.

Henderson, Mae Gwendolyn. 1990. "Speaking in Tongues: Dialogics, Dialectics, and the Black Woman Writer's Literary Tradition." Henry Louis Gates Jr., ed. *Reading Black, Reading Feminist: A Critical Anthology*. New York: Meridian/Penguin, pp. 116–42.

Homans, Margaret. 1994. "'Women of Color' Writers and Feminist Theory." *New Literary History* 25, no.1: 73–94.

hooks, bell. 1986/87. "Talking Back." *Discourse* 8: 123–28.

Hoving, Isabel. 1987. "Spreken, zwijgen en de macht van vrouwen in de orale literatuur van de Basse-Casamance." In Marijke Jansen, Jos van der Klei, Saskia van der Valk, eds., *Opstellen over vrouwen in de Basse-Casamance en Midden-Gambia.* Amsterdam: privately printed, pp. 123–41.

———. 1995. "The Castration of Livingstone and Other Stories: Reading Caribbean Migrant Women's Writing." Ph.D. diss., University of Amsterdam.

Huggan, Graham. 1990. "Philomela's Retold Sory: Silence, Music, and the Post-Colonial Text." *Journal of Commonwealth Literature* 25, no. 1: 12–23.

Hulme, Peter. 1986. *Colonial Encounters: Europe and the Native Caribbean 1492–1797.* London: Methuen.

Hutcheon, Linda. 1988. *A Poetics of Postmodernism: History, Theory, Fiction.* London: Routledge.

———. 1991. "Circling the Downspout of Empire." In Ian Adam and Helen Tiffin, eds., *Past the Last Post: Theorizing Post-Colonialism and Post-Modernism.* New York: Harvester Wheatsheaf, pp. 167–89.

———. 1995. "Colonialism and the Postcolonial Condition: Complexities Abounding." *PMLA* 110, no. 1: 7–16.

Ibitokun, Benedict M. 1991. "The Dynamics of Spatiality in African Fiction." *Modern Fiction Studies* 37, no. 3: 409–26.

Iginla, Biodun. 1992. "Black feminist critique of psychoanalysis." In Elizabeth Wright, ed. *Feminism and Psychoanalysis: A Critical Dictionary.* Cambridge, Mass.: Blackwell, pp. 31–33.

Irigaray, Luce. 1984. *Ethique de la différence sexuelle.* Paris: Editions de Minuit.

James, Adeola, ed. 1990. *In Their Own Voices: African Women Writers Talk.* London: Currey; Portsmouth, N.H.: Heinemann.

Jameson, Fredric. 1988. "Cognitive Mapping." In Lawrence Grossberg and Cary Nelson, eds., *Marxism and the Interpretation of Culture.* Urbana: University of Illinois Press, 347–60.

JanMohamed, Abdul R. 1986. "The Economy of Manichean Allegory: The Function of Racial Difference in Colonialist Literature." In Henry Louis Gates Jr, ed., *"Race," Writing, and Difference.* Chicago: University of Chicago Press, pp. 78–106.

Johnson, Amryl. 1988. *Sequins for a Ragged Hem.* London: Virago Press.

Johnson, Lemuel A. 1990. "A-beng: (Re)Calling the Body In(to) Question." In Carole Boyce Davies and Elaine Savory Fido, eds., *Out of the Kumbla: Caribbean Women and Literature.* Trenton, N.J.: Africa World Press, pp. 111–42.

Joyce, Joyce A. 1987a. "The Black Canon: Reconstructing Black American Literary Criticism." *New Literary History* 18, no. 2: 335–44.

———. 1987b. "'Who the Cap Fit': Unconsciousness and Unconscionableness in the Criticism of Houston A. Baker, Jr., and Henry Louis Gates, Jr." *New Literary History* 18, no. 2: 371–84.

Kaplan, Caren. 1987. "Deterritorrialization: The Rewriting of Home and Exile in Western Feminist Discourse." *Cultural Critique* 6: 187–98.

Kimmerle, Heinz. 1995. *Mazungumzo: dialogen tussen Afrikaanse en Westerse filoso-fieën.* Amsterdam: Boom.

Kincaid, Jamaica. 1984. *At the Bottom of the River.* London: Picador.

———. 1985. *Annie John.* London: Picador.

———. 1988. *A Small Place.* London: Virago.

———. 1991. *Lucy.* New York: Penguin.

———. 1992. "Flowers of Evil." *New Yorker* 5: 154–59.

———. 1996. *The Autobiography of My Mother.* London: Vintage.

———. 1998. *My Brother.* London: Vintage.

Kristeva, Julia. 1974. *La Révolution du langage poétique: l'Avant-garde a la fin du XIXe siècle: Lautréamont et Mallarmé.* Paris: Editions du Seuil.

———. 1980. *Desire in Language: A Semiotic Approach to Literature and Art.* Ed. Léon S. Roudiez. Trans. Alice Jardine, Thomas Gora, and Léon S. Roudiez. Cambridge, Mass.: Blackwell.

Kubayanda, Josaphat Bekunu. 1987. "Minority Discourse and the African Collective: Some Examples from Latin American and Caribbean Literature." *Cultural Critique* 6: 113–30.

Kunene, Daniel P. 1992. "African-Language Literature: Tragedy and Hope." *Research in African Literatures* 23, no. 1: 7–15.

Lamming, George. 1987 (1953). *In the Castle of My Skin.* London: Michael Joseph.

———. 1992. *The Pleasures of Exile.* Ann Arbor: University of Michigan Press.

Latin America Bureau. 1984. *Grenada: Whose Freedom?* London: Latin America Bureau.

Laurence, Margaret. 1963. *The Prophet's Camel Bell.* Toronto: McClelland and Stewart, 1988.

Lauretis, Teresa de. 1984. "Desire in Narrative." In *Alice Doesn't: Feminism, Semiotics, Cinema.* Bloomington: Indiana University Press, pp. 103–58.

Laye, Camara. 1980. *The Guardian of the Word.* Glasgow: Fontana.

Lemaire, Ton. 1986. *De Indiaan in ons bewustzijn: de ontmoeting van de Oude met de Nieuwe Wereld.* Baarn, Netherlands: Ambo.

Longmore, Zelda. 1990. *Tap-taps to Trinidad: A Journey Through the Caribbean.* London: Arrow.

Loomba, Ania. 1998. *Colonialism/Postcolonialism.* London: Routledge.

Lord, Albert B. 1960. *The Singer of Tales.* Cambridge: Harvard University Press.

Lorde, Audre. 1984b. "The Uses of Anger: Women Responding to Racism." Audre Lorde, *Sister Outsider: Essays and Speeches.* Trumansburg, N.Y.: Crossing Press, pp. 124–33.

Lotman, Yuri M. 1990. *Universe of the Mind: A Semiotic Theory of Culture.* Trans. Ann Shukman. London: I. B. Tauris.

Lyotard, Jean-François. 1993. "Defining the Postmodern." In *The Cultural Studies Reader*, ed. Simon During. London: Routledge, 170–73.

Maes-Jelinek, Hena. 1991. "'Numinous Proportions': Wilson Harris' Alternative to All 'Posts.'" Ian Adam and Helen Tiffin, *Past the Last Post: Theorizing Post-Colonialism and Post-Modernism*. New York: Harvester Wheatsheaf, pp. 47–64.

Mair, Christian. 1991. "Naipaul's *Miguel Street* and Selvon's *Lonely Londoners*: Two Approaches to the Use of Caribbean Creole in Fiction." *Journal of Commonwealth Literature* 26: 138–54.

Mais, Roger. 1974 (1954). *Brother Man*. London: Heinemann.

Makang, Jean Marie. 1997. "Of the Good Use of Tradition: Keeping the Critical Perspective in African Philosophy." In Emmanuel Chukwudi Eze, ed., *Postcolonial African Philosophy: A Critical Reader*. Cambridge, Mass.: Blackwell, pp. 324–38.

Martin, Biddy, and Chandra Talpade Mohanty. 1986. "Feminist Politics: What's Home Got to Do with It?" In Teresa de Lauretis, ed., *Feminist Studies, Critical Studies* Basingstoke: MacMillan, pp. 191–212.

Masolo, D. A. 1997. "African Philosophy and the Postcolonial: Some Misleading Abstractions about 'Identity.'" In Emmanuel Chukwudi Eze, ed., *Postcolonial African Philosophy: A Critical Reader*. Cambridge, Mass.: Blackwell, pp. 283–300.

Maxwell, D. E. S. 1965. "Landscape and Theme." In John Press, ed., *Commonwealth Literature: Unity and Diversity in a Common Culture*. London: Heinemann, pp. 82–89.

McClintock, Anne. 1992. "The Angel of Progress: Pitfalls of the Term 'Post-Colonialism'" *Social Text* 31–32: 1–15.

Meijer, Maaike. 1988. *De Lust tot Lezen. Nederlandse dichteressen en het literaire systeem*. Amsterdam: Sara/Van Gennep.

Miller, Christopher L. 1986. "Theories of Africans: The Question of Literary Anthropology." Henry Louis Gates Jr., ed., *"Race," Writing, and Difference*. Chicago: University of Chicago Press, pp. 281–300.

———. 1990. *Theories of Africans: Francophone Literature and Anthropology in Africa*. Chicago: University of Chicago Press.

———. 1993. "The Postidentitarian Predicament in the Footnotes of *A Thousand Plateaus*: Nomadology, Anthropology, and Authority." *Diacritics* 23, no. 3: 6–35.

Moglen, Helene. 1997. "Redeeming History: Toni Morrison's *Beloved*." In Abel, Christian, and Moglen, eds., *Female Subjects in Black and White: Race, Psychoanalysis, Feminism*. Berkeley and Los Angeles: University of California Press, pp. 201–20.

Mohammed, Patricia. 1992. "Tegentonen in Trinidad: de calypso's van Lady Jane en Singing Francine." *Lover* 19: 247–57.

Mohanty, Chandra. 1988. "Under Western Eyes: Feminist Scholarship and Colonial Discourses." *Feminist Review* 30: 61–88.

Momin, Prachi. "I-Dentity." In Shabnam Grewal et al., eds., *Charting the Journey: Writings by Black and Third World Women.* London: Sheba, pp. 30–31.

Moore-Gilbert, Bart. 1997. *Postcolonial Theory: Contexts, Practices, Politics.* London and New York: Verso.

Mordecai, Pamela, and Betty Wilson, eds. 1990. *Her True-True Name: An Anthology of Women's Writing from the Caribbean.* Oxford: Heinemann.

Morris, Ann R., and Margaret M. Dunn. 1991. "'The Bloodstream of Our Inheritance': Female Identity and the Caribbean Mothers'-Land." In Susheila Nasta, ed., *Motherlands: Black Women's Writing from Africa, the Caribbean, and South Asia.* London: Women's Press, pp. 219–37.

Morris, Meaghan. 1992. "Great Moments in Social Climbing: King Kong and the Human Fly." In Beatriz Colomina, ed., *Sexuality and Space.* New York: Princeton Architectural Press, pp. 1–52.

Morrison, Toni. 1982. *Sula.* New York: Knopf.

———. 1992. *Playing in the Dark: Whiteness and the Literary Imagination.* London: Picador.

Mudimbe, V. Y. 1988. *The Invention of Africa: Gnosis, Philosophy, and the Order of Knowledge.* London: Currey; Bloomington: Indiana University Press.

Mulvey, Laura. 1992. "Pandora: Topographies of the Mask and Curiosity." In Beatriz Colomina, ed., *Sexuality and Space.* New York: Princeton Architectural Press, pp. 53–72.

Murdoch, H. Adlai. 1990. "Severing the (M)other Connection: The Representation of Cultural Identity in Jamaica Kincaid's *Annie John.*" *Callaloo* 13, no.2: 325–40.

Naipaul, V. S. 1959. *Miguel Street.* London: André Deutsch.

Nasta, Susheila, ed. 1991. *Motherlands: Black Women's Writing from Africa, the Caribbean, and South Asia.* London: Women's Press.

Ngcobo, Lauretta, ed. 1988. *Let It Be Told: Essays by Black Women in Britain.* London: Virago.

Ngugi wa Thiong'o. 1986. *Decolonising the Mind: The Politics of Language in African Literature.* London: Currey.

Nichols, Grace. 1983. *I Is a Long Memoried Woman.* London: Karnac House.

———. 1986. *Whole of a Morning Sky.* London: Virago.

Niesen de Abruña, Laura. 1991. "Family Connections: Mother and Mother Country in the Fiction of Jean Rhys and Jamaica Kincaid." In Susheila Nasta, ed., *Motherlands: Black Women's Writing from Africa, the Caribbean, and South Asia.* London: Women's Press, pp. 257–89.

Nightingale, Peggy, ed. 1986. *A Sense of Place in the New Literatures in English.* St. Lucia, Australia: University of Queensland Press.

Njau, Rebecca. 1975. *Ripples in the Pool.* London: Heinemann.

O'Connor, Mary. 1990. "Chronotopes for Women Under Capital: An Investigation into the Relation of Women to Objects." *Critical Studies* 2, no. 1–2: 137–51.

Ombre, Ellen. 1994. *Vrouwvreemd: verhalen*. Amsterdam: Arbeiderspers.

Ong, Walter J. 1982. *Orality and Literacy: The Technologizing of the Word*. London: Methuen.

———. 1987. "Orality-Literacy Studies and the Unity of the Human Race." *Oral Tradition* 2, no. 1: 371–82.

Papastergiadis, Nikos. 1997. "Tracing Hybridity in Theory." In *Debating Cultural Hybridity: Multi-Cultural Identity and the Politics of Anti-Racism*, ed. Pnina Werbner and Tariq Modood. London: Zed Books, pp. 29–37.

Parry, Benita. 1987. "Problems in Current Theories of Colonial Discourse." *Oxford Literary Review* 9, no. 1–2: 27–58.

Pattanaik, D. R. 1991. "Silence as a Mode of Transcendence in the Poetry of Jayanta Mahapatra." *Journal of Commonwealth Literature* 26, no. 1: 117–26.

Perry, Donna. 1990. "An Interview with Jamaica Kincaid." In Henry Louis Gates Jr., ed., *Reading Black, Reading Feminist: A Critical Anthology*. New York: Meridian/Penguin, pp.492–509.

Peypers, Ankie. 1982. *Voor en tegen mensen*. Baarn, Netherlands: Ambo.

Phaf, Ineke. 1990. "Women Writers of the Dutch-Speaking Caribbean: Life Long Poem in the Tradition of Surinamese Granmorgu (New Dawn)." In *Caribbean Women Writers: Essays from the First International Conference*, ed. Selwyn R. Cudjoe. Wellesley, Mass.: Calaloux Publications, pp. 357–64.

Philip, Marlene Nourbese. 1989. *She Tries Her Tongue: Her Silence Softly Breaks*. Charlottetown, Canada: Ragweed Press.

———. 1991. *Looking for Livingstone: An Odyssey of Silence*. Stratford, England: Mercury Press.

Praeger, Michele. 1992. "Edouard Glissant: Towards a Literature of Orality." *Callaloo* 15, no. 1: 41–48.

Prasad, Madhava. 1992. "The 'Other' Worldliness of Postcolonial Discourse: A Critique." *Critical Quarterly*. 34, no. 3: 74–89.

Pratt, Mary Louise. 1986. "Scratches on the Face of the Country; or, What Mr. Barrow Saw in the Land of the Bushmen." In Henry Louis Gates Jr., ed., *"Race," Writing, and Difference*. Chicago: University of Chicago Press, pp. 138–62.

———. 1992. *Imperial Eyes: Travel Writing and Transculturation*. London: Routledge.

———. 1993. "'Yo Soy La Malinche': Chicana Writers and the Poetics of Ethno-nationalism." *Callaloo* 16, no. 4: 859–73.

Pratt, Minnie Bruce. 1984. "Identity: Skin Blood Heart." In Elly Bulkin, Minnie Bruce Pratt, and Barbara Smith, *Yours in Struggle: Three Feminist Perspectives on Anti-Semitism and Racism*. Brooklyn, N.Y.: Long Haul Press, pp. 9–63.

Rahim, Jennifer. 1992. *Mothers Are Not the Only Linguists and Other Poems*. Diego Martin, Trinidad: New Voices.

Ramchand, Kenneth. 1983. *The West Indian Novel and Its Background*. London: Heinemann.

Ravell-Pinto, Thelma. 1993. Gender Representation and Social Change. Paper read at Landelijk Congres Vrouwen / Genderstudies, 29 October 1993, University of Amsterdam, Netherlands.

Redmond, Roline. 1993. *Taal, macht en cultuur: machtsverhoudingen in een Afro-Caribische roman*. Utrecht, Netherlands: ISOR.

Rich, Adrienne. 1984. "Een politiek van plaats: Aantekeningen." *Lust en Gratie* 3: 9–27.

Riley, Joan. 1985. *The Unbelonging*. London: Women's Press.

———. 1987. *Waiting in the Twilight*. London: Women's Press.

———. 1988. *Romance*. London: Women's Press.

———. 1992. *A Kindness to the Children*. London: Women's Press.

Rodriguez, Maria Christina. 1990. "Women Writers of the Spanish-Speaking Caribbean: An Overview." In *Caribbean Women Writers: Essays from the First International Conference*, ed. Selwyn R. Cudjoe. Wellesley, Mass.: Calaloux Publications, pp. 339–45.

Rosello, Mireille. 1993. "Michele Maillet's *L'Etoile noire*: Historian's Counter-History and Translator's Counter-Silence." *Callaloo* 16, no.1: 192–212.

Rutgers, Wim. 1986. *Dubbeltje lezen, stuivertje schrijven: Over Nederlandstalige Caraïbische literatuur*. Oranjestad: Charuba; Den Haag: Leopold.

———. 1994. *Schrijven is zilver, spreken is goud: oratuur, auratuur en literatuur van de Nederlandse Antillen en Aruba*. PhD. diss., Rijksuniversiteit, Utrecht.

Said, Edward W. 1983. *The World, the Text, and the Critic*. Cambridge: Harvard University Press.

———. 1991. *Orientalism*. London: Penguin, 1991.

———. 1994. *Culture and Imperialism*. London: Vintage.

Scharlau, Birgit, and Mark Münzel. 1986. *Qellqay. Mündliche Kultur und Schrifttradi tion bei Indianern Lateinamerikas*. Frankfurt: Campus Verlag.

Schine, Cathleen. 1996. *New York Times Book Review*, 4 February 1996.

Schwartz, Meryl F. 1993. "An Interview with Michelle Cliff." *Contemporary Literature* 34: 595–619.

Shelton, Marie-Denise. 1990. "Women Writers of the French-Speaking Caribbean: An Overview." In *Caribbean Women Writers: Essays from the First International Conference*, ed. Selwyn R. Cudjoe. Wellesley, Mass.: Calaloux Publications, pp. 346–56.

Shinebourne, Janice. [1986]. *Timepiece*. Leeds: Peepal Tree Press.

Shohat, Ella. 1992. "Notes on the 'Post-Colonial.'" *Social Text* 31–32: 99–113.

Shohat, Ella, and Robert Stam. 1994. *Unthinking Eurocentrism: Multiculturalism and the Media*. London and New York: Routledge.

Silverman, Kaja. 1984. *The Subject of Semiotics*. New York: Oxford University Press.

———. 1988. *The Acoustic Mirror: The Female Voice in Psychoanalysis and Cinema*. Bloomington: Indiana University Press.

———. 1992. *Male Subjectivity at the Margins*. New York: Routledge.

———. 1996. *The Threshold of the Visible World.* New York and London: Routledge.

Slemon, Stephen. 1991. "Waiting for the Post: Some Relations Between Modernity, Colonization, and Writing." In Ian Adam and Helen Tiffin, *Past the Last Post: Theorizing Post-Colonialism and Post-Modernism.* New York: Harvester Wheatsheaf, pp. 23–45.

Smith, Lillian. 1963. *Killers of the Dream.* Garden City, N.Y.: Anchor Books.

Smith, Valerie. 1989. "Black Feminist Theory and the Representation of the 'Other.'" In Cheryl A. Wall, ed., *Changing Our Own Words: Essays on Criticism, Theory, and Writing by Black Women.* New Brunswick, N.J.: Rutgers University Press, pp. 38–57.

Snead, James A. 1991. "Repetition as a Figure of Black Culture". In Russell Ferguson, Martha Gever, T. Minh-ha Trinh, and Cornel West, eds., *Out There: Marginalization and Contemporary Cultures.* Cambridge: MIT Press, pp. 213–30.

Spillers, Hortense J. 1987. "Mama's Baby, Papa's Maybe: An American Grammar Book." *Diacritics* 17: 65–81.

———. 1997. "All the Things You Could Be by Now, If Sigmund Freud's Wife Was Your Mother": Psychoanalysis and Race". In Abel, Christian, and Moglen, eds., *Female Subjects in Black and White: Race, Psychoanalysis, Feminism.* Berkeley and Los Angeles: University of California Press, pp. 135–58.

Spivak, Gayatri Chakravorty. 1986. "Three Women's Texts and a Critique of Imperialism." In Henry Louis Gates Jr., ed. *"Race," Writing, and Difference.* Chicago: University of Chicago Press, pp. 262–81.

———. 1988. "Can the Subaltern Speak?" Larry Grossberg and Cary Nelson, eds., *Marxism and the Interpretation of Culture.* Urbana: University of Illinois Press, pp. 271–313.

———. 1993a. "Echo." *New Literary History* 24: 17–43.

———. 1993b. *Outside in the Teaching Machine.* New York: Routledge.

Tapping, Craig. 1989. "Oral Cultures and the Empire of Literature." *Kunapipi* 11, no. 1: 86–96.

Taylor, Mark C. 1990. "Non-negative Negative Atheology." *Diacritics* 20, no. 4: 2–16.

Tiffin, Helen. 1986. "New Concepts of Persons and Place in *The Twyborn Affair* and *A Bend in the River.*" Peggy Nightingale, ed. *A Sense of Place in the New Literatures in English.* St. Lucia, Australia: University of Queensland Press, pp. 22–31.

———. 1993. "Cold Hearts and (Foreign) Tongues: Recitation and the Reclamation of the Female Body in the Works of Erna Brodber and Jamaica Kincaid." *Callaloo* 16, no. 4: 909–21.

Todorov, Tzvetan, 1984a. *The Conquest of America: The Question of the Other.* New York: Harper & Row.

Trinh, T. Minh-ha, 1986/87. "Difference: 'A Special Third World Women Issue.'" *Discourse* 8: 3–8.

————. 1989. *Woman, Native, Other: Writing Postcoloniality and Feminism.* Bloomington: Indiana University Press.

Turner, Victor. 1967. *The Forest of Symbols: Aspects of Ndembu Ritual.* Ithaca, N.Y.: Cornell University Press.

————. 1969. *The Ritual Process: Structure and Anti-Structure.* Ithaca, N.Y.: Cornell University Press.

Walker, Alice. 1982. *The Color Purple.* New York: Harcourt Brace Jovanovich.

————. 1984. *In Search of Our Mother's Gardens: Womanist Prose.* London: Women's Press.

Ward, Cynthia. 1989. "The Rising of the Bones." *Modern Fiction Studies* 35, no. 1: 121–35.

————. 1990. "What They Told Buchi Emecheta: Oral Subjectivity and the Joys of 'Otherhood.'" *PMLA* 105, no. 1: 83–97.

Wilentz, Gay. 1992. "Toward a Diaspora Literature: Black Women Writers from Africa, the Caribbean, and the United States." *College English* 54, no.4: 385–407.

Wilson, Elizabeth. 1990. "'Le voyage et l'espace clos': Island and Journey as Metaphor: Aspects of Woman's Experience in the Works of Francophone Caribbean Women Novelists." In Carole Boyce Davies and Elaine Savory Fido, eds., *Out of the Kumbla: Caribbean Women and Literature.* Trenton, N.J.: Africa World Press, pp. 45–57.

Wittig, Monique. 1973. *Le Corps Lesbien.* Paris: Editions de Minuit.

Wolff, Janet. 1993. "On the Road Again: Metaphors of Travel in Cultural Criticism." *Cultural Studies* 7, no. 2: 224–39.

Young, Robert. 1990. *White Mythologies: Writing History and the West.* London: Routledge.

————. 1995. *Colonial Desire: Hybridity in Theory, Culture, and Race.* London: Routledge.

Zhana, ed. 1988. *Sojourn.* London: Methuen.

Zima, Peter V. 1981. *Literatuur en maatschappij: Inleiding in de Literatuur- en Tekstsociologie.* Assen, Netherlands: van Gorcum.

Zimra, Clarisse. 1990. "Righting the Calabash: Writing History in the Female Francophone Narrative." In Carole Boyce Davies and Elaine Savory Fido, eds., *Out of the Kumbla: Caribbean Women and Literature.* Trenton, N.J.: Africa World Press, pp. 143–51.

Zinsser, William, ed. 1987. *Inventing the Truth: The Art and Craft of Memoir.* Boston: Houghton Mifflin.

Index

In this index an "f" after a number indicates a separate reference on the next page, and an "ff" indicates separate references on the next two pages. A continuous discussion over two or more pages is indicated by a span of page numbers, e.g., "57–59." *Passim* is used for a cluster of references in close but not consecutive sequence.